LEARNING RESOURCES
South Campus
Tarrant County College District
Fort Worth, Texas

A00200241001

BP75.B56
1969

1228315

SOUTH CAMPUS LIBRARY

TARRANT COUNTY JUNIOR COLLEGE

FT. WORTH, TEXAS 76119

The Messenger

THE LIFE OF MOHAMMED

BY

R. V. C. BODLEY

LA ILAHA ILL-ALLAH
MUHAMMAD RASUL ALLAH
*There is no God but one God
Muhammad is a Messenger of God.*

GREENWOOD PRESS, PUBLISHERS
NEW YORK

Copyright © 1946 by R. V. C. Bodley

Reprinted by permission
of Doubleday & Co.

First Greenwood Reprinting 1969

Library of Congress Catalogue Card Number 70-92296

SBN 8371-2423-9

PRINTED IN UNITED STATES OF AMERICA

To
FLORA WHITNEY MILLER
*whose friendly help through the years
made the writing of
this book possible*

Bismillahir Rahmaanir Raheem.
Qul Hua-llaahu Ahad:
Allaahu-ssamad,
Lam Yalid wa-lam yulad,
Wa-lam ya-ku-llahu kufuwan ahad.

In the name of God, the compassionate, the merciful!
Say: He is God alone:
God the eternal,
He begetteth not, and He is not begotten,
And there is none like unto Him.

KORAN: SURA, 112.

FOREWORD

My first appreciation of what Mohammed represented came to me among the towering mountains of Kashmir. It was before the other world war, and familiarity between "white men" and "natives" was discouraged. I was, nevertheless, interested in the way my shikari stopped whatever he was doing to turn toward Mecca and say his prayers. He knew a little English, and after a while I began asking him about this God who he worshiped so conscientiously. My astonishment was great when I discovered that it was the God of the same faith into which I had been baptized. I was further astonished when I heard this rugged hunter talking familiarly of Abraham and Moses, of Jesus and John the Baptist —all prophets of his religion. That was as far as I got for the moment. General prejudice on the part of my occidental colleagues toward anything so unfamiliar as the beliefs of the inhabitants of the country in which we ruled, together with the outbreak of World War I, diverted me from what then I might have made a study.

This diversion lasted quite a while. In fact, more than ten years passed without my giving a thought to Moslems and Islam. Then, weary of the futile complications of this first postwar era, I went to live among the Arabs of the Sahara Desert. With them I remained for seven years.

A camel's-hair tent became my home, the nomads my friends, the rolling wilderness my country. What my Kashmiri had given me a glimpse of, was now spread before me in detail. I heard the Koran recited in the majestic language of Meccan Arabia. Without becoming a Moslem, I felt the spell of this faith which placed the suppliant and his Creator face to face on the desert. I heard of Mohammed as the man who had united a handful of rival Arab tribes and made of them the foundations of one of the most powerful empires of the world. I heard of him as the warm-hearted human being who had changed mundane, pagan idolaters into profound believers in one God, in the resurrection of the dead and the life of the world to come. I saw people, ninety-nine per cent of whom practiced their religion sincerely because they believed in it.

As the months and the years went by, my information about Mohammed accumulated. This was not from deliberate study. I do not believe that, during the whole of that period on the desert, I read one printed word about Allah's messenger—outside the Koran. My knowledge I obtained from conversations around campfires, during long rides with the caravans, while watching the flocks by night. In fact, it was not until long after desert days that I began to read about Mohammed. When I did I was, to a great extent, disappointed.

The simplicity of Mohammed's teaching and ideals, as reverenced in the desert, seemed to have been submerged under oceans of tradition and theology and politics. It was like reading the life of a friend written by writers who had never known him intimately. Even the Moslem authors seemed to have failed to achieve that personal touch. There were, of course, exceptions. Some of Mohammed's biographies are masterpieces of literature, but the majority are not. For those interested in this bibliography, I have appended a list of the books which I have read. But, while these confirmed and co-ordinated what I had picked up among my nomad Arabs, the basic thoughts of my story of Mohammed's life originated among the snowy peaks of Kashmir and on the golden wastes of the Sahara.

The title of this book may need explanation. Many people refer to Mohammed as, "The Prophet," and while the Arab word *Nabi*, although not strictly signifying "prophet" in the sense of the Greek ἠροφητης is often used, it is not correct. Mohammed's recognized title is "Rasul Allah," meaning "Allah's messenger."

Those who have heard the muezzin's call to prayer from the minarets of Islam's mosques may remember one of the lines:

"*La ilaha illa Allah! Mohammed* Rasul *Allah!*
[There is no God but Allah! Mohammed is his *Messenger!*]"

So I have called my story *The Messenger: The Life of Mohammed*.

In order to help with the reading of this long biography, I have included several practical appendices.

The story of Mohammed is teeming with names, the majority of which are unfamiliar to many Occidentals. In addition, therefore, to my general index, I have made a supplementary list of names of those men and women who figure prominently and contemporarily in the life of the Messenger of Allah.

With the same idea, I have prepared a roll of Mohammed's wives, giving their full names and those of their parents.

A glossary of Arabic expressions appearing in the text will be found at the end of the book. The spelling of the words as well as of the proper names, I have tried to make as simple as possible. It is difficult to convey Arab sounds in any characters but Arabic. An Arabic manuscript is made up chiefly of consonants. These consonants vary according to whether they come at the beginning or middle or end of a word. Occidental writers who try to reproduce this way of writing achieve nothing, unless it is to confuse and irritate the reader. So I have used "Koran" and "Koreish" instead of the more correct "Quar'an" and "Quraish." I have also written "caliph" with a *c*, which seems to be the tendency of approved dictionaries. Webster also spells "Kaaba" with two *a*'s, and not with the Arabic *a'*.

With the same idea, I have tried to translate literally and simply the Arab dialogue. Its poetry and cadence is outside my scope. The Koranic quotations have been based on the versions of Marmaduke Picktall and J. M. Rodwell.

To any readers who make issues of what is historical about Mohammed and what is traditional, I want to say this. In the stories of all great men there is always much tradition which can neither be affirmed nor denied. In fact, it is sometimes hard to say how certainty became certainty and how tradition became tradition. Furthermore, in all religions there is much which is not only tradition but legend. Theologians do not, however, discard the unproven merely for lack of evidence. So while, on principle, I have adhered to fact, I have not upset the balance of a sentence by inserting "it is said" whenever I was not sure whether I was slipping away from history.

I want to thank the following kind people for helping me to bring this book into being: Dr. Philip K. Hitti and Dr. G. I. Kheirallah who revised my manuscript with me. Mr. Donald B. Elder, Mrs. Morton Pennypacker, Mrs. Nada Patcevitch, Mrs. Ellen Seabrook, and Miss Ann Watkins who, in various ways, contributed to the writing of this work. To Miss Emily Davie who read and corrected the galley proofs of *The Messenger*.

R. V. C. BODLEY

Washington, Connecticut
December 1945.

CONTENTS

	Foreword	ix
	Introduction	1
I	Mecca	10
II	Mohammed's Childhood	22
III	Mohammed's Youth	36
IV	The Call	49
V	The Persecutions	63
VI	The Faith	83
VII	The Seven Heavens	104
VIII	Al Hijra—The Flight	119
IX	Medina	133
X	The First Battle	149
XI	The Jews	164
XII	The Second Battle	177
XIII	Political and Domestic Troubles in Medina	190
XIV	The Siege of Medina	204
XV	The Affair of Aisha's Necklace	218
XVI	The Koran	232

CONTENTS

XVII	The Treaty	246
XVIII	The Embassies	261
XIX	The Fulfillment of the Treaty	276
XX	The Abdication of Abu Sofian	288
XXI	The Forging of an Army	300
XXII	The Last Pilgrimage	314
XXIII	The Death of Mohammed	326
XXIV	Mohammed at Home	339
	Epilogue	346
	Principal Actors in Mohammed's Drama of the Desert	356
	Mohammed's Wives and Concubines	357
	Glossary	358
	Bibliography	360
	Index	361

THE MESSENGER

INTRODUCTION

THIS BOOK has been written more for people who want to know something about Mohammed and Islam than for oriental scholars or students of theology. This does not mean that liberties have been taken with the subject or that any details of Mohammed's life and teachings have been omitted. On the contrary, the material in these pages is perhaps wealthier in particulars than in many of Mohammed's biographies. Special attention has likewise been paid to keeping as accurately to facts as is possible in the recording of the life of any individual not personally known to the biographer. So, too, has every endeavor been made to avoid the bias of the Moslem fanatic or the misrepresentations of the Christian bigot. Legends and controversies have been given their appropriate values. For it is strange to note that, without any valid reasons, there are more popular misconceptions about Mohammed than about any of the other founders of great faiths.

While we have no contemporary records of Moses or Confucius or Buddha, while we know some fragments *of a fragment* of Christ's life, but nothing of the thirty years which prepared the way for the culminating three, the story of Mohammed is extremely clear.

Here, instead of the shadowy and the mysterious, we have history. We know as much of Mohammed as we do of men who lived much closer to our epoch. His external record, his youth, his relatives, his habits are neither legendary nor hearsay. His internal record, after his mission had been proclaimed, is no hazy tradition of some obscure or perplexed preacher. We have a contemporaneous book, absolutely unique in its origin and in its preservation, on the authenticity of which no one has ever been able to cast a serious doubt.

This book, known as the Koran, is available today as it was first written under Mohammed's supervision. For although the thoughts were scrawled at odd moments on pieces of parchment, on palm leaves, on bones and scraps of leather, the original chapters and verses were preserved. Neither was this done, as in the cases of the Old and New Testaments, centuries, or even decades, after the death of the author. Abu Bakr, Mohammed's immediate successor, had all the fragments of the Koranic "manuscript" collected, transcribed, and bound. This copy was committed to the care of Hafsa, one of Mohammed's widows.

In 646 after Christ, fourteen years after Mohammed's death, Othman, the third caliph, a friend and contemporary of Mohammed, had all unauthorized versions of the Koran, which enthusiastic disciples had compiled from memory, destroyed. Only Hafsa's master copy was retained. From this, all subsequent editions were made. Nothing has been added or subtracted since.

Neither is the work a compilation of traditions or reports of what Mohammed is supposed to have said. It is the actual text as dictated by himself, day by day and month by month, during his lifetime. It is the reflection of this master mind; sometimes inartistic and self-contradictory, more often inspiring and lyric, and always filled with great ideas which stand out as a whole.

But, if we had not the Koran, we have other links with Mohammed's times peculiar to the Arab people.

The human race has not altered physically and very little intellectually during the tens of thousands of years which history records as having preceded our times. The passions and pleasures and heartaches, the political and domestic problems of the people of those remote ages were, in all likelihood, much the same as ours.

Occidentals are apt to regard civilization as an advancing flood which has progressed steadily since the beginning of time. This is probably inexact. It is rather a tide which ebbs and flows, reaches a high-water mark and turns back again. Nevertheless, a resurrected Babylonian or an Ancient Greek would find it difficult to adapt himself to the modern way of living. The centuries which divide those eras from this are, in thought and custom, unbridgeable. This can be said of most epochs, epochs much less remote than those of Greece and Babylon, epochs separated only by a few hundred years. One bridge of time makes the exception. The thirteen centuries which lie between our days and the days of Mohammed have done less to change the descendants of the men who first decided that Islam was the way to salvation, than the time which has elapsed between General Washington and General Eisenhower.

A Moslem of the seventh century, returning to that region of Arabia, between Mecca and Medina, where Mohammed lived, would find little to surprise him. The nomad Arabs in their black tents, the travelers on their camels, the pilgrims streaming over the desert from the Red Sea would all be there as he had left them. So would the people's clothes, so would their physical appearance. The face and build of an Arab of today, of thirteen hundred or of three thousand years ago have not gone through those evolutions which refashioned the Anglo-Saxon and Latin races. The way of dressing has hardly altered at all. The seventh-century Moslem would even be able to recognize tribes pasturing around Mecca, with the same names as in the days of Mohammed. Among the tribesmen he would find men directly descended from the people of his time. If a truck did rattle past in a cloud of dust or an airplane whirred overhead, the reborn Arab would have no difficulty in attributing these singularities to djinns.

Although there are no written works by contemporaries of God's Messenger, there are several by men who had first-hand, and almost personal, knowledge of their subject. Some of these can be read today. To us, accustomed to having writers compiling biographies of living people, this does not seem remarkable. The custom is, however, modern. Until comparatively recently, biographies were, literally, post-mortems.

Numerous relatives survived Mohammed and handed down

their recollections of him to their descendants. His lieutenants carried on his political and military traditions without any break. The Arabs who overran Spain and marched halfway across France had all known men who had heard the Messenger preach.

The nomads with whom I lived on the desert did not speak of Mohammed as someone remote and mystic, as Christians do of Jesus. One never felt that intangibility, that disassociation of a being who wore different clothes and lived in a strange land among people whom the average person could not visualize. There was none of that state of mind of the old lady from Baltimore saying about the crucifixion:

"It was *so* long ago. Let's hope it isn't true."

My Arabs spoke of the founder of their faith as someone they knew. He had been a shepherd, he had worn the same kind of robes as they, he had ridden identical camels, his diet had been similar to theirs. Everything they did, they could associate with him. Mohammed was as alive to these nomads as any one of them.

It is thus easier for me to reconstitute this scene of thirteen hundred years ago than for an Oxford don to describe accurately the intimate life of an Elizabethan. It is simpler than for an American historian to write of the United States before the War of Independence. It is less difficult than for most biographers of Mohammed.

The majority of these writers have far greater claims than I to style, to erudition, to the technique of biography. But all of them lack what I possess. For, be they Orientals or Occidentals, none of them led the kind of existence which Mohammed and his followers did in Arabia at the beginning of the seventh century, and I, during the first half of the twentieth.

Neither the Asiatics nor the Europeans nor the Americans who have written of Mohammed ever ventured into those desolate regions of Arabia Deserta where the Messenger brought Islam into being.

The Occidentals did not make the experiment because they were not the kind to adapt themselves to Arab life. They realized that, unless years were given up to the nomadic existence, there would be nothing to show for the uncomfortable experience.

The Orientals would have found it even more difficult. People of the East who write are sedentary folk. They live in oases or cities. They know nothing about the desert and have little contact with the nomads. They would no more think of spending months under a camel's-hair tent than swimming the Mediterranean.

Thus, all these biographies lack something. They are incomplete. They fail to consider their subject from *all* angles. Mohammed usually appears as a kind of one-dimensional figure against a blank wall. The dimension may be spiritual or material or deceitful; whatever it is, it is isolated. There is rarely any background. The picture is like a silhouette pasted on a drab sheet of cardboard. Yet Mohammed was not flat; he was of many dimensions, and there was nothing colorless about his setting.

One author, whose biography of Mohammed I read, had evidently never been out of New England, where he was a minister of the Gospel. Asia and Africa were more remote to him than heaven or hell. Yet he covered three hundred pages with an intimate review of the life of the Messenger of Allah which, in spite of an enlightened style, and excellent knowledge of the Scriptures, and a smattering of Arabic, disclosed a surprising ignorance of how Mohammed lived and what he represented.

Throughout his book, he never referred to his subject in any way but as "the impostor," without explaining how the said impostor caused his immediate descendants to conquer an area of the world's surface three times as large as the United States and impart a culture to mankind which is alive today.

George Sale, who made a fine translation of the Koran in the early part of the eighteenth century and should have known better, prefaces the volume as follows:

We are informed by historians that famous cities, distinguished above all others for literature and commerce, contended for which of them should have the honor of being the birthplace of Homer. . . . Such a contest was commendable, as it evinced the high opinion which men of that period had of unexampled merit.

But, when the character of Mohammed is attentively surveyed, the picture is so shocking that it is a wonder the place of his nativity has not been buried in oblivion. Any country might blush to produce such a monster. So great, however, has the veneration of the Arabians for this arch-deceiver always been, that they have not left it problematical where he drew his first breath.

And so on. To which the only comment is to take the words from the pages of the afore-mentioned New England divine's story of Mohammed:

How could such a monster, such an arch-deceiver, have created a religion which, today, numbers three hundred million believers and, instead of being on the wane as so many other religions of the world, is stronger than ever, and increasing in converts daily?

What these denouncers of the false prophet seem also to have missed is that, in the beginning, there was little difference of opinion between Moslems and Christians. In the early days of his ministry, Mohammed would not have been offended to be thought a Christian. When he was being persecuted, he sought and found protection for his people with the Negus of Abyssinia who ruled over a Christian kingdom. In fact, as will be shown later in this book, it was only a matter of chance that Islam did not become an obscure Christian sect like the Maronites or the Corinthians. The misunderstandings with the Christians did not begin until toward the end of Mohammed's life and not seriously until the early wars brought on by the Crusaders. From then on, they increased so that "Mohammed" became practically synonymous with blasphemy. In the minds of the contemporaries of Shakespeare, "Mammetry" grew to mean any false religion, especially one which worshiped idols. "Maumets" was used currently to *signify* idols. "Mahomerie," and thence "mummery," are derived from the same source.

Some of the accepted ideas of these times were fantastic. For example, in a twelfth-century poem, Mohammed was shown as a feudal lord who took Christian Holy Orders. He was created a cardinal, but, failing to be elected to the papacy, revenged himself by starting a new religion.

The idea that Mohammed's coffin hung suspended between heaven and earth was believed until comparatively recently. Historians have stated unblushingly that Mohammed was buried in Mecca. Others have said that he died of drink and that his body was eaten by pigs. Whereas, in fact, Mohammed declared pork unclean and forbade his followers to touch liquor; while his body has remained where it was laid to rest in Medina thirteen hundred years ago.

The proverbial saying about Mohammed and the mountain has no connection with Arabia of the seventh century. Its first mention is probably not before Bacon's essay, "Of Boldness," which he published about 1597 after Christ.

Occasionally one comes across writers of those times, like John Selden, who took the trouble to investigate this Arab faith.

"They called images Mammets and the adoration of images Mammetry," says this seventeenth-century scholar, "that is, Mahomets and Mahometry, odious names, when all the world knows that the Turks [synonymous then with Moslem] are forbidden images in their religion."

But such statements of fact were rare, and the general conviction prevailed that any self-styled religion which had come into being since the death of Christ must be an imposition.

There are also biographers who have gone to the other extreme and have made Mohammed out to be a saint, if not a god—biographers who have attributed to him miracles and supernatural performances and divine powers which are no more true than the accusations of George Sale and his school of thinkers. One of Mohammed's last requests before he died was:

"O Lord, let not my tomb be ever an object of worship."

He would have been scandalized if he could have foreseen the mass of superstitions which writers would manufacture at his expense.

That is the trouble with Mohammed's biographers. They have

either believed in him or disbelieved in him, with varying degrees of fanatacism. Very few have told the story of the man impartially, stressing neither his vices nor his virtues. Practically none have brought out the influences of country and climate and customs which, after all, make the greatest differences to anyone's way of living.

My attempt, therefore, has been to present Mohammed as he really was—an Arab like many I knew in the desert; a man of simple tastes, but of great personality, with the good of his people at heart; a man who was inspired, but thought out all he did logically; who had tolerance for the weakness of men and women, because he was often weak himself. Not a god by any means.

The expression "Mohammedan" or "Mohammedanism" was never used by Mohammed and his disciples. In spite of the reverence for their master, these designations have always been rejected by the Faithful. "Moslem, one who surrenders himself to the will of God," is the only correct term to apply to a member of the religion which Mohammed founded.

Mohammed's tastes were simple to asceticism, but he was also a man of the world. Neither was it a world of the remote past. Mohammed would not have felt ill at ease in society, occidental or oriental. He loved as we do, he had children, he was a fine horseman, he could make his own shoes and mend his own clothes. He had a good sense of humor. He knew himself to be a leader, but he was never showy and never tried to create anything resembling a court. He never led anyone to believe that he had supernatural or divine gifts.

To return to my earlier statement: human beings have little changed throughout the centuries of recorded history. They have made life more complicated, but they have retained the same shapes and the same primitive instincts. Therefore, because this book is about the Messenger of Allah, the founder of Islam, it should not be considered as something outside the interest of the casual reader. Mohammed's biography could be that of any famous figure in history or fiction. It has all the elements of drama and conflict and romance essential to good storytelling.

So, let the reader forget Islam and Moslems and the seventh century and Arabia. Let him consider a man who set out to make good, and *made* good in spite of every possible obstacle in his way. The only difference between Mohammed's and anyone else's thrilling success story is the setting, and that adds to the excitement and the glamor.

There is nothing startlingly new about Mohammed in this biography. All that may have been introduced which is fresh is to show how circumstances made Mohammed do some things which to Occidentals have remained obscure. This has been possible owing to my long association with the Arabs, to my friendship with them.

I know the Arabs intimately and I like them. I have lived in their tents and liked it. I once took a practical interest in the Moslem faith. I have an idea that I can think and feel as Mohammed did. I certainly understand his problems. For that reason I have told the good with the bad impartially. I feel that Mohammed is big enough to carry his faults as well as his merits and still remain great. I doubt whether any man whose external conditions changed so much ever changed himself less to meet them.

CHAPTER I

MECCA

(Sixth Century After Christ)

ENFOLDED in the wildernesses of Arabia Deserta, halfway between Yemen and Syria, in a land wasted by winds and secular rains, lies Mecca, the holy city of Islam. A savage valley, enclosed between two sharp and arid chains of rock mountains, makes its position so secluded that not until the pilgrim is looking down into its streets does he know that he has arrived. It is as if nature had co-operated with the Moslem faith to guard the secrets of this hallowed spot from the unsanctified.

It is an uninviting place, unfriendly too, in the midst of many little hills, stony and black and all of equal height. For miles around there appears to be no end to these barren hills, no end to the glittering, glaring desert, no respite from the fiery heat. Like smoldering coals, the pebbles and flints shine vaporing under the blazing skies.

Except for occasional thorny acacias, everything living seems to have been blasted from this wilderness. The desolation is absolute. The only sound is the hissing of the breathless wind. The only relief to the monotony of the landscape is the sand columns whirling over the plain like angry djinns. There are not even mirages to lure travelers to their reflections of palms and cool gardens. There are no palms or cool gardens to reflect. Nothing grows in this holy city of the Messenger of Allah. Night is the only respite from the scorching of the sun.

The city itself is the same color as the surrounding country. Houses of all shapes and sizes, built of stone, climb up the steep sides of the valley, packed and crammed together like the cells of a honeycomb. Here and there an outlying building on the summit of a wind-polished rock looks as if it had been crowded out and waited for a chance to squeeze into the confusion below.

In the heart of the city is the Great Mosque, Beit Allah, consisting of an immense pillared courtyard in which are numerous sacred shrines. Beit Allah means House of God and is situated, according to Arab tradition, in the center of the world and immediately beneath the throne of the Almighty. Almost in the middle of the court, and in a depression, stands the Kaaba. The Kaaba is a windowless, cube-shaped, flat-roofed building made of gray stone, forty feet high. Enveloping it is a huge black brocade cover, like a tea cozy, on which verses from the Koran are embroidered in gold. Every year the cover, which is called Kesoua, is renewed. The Kaaba is the focal point of Islam toward which Moslems all over the world turn five times a day to pray.

The Kaaba has been an object of worship since the dawn of history, but its origins have been forgotten, lost in the mists of fable. Its association with the name, Beit Allah, shows that it might, in its first rude shape, have been erected by some ancient patriarch to commemorate a vision of angels. Jacob called his pillar Bethel, or Beit Allah.

Arab legends suggest that the first Kaaba dates back to Adam. This one was destroyed by the Deluge, and another was rebuilt by Abraham and Ishmael. After that it fell into the hands of idolators who built other editions until Mohammed came and restored its ancient dedication to one God.

Sunk in one of the sharp corners of the outer wall of the Kaaba is the Black Stone.

The Black Stone is really a number of fragments—twelve, to be exact—united by dark cement and held together by a silver band. The whole is oval and about seven inches in diameter. What these stones or fragments are made of no one seems to have ever definitely established.

Tradition asserts that the original stone came from Paradise and was handed by the angel Gabriel to Abraham and Ishmael when they were building the Kaaba. At that time it was snow-white. Its present color is the outcome of having been kissed by the millions of sinners who yearly make the pilgrimage to Mecca. This, however, does not clear up the question of its composition. The obstacle to so doing is that the vast majority of the men who go to Mecca accept the Black Stone as a holy emblem and do not worry about its geological history. Those travelers who have examined the stone with curiosity as well as reverence differ in their opinion. Some say that it is a chip of rock from the Abu Kobeis hills to the east of Mecca. Some say that it is a meteorite. Others insist that it is of volcanic origin.

None of this is of any real importance, in spite of the controversies which the subject has given rise to on various occasions. Whatever it is made of, the stone has been there for a long time. Maximus Tyrius, writing in the second century after Christ, tells of "Arabians praying to a god which they represent by a rectangular building in which there is a black stone."

Today the Black Stone is venerated as much for the sake of tradition as anything else. Before the acceptance of Mohammed's teaching, the Arabs had a frenzied cult for stones. The interior of the Kaaba was filled with all sorts of crudely hewn blocks of granite, among which were effigies supposed to represent Jesus and Mary and Abraham and Ishmael. Three hundred and sixty rough stone idols were said to have cluttered up the windowless sanctuary of the shrine. The stone remains, therefore, without Moslems associating its origin with idolatry, any more than Christians associate church spires and Gothic arches with phallic symbols.

Seven smaller buildings are disposed around the Kaaba. The most important contains the well of Zemzem. This is where Hagar, when she was expelled from the tents of Abraham through the instigation of Sarah, decided to die. Wandering over the desert, she had reached the stony valley of Mecca. Her provisions had given out, her gourd was empty. Frenziedly she ran to and fro, looking for water. Then, nearly dead from thirst, she flung herself on the parched ground and pushed her baby under a thorny acacia.

"Let me not see the death of my child!" she cried, as she covered her head with her mantle.

But before what seemed inevitable happened, an angel appeared and showed Hagar that she was within walking distance of a well. Hagar could no longer walk, but she crawled over to the water, which saved her and Ishmael's lives. This Zemzem is the same, identical well, so called because of the bubbling sound which it made when Hagar found it. If we are to believe the Book of Genesis, it is probably one of the oldest existing wells of the world. The Arabs have no doubts on the matter. They say that it is as clear as day that Mecca stands on the site of this place. There is no reason why this should not be.

Abraham was a nomad who lived in a tent. Anyone driven out alone onto the desert without a camel would not stand much chance of survival if water were not found. While there were water holes and wells then as there are now, someone who was not a shepherd and unfamiliar with the lay of the land would miss them, especially if distressed and worn out. The story is more likely than many in the Old Testament. It was probably this very water which brought Mecca into being. In such a desolate wilderness a well would attract caravans along with shepherds. After a while it would become a resting place for the night and, by degrees, develop into a trading center.

If we are to accept legend, the history of the Arabs can be said to begin at this point. Not long after the dramatic repudiating of Hagar came the no less dramatic disinheriting of Esau by Jacob. As an indirect result of these two tragedies, Esau married Makalah, the daughter of Ishmael. From this union sprang the Edomites, the Amalekites, the Ishmaelites who are the ancestors of the peoples of Arabia.

In another building, not far from the Zemzem well, are the tombs of Hagar and Ishmael. In yet another is the stone on which Abraham stood while he superintended the rebuilding of the Kaaba.

The present tense has been used to describe Mecca because,

while only certain parts of the seventh-century city remain, its aspect has little changed since the days of Mohammed.

The houses are still made of the local gray stone and are taller than in most oriental cities. They have flat roofs and enclosed, projecting balconies. The streets are winding and narrow. Some wander steeply up the sides of the hills which surround Mecca. Now, as then, they are never deserted. People seem to be always going on some errand or visiting friends or returning from a journey. Camels pad disdainfully over the rough cobbles, pushing aside the heavily laden donkeys and mules. There are chatter and laughter and always dust. Although many of the original buildings have been destroyed by torrential rains which turn the lower levels of the narrow valley in which Mecca lies into raging torrents, other similar structures have taken their place. Those, however, above the reach of floods still stand. Today Mohammed's birthplace and the home where he lived after his marriage are shown to pilgrims as the originals. This is not necessarily a stretch of pious imagination. In that dry climate, masonry resists disintegration much longer than in countries of fog and drizzle. An idol worshiper, therefore, of pre-Islamic times or one of Mohammed's contemporaries, returning to the Holy City, would have no trouble in recognizing landmarks in the streets which he had left from ten to twenty centuries before.

Neither would he find the *way* of living different. The shops, the boardinghouses, the eating places are as they were thirteen hundred years ago, and earlier. By the sixth century Mecca had become important. Her Arabic was considered the most cultured. Her people regarded themselves the most refined. Merchants and pilgrims came there from all over Arabia. It is much the same today. The Meccan dialect is still the standard language and, while other cities have developed as centers of fashion, the trans-Arabian caravans and the pilgrims continue to be the main sources of revenue for the Meccans. As then, they exploit them, fixing their rents and tariffs according to the number of people in the city. The speculation in rates of exchange, the monopolizing of commodities, the gambling on harvests goes on, as it has from time immemorial.

It was from these idolatrous, money-conscious, aristocratic Meccans, from these townspeople living in the midst of that hideous wilderness, that Mohammed sprang. He was not a nomad; his spiritual horizon was entirely different to that of the bedouins. Yet it was the nomadic tribesmen who became his stanchest converts. It was the desert people who carried Islam round the world.

This may not seem peculiar to any who have not lived among Arabs. Actually it is one of Mohammed's achievements which is near to being miraculous.

All Arabs are divided into two classes, those who are sedentary and those who roam. The oasis or city people, the nomads or bedouins.

The oasis dwellers, or sedentary Arabs, have always been the scholars, the merchants, the administrators. It is they who have guided the political destinies of the Arabs in spite of being in a minority.

The nomad is the fighter, the wanderer, the pioneer who has carried Islam to the ends of the earth more from love of adventure than from a wish to inspire with his Arab culture. The nomads and the sedentary Arabs are as different as possible, but they make up an entity like a father and a mother.

The oasis or city way of living is quite unlike the desert way.

The oasis may be a vast garden of date palms and flowers in the middle of the wilderness, as Medina, or just a town which has sprung up round a desert well, as Mecca. Whatever kind of oasis it is, living there bears no resemblance to living anywhere else. It is rather like being on an island among people whose every thought is centered on that island. The oasis city folk are more stay-at-home than the inhabitants of any American country town. They have nothing in common with the nomads.

To the nomad warrior the vast expanses of the desert, with their dangers and privations, are essential. They bring out all his fine characteristics, his honesty, his sense of humor. His wandering life gives him little time to be anything but a man of unpremeditated action. If he loses his camel or his horse and is, in consequence, immobilized and has to become sedentary, he is humiliated and quickly degenerates. He does not despise the oasis dweller, neither does he fight him, but he considers him a subordinate and does not wish to be like him.

That is why Mohammed's ascendancy over the nomads was so remarkable.

Although all Arabs were ruled by nearly identical codes and spoke the same basic language and had a kind of pan-Arabian patriotism, they were divided into independent tribes. Each of these tribes had its own particular customs, its own dialect, and was always ready to defend its own special group of tents. This goes on today and explains why there is no central Arab government.

That a desert man should have become the leader of these tribes to the extent of having them unite and die for his cause would have been astonishing. That this man should have come from among the despised city people was fantastic. In fact, until the appearance of Mohammed the nomads were so jealous of their freedom that they drove out anyone, bedouin or otherwise, who showed signs of monarchial tendencies.

The Arab in general, and the nomad in particular, is a socialist by instinct and tradition. The chief and the shepherd meet on an equal footing. In the tribal confederations there are opportunities for all. No one is better than anyone else, except by outstanding merit. The deserts of the Arabs are the only places in the world where democracy is really put into practice. But while the Arabs maintain these principles in their own circles, they have always considered themselves the noblest of all peoples. They believe themselves to be the original race of the world.

According to Arab tradition, Adam and Eve, after their expulsion from the Garden of Eden, wandered over the earth separately for years. When God reunited them, it was on Mount Arafat, which is close to present-day Mecca. One of Adam's first duties was to build the Kaaba. The primitive population of Arabia is thus traced to Adam's immediate descendants, to Noah and especially to Noah's son Shem. It was Shem's great-grandson who founded the kingdoms of Yemen and the Hedjaz, where Mecca is, and Abraham, the father of Ishmael, was the great-grandson, several times removed, of Shem.

That, at any rate, is the Arab tradition. The part about Ishmael is also in the Old Testament.

"And God said [to Abraham] as for Ishmael, I have heard thee. Behold I have blessed him and will make him fruitful and will multiply him exceedingly. Twelve princes shall he beget, and I will make him a great nation."

And the angel in the desert confirmed this to Hagar while she panted for water:

"Arise, lift up the lad, and hold him in thine hand, for I shall make him a great nation."

The twelve sons of Ishmael are referred to in Genesis as living from "Havilah unto Shur, as thou goest towards Assyria"—which has been identified with that part of the Hedjaz near Mecca. So has Paran, likewise given in Genesis as the name of the wilderness where Hagar and Ishmael settled.

The description of the people also indicates them to be Arabs: "Some lived in towns, others dwelt in tents."

And the tents about which David laments in the Psalms belonged to Ishmael's second son, Kedar, from whom many Arabs trace their beginning.

Jeremiah, writing on the same subject, mentions "the wealthy nation that dwelleth without care, which have neither gates nor bars and dwell alone."

If, therefore, the Old Testament is to be relied on and the biblical places can be made to fit with the cities and wells of Arabia, all that the Arabs tell us must be so.

As a matter of fact, omitting the Adam legend, the history of the Arabs goes far behind the times of the biblical patriarchs. Their pre-Islamic religious beliefs alone prove this. In addition to the traces of Christianity and Judaism and their numerous idols, they practiced phallic worship, as well as the veneration of the sun and the moon and the stars. Herodotus does not actually mention the Kaaba, but he writes of Alilat, or more correctly, al-ilat, which signifies "The Goddess," one of the principal Arab deities who lived in the windowless shrine.

Yet, in spite of these ancient traditions, the Arabs did not count in this world of the twilight of the sixth century. As a matter of fact, no one counted very much. It was a moribund period when the great empires of eastern Europe and western Asia had already been destroyed or were in sight of the end of their imperial careers.

It was a world still dazed by the eloquence of Greece, by the magnificence of Persia, by the majesty of Rome, with nothing yet to take their places, not even a religion.

The Jews were drifting all over the world, with no central leadership, tolerated or persecuted according to circumstances. They had no country to call their own and about as nebulous a future as they have today.

Outside the spheres of influence of Pope Gregory the Great, the Christians were discovering all kinds of complicated interpretations to their once simple creed, and cutting each other's throats in the process.

In Persia, a last flicker of empire building remained. Chosroes II was actually spreading his rule. Defying Rome, he had occupied Cappadocia, Egypt, and Syria. He had sacked Jerusalem and stolen the Holy Cross. By 620 A.C.,* when Mohammed was about to emerge as a public figure, he had restored the mighty sovereignty of Darius I.

It looked almost like a new lease of life for the splendors of the Middle East. But not quite. The Byzantine Romans still had a little of their old vitality. When Chosroes brought his armies to the walls of Constantinople, they made a final effort.

The Emperor Justinian, husband of the notorious Theodora, had died in 565 A.C., just before Mohammed's birth. He had been

*Throughout this biography A.C. stands for "after Christ"—not, of course, the usual "ante Christum."

succeeded by a series of unimportant rulers until 610, when Heraclius was proclaimed emperor. Heraclius was a different type to his predecessors and wasted no time in taking action against the Persians. These he finally defeated in 627 A.C. He retrieved most of what Chosroes had seized and returned the Holy Cross to Jerusalem. But his triumph was not long. In a few years he had to meet the onslaught of Islam. It was short and fierce. To the war cry of *"Allahu Akbar!"* the Roman eagle was, for the last time, rolled in the dust and trampled on by the soldiers from Arabia Deserta.

Farther away to the east, the march of events was leaving few landmarks. India was still a country of many unimportant states which struggled politically and militarily for power.

The Chinese were, as usual, fighting among one another. The Sui dynasty came and went and was replaced by the Tang, which remained for three centuries.

In Japan an empress sat for the first time on the throne. Buddhism was beginning to take root and influence Japanese ideas and ideals.

Europe was gradually merging into the Frankish empire, which would eventually comprise France, northern Italy, and most of the countries east of the Rhine as far as the present Russo-Polish borders. Clovis was dead and Dagobert, the last great ruler of the Merovingian dynasty, was soon to be crowned.

Spain and England were unimportant little states.

Spain was under the control of the Visigoths, who had lately been driven out of France, which they had occupied as far north as the Loire. They were persecuting the Jews, who would, consequently, do much to facilitate the Moslem invasion which was less than a century away.

The British Isles were divided into independent principalities. One hundred and fifty years had passed since the departure of the Romans, who had been replaced by an influx of Nordic people. England herself was made up of seven separate kingdoms. Scotland was the home of the warlike Picts, though Columba's recent visit had converted their king to Christianity and given the people contact with the civilized world.

The Druids still carried out their ancient rites in Wales. The majority of the Irish lived much as they do now. The others belonged to a brilliant monastic group and sent out apostles to establish other great Celtic foundations on the continent of Europe.

The history of North Africa was tied up with that of the Byzantine Romans. Belisarius had driven out the Vandals, and restless peace brooded over the southern shores of the Mediterranean. It was the lull before the storm of the Moslem armies.

Although the European had not yet set foot on the continents of America, there were people there with a civilization of their own. The Mayas, at the time of Mohammed, were advanced in architecture and astrology and mathematics. Farther north, the migrations were still taking place across the Bering Strait from Asia. The newcomers were fighting those already settled and pushing them farther east. The aborigines were practicing their phallic rites, their sadisms, and their masochisms with the enthusiasm of a people whose days are numbered.

The South Sea Islanders lived contentedly on their atolls, exactly as those who have not been corrupted by the coming of the white man live today.

In fact, as far as mentality goes, the world differed little then from what it is now. The bane of empires and imperial greed were causing men to kill one another as lustily in the six hundreds as in the nineteen forties. The massacres and executions and barbarities in the name of one brand of imperial civilization and another brand of imperial civilization had the same aspect in the days of Mohammed and Heraclius as in the days of Pius XII and George VI. The human race had learned no lessons from what had been its food and drink for the past two thousand years and was to learn nothing further during the next fifteen hundred.

It was, nevertheless, a kind of pause in the convulsions of war and religious strife, a condition fertile and, at the same time, delicate for the planting of an idea which *might* lead to an irresistible ideal. Only someone with personality and courage, with tenacity and faith in himself, would have dared to attempt such an experiment. Only one with kindness and understanding, as well as fanatic enthusiasm, could have succeeded in winning to his side a people which had, from all times, been raised in the traditions of tribal organization, in individualistic freedom and indifference to dogmatic religion.

Of this man is our story.

CHAPTER II

MOHAMMED'S CHILDHOOD

(570 After Christ)

OUTSIDE of some extremely improbable legends, there are no mysteries surrounding the birth of Mohammed, no evidences that he was one of God's chosen, no premonitions by his mother, no visitations by angels. Mohammed was begotten and born like anybody else. His father and mother were well-to-do Meccans who belonged to an illustrious clan known as the Koreish. The Koreishites were, for the most part, merchants, and, like them, Mohammed and his forebears were all in business.

Mohammed's father was called Abdallah. He is reputed to have been the best-looking, the most charming, the most worthy young man in Mecca. It is said that when he became engaged to Amina bint Wahb the hearts of many young Meccan ladies were broken.

Abdallah had several beautiful sisters and eleven brothers. Four of these were to play important roles in the world revolution which the child of Abdallah's marriage was to bring about. The names of these four were Abu Taleb and Abu Lahab, contemporaries of Abdallah, and Al Abbas and Hamza, considerably younger. Their father was a distinguished Meccan called Abd al Mottaleb. The name of *his* father was Hashim.

That is as far back as it is necessary to go in Mohammed's genealogy. The only reason for mentioning Hashim is his position in Mecca and the effect it had on his great-grandson.

Hashim had money and position. He was a respected merchant and the official tax gatherer of Mecca. Like all Arabs, he was practical. He realized what a desolate place Mecca was, and how unattractive, with its abominable climate and its horrible heat.

If it had not been for its holy associations, he and everybody else would have left the place to be buried in sand, ages before. But he had to stay and, therefore, made the best of it.

While appreciating the value of the pilgrimage, Hashim added to the city's revenues by other means. It was he who started sending out the two great yearly caravans from Mecca, one in winter to Yemen and the south, one in summer to Syria and the north. It was Hashim who encouraged the smaller caravans to break their desert treks at the Holy City. It was he who made the trading safe by concluding treaties with the Byzantine Romans and with the Amir of the Syrian Arabs while, at the same time, establishing commercial agreements with the Persians and the Abyssinians. It was he who saw to it that the pilgrims were not pillaged of *all* they had, and received something in return for the money they spent. This balanced foresight did well for Mecca. It did well also for the Koreish notables. It, incidentally, put money into the coffers of old Hashim.

Thus, in spite of its dust and heat and remoteness from other cities, Mecca was not stagnant or behind the times. It was exciting, it had movement, it was filled with contrasts. Great wealth and starving poverty, luxury and asceticism lived side by side. The merchant bankers, dealing in oils and linens and perfumes, in precious stones and slaves, had built up an aristocracy rather like that of Venice of the future. They thought of little else but commerce and the gayest way to spend the money they made. Neither was this money-making a dreary office routine. The primary instinct of all Meccans was gambling. They speculated, selling and reselling goods which existed only in their minds or had not yet been delivered. They played the market on the rise and fall of commodity prices, on what the caravans might bring in from Yemen and Syria, on the crops, long before the harvest. Firms made fortunes and went bankrupt overnight, adding to the excitement of the business.

Women also had their fingers in the affairs of Mecca. Many of them were active participators in these commercial speculations. The majority, however, contented themselves with helping the merchants to spend their profits. In doing so they had the calculating attitude toward love of most Arab women. Their passions rose and fell with the market.

The smaller shopkeepers followed the example of their richer colleagues and speculated among themselves and cheated the simple-minded nomads. The nomads despised the tradesmen. They said that *"Koreish"* was synonymous with "shark," which indeed it was, the derivation of the word signifying "large fish"; but they had to deal with them to dispose of their sheep and their camels and their wool. The poor people lived as best they could and hoped for something better. Their state of mind was fertile for the planting of any creed which would promise rewards in a future life. No such offers had come from the gods of the Kaaba. These also were the perquisites of the rich and especially of the Koreishites.

In addition to being a member of the gilded aristocracy of this gilded community, Hashim had religious duties. He was one of the guardians of the Kaaba and the shrines which went with it. It was a family affair dating from centuries back. Like the Levites in Jerusalem, only Hashimites could hold this holy as well as lucrative office. Today, even, in Mecca and Medina the chief magistrates, who must belong to the family of Mohammed, are styled Princes of the Hashimites.

So old Hashim is important, or was important, as a background to Mohammed. He would probably have disapproved of his great-grandson. He would certainly have been scandalized if he had imagined that a descendant of his would revolutionize everything in Arabia. He would have been humiliated if he could have foreseen the desecrating of the Kaaba and the destroying of the idols of which he was the guardian. He would undoubtedly have been one of Mohammed's persecutors. But he died before any of these things happened, and his ministry and fortune passed to his younger brother Al Mottaleb.

Al Mottaleb played no direct part in Mohammed's life either. He continued in his brother's footsteps for ten years, when he died also. He was succeeded by his nephew, Abd al Mottaleb,

Hashim's son and Mohammed's grandfather. The *abd* prefix to his name, in fact the whole combination of his name, came about through a misunderstanding. He had been in Medina with his mother at the time of his father's death. There he remained until he was grown up, when his uncle brought him to Mecca. Here the idea got abroad that he was Al Mottaleb's slave. Hence the prefix *abd,* which means "servitor." When the mistake was found out, the prefix remained together with the name of his uncle. However, he was really called Shaybat.

Abd al Mottaleb was a fine type of Arab. Like his father and his uncle, he was a merchant, but he was also a warrior. Shortly before Mohammed's birth the Abyssinians invaded Arabia with elephants and all manner of contrivances which the Arabs had never seen. Abd al Mottaleb led an army against the invaders and drove them out of the country.

He was, however, chiefly famous for rediscovering the Zemzem well, which the ever drifting desert sand had buried. One of his duties as custodian of the Kaaba was to furnish the pilgrims with water. Getting this water from the cisterns around Mecca was quite a task. Abd al Mottaleb knew that Zemzem and the Kaaba must have been on much the same sites. They had to be if the stories of the founding of Mecca were true. So he began to dig. One day he found the well. He also found two golden gazelles, some swords and suits of armor. These turned out to have belonged to the last of the Jurhumite kings who had ruled in Mecca up to the end of the third century A.C.

After a certain amount of discussion, and invocation of divine advice from the great god Hubal, carved from a solid block of red agate, the treasure was assigned to the Kaaba and the well to Abd al Mottaleb. This was all he wanted. Being in charge of this convenient, as well as historic, water supply solved his problems and raised his prestige. That it was bitter and had the properties of Epsom salts did not bother him. It had saved Hagar's and Ishmael's lives. It would probably do a lot of good to the pilgrims.

Abdallah was Abd al Mottaleb's favorite son. He would undoubtedly have succeeded to his father's fortune and position in Mecca, but he died soon after his marriage to Amina, while on a business trip to Medina. He never saw his son, who was born some months later in August of 570 after Christ.

For some reason, probably because his grandfather was still alive, Mohammed received none of the inheritance which might have been expected. In fact, all that the handsome Abdallah left him was a small house, five camels, a few goats, and an Ethiopian Negress called Baraka. This was not much for anyone to start life on, and disappointing for the descendant of all the Hashims.

However, Abdallah had gone to wherever God, the compassionate, consigned those who had not yet learned about Islam or Christianity or Judaism, and there was not anything for Amina and Mohammed to do except count on the generosity of the family. This seems to have been intended. Seven days after Amina's child was born, Abd al Mottaleb gave a party in his honor. All the Koreish relatives and everyone else of note in Mecca were invited. Many of them, if they had had second sight, would have gladly strangled the baby then and there. But none of them had second sight and smiled complacently when the red-faced mite was carried into the dining room with the dessert.

The baby's birth name was Kothan but, after giving thanks to the Kaaba gods for blessing him with a grandson, Abd al Mottaleb introduced him as Mohammed. The guests were surprised. The name was not unknown among the Arabs, but it was rare. One of them asked the reason for dropping the custom of using the family name. To which Abd al Mottaleb replied:

"May the Most High glorify in heaven him whom He has created on earth!"

This seemingly obscure remark probably referred to the meaning of the word Mohammed—"The Praised." Or it may have been that old Abd al Mottaleb was one of those who *could* see into the future. Whatever the reason, the baby was now Mohammed, a name which, in varying forms, has since been given to millions of little boys born into the faith which the son

MOHAMMED'S CHILDHOOD

of Abdallah and Amina was destined to found and spread all over the world.

For the moment no one had any such ideas. Abd al Mottaleb had chosen a fancy name for his grandchild, and he was sufficiently important to do as he pleased. Mohammed was an infant with nothing in the world to call his own except a mother, a few camels and goats, and a devoted black slave. Even his mother was not much good to him. The death of her husband had made her very unhappy, so that her milk turned sour and dried up. The murderous climate of Mecca was showing its effects on the baby. It looked as if the name with the high-sounding significance would be all that Mohammed would ever be able to boast about. Even this seemed unlikely. If something were not done quickly to feed the child, he would surely follow his father to the grave. For a few days he was suckled by a slave of his uncle Abu Lahab, called Thuweiba. But this could only be a temporary expedient.

Owing to the trying temperature of the Holy City, it was a Meccan custom to put well-to-do children out to nurse with the desert tribes. Twice a year the bedouin women, who were strong and healthy from living always in the open, came to the city to offer their services to the rich mothers of Mecca. But Amina was not rich, and these ladies of the desert did not give their milk for charity or even for the honor of suckling a baby of noble parentage. Amina was in despair, but at length found the wife of a shepherd of the Sa'adite nomads called Halima, who agreed to look after Mohammed. So one morning the baby boy who was to rule Arabia was carried out to the grazing country of the Beni Sa'ad on the back of a donkey. Mohammed had become a wanderer of the desert.

For five years he lived among the black tents. The Sa'adites belonged to one of the oldest tribes of Arabia. They were powerful, and their pastures were extensive. Mohammed's first words were spoken, his first steps were taken among these gentlemen of the wilderness who would one day fight him and later submit to him and finally carry his name to parts of the world which, at that time, none of them had heard of.

Mohammed was not precocious, but his mind and body were active. He walked before other babies of his age, and speech came to him easily. He thought more clearly than the average children of shepherds. This was not abnormal. Nomads, at the best of times, are not as quick as townspeople. As soon as his legs were long enough, he rode a donkey. He learned to use a small bow and set of arrows which his foster parents made for him.

The life Mohammed led was altogether in the open air. With the nomads ever roving in search of fresh pastures, his tent home was rarely in the same place for more than a few days at a time. His food was the simple fare of the desert: camel's milk, rice, dates, occasionally a piece of mutton or gazelle. Sometimes there were desert birds. After a locust storm he ate locusts fried in fat. He learned to rise with the day and go to bed when it was dark. He learned to respect the sun and give thanks for the rain, to meet the sandstorm and the fiery simoom with his face covered. He learned the primitive lore of the nomads, the code of an eye for an eye and a tooth for a tooth. He witnessed the summary justice, the expulsion from the tribe which was tantamount to sentence of death. He helped the shepherds and cameleers with their flocks and herds.

Those years which Mohammed spent in the hard school of the nomads had a marked effect on his character. The desert left its stamp. However sedentary a one-time nomad may become, the freedom of the open plain, the black tent as the only home, the struggle against the vagaries of nature remain in his mind. Again and again Mohammed showed evidence of the bedouin instinct.

Although the Sa'adite nomads declared that luck had been with them ever since Mohammed had become their guest, Halima decided that she must return her foster child to his mother. When he was six, therefore, she took him to Mecca and delivered him to Amina. Amina was glad to have her baby home, and pleased with the healthy change in his body. She decided that this would be a good time to show him to the other branch of the family which lived in Yathrib. Yathrib was an oasis town about two hundred miles from Mecca. It was here that her husband had died seven years before. One day it would be named after their son, Medinat en Nabi, the City of the Prophet.

It was a long and tiring trip across a wicked desert, alternating narrow gorges of hardened sand and stony, desolate plains. However, Amina and Baraka equipped a camel with provisions and a kind of wicker cradle protected from the sun by an awning in which they could sit with the little boy. With this done, they joined one of the weekly caravans making the northerly journey from Mecca.

Yathrib was a comforting contrast to the desert and Mecca. Instead of the glaring plains, instead of the jagged hills, instead of the gray houses baking in the fierce sunshine, here was something cool and green. In the hollow of an immense plain covered with fertile fields and dateries, the town lay white and tempting. There was nothing harsh about the picture, none of that sensation of always being at the mercy of burning daylight, none of that starving for water. In this land, the trees and shrubs were green and afforded shade, while water flowed gurgling through irrigation channels. For the three travelers it was like a vision of the Garden of Eden.

The change did Amina good. She showed off her son to his relations and took him to the house where his father had died. For a month Mohammed enjoyed the cool air, played with his cousins, and, strange for a little desert boy, learned to swim. If it had not been for the family being primarily Meccan, Amina might have stayed in this oasis and changed much of Arabia's history. But Mecca was the home town and returning was essential. Once more they sat in the swaying cradle on the back of the camel. The journey was delayed by sandstorms and burning winds. These were too much for Amina's never robust health. One night she died by the roadside. Baraka transported the body to a nearby village called Abwa, where it was buried.

Then she continued mournfully with Mohammed to Mecca. Here she presented him to his grandfather.

Abd al Mottaleb was now very old, but he was glad to have his grandson with him. For two years the patriarch and the stripling kept house together.

When the old man felt that he could not live much longer, he called his son Abu Taleb and bequeathed him Mohammed. Soon after, he died. Once more Mohammed changed his home. His life was developing into a series of violent contrasts.

The black tents of the desert, the modest quarters of his mother, the gardens of Yathrib, the comfortable home of his grandfather had succeeded one another rapidly. Now, with his uncle, Mohammed found himself in a kind of commercial household which, at the same time, was much mixed up with the sacred duties of the Kaaba.

Abd al Mottaleb had assigned his pious obligations to two sons. The Sikaya, or guardianship of Zemzem, with the distribution of the bitter water to the pilgrims, to Al Abbas. The Rifada, or poor-tax administration, which provided food for indigent pilgrims whom the city accepted as guests of God, to Abu Taleb.

In the desert Mohammed had lived in an atmosphere of nature worship. The stars, the sun, the moon, the storm were all the nomads respected. With Amina he had probably not been bothered with much religion. In his grandfather's home the ritual was far above his head and rather frightening. Now he met dogma and church politics at close quarters. He watched the ceremonial, he listened to the superstitions, he may have compared them to the simpler ideals of the desert people, but he was not specially interested. He was only a little over ten, and he had other things to think about than the merits of idols versus sun and moon. He played with little boys in the same way as other little boys have played together throughout the ages. He probably taught them things he had learned in the desert and found out a lot of things which only city-bred children would know.

But he was restless. For a Meccan child, he had seen quite a lot of the world. He felt enclosed by the streets and tall buildings. The barren hills around Mecca barred his views of the broad horizons of Arabia Deserta. His only contact with the outside were the caravans. Whenever these came into Mecca, Mohammed was there to greet them. He looked with awe at these sun-bronzed men who had dared the dangers of the long desert journeys. When a caravan was forming to leave, he was there too, envying the careless way these Arabs set out into the great unknown. Sometimes he talked to these cameleers and traders and discovered much about what was going on beyond the confines of the glittering desert. The more he discovered, the more he longed to go out and see things for himself. He wanted to become a camel driver, a merchant, a traveling salesman—anything to get away. One day his wish was granted.

Abu Taleb, in addition to being an official of the Meccan shrines, had other occupations. He kept an up-to-date clothing store and sold perfumes. The pre-Islamic Arabs were dressy and liked to turn out in elegant outfits which came from foreign lands. They also delighted in sweet-smelling essences, both for themselves and for their women. Abu Taleb, therefore, had business inside and outside the harems. But he did not let his activities hold him to the stores. He was a merchant by instinct and took a close interest in the caravans which his grandfather, Hashim, had initiated. Frequently he led the caravans himself. It was when Mohammed saw his uncle setting out that he longed to escape from the dusty streets and see what happened out there to the north and to the south.

These arrivals and departures of caravans were important events in the lives of the Meccans. Apart from the excitement of welcoming or bidding farewell to husbands and lovers and sons and nephews, there was the financial aspect. Almost everyone in Mecca had some kind of investment in the fortunes of the thousands of camels, the hundreds of men, horses, and donkeys which went out with hides, raisins, and silver bars, and came back with oils, perfumes, and manufactured goods from Syria and Egypt and Persia, and with spices and gold from the south. Mohammed had no investments, but he was none the less interested.

One morning he accompanied Abu Taleb to the assembly point of the caravans with even greater interest than usual. The market square was seething with gurgling, grunting camels, with patient donkeys and spirited horses. Arabs and Syrians and Persians, black men and Hebrews, jostled one another in a babel of tongues. It was not quite dawn, and the flaring torches added to the excitement of the scene. The appearance of Abu Taleb was the signal for the final settling of loads and tightening of girths ready for the order to move. As Abu Taleb was mounting his camel, Mohammed suddenly seized his uncle's hand and begged to be allowed to come too. His entreaty was so sincere that the kindly Abu Taleb smiled and let Mohammed join him on his camel. Then he gave the signal to go. For the third time in his young life Mohammed the son of Abdallah was leaving the shelter of Mecca.

In a few moments the mauve dawn crept across the desert. Deeply the animals drank the cool morning air as they came slowly up out of the rocky cup in which Mecca lay. Mohammed, too, breathed deeply as he viewed this new day which would bring him closer to a new world.

This first trip made a strong impression on Mohammed. His roamings with the nomad shepherds had never taken him very far, and they had always been in a country where there were wells and scrub pasture. Here, however, he found himself in the vastness of the waterless desert where any mistake in the route would lead to death from thirst. The landscape had that openness of the sea. Not a rock or a bush or a tree relieved the monotony of the horizon. There was no shelter from the wind or the sun. It was the land of flints, of stony nakedness blackened by prehistoric fires. Every pebble had been ground down and polished by the ever drifting sand. It was the haunt of djinns, so the cameleers told, the homes of weird creatures who alone could live on these plains of eternal silence.

The journey was dreary and slow. The stately pace of the

camels could not be hurried, and at the end of the day the monotonous scenery gave the impression that no progress had been made since the night before. It was a relief, therefore, that one evening, the shimmering wilderness was left behind. Soon the caravan was crossing into what is now Trans-Jordan. At a place called Bosra the first long halt was made.

This Bosra was a trading place where Greek merchants came to barter with the Arabs. In exchange for the rawhides from the desert and the raisins from the oasis of At Tayef and the silver from the mines of Beni Soleim, they gave brocades and linens and spices and perfumes and jewelry. Everything was bustle and laughter. After the harassing journey through the land of thirst, it was like waking from a hideous dream. Mohammed was even more excited than the others. Everything was so new, so unexpected. He was meeting different kinds of people also, people unlike any he had ever seen before, people with ideas foreign to any with which he had ever been in contact.

Near the Bosra market was a monastery of Nestorian monks—Christians. They knew Abu Taleb and offered him and his nephew hospitality. One of the monks, whose name was Bahira, took a special interest in Mohammed. His inquiring mind, his eagerness for knowledge, his lucid thoughts impressed him. He talked to the Arab boy as if he was a contemporary. He told him about the creed of the followers of Christ. He denounced idolatry. Mohammed listened. All that this man was giving him was so strange, so different from what he had been brought up to believe. The only other person who had ever suggested anything of the kind was his Ethiopian slave-nurse, Baraka. But her Christianity was garbled, and he had not rightly understood what she was talking about. What he was hearing now was much clearer. Idols and the worship of the elements did not seem to make so much sense. This was something alive, real, leading to a future.

It is not in the least likely that Mohammed had at that time any ideas about religion and the way it might apply to himself. In fact, up to his middle age, there is nothing to show that any serious scruples had occurred to him about the worshiping of the Kaaba idols. On the other hand, he did not forget what the Nestorian monk had told him. He kept it stored in his mind, and, when the time came, there was this groundwork of Christianity of which he made full use.

The monk was not the only new influence at this time. One of the principal fairs in the neighborhood of Mecca was at 'Okaz. Here, in vast hostile confusion, converged monotheistic Jews and Christians, and idolatrous Arabs and fire-worshiping Persians. The rivalry and hostility, however, ceased with the opening of the fair. Religious tolerance was demanded, personal quarrels were made up, prisoners were exchanged, and all differences were forgotten in a kind of Olympic Games atmosphere. A certain amount of business was contracted, but the main attractions were the side shows. Every kind of entertainment was furnished, from races and poetry contests and drinking and dancing to sermons.

Among the preachers was Kuss ibn Saida, Christian bishop of Nejran. Daily, from the back of his tall camel, he spoke of his faith. For hours he would talk of the futility of this life and of the glories of the world to come. Mohammed only listened to fragments of these orations, yet often in later years he preached from the back of his own camel and his sermons had many of the exhortations of this Christian prelate.

Abu Taleb had heard all this kind of talk before and was not impressed. He did not understand what it was all about and did not suppose that his nephew paid any more attention than he did. In this, he was right—up to a certain point. Mohammed was a normal boy, and if he was more than usually impressed it was because it was all so fresh. For the first time, he had caught a glimpse of a new world, a world where the sun was not an enemy and the rain a kind of miracle which everyone prayed for but no one expected except in the form of a cloudburst. He had seen grass and trees, and people who led leisurely lives given up to more constructive things than constantly fighting nature. He had heard people talking on other subjects than pilgrimages and money and Kaaba politics.

Mohammed was to have little formal school education, but he was learning more than any of the scholars who spent their days in classrooms. He had no wish for schooling, either. He had tasted adventure, and he wanted more. If ever a man was to have a longing granted, it was he, the heir to the Hashimite guardians of the idols of Mecca.

CHAPTER III

MOHAMMED'S YOUTH

(586-597 After Christ)

MOHAMMED EMERGED from boyhood rapidly. Before he was sixteen he had done more traveling than most Meccans in a lifetime. He had also been to war. His eldest uncle, Az Zubeir, was a commander of the Koreishite armies. During a long-drawn-out campaign against the Hawazinite tribe, he frequently took his nephew with him. Mohammed did not have much to do and had no opportunity to distinguish himself. His chief occupation was to pick up arrows shot by the enemy and hand them to his uncle. Nevertheless he had acquired another experience more maturing than years at school.

The caravans too were giving him a healthy joy of living. Every mile he covered—and he had covered many before he was twenty—increased his enthusiasm and made him want to go further. Arabia, from Yemen to Syria, Palestine and north toward Persia, had become as much of a routine as his contemporaries' visits to the Kaaba. Those journeys are arduous enough today with the aid of trucks and automobiles; in Mohammed's time they lasted weeks and months. The men who undertook them had to be able to stand the grueling climate, to fight raiders, and bring their animals with their precious loads in a fit condition to their destinations. Being a commercial traveler in the five hundreds was a man's job.

Mohammed soon found himself representing other merchants as well as his uncle. His reputation for hard work and honesty had spread. Before he was twenty-five, he had become one of the most active traveling salesmen in western Arabia.

Where, however, he was different from the average businessman was that he was interested in things outside the filling of orders for linens and silks and sugar and rice. When the day's work was over he sat in the market squares or in a friend's house and listened. Here were musicians and storytellers and poets. Philosophers, too, who engaged in discussions, and holy men who discoursed on the subjects of their faiths. As trip succeeded trip, Mohammed accumulated knowledge of the traditions and religions and history of these parts of Asia. He also acquired the kind of worldly wisdom which is characteristic of men who spend their time "on the road," whether on camels or in carts or in Chevrolets. As one studies his story, this common sense stands out like a searchlight. Mohammed gives the impression of someone belonging to another age. There are occasions when his laws and judgments, his approaches to current problems, startle one by their modernness. His whole attitude to life is far in advance of the people with whom he lived.

The fact of the matter is that Mohammed's contacts with foreign places and peoples made him think. Unlike other prophets, his thoughts were not limited by divine horizons. He saw the world and its problems as they were. When he came to spiritualizing his ideas, he did not leave the practical, the mundane, completely out of what he was trying to build. He avoided the pitfalls of preceding evangelists who had tried to send their flocks to redemption over unfamiliar roads. Mohammed's roads were those of a traveling salesman. Along these he directed his followers, adding God to the caravan and Paradise as the final market place.

But while Mohammed's mind and body correspondingly developed, he does not seem to have made much money for himself. He presumably received a salary and earned his commissions, yet he was not well off. Money never interested him, and there were times when he became weary of traveling in close association with other men and wanted to be alone. As he could not afford unpaid leisure, he accepted temporary jobs as a shepherd. Like Moses and David, he used to disappear for long spells into the desert. For weeks he would have nothing on his mind but keeping his flocks on the move. Years later, referring to this, he said:

"Verily, there have been no prophets who performed not the work of shepherds."

But, whatever he was doing—trading perfumes or carpets in Damascus or watching over flocks in the silences of the desert—his character remained the same. His honesty, his truthfulness, his virtue were never spoiled. From the earliest days, his friends called him Al Amin—The Trusty. Women could do nothing with him. He had no special principles about chastity, he was just not interested. The sex instincts which were to invade the last years of his life were dormant. But he was at ease in society. He had a ready wit. A pleasing way of speaking made him popular. He was always carefully dressed.

On the road and in the camp he had to suit himself to circumstances, but at home he took pains with his personal appearance. He tied his turban with care and drew the *tailasan*, or scarf which covered it, low over his face. His tunic and his cloak were always well laundered, and though, in later years, he went in for greens and yellows and reds, white was always the foundation of his costume.

He had a special horror of people with dirty teeth. His own were of singular brilliance, but unusual. Though symmetrical, they were like the teeth of a saw, and some distance from each other. But the fact that his teeth were naturally good was not enough. He had a mania for keeping them perfect. Wherever he went, he carried toothpicks. He kept some always by his bed and never traveled without his supply.

The strong white teeth were in keeping with the rest of Mohammed's physical appearance. He was of average height, with a well-molded, strongly built frame, broad shoulders, and narrow hips. No superfluous flesh covered his bones; on the contrary, he inclined to leanness. He walked rapidly as a man who knows where he is going and wants to get there. His head was large and well formed and set on a slender neck. His hair, glossy and black and inclined to curl, he wore long. Sometimes it reached to his shoulders like a flowing mane. Great black, restless eyes shone from under heavy lashes. A beard, which, as he grew older, was allowed to spread to an impressive size, was dark and curly. The mustache was kept clipped and did not hide the graceful, sensual mouth which had the ripe redness of a freshly cut pomegranate. He had a thin, aristocratic nose, Semitically aquiline. His face was lean and rosy, with a clear skin almost of a woman's. As with all Arabs, his hands and feet were small and well shaped.

In two ways Mohammed was physically different from other men. Between finely arching eyebrows, which mutually approached but did not meet, was a strongly marked blood vessel which, when he was angry, would turn black and throb. Also, in the middle of his back, a little above the shoulder blades, was a large mole, the size of a pigeon's egg. This was held by the faithful to be the divine seal of prophecy. Mohammed never referred to this birthmark, probably because he could not see it, and nothing he said ever suggested that he thought it had anything to do with his prophetic calling.

When he laughed, he laughed heartily. He was amused and did not want to disguise it. But his chief charm was in his smile. The muscles of the mouth and cheeks had a way of contracting which made the most hostile pause when a quarrel was on the way.

His handshake was as genuine as his laugh. He grasped the offered hand firmly and was never the first to withdraw. Throughout the whole of his life, he never changed his allegiance to a friend. He was sincerely fond of animals and children. Little boys and girls always crowded round him when he walked. He would not allow his followers to ill-treat dumb creatures.

In spite of this cordiality, however, Mohammed was not much of a talker. That is to say, he had that admirable Arab gift of speaking only when he had something which he thought was worth while making a basis for conversation.

"The beauty of man's Islam," he declared, "is that he shuns discussing unnecessary things."

But, with all these physical gifts and fine family background, there was no evidence, up to the age of twenty-five, that Mohammed would ever be anything more than a reliable traveling salesman, or a shepherd who could be counted on not to run off with his employer's flocks. To the people of Mecca he was a good-natured, capable, rather above the average young man, whose morals were better than most. "He was more modest than a virgin behind a curtain," was said of him by one of his friends. There is no record of his having done anything outstanding, probably because he *did* nothing outstanding. Such an anecdote as the following, often quoted as evidence of unusual sagacity, does not prove anything beyond that Mohammed had more common sense than his fellow citizens.

Unremitting floods from cloudbursts over the Mecca hills had undermined the Kaaba. Its foundations were tottering, and rebuilding a good deal of it was necessary. After some anxious discussion, certain carefully selected Koreishites took pick and shovel and set to work. No divine vengeance attacked them, and the removal of the Black Stone from its niche passed unchallenged. But when it came to replacing the fetish, an argument developed. Who should have the honor? Who should have this extra-special honor of touching the idol of idols and carrying it back to where it belonged? When no satisfactory solution to the question could be arrived at, someone suggested asking the advice of the first man who walked into the courtyard of the Beit Allah. This was agreed to, and the group of men relaxed and watched the gate. In a little while Mohammed strolled in. He was immediately hailed and had the problem laid before him. After a moment's reflection he took off his cloak and spread it on the ground.

"Place the Black Stone on my cloak," he suggested, "then each one of you take a corner and lift it. In this way you can all share in carrying the Stone to where it comes from."

This the men did. When the wall of the Kaaba was reached, Mohammed thrust the Black Stone into the hole where it belonged before anyone could start another argument.

However simple was this solution, it raised Mohammed in the estimation of the older men. Arabs flare up quickly, and the Black Stone problem might have led to a fight and, thence, to a blood feud. This Mohammed had averted.

Nevertheless, in a general way his life was drifting into an obscure routine which showed no indication of ever being more than an obscure routine. Then, when he was twenty-five, something happened which was not only to alter his whole existence, but, indirectly, have repercussions all over the world.

Living in Mecca at this time was a lady of middle age called Khadija bint Khuweilid. To be precise, she was forty. She was of the Koreish clan, and a cousin of Mohammed through a mutual great-great-great grandfather. Being, however, of an elder generation, she was unacquainted with her kinsman. Two husbands had predeceased her, both of whom had left her their commercial banking houses, which their widow had merged. The merger had been successful and had prospered under the new management.

Khadija's business methods were modern. She loaned money to reliable Koreishite merchants, in return for which she became a partner in the transactions which she had backed. She also invested the money of her smaller depositors in caravans. When the caravans returned from their trading expeditions, the profits were shared in proportion to the investments. Khadija also had her employees, in the town office and on the road, financially interested in her various business enterprises. They thus found themselves, at the same time, her employees, her creditors, and her shareholders. The success, therefore, of everything which the firm undertook was to the interest of all, from the president and managers to the accountants and the lowliest cameleers.

However, being a career woman did not deprive Khadija of charm. While in Arab reckoning she was already old, in her reckoning she was as young as she felt. Neither had she any idea of giving in for a while. True, she was running to plumpness, but her skin was fresh, her hair was glossy and black, her eyes large and twinkling. She wore her dark robes and her rich cloth mantle becomingly. The silver-and-turquoise jewelry which adorned her hands and ears and neck was always in good taste. She was, in fact, still desirable physically as well as very rich. The only thing lacking was the right man.

Although Khadija's mind was as alive as her body, she felt that she needed someone experienced in business, trustworthy, and energetic to look after her affairs. Especially she wanted someone to take charge of her trading caravans. She was cautious, though, and had no intention of entrusting her fortune and her trains of camels and mules to someone who might disappear into Syria or Egypt and never be heard of again. So for a while she presided over the firm herself.

Khadija had a nephew called Khuzaima who was about Mohammed's age. He had been his traveling companion on several trading expeditions and, like all those who came into contact with him, appreciated his ability and his integrity. He spoke to Khadija about his friend.

About the same time Abu Taleb had been advising his nephew to expand his connections and aim at representing the biggest firms in the city. When, therefore, the opening with Khadija was suggested, Mohammed applied for an interview.

His good looks and charming smile undoubtedly did as much to help the already good opinion which Khadija's nephew had promoted as his business credentials. Khadija was also impressed by the young man's not accepting the post immediately. Mohammed was not one to jump to decisions. Whether it was a matter of business or battle or religion, he always thought things out. Before giving his reply to the banking widow, he consulted his uncle. Abu Taleb felt that this was the very thing for his nephew, and when he heard that Khadija was ready to give him double what he had been receiving, he urged him to sign on at once.

Mohammed accordingly entered the service of Khadija and, in so doing, placed his foot on the first rung of the ladder which would take him to the sovereignty of all Arabia.

To begin with, Khadija sent her nephew and her personal slave, an Ethiopian called Maisara, with Mohammed. She was a sensible woman and wanted to make sure that she had not allowed personal feelings to overrule common sense. She need not have worried. The way Mohammed discharged his duties and the excellent business he did for his new employer made her again raise his wages. A few months later she appointed him head of all her caravans.

For the next two years Mohammed traveled on behalf of Khadija to most of the places to which caravans had, at that time, penetrated. Damascus, Aleppo, Antioch, Jerusalem, Beyrouth, Palmyra, Baalbek—all were on his beat. Soon there were added other responsibilities: the management of the whole firm. When he was not on the road, Mohammed would be at the office looking after the administrative side of the business. Here would come Khadija to listen to suggestions from her handsome director which always led to increase of income for her trading concerns.

And, outside the money-making aspects of the association, Khadija was happy. She looked forward to these talks. She counted the days to the return of the caravan. She waited eagerly until Mohammed, bathed and in clean white clothes, his hair and beard dressed and perfumed, came to give her the news. Gradually she found herself becoming less interested in the business and more interested in her charming and virile manager. She found herself no longer satisfied to wait in her house or office for the news of the arrival of the caravan. She would go up to the terrace roof of her home and look out over the barren hills for the first glimpse of the camels padding slowly down the rocky road. For the first time in her life, Khadija was falling in love.

But how could she convey these disturbing feelings to the object of her affections? How? She was now forty-two and old enough to know better. How could she explain these violent emotions for a man fifteen years her junior? Not only that, but an employee of hers. An employee who had not a dirhem in the world which he did not earn from her! And what would her family say about it? What would Omar ibn Assad, her aged uncle and guardian, say about it? She knew exactly. He and everyone else would laugh and tell her not to be an old fool. Everyone would say that she had been lucky enough to bury two rich husbands amicably and not to experiment a third time with someone who was young enough to be her son. As far as her family was concerned, she knew their exact reactions. If she let one of them suspect what was on her mind, the little chance there was of her getting Mohammed would be gone. She must think up other methods. The trouble was that she had no idea of what Mohammed thought of her.

Mohammed felt just nothing. He was doing the kind of work he liked. He was earning good money and being given credit for his enterprise. Khadija was a fine employer. He admired and respected her. That was all. The fact of the matter was that, up till then, women had still made no impression on Mohammed's life. It would have required the courage which he had not to make advances to any girl. To do such a thing to his revered employer was no more in his mind than that he might one day be ruler of Arabia. Yet the employer and Arabia were both within his reach.

Khadija sensed this shyness and decided to act herself. For this purpose she commissioned her slave Maisara.

Maisara had accompanied Mohammed on many of his journeys. In spite of the difference in their respective positions, the close associations and shared hardships of desert journeys had made them friends. Mohammed, then, as in the days of his future greatness, was of easy access and never had any ideas of being better than, or socially situated above, anyone else. Maisara had, therefore, no compunctions about talking informally on the subject of marriage.

How was it, he asked, that a man of nearly twenty-eight, with ability and good looks and a fine family background, had never married? Mohammed replied, with equal candor, that he had never thought much about it. He had been too busy. He was glad, too, that he had not; for how could a man who spent his life on the road, dependent on a salary and commission, establish the kind of home which would be expected of someone of his age and upbringing? Maisara countered this with the suggestion that he might "marry money." This amused Mohammed. How could a traveling salesman meet a wealthy woman, and if he did how could he even suggest marriage?

Maisara laughed. "But supposing a wealthy lady asked you to marry *her?*" and added, "A good-looking lady and of the best family?"

Mohammed was still more amused. Who was this dream creature whom Maisara had in mind?

He could not have been more taken aback when Maisara replied unhesitatingly: "Khadija!" and continued before Mohammed had time to recover from his astonishment. "If you'll leave it to me, I will arrange everything."

It took a while for Maisara to convince Mohammed that the idea was serious. It took him a further while to make him see that the idea made sense. As soon as he had done this, an interview was planned between Mohammed and Khadija.

They had often met alone before, but always in the firm's office. Today the talk took place in Khadija's own apartments. Mohammed was shy, and Khadija had to do all the explaining. When she had finished, Mohammed gratefully accepted the proposal. Everything seemed set for an immediate wedding. But not yet! Mohammed had been won, the family had not.

When Omar ibn Assad, the uncle and guardian of the bride-to-be, heard of the intended alliance, he flew into a rage. Then he said No with definiteness. He pointed out that everything was against such an idea: Mohammed's age, the fact that he was in Khadija's employ, and, above all, that he had no money. In Omar's mind this marriage was merely a means of dispersing the wealth of Khadija instead of keeping it in the family. It was the basis for the old squabble among relatives which has gone on ever since material values and tokens for values were thought of.

Khadija had anticipated all this and had counterarguments to her uncle's objections. These, however, had no effect on the old man, and it looked as if Mohammed might, after all, spend the rest of his life on the road.

It may be wondered why Khadija, forty-two and a widow, was still under the tutelage of her uncle. The explanation is that a custom existed whereby a daughter without a husband, whether maid or widow, remained under the guardianship of the head of the family. Without his consent, a marriage could not take place.*

But, though annoyed, Khadija was not discouraged. She had her uncle's obstinacy, and she also had her woman's wit. She let the matter drop. She let the storm pass. When everyone was off guard, when the atmosphere was serene, she gave a dinner. To the dinner she invited all her nearest relations, including her uncle. She also asked two of Mohammed's uncles, Abu Taleb and Hamza, and several other important members of the Koreish clan. She asked, of course, Mohammed and her nephew, Khuzaima, who had first introduced them.

The dinner had been specially ordered and carefully cooked. With it were served quantities of imported wines and liqueurs. Soon everyone was in high spirits. Toasts were being drunk, speeches were being made, the warmth of a well-wined gathering was everywhere. The only diners who were completely sober were Khadija and Mohammed.

Choosing her time, Khadija made a speech herself. She spoke of Mohammed as the mind which had made her business prosper, as the man who, by his enterprise, had greatly increased her fortune. She spoke of his integrity, of his noble lineage. She concluded that it would be an honor for any woman to marry such a man. All the guests applauded. More wine was poured. A cousin of Khadija called Waraka jumped up and seconded what Khadija had just said. There was more applause and more wine. Abu Taleb and then Hamza concurred with Khadija and Waraka. Before Omar ibn Assad knew what it was all about,

---

*Many biographers substitute Khuweilid, Khadija's father, for Omar ibn Assad. While this is of no importance to this story, Khuweilid actually died before his daughter met Mohammed.

he had made a speech himself approving of the engagement. Mohammed at once clothed the old man in the robe which, according to tradition, a son-in-law gave his father-in-law at a wedding. At the same time Khadija anointed her uncle's hair with saffron and ambergris perfumes. The applause echoed round the courts of Khadija's house. As far as custom was concerned, Mohammed and Khadija were married.

But Khadija was not taking any risks. She knew how much wine had had to do with this cordial spirit. She was familiar with the reactions of mornings after. So, while everyone was patting everyone else on the back and toasting and boasting, she had the lawyers come in. In the same friendly atmosphere the marriage contract was drawn up, the dowry arranged, and everything else settled. According to the laws of Mecca, Mohammed and Khadija were bound and tied as man and wife. When the party broke up, Mohammed said good night to the guests and remained with his bride.

It is said that Omar had a headache next morning and grumbled over his ward marrying a nobody when she could have had anyone in Mecca. But Mohammed's uncles cut him short with the rejoinder that the grandson of Abd al Mottaleb was also good enough for anyone in Mecca, and outside Mecca too. In any case, what Omar thought or did not think no longer mattered. The marriage had been legally performed, and nothing could undo it.

The general wedding festivities followed quickly after the nuptial rites. Mohammed killed a camel and distributed the flesh to the poor. Khadija declared "open house" to her friends and to the friends of Mohammed. Dancers danced and musicians played from dawn to dusk and from dusk to dawn. Never had there been such merriment in the home of the president of the illustrious firm of Khadija, Inc. No one enjoyed it more than the plump hostess. Maisara was in attendance at the party; so was the faithful Baraka. Halima, Mohammed's foster mother, was brought in from the desert. Khadija made her a present of forty sheep and sent her back to the camp, proclaiming again that her charitable action in nursing Amina's sickly baby had brought luck to the Sa'adite tribesmen. Finally the revelry stopped and Mohammed was able to turn his attention to the more serious matter of managing his wife's business—while Khadija relapsed into an ecstatic state, as she gazed at this engaging and handsome husband.

It was the beginning of an extremely happy marriage. Khadija was passionately in love with Mohammed. Mohammed's feelings were more of affection and attachment for his bride. In a different way, he probably loved her more deeply than she loved him. He certainly cared more about Khadija than any other woman, perhaps more than any other person, in his life. During the twenty-one years they were married, she received his undivided attention, and that in a country where polygamy was practiced and recognized. Whatever may have been the bases of Mohammed's subsequent love affairs, Khadija was his first woman and, in his mind, she certainly remained his last.

CHAPTER IV

THE CALL

(599–611 After Christ)

MOHAMMED'S UNION with Khadija did not immediately affect his way of living. He continued as head of the firm and did not give up his trips with the caravans. Some of Mohammed's most distant journeys to fairs and to markets of Asia Minor were undertaken after his marriage. Nevertheless, the business of the late house of Khadija did not improve. It fact it deteriorated. There were no heavy losses, and Khadija continued to be one of the richest in Mecca, but her commercial methods had lost their sting. In other words, Mohammed had lost *his* sting. He had lost interest in something which he had been doing because he had to.

With the relief from the daily necessity to earn, Mohammed was finding time to think about all kinds of things which had been accumulating in his head. Sometimes, when he should have been signing a contract or martialing a caravan, his wife would find him lost in a daydream. It was not laziness. It was not the case of a man suddenly introduced to wealth letting things slide. Mohammed was not lazy. From his childhood to his death, sloth was never one of his weaknesses. It was rather the case of a good mind, which had been obliged to concentrate on uncongenial subjects, unexpectedly finding its freedom. Khadija, being a wise woman, sensed something of what was stirring in her husband. Being a tactful wife, she did not nag. She let him be. Thus, once more, she was helping to lay the foundations of Islam. In this she had an enthusiastic abettor in her cousin Waraka, who had backed her up at the wedding feast.

Waraka was somewhat of a mystery man. Without anything

to gain by it, he had been the only member of Khadija's family to take her side when she wanted to marry Mohammed. He was the first also to support Mohammed when he began to have ideas about a mission. What he believed in himself is uncertain. He was born a pagan, then he became a Jew, and later on a Christian. The first translation into Arabic of the Old and New Testaments is attributed to Waraka. Much of the knowledge which Mohammed had of the Torah and the Talmud of the Jews and of the Christian Gospels came from this man. It was the outcome of talks with Waraka, together with what he had picked up during his travels, which made Mohammed dream in his office and loll on his camel.

Up to that time, he had never seriously questioned the ritual of the Kaaba. He and his wife were conventional idolators who prayed to Allah Ta'ala and his consort Allat, as well as to the other gods and goddesses. That they were made of stone did not particularly worry Mohammed. His grandfather had found them deserving of his attention, which seemed a good enough recommendation. As a matter of fact, Mohammed had never given the subject more than occasional thought. Except when he was pasturing sheep, he had not had much opportunity. Now that he had the leisure to turn over in his mind what Waraka discoursed about, what the Nestorian monk at Bosra had said so many years ago, what the bishop of Nejran had preached about, what he had heard in the distant cities of Asia Minor, the Kaaba and all that went with it seemed to lack something.

The great desert shrine was like an overcrowded hen coop after sunset. Three hundred and sixty rude stone figures encumbered its dimly lit interior. They had been brought from all corners of Arabia. Some were from Syria and Egypt. The statues of Abraham and Ishmael, which had been nothing more than reminders of the founders of the Arab race, had become part of the pagan worship. Mary and Jesus were there with divining arrows thrust into their cold hands as symbols of magic.

The absurdity of the whole thing surged over Mohammed like the dawn of a new day. It was impossible to reconcile the mystic thoughts which his mind was generating with this worship of grotesque and shapeless figures of stone, some of which were nothing more than phallic emblems, some no more than shapeless blocks of rock. Still he had no solution. The more he considered the matter, the more baffled he felt.

After a while, which must be measured in years, the negative conclusions faded and rematerialized into constructive ideas, into ideas for religious reform. Vaguely, and then lucidly, Mohammed reasoned, and his reasoning took on something of this order.

To Adam must have been revealed the bases, the origins, of all religions. These must have been simple and inartificial; they had had to do with one God. That God was still there? He must be if He was the God who had created the universe. The universe was the best evidence of God. Therefore, presuming that He was there, He should be worshiped, He should be consecrated as the source of everything now and in the hereafter. Neither did it require a great deal of thought to identify Him right there in Mecca. He was Allah, the Lord of the Kaaba, the God who was reverenced above all the vague deities whom the Arabs worshiped.

In deciding this, Mohammed was not falling back against the line of least resistance. He was not adapting one of the idols to suit his theory. Allah was not a name like Baal or Zeus, it was a contraction of Al Ilah, which signified "*The* God," in the same way as "Allat," contracted from "Al Ilat," signified "*The* Goddess." Allah Ta'ala, as He was also referred to, meant "The Most High God." The situation was rather like that of the Athenians whom Paul found dedicating an altar, among their many altars, "To the Unknown God."

These thoughts arranged themselves slowly in Mohammed's head like the figures of an intricate mathematical problem, but without there being any clear conclusion. Mohammed was no scholar, and the mind of a traveling salesman could not suddenly change the way it had reasoned for twenty years. Besides, he was not going to proclaim a theological doctrine until he was sure of it. He was not yet an inspired preacher. He was more or less of a retired businessman with the shrewd instincts of his profession. He was, above all, a man of good faith.

There was a further reason for not broadcasting these new ideas. While Mohammed had many friends, he had but few intimates. Outside his wife, there were really only three. These were all as different as possible in temperament and age and background. If it had not been for Mohammed, they would probably never have come into contact.

The youngest was Ali. He was the son of Abu Taleb and thus the first cousin of Mohammed who had also adopted him to ease the financial strain of his uncle's overcrowded household. Ali was a lively, husky boy of fourteen who, from the earliest days, hero-worshiped his cousin and foster father.

Mohammed's closest and only contemporary friend was Abdallah ibn Othman. No one, however, knew him by that name. He was usually referred to as As Siddik, "The True," or more often as Abu Bakr, "father of the young camel." It is uncertain when he adopted this last designation, but it is the one by which he has gone down to history and which I will use.

Abu Bakr was a wealthy merchant who had made a position and fortune from humble origins. He was shrewd and intelligent, and though lacking Mohammed's emotional enthusiasm, in some aspects a greater character. Short and spare, with a fine eaglelike head, his face was reddish and partially covered by a thin beard. Although his money gave him access to Mecca's luxuries, although he remained Mohammed's right-hand man from the beginning of his mission to his death, although he became the first caliph of Islam, his ways of thinking and living were those of an ascetic. His character, in many ways, resembled that of his descendant, Othman Ali, the present Nizam of Hyderabad.

The third of Mohammed's intimates was Zaid, a Christian convert whom a nephew of Khadija had captured during a raid into Syria. Mohammed had taken an interest in the young man, so Khadija had assigned him as personal slave to her husband. Zaid was then twenty, small and dark and rather ugly, but diligent and devoted to his master. When, one day, his family, having traced him to Mecca, came with the necessary funds to redeem him, Zaid declared that he was happy where he was and refused to go home. This devotion touched Mohammed, and he led him at once to the Kaaba. Here, in the presence of Zaid's father, he laid his hand on the Black Stone and swore:

"Bear testimony, all ye that are here present. Zaid is my son. I will be his heir and he shall be mine."

With that he formally adopted him and freed Zaid from slavery, but tied him up in another way by marrying him to his old nurse, Baraka. She was twenty years the young man's senior, nevertheless she bore him a son who was named Osama and became a distinguished general in the armies of Islam.

But, although these three were nearly always with Mohammed, he did not confide in any of them yet. During the twelve years which succeeded his marriage, no one knew of the spiritual changes which he was undergoing except Khadija.

The middle-aged wife was still blissfully happy. Mohammed's tenderness toward her had increased; his consideration had remained at the same level as on their wedding night. At no time did he suggest insulting her presence in the harem by introducing a rival. Khadija did not know what exactly was going on in her husband's mind, but she did not ask questions or let the matter worry her. She did not really have the leisure. In addition to keeping her eye on the business, she was occupied by having babies. Contrary to all expectations, this comparatively old lady bore Mohammed two sons and four daughters.

The eldest of the sons was Kasim. Some oriental writers still refer to Mohammed as Abu Kasim, the father of Kasim. But Kasim died, and his death drove Mohammed more and more into himself and to weighing his misgivings about what he had been brought up to believe. The other boy died in infancy. All of the daughters grew to maturity, but three predeceased their father. Only one of the children survived him. This was Fatima, who became the wife of her cousin Ali. Today she is revered by the Shia Moslems as the ancestress of Islam's denomination, and one-time dynasty, of the Fatimides. They regard her, moreover, as the mother of the hereditary line of caliphs.

Had Mohammed's sons lived, it is possible that his cares might have been quite different.

But there were no little boys to bring up, so he continued to ruminate on his ideas for a religious reformation in Mecca. Again and again he went back over all he remembered hearing during the caravan days. These thoughts brought him to a second conclusion.

The primitive and pure faith of Adam had been corrupted by men. In order to counteract this, a succession of prophets had been sent to the world by God. Noah had been one of these, so had Abraham and Moses, so had John the Baptist and Jesus Christ. Abraham especially appealed to Mohammed. Unlike the other envoys of the Almighty, he did not represent any dogmatic teaching. According to Mohammed, he was neither Jew nor Christian. He was certainly a purist.

These theories led Mohammed to further thought. Had not nearly six hundred years passed since the death of Christ? Was it not time for another prophet to appear to reform the world? The 360 idols cluttering up the Kaaba certainly suggested it.

The moment that notion took hold of Mohammed, all interest in business faded. Soon it died. Solitude became an obsession. He had had such addictions during his traveling-salesman days which he had satisfied by having himself hired to pasture sheep in the desert. But now, as one of the most important citizens of Mecca, this was impossible. So he just avoided society and rarely appeared among his former companions of the road. He even took to absenting himself from his home. Khadija did not interfere. She did all she could to help. But there was nothing much to do. With what was seething inside of him, Mohammed needed complete severance from human associations.

The place he chose for his retreat was Mount Hira, a few miles outside Mecca. Mount Hira was really a gigantic rock polished by sand and wind and rent in the middle by a great cleft. It stood

THE CALL

alone in the dazzling white glare of the Arabian sun, shimmering and barren and waterless. Within its rocky side was a small, dark cave. Here Mohammed spent days, sometimes days and nights, in silent meditation. He ate little, he slept little, and gradually developed a nervous tensity which had nothing of the carefree businessman of a few years back.

These fasts and vigils naturally affected the health of one who had been accustomed to plenty of food and exercise and a life in the open. Mohammed's rare sleeps became troubled with strange dreams, which he remembered vividly on waking and told to Khadija. Sometimes he lost consciousness and lay on the ground like one dead. Sometimes he went into convulsions.

It is from reports of these attacks that has sprung the story that Mohammed was epileptic. This is still a matter of controversy. A majority asserts that Mohammed suffered from epilepsy. There are many, however, who affirm that these fits were veritable trances brought on by the realization that there was something infinitely higher and better than the cult of the Kaaba. In view of what is known today about Yoga and the conditions into which Indians can project themselves, this theory seems valid.

The facts of Mohammed's case, according to contemporary traditions and the evidence of Khadija, are these. Shortly before he had his first revelation—that is, when he was thirty-nine to forty—and then on through his life, he was seized with violent trembling, followed by a fainting spell. This was accompanied by heavy perspiring, even in the coldest weather. On some occasions he would lie for appreciable periods with tightly closed eyes, moaning.

Mohammed knew that he had these attacks and was self-conscious about them. Few people except Khadija and his subsequent wives saw him in this condition. It must be noted, moreover, that Mohammed never said anything of importance while these paroxysms lasted. Every word of the Koran was dictated clearheadedly after the revelations had taken place. Any medical man will confirm that an epileptic does not come out of his fit with lucid thoughts. Neither is such a one in the fine physical health which Mohammed enjoyed until a week before he died. There is no reason why these symptoms should not have been brought on by malaria or some other fever or that they came from sheer exaltation.

However, whether it was epilepsy or malaria or a spiritual trance does not seem to matter, in spite of all that has been said on the subject. Epilepsy never made anyone into a prophet or a lawgiver or raised anyone to positions of esteem and power. In those days, especially, such a state would suggest someone possessed or insane. If ever there was a man who was clearly sane, it was Mohammed.

The first of the divine revelations took place in the year 610 A.C. It was during the month of Ramadan, and Mohammed had gone to his cave on Mount Hira to fast and pray and meditate. The sun had set on the night of Al Kadar. Al Kadar, according to the Koran, is the night which is better than a thousand months, bringing peace and blessing until rosy dawn. The Arabs say that on this night angels visit the world and Gabriel brings down the decrees of Allah from heaven.

Wrapped in his mantle, Mohammed lay on the rock floor of his cave half asleep. Suddenly a voice—a strange, clear voice unlike any he had heard before—roused him. Twice the voice called, each time more urgently. Mohammed, with his superstitions about djinns, tried to close his ears to the voice. But it persisted and grew louder. The effect was so disturbing that Mohammed fainted. When he came to, he saw a dazzling angel in human form standing before him. The same voice spoke once more:

"Read thou!" it commanded.

"I cannot," replied Mohammed.

"Read thou!" insisted the angel. "Read thou, in the name of the Lord who created all things, who created man from a clot; read in the name of the Most High, who taught man the use of the pen, and taught him what before he knew not."

These words Mohammed, now strangely elated, repeated

until he knew them by heart. When he had finished, the angel said:

"O Mohammed, truly thou art the messenger of Allah, and I am his angel Gabriel."

With that he vanished.

Mohammed's reply to the angel that he could not read raises another controversy which has been much debated by opponents and partisans of the founder of Islam. Some say that he was illiterate, others say that he was not. There is no evidence to prove or disprove either contention.

At this time literacy was not uncommon among the Arabs. Ali, Mohammed's cousin, could write, so why should Abu Taleb have had his son taught and not his nephew who lived under the same roof? Why should the education of a descendant of merchant aristocrats like Hashim and Abd al Mottaleb have been so neglected? The only possible suggestion is that Mohammed's early start in business gave him no time for a formal education. But the fact that he did not begin traveling until he was in his teens does not make this particularly convincing. Yet illiterate he is affirmed to have been, and one of the greatest arguments in favor of this theory comes from Mohammed himself!

Mohammed always insisted that he could not read or write! Perhaps he could not, or perhaps he thought such a reputation made good propaganda. An unlettered Arab giving out something in the nature of the Koran would create a far greater impression than if it had come from a scholar.

In some translations of the Koran, "Recite" or "Cry" is substituted for Gabriel's order, "Read." "*Qaraa*," which is the root of "*Koran*," can mean "to recite or address." But like the question of the epilepsy, it is of no consequence whether Mohammed was illiterate or not. It does not affect his story or his greatness. In whatever way the Koran came into being, it is a masterpiece. Whether Khadija or Ali or Zaid copied it from Mohammed's dictation makes not the least difference.

As soon as Mohammed had recovered from the celestial apparition, he thought of Khadija. So he gathered himself up from the floor of the cave and ran out onto the desert. The dawn was creeping stealthily over the horizon as he stumbled over the sagebrush and into the narrow streets of Mecca. Trembling and agitated, he tottered into Khadija's room and, waking her, told her of his vision. For a moment he remained staring at her, but before she could sufficiently recover from her surprise to say anything, he suddenly let out a cry of distress. Something unexpected had occurred to him.

Mohammed had always expressed his contempt for soothsayers. Trading on the supernatural was a trick which he despised. Yet here he was appearing himself like a kind of medium. Furthermore, now that he was back within the four walls of his wife's room, with the sun glinting through the shutters, he was not sure whether he had not just dreamt it all or, worse still, had been possessed by a devil.

Khadija loved her husband. Twelve years of marriage had only increased her attachment. As he stood before her now, haggard and questioning, his hair and beard uncombed, the dust of the cave on his clothes, she felt a deep, motherly compassion for him. He was her man, and her man was troubled. Khadija's affection welled in her. Laying her hand on Mohammed's arm, she said earnestly:

"God is my protection, oh Abu Kasim!" This was the term of endearment between the husband and the wife referring to the boy Kasim who had died. "Rejoice, dear husband, and be of good cheer. He in whose hands stands the life of Khadija is my witness that thou wilt be the Messenger of His people!" Then she added, "Hast thou not been loving to thy kinsfolk, kind to thy neighbors, charitable to the poor, hospitable to the stranger, faithful to thy word, and ever a defender of the truth?"

Mohammed's strained expression relaxed. Then he smiled. Khadija put her arms around her husband and held him for a moment. Then she suggested that he rest awhile. With that, she ran off to tell Waraka what had happened.

Waraka was now very old and infirm and blind. He hardly left his mat, but he roused himself at Khadija's news. Without hesitation he assured her that all Mohammed had said must be true, that her husband was God's elect. Khadija, bursting with excitement, hurried back to Mohammed with her cousin's message. Nothing could have impressed him more. He believed in Waraka and had always felt that he was a man who spoke with authority.

Once more he slept. Khadija covered him with his cloak and watched beside his mat. Soon he began to moan and tremble. Beads of perspiration appeared on his forehead. Khadija laid on more coverings. For a while he continued to moan and mutter. Then he sat up, tense. He stared before him as if listening to someone. After a time, he spoke as if repeating a lesson:

"O thou, enwrapped in thy mantle! Arise and warn! Arise and magnify thy Lord! Purify thy raiment and depart from all uncleanliness!"

Mohammed's voice died away. He continued to stare as if he expected further revelations. As none came, he turned to his wife.

"Oh, Khadija," he said, "the time of rest and sleep has passed, Gabriel has ordered me to warn the people and call them to God and His worship!"

With that, he rose and hurried off to speak to Waraka. The old man was waiting anxiously and, after hearing Mohammed, confirmed what he had said to Khadija, adding:

"I swear by him whose hands Waraka's life is, God has chosen thee to be the Prophet of his people. The great Nomos, the confidant of Allah, has come to thee. They will call thee liar, they will persecute thee, they will banish thee, they will fight against thee. Oh that I could live to those days. I would fight for thee."

Then he kissed Mohammed's forehead. Mohammed thanked his kinsman and walked thoughtfully home. Waraka's spontaneous enthusiasm had encouraged him. What had happened in the cave seemed as real as when he had seen it.

This reassurance was important to Mohammed. He was an honest man, and he wanted to be certain that the messages which he proclaimed did not come from himself. He wanted to speak always in the name of the Lord. In fact, so careful was he lest there should be any suggestion of human influence in what he declared, that every so often he prefaced his words with God's injunction: "Speak" or "Say."

For example, selecting from the Koran at random, we have:

"Say: The angel of death who is charged with you shall cause you to die: then shall ye be returned to your Lord."

Similarly, every chapter of the Koran except one opens with:

"In the name of God, the compassionate, the merciful!"

What may be wondered is why Waraka came out so unhesitatingly with this affirmation that Mohammed was the Messenger of God. Was it that, having recanted his faith three times, he thought it might be a good idea to do it a fourth? Or was he inspired, and did he really sense the greatness of Mohammed? Whatever was the cause, we can attribute a great part of the initial headway of the new religion to Waraka.

However, although comforted and encouraged, Mohammed did not quite know what to do next. A feeling of anticlimax began to settle over him. After a few days he began to worry.

What if this *had* been a celestial practical joke? What if there were to be no more revelations? Anxiously he waited for the angel to give him a further sign. But no angel came. Mohammed became nervous, then frightened. Finally, desperate, he went back to Mount Hira. It looked as it always had, arid and white and shimmering under the desert sun. Mohammed decided that he had made a fool of himself. He had done the very thing he had scoffed at. He had declared himself a soothsayer, he had let his wife believe him to be a prophet with a divine mission. Mohammed writhed with shame and climbed quickly to the top of the glittering crag. There was only one thing left for him to do. But, as he made ready to take the first step which would send him to some sort of eternity, he saw Gabriel, who halted him with raised hand. In those clear and unmistakable tones, the angel cried:

"I am Gabriel and thou art Mohammed, the Messenger of Allah!"

The angel vanished, leaving Mohammed rooted to the edge of the precipice. He tried to move, but he felt as if his limbs were paralyzed. His voice had gone. He was like a statue made of marble. It looked as if Gabriel had saved him from being dashed to pieces, only to condemn him to die of starvation. This he might have done had it not been for Khadija.

Khadija knew that her husband was in a disturbed state of mind. When, therefore, he tramped out onto the desert, she had a notion where he had gone. Accordingly, when he did not return, she sent a man to look for him. The man found him in a kind of trance on the edge of the precipice and brought him home.

Once again Khadija was unwittingly saving Islam. If Mohammed had been alone, it is possible that he might have worried himself into taking his life. That he did not was partly due to his own character and a great deal to the kindness and understanding of his now aging wife. She never showed the smallest sign of distrust. At all times she encouraged him. It was probably this devotion which caused Mohammed later to write as part of the Koran:

"By the midday splendor and by the stilly night, the Lord does not reject him, and will not forsake him, and the future shall be better than the past. Has he not found him an orphan and given him a home, found him astray and guided him into the straight path, found him so poor and made him so rich?"

There were to be other women in Mohammed's life, but none for whom he had so genuine and sublime emotions as for Khadija. Her simple belief in the man she married, because she loved him, gives credence to these first stages of the faith which today claims one in every seven people of the world's population. Some of Mohammed's biographers cannot determine whether Mohammed began his career as an inspired enthusiast or a designing impostor. Khadija seems to answer their question.

It does not seem likely that a person like Khadija would have chosen as leader of her caravans, then as manager of her important business, and finally as her husband a man who was a designing impostor, or even an impostor who was not designing. Neither does it appear probable that an impostor with so much family influence would have made so little out of such obviously golden opportunities. Neither is it likely that such a character, having married his wealthy employer, would have remained faithful to her until she died or neglected the money-making aspect of their alliance for some intangible spiritual revelation.

I stress this here, as what follows is, in the light of history, really the commencement of Mohammed's life. A number of Mohammed's chroniclers, in fact, dismiss these forty years before the "call" in a few pages, some in a paragraph or two. To my way of thinking, however, they are the explanation of Mohammed, the exposition of Mohammed, the substance of the founder of Islam.

CHAPTER V

THE PERSECUTIONS

(612–619 After Christ)

THE SAME WRITERS who represent Mohammed as a designing impostor ridicule his visions. Against such ridicule nothing can be said, as proof or disproof to the contrary, except this.

In almost every chapter of the Old Testament and in many of the New, occurrences are reported which are no more peculiar than those which are supposed to have taken place on Mount Hira. The fact that they belong to periods of history bordering on the legendary has no bearing on the matter. Miracles and supernatural revelations, if they are to be believed, belong to any age—two thousand years before Christ or two thousand years after. Those, therefore, who scoff at Mohammed on Mount Hira must likewise scoff at Moses on Mount Sinai and Jesus on the hills of Galilee. They must scoff at Joan of Arc in her Domremy highlands and at Bernadette Soubirous in the Pyrenees. The accounts of the Transfiguration and of Michael speaking to Joan and of the Blessed Virgin appearing at Lourdes were all given in good faith. So were those about Mohammed ibn Abdallah and the angel Gabriel.

As far as the story of Islam is concerned, it is of no particular significance whether Mohammed met Gabriel or did not meet Gabriel. It is of no more significance than the epilepsy and the illiteracy controversy. According to tradition, it was an angel who set Mohammed on his way. According to tradition, it was a burning bush which started Moses. According to tradition, it was John the Baptist, assisted by a dove out of heaven, who sent Jesus preaching. However, had there been none of these mystic accessories, there is no reason to suppose that the three men would have been any less zealous.

Moses, we know, built his religion on what he had learned from his Arab wife, Zipporah. This religion rested basically on the worship of an austere desert god called Yahu who lived in a tent. The rites which Yahu demanded applied exclusively to nomadic people of the Arabian wildernesses. Moses adapted these rites to the Israelites, changed Yahu's name to Jehovah, and gradually constructed the Jewish faith. When he became convinced that he had been filled by the spirit of God, he probably had no clear recollection of how the commandments had developed in his mind.

About the beginnings of Jesus we know very little. They were, in all likelihood, much like Mohammed's. Jesus was an intelligent boy, learned quickly and, the chances are, found employment as easily as did Mohammed. He had the same receptive mind or spirit as Mohammed in which ideas subconsciously took root. In the same way as with Mohammed, these ideas remained dormant for many years. The power of these ideas was never consciously clear to either man until they emerged as soul-shattering revelations. *Neither Jesus nor Mohammed could recognize his own reminiscences and thoughts in their new form.* They genuinely felt the inspiration of God. They probably had it.

Thus the Mount Hira episode is no more worth arguing about than the burning bush or the dove over Jordan. Mohammed tells us what he believed took place, and this we must accept like the forty days and nights in the wilderness and the tables of stone.

As a matter of fact, Mohammed was, to begin with, cautious about letting anyone know of his adventure in the cave. Outside Khadija and Waraka, he told no one except Zaid. He did not really tell Zaid. Zaid found out. His position in the household as adopted son led him to overhear conversations between his foster parents. When he understood that Mohammed's religious ideals were closely related to his own Christianity, he declared himself a believer and disciple of the man who had freed him.

THE PERSECUTIONS

In the same way, Ali one day came upon Mohammed and Khadija praying in the new way. Although he had been brought up in the polytheist traditions of the Hashimites, he did not hesitate to range himself on the side of his cousin.

Soon a few other near relatives were let into the secret and made the profession of faith with their slaves.

There were Saad, the nephew of Amina, and Az Zubeir, Khadija's nephew, and Talha, a cousin of Abu Bakr. Then Othman ibn Affan, a future caliph, and grandson on his mother's side of Abd al Mottaleb. Also Abd ar Rahman and Obeida and Abu Selama and a few others who were to distinguish themselves in the cause of Islam.

The reason why Mohammed had to be so cautious was on account of the Kaaba people—that is, the officials of the shrine, the administrators of the city. With them officially against him, he would have little chance of making any headway in Mecca. The Kaaba people were divided into rival groups, those descended from Mohammed's ancestor Hashim and those descended from another patriarch of the same generation called Abd Shems. The Hashimites were in power. The Abd Shemites wanted that power. If they could bring charges of heresy or impiety against the guardians of the Kaaba through their Hashimite kinsman, Mohammed, it would suit their purposes well.

The head of the Abd Shemite faction was Abu Sofian. He was a rich merchant banker whose family and fortune had been traditions in Mecca for generations. A custodian of the national standard, under which the Koreishites marched to battle, his official position corresponded to that of commander in chief. His appearance was in keeping with his military position. Abu Sofian looked like a leader and warrior. He was tall and slim with fine, clearly carved features. His beard was trimmed short and very black. His eyes, of the same color, glowed beneath a broad white forehead. He was attractive to women and was married to a beautiful, passionate Meccan called Hind. Hind, like Khadija, was a career woman and spent most of her time speculating or financing nomads at exorbitant rates of interest.

Abu Sofian had an important say in all that went on in the city, and usually that "say" carried any controversy. Partly from personal reasons, partly because of family jealousy, he harbored a hearty dislike for Mohammed.

Mohammed knew where the danger lay and worked discreetly and slowly. During the first four years of his mission, he gathered no more than forty converts. These, outside the relatives and their households, were mostly unsuccessful businessmen and other discontented folk. Not that the new teaching offered an easy solution to life's troubles. On the contrary, the gospel of Islam demanded great sacrifices and much drudgery. But it held out something more tangible and realistic than what these desert people had known before. Speaking in later years of these early converts, Mohammed said:

"I never invited anyone into the faith who displayed not hesitation and perplexity, except only Abu Bakr."

But Abu Bakr was one of those rarities who are sure of their own minds. Although his name is little known outside students of Islam, it was almost entirely because of him that the Mohammed tradition was carried on after Mohammed's death. Abu Bakr was a man who really believed, a man who accepted the Moslem doctrine literally and practiced all it ordered. Of him, also, Mohammed declared that if the faith of all men were weighed against that of Abu Bakr, his would tip the scales.

Nothing remains secret for long in an Arab community. Although Mohammed did his best to change the places of the meetings from friend's house to friend's house, even to the desert, leakage of what was going on began. Soon the gatherings of believers were being broken up by rowdies and often degenerated into fist fights. One of the bitterest opponents of the new sect was Mohammed's own uncle, Abu Lahab. His son, Otba, had married Mohammed's and Khadija's daughter Rokaia. But, whatever friendliness this kinship might have created, it was counterbalanced by Abu Lahab's wife, Omm Jemil, who was the sister of Abu Sofian. She never ceased to encourage her husband's resentment against what he considered the ridicule his nephew was bringing onto an ancient Meccan name.

To Mohammed these feuds were specially distressing. He had always believed in family unity, and now, because of something which was beyond his control, a kind of civil war was being generated among his own people. The nervous strain began to tell on him. He avoided contact with his old associates and spent long spells on Mount Hira. Perhaps he hoped he would have some further revelation which might solve these painful problems, perhaps even give him a loophole of escape. But if he did wish this, he was disappointed. The angel Gabriel appeared to him again but only confirmed the order to go out and preach. The definiteness of this order could not be questioned. There was nothing which Mohammed could do but return to Mecca and open his campaign. The date of this resolution was 612 A.C., Mohammed being then forty-two.

As a first step he persuaded the Kaaba people to meet him on the heights outside Mecca to hear his cause.

Many came. The stony hillside was thronged with white-robed men waiting to hear what their kinsman could possibly have to say. There was not much talking as the sun, setting in a furnace of scarlet and gold, slowly stretched shadows over the desert. Mohammed, standing on a slight eminence, seemed to be clothed in bright rays of triumphant fire. Looking down on the men and women who waited questioningly, he said:

"O people of the Koreish, were I to tell you that an army was advancing to attack you from yonder hills, would you believe me?"

"Yes!" everyone answered. "We have always known you to be truthful."

Mohammed inclined his head. Then, raising his voice, he continued: "I have come to you as a warner, and if you do not respond to my warning, punishment will fall upon you." Looking around the crowd of listeners, he named each subdivision of the Koreish clan. As each sonorous Arabic title rolled out, the people indicated stirred. Dramatically Mohammed went on: "I have been commanded by God to warn you, my kinsmen, that there is no benefit for you now and forever, unless you acknowledge that there is none worthy of worship but the One and Only God!"

The sun had almost gone now and, with its vanishing, the evening breeze whispered through the desert scrub. Otherwise there was no sound. Mohammed's declaration had stunned the most unimaginative. Glancing anxiously from one to another, the Arabs waited for someone to take up the challenge. Mohammed began to speak again, but before he had said more than a few words, Abu Lahab interrupted him. Again Mohammed tried to talk, but Abu Lahab's interruptions became insults. Then, as Mohammed still persisted, he started throwing stones at him. Mohammed's expression set. His face turned ashen. He was, above all, a man, a man who had been accustomed to command and with no highly developed ideals about turning the other cheek. He had stood much from this ill-mannered, bigoted old uncle. The moment had come when he could stand no more. His even temper left him, and he cursed his uncle and his aunt. He cursed them loudly and definitely. He told them picturesquely to go to hell and stay there eternally. He added that one of the infernal duties of Omm Jemil would be to supply the fuel that would keep the flames alive to roast her husband. He left none of the horrors of infernal fire to the imagination. Everything he said he obviously meant.

Later on, he embodied these maledictions in the 101st sura of the Koran:

Let the hands of Abu Lahab perish, and let himself perish!
His wealth and his gains shall avail him not.
Burned shall he be at the fiery flame,*
And his wife laden with firewood,
On her neck a rope of palm fiber.

The Arabs are superstitious, and Mohammed's curses were as eloquent as they were specific. Abu Lahab left the meeting with Omm Jemil. The other Koreishites followed. Mohammed remained on the darkening desert with a few converts. As there

---
*This is a pun. "Abu Lahab" means "father of flame."

was no one to preach to, he also went home. Here he found more trouble. Otba had repudiated his wife and sent her back to Khadija, weeping. This, as it happened, was fortunate for Rokaia. Soon after her divorce, she was married to the new convert Othman ibn Affan, who one day would be the third caliph of the Arab empire.

Although Othman played an important role in the building of Islam, he lacked the picturesque dash of most of Mohammed's immediate lieutenants. He was a fine-looking man, tall and swarthy, with a long black beard, but he kept his own counsel and spent much of his time studying the Koran. His adoption of the new faith was, nevertheless, politically important. On one side he was related to Abu Sofian's branch of the Koreishites, the Ommeyades, on the other to that of Abd al Mottaleb's. He also became doubly allied to Mohammed by marrying another of his daughters. This one was called Umm Kulthum, who, in the same way as her sister, had been repudiated by Abu Lahab's second son Otabayah.

For the moment, however, Othman was just another brave man who had declared himself for this unpopular cause. He did not know why. All that he was certain of was that Mohammed, without anything more than his word, had convinced him that this was the road to salvation.

Mohammed himself was discouraged. Yet his orders were formal, and he must do something to fulfill them. The only thing he could think of was to call another meeting and endeavor to hold the attention of these narrow-minded old men. This time he made it a private affair and invited only the leading Hashimites to supper in his own home.

When he had fed his guests on mutton and milk, he made a short speech explaining more specifically what was at stake. He closed his remarks with an assurance of the blessings which awaited any who stood by him now. No one spoke or applauded. The silence was awkward and icy. Almost despairingly, Mohammed exclaimed:

"Who will share the burden of my office? Who will be my brother, my lieutenant, my vizier?"

No one paid any attention. The silence became more awkward. Then Ali stepped forward. Looking defiantly at the older men, he said he would be anything Mohammed wanted him to be. Mohammed threw his arm around his cousin's shoulder.

"Behold my brother, my vizier, my viceregent!" he cried. "Let all listen to his words and obey him!"

The remark undid the silence, but the wrong way. Everyone laughed. Someone asked Abu Taleb if he intended doing homage to his young son. Abu Taleb shrugged his shoulders and evaded the issue. He did not hold with Mohammed's way of acting, but he was loyal to the memory of the boy he had brought up. The meeting dispersed peacefully, but without accomplishing anything. That is, it accomplished nothing which Mohammed had hoped for. On the other hand it had the definite effect of bringing him out into the open. Everyone knew now what he had on his mind. There was only one course left to him, and he took it. Without preface or apology, he boldly announced to all that he was the Messenger sent by God to preach His unity and put an end to idolatry. War had been declared on the Koreish, a war which would literally be fought out to the unconditional surrender of one of the parties concerned.

With that settled, Mohammed had to turn to meet hostility from another direction. This one was even more difficult to cope with, because it was that of former friends. To these it seemed absurd that someone who, a few years ago, had been a companionable traveling salesman, a jovial businessman, a good sport, should now be telling them about what went on in heaven! It could not be taken seriously. All these meetings with angels, this declaration that their one-time colleague was God's appointed representative, sent to reform a religion which had stood the test of centuries, was pure nonsense. It was grotesque! It was laughable! And how these men laughed. They laughed in their homes and they laughed in the street. When they met Mohammed, they laughed all the more. They called him "driveler," "star gazer," "fake"!

The situation was much the same as it had been with Jesus,

as with any reformer in those conservative times when tradition was law. Today a Mohammed would find every outlet for his zeal. He could preach or become a lay missionary. He could take holy orders of his own invention. A good-looking, amiable traveler in razor blades or hair tonics would find easy relief for an attack of fanaticism, for an urge to deliver a message. Few would scoff at him, many would listen, everyone would be sympathetic or compassionate. He would not found a great religion, but no one would mind his thinking he was the Messenger of God.

In Mohammed's time, this tolerance could not be. There was too much involved.

To begin with, the Meccans were snobs. They were particularly snobs about money. Mohammed came from a good enough stock, but he had never risen by his own efforts to any position in Meccan society. Although he had married the richest widow in Mecca—and this did not advance his popularity—he had never aspired to anything higher than commercial traveling. He had always been a wage- and commission-earning employee. Why, therefore, should a deity choose a person of such insignificance to alter the century-old traditions of the Holy City? If the new apostle had been one of the upper four hundred, if he had been a wealthy club member, one of *the* Mottalebs who lived around the Kaaba, or even one who joined in the gay life of this gay city of the desert, his ideas might have been considered. But he was not. He was just the reverse.

This aloofness from the dining and wining and lusting was one of the greatest objections to Mohammed. These men were afraid that his attack on their beliefs would not only wreck the Kaaba cult, all-important to Mecca's prosperity, but would also deprive them of the joyous sensuousness of their existences.

Secondly, there was a situation not dissimilar to that which had existed six centuries before between the high priests and Jesus. If this doctrine made any headway, the prestige of the Kaaba would go and, with it, the Koreishites and their source of revenue. This would further disrupt business, stop the caravans, and put an end to pilgrimages. Neither was there any question of idolatry having been found wanting or being in a state of decline. On the contrary, these ladies and gentlemen, these procreative emblems of both sexes which passed their lives in the suffocating silence of the great shrine, had brought prosperity to Mecca. It would be sheer folly to slight them by showing an interest in another god whose only sponsor was an ass who had not the sense to appreciate when he had all the luck on his side. In fact, the whole notion was ridiculous and must not be given a hearing. So the old friends jeered, and the more boisterous broke up the meetings with ribald songs and catcalls, while the vindictive threw stones and punched the heads of the members of the Moslem congregations.

Occasionally a group of more tolerant men would assemble, ready to have a discussion with Mohammed. Both sides would show where the other was wrong. When neither faction had been convinced by argument, the dissenters would suggest that they might believe if Mohammed would give them some tangible proof that he had been chosen by any deity for this mission. If, for example, he would perform a miracle. They cited Moses and Jesus, who turned out miracles whenever circumstances demanded. Like Christ in the wilderness, Mohammed refused to be caught.

His unvarying reply was that he had been commanded by God to preach, not to perform miracles. He added that if visible evidence was required that he had been given this charge, all the doubters need do was to read the Koran. Therein they would find revelations being recorded daily which could only come from God. The making of the Koran was a miracle in itself.

The arguers shrugged their shoulders. They wanted real miracles. They wanted to see the dead raised, the dumb to speak, and water gushing from the desert. When Mohammed continued to shake his head, they suggested that the Koran might become a miracle if they could see the angel bringing the revelations to Mohammed.

Mohammed remained steadfast in his refusal to do anything supernatural. He declared and redeclared that he was nothing more than a man who had been chosen like any of the other prophets in history to help the people to salvation. He did not know *how* to perform miracles!

This he continued to assert all through his life, and to deny that he had any divine attributes. He was a human being like any other and never anything more than the mouthpiece of the Almighty.

This again shows that practical-mindedness and sincerity which were to carry Mohammed so far. A stupid man or an impostor would have probably put on some act to impress his persecutors. But not Mohammed. He knew what he was about, he believed in what he was about. On that belief he was going to live or die. He followed the old adage of being primarily honest with himself.

No one thought of this, of course, and the lampoonings and the physical affronts continued and increased. Some of Mohammed's bitterest detractors were men who, in later years, became his most fanatical supporters.

There was Amr' ibn al As, the son of a beautiful Meccan prostitute. All the better Meccans were her friends, so that anyone, from Abu Sofian down, might have been Amr's father. As far as anyone could be sure, he might have called himself Amr' ibn Abi Lahab, or ibn al Abbas or ibn anyone else among the Koreishite upper ten. According to Meccan standards of that time, it did not matter who had sired him. His youth and good looks and wit made up for any lack of family background. But what made him most acceptable to the Koreishites was his gift for writing poetry. Such a man was a godsend to Mohammed's defamers.

Mohammed, who was no poet and had no great sense of repartee, withered under the lyrics and songs composed by this Amr'. Yet one day the lampooner was to become one of the most distinguished generals of the Moslem armies and lead them victoriously against the Byzantines in Syria and in Egypt. It was Amr' who, in 639 A.C., was to originate the idea of digging the Suez Canal. It was he who captured Alexandria and pitched his camp on the site of what would become Cairo. But, although

Mohammed was to speak of him as "the truest of Moslems, steadfast in the faith," today his time was given to making anything to do with Islam the subject for fun.

There were also many who wanted more than lampooning. They wanted Mohammed's death. Many converts were standing their ground in spite of persecutions, and every week a few more declared their allegiance to Mohammed. As long as this went on, the discrediting of the Kaaba remained a menace.

Some of the more moderate among the persecutors warned Abu Taleb of what was in the air. Abu Taleb still disapproved of his nephew's notions and what he was stirring up, but he still loved him. So he went to him and begged him to withdraw while there was still time. Mohammed thanked his uncle and assured him respectfully that nothing anyone could say would deflect him from the course he was now following. Abu Taleb could not help being impressed. He took Mohammed's hand and promised him that, while he could never be converted to this new religion, his nephew could count on him to protect him to the best of his ability and never take the side of his enemies.

This assurance gave Mohammed fresh confidence, but it did not lift the menace of the Kaaba people. To have anything to do with Mohammed now meant running the risk of being killed. This threat especially affected Rokaia and Othman, whom she had now married. Accordingly in 615 A.C. Mohammed gathered a band of about one hundred converts and sent them under Othman to Abyssinia. The Abyssinians were Nestorian Christians and tolerant to other creeds. In this way was formed a small nucleus of men and women on whom Mohammed could depend and fall back on as a refuge if the worst came to the worst and he had to flee.

With these people safely away, Mohammed turned once more to face the storm. His most violent opponent now was a fanatic called Abu Jahl, which appropriately means "father of ignorance."

Abu Jahl's mother, another of these Meccan career women, did a rich business in perfumes. She was one of those, therefore, who had reacted violently against a reformer who wanted to put an end to that side of Mecca's life to which she catered.

Abu Jahl was himself a small, square, strong, ugly man. Unlike most Meccans, he had fiery red hair and a tawny beard. To the Arabs he suggested the devil. Abu Jahl wanted nothing less than Mohammed's head. Whenever he saw him, he went after him with a group of bullies and beat him up. One day when the trouncing had been more than usually severe, Mohammed turned grimly on his attackers. Hardly raising his voice, he said:

"Men of the Koreish, I will surely repay you for this with interest!"

With that, he went on his way. No one followed him. The quiet words had had a menacing conviction of someone seeing into the future. Had the men themselves been able to see, they would have been even more apprehensive. As it was, immediate repercussions to this maltreatment of Mohammed were about to explode.

Hamza, another of Mohammed's uncles, had no particular feelings one way or the other about his nephew's behavior. He was his contemporary and doubly related. His father, Abd al Mottaleb, had married, late in life, a cousin of Mohammed's mother. This marriage and that of Mohammed's parents had taken place within a few days of each other. The two boys had shared the same wet nurse before being sent out to their nomad foster mothers and, although as different as possible in appearance and character, had remained friends.

Hamza was essentially a fighting man, a warrior of great physical strength. Tall and bearded and fiery-eyed, he was not one with whom anyone wittingly picked a quarrel. While he had no ideas about sponsoring his nephew, he admired his courage in the face of persecution. When, therefore, he heard about Abu Jahl's attack, he became very angry and went to look for him. He found him before the Kaaba, boasting to a group of Koreishites about what he had done. This further loosened Hamza's temper. In his hand he was carrying his unstrung bow. With this he now proceeded to crack Abu Jahl over the head until he fell on the paved courtyard. The other Koreishites turned to the defense of Abu Jahl, but Hamza waved them back. With eyes blazing, he exclaimed:

"And I also do not believe in your gods of stone!"

Having made this statement, he stared unseeingly before him. The words spoken in anger had revealed to him what he really felt. Turning on his heel, he left the sullen Koreishites and went to his nephew, to whom he declared himself a convert.

This conversion was of paramount importance to Mohammed. He now had with him one of his uncles who was also a man of unquestionable character and legendary courage. It was a conversion which would give the cause more prestige than a hundred ordinary ones. It would also increase the animosity of the Kaaba people.

By the time that Hamza was out of sight, Abu Jahl and his companions realized that they had not shown themselves at their best. The beating up of Mohammed had been balanced by the chastising of Abu Jahl. The change of mood of Hamza had dealt a severe blow to means of destroying Mohammed. Something must be done quickly before this triumph could be capitalized by the Moslems.

Abu Jahl had a nephew called Omar ibn al Khattab. He was a man of great stature, so huge, they said, that when he sat he was taller than those who stood. His face was swarthy and partly hidden by a curly black beard. He was ambidextrous, and his strength was in proportion to his size. He had a savage nature too, and no one dared to cross him. While he was a puritan and not one of those who joined in the Meccan night life, he did not approve of tampering with tradition. Abu Jahl traded on this, and worked his nephew up against Mohammed until he had made a vow to destroy him. Promising to bring back the trouble maker's head, he set out to find him. The Koreishites sat back and waited hopefully. When Omar undertook to get rid of someone, he wasted no time.

However, on the way to the house where Mohammed and his followers regularly congregated, Omar met another Koreish-

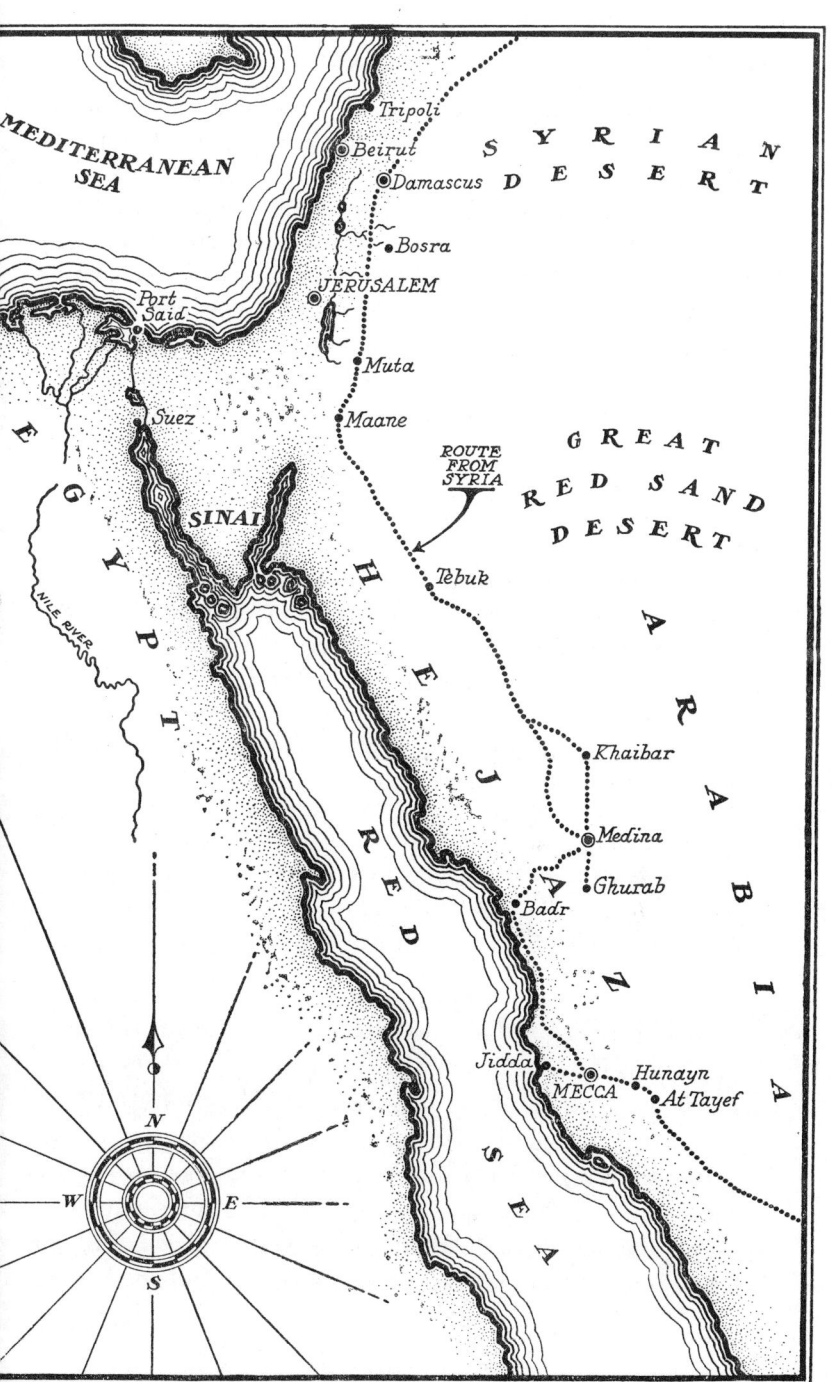

ite who had lately been converted to Islam. Omar did not know this and, gloatingly, told the man what he was going to do. The man nodded nervously, but suggested that before Omar took that kind of justice into his hands, it might be a good idea if he made sure that all was as it should be with his own kin. Omar asked for an explanation. The man then revealed that Omar's sister Amina and her husband Said were both converts. Without a word, Omar retraced his steps and went to his sister's place. The man, in the meanwhile, hurried to warn Mohammed.

Omar found his sister and her husband reading the Koran from a piece of lambskin. Omar's anger boiled. He knocked Said down and made ready to behead him. Amina tried to intervene and was sent staggering across the room with a bleeding lip. But she showed no fear. Looking coldly at her brother, she said:

"In despite of thee and thy violence, I persevere in the true faith," and added ecstatically, "There is no God but Allah, and Mohammed is his Messenger!"

Omar looked at his sister, surprised. There had been something brave and arresting in her voice. He let Said up and asked to see what Amina had been reading. Reluctantly Amina handed him the holy scroll. Omar began to read:

"In the name of the most merciful God! We have not sent down the Koran to inflict misery on mankind, but as a monitor, to teach him to believe in the true God, the creator of the earth and the lofty heavens."

Omar seated himself and continued to read. After a while he sheathed his sword and left his sister's house as unexpectedly as he had come. Rapidly he made his way to his original destination. Mohammed, warned of the murderous intentions of Abu Jahl's kinsman, was waiting for him with a number of converts, including Hamza. But instead of bursting down the door, as was expected, Omar knocked. Mohammed bade him enter and, when he stood filling the threshold with his gigantic frame, asked him what he wanted. Soberly Omar replied:

"I have come to enroll myself among the believers in God and His Messenger."

While the other Moslems could barely control their exclamations of astonishment, Mohammed showed no emotion. After a few brief questions, he had Omar make the profession of faith.

Omar's conversion was not only one of tremendous and immediate importance to the Moslem cause, but it was also to leave its mark on Moslem history. Omar became the second caliph of Islam after Mohammed's death, Abu Bakr having been the first. He was the first to assume the title of "Amir al Momirin"—Commander of the Faithful—which survived until 1922. It was under his reign that the mighty foundations of the Saracenic empire were perfected. It was in his memory that the famous Mosque of Omar was erected in Jerusalem. Omar ranks second only to Mohammed in the annals of Islam. He had none of the Messenger's humor, none of Abu Bakr's tolerance, but a fanatic enthusiasm with which he inspired his subordinates and sent them fearlessly to conquer the world.

There was a moment of tense excitement when Omar said: "And Mohammed is His Messenger." This was the kind of windfall which the most optimistic had not considered. It seemed unbelievable and must be capitalized without delay.

No one was more eager to do so than Omar. As soon as Mohammed had accepted his profession, he suggested that this should be made official at the Kaaba. No one dissented. A procession was formed. The disciples who had gathered round Mohammed to defend him against Omar now marched behind their would-be murderer. On his right and left were Mohammed and Abu Bakr. Immediately behind was Hamza.

Abu Jahl and his supporters were dumfounded. They had been waiting confidently to have Omar fling the bloodstained head of Mohammed at their feet. Instead they saw their champion not only almost arm in arm with their enemy, but actually going through the despised Moslem ritual. Neither was there anything which anyone could do. Men who valued their lives did not pick quarrels with men like Omar, especially when they were backed up by men like Hamza.

The next day Omar went alone to the Kaaba to pray in the new way, and again no one dared to say a word or raise a hand. From the point of view of the Koreish, this was a mistake. The assassination of Omar would have created violent blood feuds. It would, however, have deprived Mohammed of a weapon which did as much to destroy idolatrous Mecca as his own convictions. Later on, he used to say:

"If the devil himself were to meet Omar in the street, he would dodge into a side alley."

For the moment it was the Koreishites who dodged into alleys whenever Omar was seen coming.

But, while keeping their mouths shut and their swords sheathed, the men of the Koreish were in no friendlier moods. Their resentment in fact increased and was now aggravated by something else.

A second immigration of converts to Abyssinia had taken place, and the story began to circulate that Mohammed was planning to have the Abyssinians invade Mecca. To his other offenses against the community, he was adding that of turning traitor. His death was demanded, regardless of consequences. To bring this about, Abu Sofian issued a decree ostracizing the Hashimites until they had delivered their kinsman for execution. The situation was beginning to look ugly until Abu Taleb came to the rescue. Outside of Mecca, he owned a kind of family stronghold. In this, he had Mohammed and his partisans take refuge. Here they remained for some time in the greatest discomfort. The Koreishites tried to starve them out, and the only food and water they obtained was through the help of a few loyal friends who had stayed in Mecca. But as with all persecuted persons, their courage and determination to vindicate themselves grew stronger.

After a while the situation degenerated into a stalemate. Then it began to raise dissension among the various Meccan factions. Gradually the tide turned against Abu Sofian. There had been no invasion by Abyssinians. Neither Mohammed nor his companions had shown any signs of giving in, and the feud among the

THE PERSECUTIONS

Kaaba people was causing all sorts of embarrassing situations. Abu Sofian realized that he must compromise. For this he found a plausible excuse in the fact that white ants had destroyed the decree against the Hashimites. With the indictment gone, Mohammed and his besieged garrison were permitted to go back to their homes.

The return was the signal for a number of conversions which, for the moment, the Kaaba people thought wiser to ignore. This did not mean that there was peace. There was no peace, only a truce while Mohammed's antagonists waited to see what they could do next. Mohammed also waited and watched. He had been through a great deal during the past eight years, and he was more than ever convinced that he was not on the wrong track. But, while he no longer had to creep about Mecca expecting to be attacked at every street corner, other more intimate troubles awaited him. It seemed as if everything were being done to test his spirit.

Soon after coming back to Mecca, Khadija fell ill. She had been worn down by the persecutions and hardships to which she was not accustomed. In a short time she died. During the three days of her agony, Mohammed never left her. As she drifted toward unconsciousness, he promised that she would be considered among the most honored women in paradise. Believing everything her husband said until the last, loving him as she had from the first day she saw him, Khadija drew her last breath in his arms. It was the month of December 619 A.C.; Khadija was sixty-five years old, Mohammed was not quite fifty.

Before Mohammed had time to appreciate this loss, he had another tragic bereavement. Abu Taleb died. Mohammed was with him to the end. He did his best to persuade his octogenarian uncle to make his profession of the new faith. But the old man remained obdurate. His moral and physical support of Mohammed during these years of persecution had been the outcome of affection and duty. But he had never approved of his nephew's thoughts or actions in regard to founding this revolutionary religion. He died as he had been born in the ancient belief of the idolatrous Koreishites.

This second death within one year almost shook Mohammed's faith in himself. It seemed impossible that anyone with so many obstacles in his way could be intended to succeed. Not only was the world against him, but he had lost his dearest and best friends. The moral support and the affection which meant so much to him were gone, and, even more important to his cause, their protection. As long as Abu Taleb was alive, many of his associates had scruples about declaring themselves against his nephew. In the same way, for form's sake, Khadija's family had refrained from open attack on their kinsman by marriage. But now these scruples were gone. Mohammed stood alone with his small band of converts. He had not even any money. During these years of persecution, Khadija's business had continued to deteriorate. Mohammed was too preoccupied to consider this and Khadija did not tell him. She had savings, and on these they had lived. It was not until she was dead that Mohammed realized that, in addition to all other misfortunes, he was practically a pauper.

That he did not give in now is again evidence of his detachment from things of the world. It would have been easy and profitable for him to go to the Koreish and confess that he had made a mistake. Every member of that arrogant clan would have offered him his hand. He would have been reinstated in business, possibly made a guardian of the Kaaba. A bride with a rich dowry would have been found him. But, although he once wavered to the extent of suggesting that Al Uzza, Allat, and Manat might be recognized in conjunction with Allah, he quickly retracted this concession. He saw that in the enterprise which he had undertaken there could be no compromise, no easy way out. He had started on this road and he was going to follow it to its end, however heartbreaking. In this he had the unwavering support of those few faithful friends, Abu Bakr, Omar, Hamza, Zaid, and Ali. With them he reaffirmed his intention of proving that there was no God but Allah, and that Mohammed was his Messenger.

CHAPTER VI

THE FAITH

Over a seemingly harmless statement that he had been appointed the Messenger of Allah, Mohammed had stirred up more turmoil in Mecca than it had known for centuries. Before one hundred years had passed, the turmoil had increased and spread over most of the then civilized world. Today, thirteen hundred years later, that turmoil is still apt to bubble up whenever Moslems and non-Moslems are thrown together.

Why? What had Mohammed evolved in his mind during those ten years since the first revelation on Mount Hira which was so disturbing? Why did his doctrines spread so much more rapidly than those of the Jews or Christians? What was the difference in Mohammed's teaching and that of Moses and Jesus? Why is the ratio of *practicing* Moslems greater than the ratio of *practicing* Jews or Christians?

There is no one-paragraph answer. If this book fulfills its purpose, the explanation should be found on its pages. What can be, and will be, explained now, are the main principles of Mohammed's new faith, the name of which is *Islam*, not Mohammedanism.

To say that a man or a woman is a Mohammedan is incorrect. Mohammed never, at any time, suggested that the religion which he preached was his idea. He never attributed to himself anything godly. None of his followers ever worshiped him. According to his lights, he was a prophet like Noah or Moses, sent by God to restore into the right path His people who, from time to time, strayed. He said:

"We believe in Allah and what has been sent down to us, and what has been sent down to Abraham and Ishmael and Isaac and

Jacob and the patriarchs, what has been given to Moses and Jesus, and what has been given to the prophets from the Lord; we make no distinction between any of them." (Koran: Sura 2.)

And again:

"I am a man like unto you, only the word of God has been revealed unto me."

The thesis of Islam had little to do with Mohammed. It was founded on a ready-made theory of revelation which had resulted from the gradual development of the religious history of Judaism and from Christianity. Mohammed was a realist. Had he lived in the twentieth century, he and his theories would have fitted in comfortably with those of the Modernists. He would most likely have been their leader. But he would not have said anything, any more than he did in the seventh century, to indicate that he thought himself better than his predecessors. He certainly would never have advocated that the religion should be named after him.

The men and women who adopted the teachings of Mohammed were, and still are, called Moslems. *"Moslem"* signifies "one who submits or surrenders himself." It is derived from *"Salama,"* which is the root of *"Islam,"* denoting the Moslem faith.

"Salama" means, in the first instance, to be tranquil, at rest, to have done one's duty, to have paid up, to be at perfect peace and, finally, to hand oneself over to the care of Him with whom peace is made.

The more concise translation of *"Islam"* is "submission to God." Not an *absolute* submission to Him, rather a striving after righteousness. It is actually the main principle of all earnest faiths. As Goethe remarked, "If this is Islam, do we not all live in Islam?"

The expression *"Salaam,"* used rather loosely by some Occidentals on meeting and parting, comes from the same root. It means "greeting and peace." The full salute is, *"Assalamu Alaik"* or *"Assalamu Alaikum"*—"Greeting and peace to you," according to whether one person or more is being saluted.

The whole of Islam hangs on the simplest of fabrics:

There is no God but Allah, who is the King, the Holy, the Peaceful, the Faithful, the Mighty, the Most High, the Provider, the Fashioner, the Wise.

In the words of the 112th sura of the Koran:

He is God alone, God the eternal! He begetteth not, and he is not begotten, and there are none like unto him.

According to Mohammed, there is no sin to compare with the belief in godly associates or other gods. This is specified many times in the Koran and particularly in the second sura:

God! There is no God but He, the Living, the Eternal. Nor slumber seizeth Him, nor sleep; His, whatsoever is in the Heavens and whatsoever is in the earth.

To this must be added that Mohammed is the Messenger of Allah. Not "Prophet"—"Messenger."—For while *"nabi,"* meaning "prophet," or "preacher," is often used with reference to Mohammed, the word in the creed is *"rasul,"* which signifies "messenger."

This tenet is important, for, while Mohammed declared himself to be as mortal as any other Arab, he made the belief in himself as the Messenger of God imperative. Again in the words of the Koran:

The belief in God is inseparable to that of Mohammed.

To begin with, Mohammed's conception of Allah was of something unimaginable. He was Rabb, the Lord, a remote God who exercised absolute dominion from afar. Then Rabb was used less frequently, and Allah (*Al Illah*—The God) took its place. God was now closer. Gradually His presence was felt wherever man turned. Soon his personality came even nearer. Mohammed began to say:

"God is fourth when three are met together, sixth when five are met together. When praying there is no reason to shout. God can hear the lowest whisper."

Finally he declared that God was not only over all and about all, but in all people.

One of the strongest impressions I had when I first lived with the Arabs was the "everydayness" of God. He ruled their eating, their traveling, their business, their loving. He was their hourly thought, their closest friend, in a way impossible to people whose God is separated from them by the rites of formal worship. This belief that God was there with us in the desert was accepted by everyone from the chief to the shepherd's son. Everyone from the beggar to the wealthy merchant could discuss God and Islam intelligently. Nothing was begun or ended or promised or invoked without God being called upon to help or witness or receive thanks. As Mohammed had declared, God was all about us.

None of this is admittedly new, but it was new to Mohammed. In spite of the many ancient traditions and doctrines which he now expounded, the common complaint that Mohammed plagiarized the Bible is untrue. He had never seen it. With the possible exception of fragments of Waraka's incompleted version, there was no Bible for him to see. It is, moreover, most unlikely that he saw these. The earliest official Arabic translations of the Old and New Testaments were made centuries after Mohammed's death.

The fact that the germinating forces in the two older religions are apparent in every phase of the younger are the outcome of what Mohammed had heard during his travels. They belong to the teachings of Bahira and of Waraka, to Kuss ibn Saida, the bishop of Nejran. Mohammed's was the case of a pagan, converted to monotheism, who had absorbed its theory and practices by attending the assemblies of worshipers, by listening to preachers, but never studying a line of Scripture.

Many people are surprised to find that Islam has so much in it of the Jewish and Christian religions. But, to Mohammed's way of thinking, these faiths had evolved one into the other and would now evolve into something else. He believed that the revelations of Jesus were those of a prophet sent by God to confirm or verify the revelations of Moses. According to him, God said:

"We gave Moses the Book, we gave Jesus the Evangel, we gave Mohammed the Koran."

Mohammed undoubtedly thought that he had been made the messenger of the one God of the world to all members of the human race. He further believed that he would succeed in bringing to full realization the work begun by Moses and continued by Jesus. It was a legitimate thought. The two earlier religions which had succeeded each other had been begun by men who had lived in the same region as Mohammed. To Mohammed, moreover, this region represented the world. His caravan trips had taught him that there were countries beyond the Mediterranean and the Red Sea, but only in a vague sort of way. He was more traveled than Moses or Jesus, but that is the most we can say.

That Mohammed failed to get the Jews and the Christians to accept him or, at least, align themselves with him was partly due to his idealisms and partly to his imperfect knowledge of their doctrines.

He approached the Jews, appealing to their Scriptures, which, he assured them, he had not come to destroy but to fulfill. He adapted the fasts and feasts of his new religion to their model. He tried to make them enter into his views of a great catholic creed embracing Jews and Christians and Moslems. Until he could no longer hope for Jewish collaboration, he allowed Jerusalem to remain the point toward which Moslems had to turn when praying. He could not appreciate that if the Jews accepted his proposals it would be tantamount to their confessing they were wrong in the subject of their main controversy, Jesus.

Mohammed believed in Jesus and his claim to being the Messiah. In the Koran he wrote:

"Say unto the Christians, their God and my God are one."

It would not have taken a great deal to make Mohammed into a Christian. Although not approving of some doctrines of the

Christians, he never declared himself against them. He put no obstacles in the way of Moslems marrying Christians. The mother of one of his sons was a Christian. He undoubtedly hoped for a while that, somehow or other, Islam and Christianity would come to an understanding. That he was no more successful than with the Jews was chiefly due to a quibble. A serious and complicated quibble, but, nevertheless, a quibble.

Mohammed was trying to impose a monotheistic faith on a people who had been used to worshiping a multitude of gods. The Christians, for whom he had the highest esteem, seemed to have complicated their fine, simple dogmas with something unnecessary and incomprehensible. To Mohammed, the mystery of the Trinity and Incarnation appeared to contradict the principles of Divine unity. In their obvious sense, they introduced three equal deities and transformed the man Jesus into the substance of the son of God. In the fourth sura we read: "Believe, therefore, in God and his Apostles, and say not: 'There is a Trinity.—Forbear. It will be better for you. God is only one God.'"

Then the Christian reverence for saints and images did not seem to be so far removed from the Kaaba with its 360 idols of stone. Mohammed hated images. Every mosque in the world of Islam bears witness to this. What we call arabesques, the geometric decorations, works of art in themselves, and interwoven inscriptions from the Koran are the outcome of Mohammed's iconoclasticism. He would not have the likeness of anything alive reproduced by man. This was not original. He borrowed it from the second of the ten commandments.

Thirdly, he considered making of God the father of Jesus a blasphemy. He insisted that God was unlike anything, and could not beget. Neither did he believe that God would have allowed Jesus, who was a superior being whether he was the son of God or not, to be put to death. He declared that another person took the place of Jesus and was crucified. This person may have been one of the disciples, perhaps Judas, who thus paid for his treachery. Jesus himself was carried to heaven. In the words of the fourth sura of the Koran: "*And they* [the Jews] *did not really slay him, but God took him up to Himself.*" And again: "*Yet they slew him not, and they crucified him not, but they only had his likeness.*" The Jews, he added, did not know this and thought that Jesus died on the cross.

However, outside the question of dogma, there was an even greater obstacle in Mohammed's mind to compromising with the Christians. Christianity, as Mohammed saw it in Arabia and the adjoining countries, had been tried and failed. During the three hundred years that it had been known to the Arabs, it had been unable to weaken or overthrow the idolatry of the inhabitants. In this, Mohammed had every argument on his side.

At this time the Christian religion was divided into a great number of dissensions. Each of these dissensions had a doctrine peculiar to itself. Today the Church of Christ is dispersed under the heading of many denominations, but it is nothing to what it was in the seventh century. Some of the beliefs were unreconcilable with anything Jesus had taught a comparatively short time before. To Mohammed, they made no sense.

There were:

The Sabellians, who said that the Trinity expressed three different states, Father, Son, and Holy Ghost, of one person all forming a single substance, as a man consists of body and soul and subconscious self.

The Arians, who declared Christ the son of God, but distinct from Him and inferior to Him.

The Nestorians, who maintained that Christ had two distinct natures, divine and human. Mary was only his mother, and it was an abomination to style her the mother of God.

The Eutychians, who said that Jesus was entirely God before incarnation and entirely man during.

The Collyridians, a sect of females who worshiped the Virgin Mary.

The Mariamites, who reverenced the Trinity as God the Father, God the Son, and God the Mother—Mary.

And many more dissensions with no less variant beliefs.

But, in spite of these contradictory creeds and apparent paradoxes, Mohammed had strong sympathies for Christ. He said that he was the greatest of all prophets. He was convinced of his miraculous powers, he was the Word proceeding from God, that his name was Messiah. He accepted the immaculate conception and agreed that the birth of Jesus was a miracle. He announced that, before the end of the world, Jesus would return and slay Antichrist. After that, there would be universal peace. Christ would then die and be buried beside Mohammed. At the resurrection, both Mohammed and Jesus would rise and be judged. Jesus would also take this opportunity to denounce the Jews for not having received him as a prophet and the Christians for having worshiped him as a god. Mohammed emphasizes in the third sura that Jesus never indicated that he should be worshiped. The worshiping came after Christ's death through ignorance and misinterpretation of the Scriptures.

Thus Mohammed placed Jesus on a level with himself. Even today it is not true that Moslems regard Jesus with hatred or contempt. The name Isa, which is the Arabic for Jesus and comes from "Ischo" of the Nestorians, is never mentioned without adding, "on whom be peace."

With all these sentiments, therefore, about Judaism and Christianity, it was a disappointment to Mohammed to find the two great monotheistic faiths, which had gone before, unwilling to join him in any kind of compromise on their beliefs.

However, having resigned himself to the impossibility of fusing the three religions, he set to work on Islam. In doing this he kept only what was best in the ancient doctrines of the Arabs and selected what he thought good in the Jewish and Christian teachings.

One of his first problems was to come to a decision about the Kaaba. He sensed the dangers of Kaaba worship and thought of abolishing it. Then he remembered its remote traditions, its connections through the Hashimites with him and his family, its importance to his home town. Accordingly he did away with the idols and many of the pagan rites, but left in a few which are really out of keeping with Islam.

In this he acted in the manner of Christ, who did away with some of the Temple abuses, but did not sweep away the Temple itself.

With regard to polygamy, he compromised. As the Old Testament tells us, it was a custom in the Orient dating from time immemorial. The Arabs had always been polygamous. Mohammed did not approve, but there was not much he could do. It was one of those things, the condemning of which would have cost him many followers without doing him or his cause much good. So he let the system continue and limited the number of wives.

One of the most unjust criticisms by non-Moslems of Mohammed is in this matter of polygamy. I have often heard it said that Islam is successful because of its sensuality. Apart from the fact that no great religion could owe its success to any such accompaniment, Mohammed had nothing to say in the matter. He did not make the manners of Arabia, and he was too astute to imagine that he could remake them or unmake them at once. It must never be forgotten that what in Judaism and Christianity were the results of long and gradual development, in Islam was accomplished by the deed of a single man, and was completed in a single generation. This is apt to be lost sight of. But the feat is stupendous. Not even Jesus can be credited with anything approaching a similar achievement. Not even Paul.

Moses did not abolish institutions of primitive society. He only mitigated their worst evils.

Neither did Christ revoke traditional institutions. According to Matthew, he advocated the contrary:

"Think not that I come to destroy the law or the prophets. I am not come to destroy but to fulfill. For, verily I say unto you, till heaven and earth pass, one jot or one tittle shall in no wise pass from the law, till all is fulfilled."

Jesus contented himself with planting principles in the minds of his followers which would in time eradicate those aspects of ancient rites which he considered outdated.

It is no more fair to represent polygamy as part of Islam than, for example, to represent slavery as part of Christianity. Slavery coexisted with Christianity and tried to justify itself by Christianity even until the end of the nineteenth century. The same can be said about polygamy and Islam, with the difference that polygamy united families instead of disuniting them and made of the home a sacred institution.

In the same way as polygamy, circumcision has nothing to do with Mohammed. He was born among people who were used to being circumcised, and he saw no reason to interfere. But circumcision is not a rite of Moslem origin.

There is no priesthood in Islam. There are Moslem religious teachers and preachers and mosque officials, but there are no intermediaries between the believer and God. There is no obligation even to worship in a mosque. A Moslem is in direct relationship with Allah, and his relationship is left a good deal to his conscience.

The mosque is there, the imam is there to lead the prayer, but going there is not evidence of being a good Moslem or not going there the sign of being a bad Moslem. The problem is one of preferring to pray in private or in public. Religious observance is not a dress parade, a social gathering, an excuse to gossip. There is none of that flocking to churches on one day of the week to make up for the lack of spiritual nourishment during the other six. There is none of that separating business from religion. In Islam attending to one takes up as much concentration and time as attending to the other.

The Moslems appoint Friday as a special day for prayer, but it is not a day of sloth, of getting up late, of playing a round of golf or going for a swim. Work goes on as usual as soon as the praying is over. The Arabs have none of that mechanical worship carried out by professional clergymen who earn their living by interpreting God as they see Him. A Moslem speaks to Allah with the respectful familiarity of a son to his father. He lives beside and inside the faith.

Various reasons influenced Mohammed in his attitude toward priestcraft. He did not like the idea of men taking to asceticism and penances and chastity because of their faith. He felt that a man could be an exemplary Moslem, and remain normal in his way of living. He did not believe that enforced chastity was natural or made anyone a better man or woman or any more acceptable to God than someone whose sex life followed the laws of nature.

In other religions he had seen the evils of priestcraft, the abuse of priestly power, the priestly distortion of religious facts. Those Christian sects with all their contradictory beliefs were evidence to him of what damage human dictates could have on a faith. He saw its wicked influence on simple-minded believers, frightened by threats of punishment if they did not do as their spiritual advisers told them.

The third reason for Mohammed's feelings on this subject was, like many things in Islam, due to circumstances. He had been born and raised in desert surroundings. With the exceptions of Syria and Palestine, he knew little about any other way of living but in the desert. So he was aware that it would be impossible for a nomadic people, the majority of whom knew no home but a tent, to find a mosque or a ritualist when the moment came to worship. So he ordained prayers for specific hours, but added that they could be said without outside guidance and wherever the worshiper happened to be.

The influence of the desert on Islam must always be borne in mind. Arabs allot to God a far larger place in their design for living than that usually allowed Him by people whose religious settings are overcrowded with woods and rivers and seas. Moslems feel the continual need of God's protection. They depend on Allah for everything, and Allah rarely disappoints them.

Many of the other Islamic codes were brought into being by local circumstances.

The eating of pork was banned because the pig in the Orient is an even fouler feeder than in the Occident. The Arabs did not know how to cure the meat and might not even cook it properly.

The restraint on drinking alcohol was due to the Arab weakness for a raw alcoholic spirit made from the fermented sap of the date palm. Had Arabia been a wine country, it is possible that this prohibition might not have been thought of. But it was not a wine country, and wherever Islam goes drinking disappears. What the United States and other countries have tried to stamp out by laws and material punishments, Mohammed abolished by making it a sin.

The removal of the shoes instead of the headdress on going into a mosque or holy place had a practical reason. An Arab turban could not be taken off like a hat, while the slippers without laces came off easily. The floor of the mosque was declared sacred ground and must not be soiled. But, before such decrees, an Arab always took his shoes off on entering a building or a tent. He wanted to protect the carpets on which he sat and slept.

Making almsgiving a tenet of the faith would very likely not have occurred to a man living in a town among sedentary people. But it was difficult to levy taxes from the wandering tribes which came and went with the seasons. So the payment of a percentage on property or income toward the maintenance of Islam became a religious observance.

The order to the well-to-do to care for the needy insured the protection of the destitute. The duty of being kind and helpful was specially stressed. This came as a result of Mohammed's recollections of the social injustices of Mecca, where the poor and unfortunate were trampled on by the wealthy merchants. Mohammed always felt deep concern and compassion for those for whom life was a struggle. He was the first religious reformer to be practical about charity, to consecrate it and make it an article of the faith which amounted to causing it to be a law.

Islam is the only organization where communism, in its true sense, is observed. It teaches that everything in the world is the common property of all. There can, therefore, be no complete individual ownership of anything. Islam declares the share of the poor in the wealth of the rich as a right. And in the thirteenth sura of the Koran, it says:

> "Give to the kinsman and to the poor and to the wayfarer their due out of your wealth."

This democratic spirit, moreover, has been carried to all parts of the universe where Islam has penetrated and has been made applicable to nations as well as to individuals. In other words Islam does not believe in imperialism. It sees no reason why races which consider themselves culturally superior, and have the material means to do so, should subjugate other peoples on the grounds of improving their ways of living. Wherever the Moslem armies went during the centuries succeeding Mohammed's death, they never made vassals of the conquered, they never exploited their natural resources for their selfish benefit. On no occasion did they follow the white man's principle of going to the rescue of the uncultured in places only where such generosity would be richly rewarded. On the contrary, the Moslems knew nothing of the world over which they were spreading or what it might give them. They naturally took full advantage of what they found, but always in conjunction with the local inhabitants. These, for the most part, had become Moslems and were consequently, by that fact, brothers and allies. The proof of this friendly relationship is that, with the exception of Spain, all the countries which the Moslems penetrated between the seventh and fourteenth centuries have remained faithful to the cause of Islam, and regard Mecca as the center of their civilizations.

Mohammed's views on fatalism and predestination have been misrepresented. These misrepresentations are based on his own statements: *"God created man and all his actions"*—*"The fate of every man is bound about his neck."* However, the belief in absolute foredoom which turns men into puppets was not what Mohammed had intended. He declared, many times, that a man was a free agent, free to refuse or free to accept the divine message; responsible for his acts and, therefore, deserving of punishment and reward.

He said: "The most prosperous man is he who becomes prosperous by his own exertions; and the most wretched man is he who becomes wretched by his own actions."

However, whatever may have been Mohammed's feelings

about predestination, he would have been obliged to compromise with them as he did with those about polygamy. Fatalism belonged to an era far removed from Mohammed. The Arabs had been fatalists since the beginning of recorded time. To say, therefore, that fatalism and Islam are one and the same thing is nothing more than invention.

On a par with the idea that the Moslem religion has chiefly to do with polygamy is the notion that the Moslem paradise is a place where the practice of polygamy has been perfected. As a matter of fact, nothing so tedious as marriage is mentioned as a phase of future life. What Mohammed did offer his followers was a final resting place where they would find all that they had missed on earth: rivers and lakes and green grass; and fruit trees with fruit always ripe; and wine to drink which exhilarated and did not intoxicate; plenty to eat too, without indigestion, without even the tiresome process of elimination. Mohammed assured his people that they would not have to make the effort of blowing their noses or washing. All bodily impurities would be disposed of by sweet-scented perspiration.

The inhabitants of this labor-saving home could recline indefinitely on couches, the linings of which would be made of silk. There would be none of that thirsty, ceaseless toil of the desert, none of its hardships. Seventy-two houris, black-eyed girls of resplendent beauty, of virgin purity and exquisite sensibility would be at the disposal of every Moslem believer. Neither did this exclude women less resplendent or less pure from entering paradise. There are repeated declarations in the Koran contradicting the general opinion that Islam denies females the possession of a soul. Mohammed thought too highly of women to inculcate such a doctrine. So he declared that the gates of heaven would be open to both sexes. He did not, however, specify the male companions for the chosen ladies. He probably did not want to alarm the jealousies of the former husbands or disturb their happiness by a suspicion of an everlasting marriage. He evaded the issue as tactfully as Christ when cornered on the same subject.

THE FAITH

As a matter of fact, one has only to consider the splendid mausoleums erected by Suleiman the Magnificent in Constantinople and by Shah Jahan in Agra for their wives to appreciate the regard which Moslems can have for their women. It would have been stupid for men who did not believe in a future life for their ladies to spend millions on masterpieces of oriental architecture like the Suleimanieh Mosque and the Taj Mahal.

Mohammed was given to great courtesy when speaking to women. One remark of his must hold the record for tact and politeness. To an old lady who asked him how she could enter paradise, he replied:

"Old ladies do not enter paradise. When you reach paradise you will be young!"

According to the Koran, paradise will have two gardens:

"In each two fountains flowing,
"In each two kinds of every fruit.
"On couches with linings of brocade shall they recline, and the fruit of the two gardens shall be within easy reach. Therein shall be the damsels with retiring glances, whom nor man nor djinn hath touched before them. . . ."

and so on, throughout the fifty-fifth sura.

Being a lover of animals, Mohammed further asserted that animals would share in the general resurrection. This idea also belonged to pre-Moslem times. The camel tethered to the Arab's grave was an indication that he expected to take his desert companion with him into the next life.

In making this picture of paradise attractive, Mohammed was giving way neither to sensuality nor materialism. He wanted Moslems to look forward to a practical reward which they would understand. Speaking of the hereafter, he used to say:

"The world is as a prison and as a famine to Moslems, and when they leave it, you may say they leave famine and a prison."

In this attitude, he was again showing his wisdom. In all faiths, the world to come is what the believer would like to live with forever.

The red Indian dreams of a heaven behind cloud-shrouded hills where he and his trusty dog will find happiness in silent forests. The old Norsemen looked forward to the Halls of Odin and a never-ending drinking bout with the skulls of their enemies in place of goblets. The devout Dissentor's paradise is a place "where congregations ne'er break up and Sabbaths never end." The average Christian longs for something more comfortable and less worrying than the restless life of this world. It may be oblivion. It is certainly not a kind of cloudy, drafty, disembodied Sunday school.

A polygamous people, therefore, could hardly have pictured a heaven without polygamy. None of them had known a society without it, so that a different condition seemed unbelievable. No Christian who has deep feelings about home ties can favor the doctrine, according to St. Matthew, that in the future world there will be no physical attachments.

Mohammed had much worldly experience. He had loved and he had suffered. His life had been a struggle. So he wanted a heavenly recompense, a divine resting place where all he and his companions had missed on earth would be found.

What most Christians do not realize is that many of these pictures of the so-called sensuous paradise *came* from a *Christian!* His name was St. Ephraim, and he lived in Syria during the fourth century after Christ. In his hymns about paradise he has all Mohammed's predictions, including the lovely ladies who, he adds, will recompense holy men for their earthly chastity.

The following is an extract from these hymns:

I saw the dwelling places of the just, and they themselves, dripping with ointments, giving forth pleasant odors, wreathed in flowers and decked with fruits. . . . Whoever has abstained from wine on earth, for him do the vines of paradise yearn. . . . And if a man has lived in chastity, the women receive him in a pure bosom, because he was a monk and did not fall into the bosom and bed of earthly love. (Hymns of St. Ephraim, Vol. III, p. 563)

With the same motive of forewarning, Mohammed's picture of hell was an aggravation of all the discomforts of the desert. He says:

"*They* [the sinners] *shall dwell amid burning winds and scalding water, under the shade of black smoke, neither cool nor grateful; and they shall drink boiling water, even as the thirsty camel drinketh. . . . They shall have garments of fire fitted unto them, their bowels shall be dissolved thereby, and also their skins, and they shall be beaten with maces of iron.*"

And, as if anticipating George Sale and his fellow scoffers, the Koran goes on to say:

"*Woe be it on that day to those who accused the prophets of imposture. It shall be said unto them, Go ye into the shadow of the smoke of hell, which, though it ascend in three columns, shall not shade you from the heat, neither shall it be of service against the flames. But it shall cast forth sparks as big as towers, and their color shall be like unto red camels. Woe be on that day unto those who accuse the prophets of imposture.*"

But, unlike the hell of the Jews and the Christians, the Moslem hell is not one of eternal damnation. It is rather like a nursing home where people are sent to be cured of spiritual ailments contracted on earth. When they are well, they will go to heaven. As Mohammed said:

"*A time will come over hell when its gates will clash against each other because there will be no one left in it.*"

To Christians also is offered a hope of redemption through the intermediary of Jesus Christ.

Paradise was, thus, an exaggeration of what Mohammed had glimpsed during his travels outside Arabia, with a few ideas possibly borrowed from Father Ephraim. Hell was a similar exaggeration of the glittering, waterless deserts around Mecca.

The picture was much the same as that in the minds of Moses

and Jesus, who knew these same arid countries. Green pastures were synonymous with heaven, fire and brimstone with hell.

In order that the converts to Islam should know what their new religion entailed, Mohammed established a creed of which the following is a summary:

1. I believe in God.

La ilaha illa Allah—There is no God but Allah.

2. I believe in God's angels.

Of these, the four principal are: Gabriel, the medium of revelation; Azrael, who receives the souls of the dead departed; Azrafel, who is in charge of the trumpet; Michael, who cares for all created human beings.

Among the other angels are two who are black. These interrogate all souls immediately the body is buried: "Who is God? Who is his Messenger? What is your religion? On what side was your Kibla?" (The Kibla is the niche in every Moslem home showing the direction of Mecca.)

Those souls whose answers are unsatisfactory have to remain with their bodies in the grave until the day of judgment.

3. I believe in His books.

Allah revealed a great number of books to Adam and the succeeding prophets, all of which were lost except the Pentateuch of Moses, David's Psalms, the Gospel of Jesus, and Mohammed's Koran.

4. I believe in his Prophets.

God sent to the world since its creation 200,000 prophets, twenty-five of whom are referred to in the Koran. The greatest of these are Adam, Noah, Abraham, Moses, Jesus, and Mohammed. Prophets are to be regarded as free from sin, the most sinless of all being Jesus. Mohammed speaks of him as the Word of God, the Spirit of God, born of the Virgin Mary, and Worker of Miracles.

5. I believe in the resurrection and the last day.

The actions of all men will be weighed on that day and judged accordingly. The sign of its approaching advent will be the return of Jesus Christ. The resurrection will be definitely physical.

(The pagan Arabs of Mecca contested this violently, asking Mohammed how it could be possible to collect all the bones of the dead departed and put them together again. To this Mohammed replied that if God was able to create a human being from a drop he could as easily do the other.) At this resurrection, intercession for non-Moslems will be useless. Allah sent his Messenger to guide men into the right course. If they have refused to be guided, that is not Allah's fault. He has done his best. Moslems, after being purged, will enter paradise.

6. I believe in the predestination of good and evil.

Allah's will explains and accounts for everything that happens, all that has been and all that ever will be.

In addition to their creed, Mohammed gave his people five obligatory duties.

I. The recital of the creed. Condensed to its shortest, it amounts to:

"I testify that there is no God but Allah, and that Mohammed is the Messenger of Allah."

"*Ash-hadu La ilaha illa Allah, Mohammed rasul Allah.*"

II. Prayer five times a day. At dawn, noon, midafternoon, sunset, and two hours after sunset.

Mohammed had great faith in prayer. Often he used to say: "The five daily prayers are like a fresh river which runs by the door of one's house. He who washes in it five times a day will keep himself pure and clean."

This, however, did not prevent him from being particular about bodily cleanliness. Before praying, the worshiper has to go through prescribed ablutions. Furthermore, Mohammed, aware that water was not always available in his country, allowed sand to be used as a substitute.

These prayers are not petitions. Mohammed said that if God is all-powerful, He knows the needs of mankind. It would, therefore, be impertinence to tell Him. So the prayers are praises and thanks and begging forgiveness.

III. Fasting. This is observed throughout the month of Ramadan. During these thirty days, nothing can be eaten or drunk from before dawn until after sunset. That is, *"before, and until after, a white hair and a black hair held at arm's length are indistinguishable."*

Owing to the Moslems observing a "lunar year," the months do not recur at the same seasons. Hence when Ramadan falls in June, the fasting during the long, torrid day can be most trying.

Like fasts in other faiths, the underlying idea is to discipline the faster to privation and discomfort, to place the rich and the poor on the same level. However, whereas, among Christian denominations, the privations depend much on the conscience of the Lenten observer, with the Moslem the complete abstention from food or liquid is unconditionally compulsory during the prescribed hours.

IV. Pilgrimage to Mecca. This had been a custom dating back to the oldest days of the Kaaba. Mohammed had made up his mind that he must keep the Kaaba as part of his new religion. He saw also that this pilgrimage would bring the faithful from all parts of the Moslem world to a common meeting ground once a year. However, with his usual practical attitude towards life, he added a rider to this obligation, absolving any who could not afford the journey and the upkeep of the home while absent.

V. Almsgiving. These are legal alms to the community chest and non-obligatory, but recommended, alms to the destitute. This latter formal charity is conscientiously practiced by the majority of Moslems.

In brief, therefore, those are the principles of this new ideal for which Mohammed was risking his life in Mecca. He was offering his people a God as sublime as the Christians', but more intense, more in keeping with their harsh lives. It was the religion of the shepherd and the warrior, of the burning, boundless wilderness.

Christianity contains whole fields of morality and whole realms of thought which are outside the religion of Mohammed. The fundamental ideal of Christian life is more ethereal, even as the founder of Islam's is more material than the life of the founder of Christianity. There is in Islam no ethereal life, in the true sense, for Mohammed's character was admitted by himself to be not ethereal. That is possibly one of the reasons for its popularity and its ever increasing strength.

Nevertheless, Islam is not an easy religion. With its fasts, its numerous daily prayers, its solitudes, its pilgrimages, its almsgiving, it is not made to appeal to the lazy or the selfish. There is no outward show and there are no worldly rewards as in some of the earlier faiths. Mohammed, in his capacity of temporal ruler, never gave material rewards to his followers outside the spoils they had earned, at the risk of their lives, in battle.

It has been argued that Islam is less absorbing than other religions. This may be true. Islam *is* made up of ideas which existed before; and, if that were all there was to it, it would be as uninteresting as it is unoriginal. *But the element one cannot and must not forget is Mohammed himself.* That is what created Islam, that is what gave it its driving force and made it thrive and prosper through the thirteen centuries since it was first presented to the Arabs. Mohammed *is* Islam, much more so than Moses is Judaism and Jesus is Christianity. The history of this religion would be nothing without the story of its founder.

CHAPTER VII

THE SEVEN HEAVENS

(620 After Christ)

However hard the beginning, however long the road, most men have reached their goals by the time they are fifty. Mohammed is an exception. More than half of his life was spent in obscurity, a quarter of it in persecution, a sixth of it only in the realization of his purpose. All the things for which Mohammed is best remembered took place during the last ten years of his life and when he was over fifty-two. Many people who have a superficial knowledge of Islam are astonished to hear of all that happened before his fiftieth birthday. But although, so to speak, Mohammed's life began at fifty, the early backgrounds are essential to complete the full-length portrait.

One of the most disappointing features in the generally accepted life of Jesus is the lack of detail concerning his youth. We hear of him being born and, almost immediately, he is a man of thirty performing miracles. Three years later he is dead. The story of Moses has the same failing. So has that of John the Baptist and of Paul. We know them at the heights of their careers. What they did in their teens and twenties is a blank. This, with their adult effigies in glass and wood and stone, gives them an almost mythological character. Mohammed starts making history later than the others, but there is nothing obscure about his youth for those who take the trouble to inquire into it.

Soon after Khadija's death, Mohammed did an unexpected thing. He married. He married twice! Neither of the unions was for love. One of the brides was a child of seven, the other a middle-aged, unattractive widow of an immigrant who had fled to Abyssinia in 614 and had died there. The reasons for both these marriages were primarily practical.

The child bride was Aisha, the daughter of Abu Bakr, the close friend, the first convert. The idea of such a match had nothing to do with Mohammed. He was too distressed at Khadija's death and overworked by his persecutions to think about women and homes. The suggestion came from his aunt, Kwala bint Hakim, the sister of Amina. She pointed out that while, for the moment, the marriage of Aisha could be regarded as nothing more than a betrothal, it would insure the daughter of Mohammed's most faithful follower becoming a member of the family. Aisha, she added, showed every sign of growing up a beauty. Mohammed agreed, and the marriage took place. Although it was not consummated until some years later, this strange union of the aging preacher and the little girl was to have far-reaching effects on Islam, and not always to its advantage. Aisha survived her husband by many years and was the first of the intriguers to set Moslem against Moslem.

I mention this here because some biographers criticize Mohammed for this marriage. Not only did Mohammed not originally think of it, but there was never any question of its being a compulsory, lustful relationship of an old man and a virgin child. From the day Aisha set foot in Mohammed's home, she made herself felt. At times she was as great a worry to Mohammed as to his successors. If ever a woman fulfilled the title of mistress in every sense of the word, it was Aisha bint Abi Bakr.

The other bride, Sawda bint Zama, came into Mohammed's family circle more as a housekeeper than anything else. She was a large, heavy woman for whom Mohammed never had any emotional feelings. But she had been one of the first converts, whose husband had died in exile for the cause, and Kwala told her nephew that the least he could do for her was to marry her. She hardly ever lived with her second husband, and on several occasions Mohammed tried to get rid of her, but she begged to remain without privileges. She finally died in the harem, unmourned and unnoticed.

But if he had found brides. Mohammed had not found peace. With the death of Abu Taleb and Khadija, Abu Sofian and Abu Jahl made up their minds to be more practical in their methods for ridding themselves of the disturbing impostor. Without mincing words, they let the city know that nothing less than the man's dead body would satisfy them. Once more, Mohammed had to flee.

This time he took no one with him but Zaid. As there was no longer any refuge like the hospitable castle of Abu Taleb, they had to put distance quickly between them and Mecca. So they mounted their camels and traveled to the country of the great Hawazin tribe, seventy miles to the east of Mecca. It was a hilly district much favored by the wealthy Meccans, who went there to escape the summer heat. The scenery was as different as possible from the glittering aridity of the wilderness about the Holy City. There was abundant water, and the inhabitants lived by agriculture. Date palms and fruit trees and gardens, through which gushed green rivulets, covered the hillsides. After the desert, it was like paradise. Mohammed felt grateful relief as he rode up the shady avenues. But his relief was short-lived.

His first disillusion was to learn that the citizens of At Tayef, the principal city of this oasis district, had never heard of him and his doctrines. The second, that they were not interested in new cults. They were satisfied with their stone goddess, Allat, who gave them all they asked for. To Mohammed as a person there was no objection; as an antagonist of Allat, or Al Rabba, as she was also called, there was a great deal.

Mohammed, as usual, refused to back down or compromise. It would have been simple for him to give himself a holiday and rest from thoughts of Islam while he rebuilt his strength. But such an idea never occurred to him. He chose the difficult course, and began to preach. The results were disastrous. Everyone set on him. Jeers were followed by insults, insults by stones. In a short while he was driven out of the cool gardens, away from the comforting water, out onto the grilling desert. Once more it looked as if there must be something wrong with this mission. No man could be expected to survive such systematic adversity.

But Zaid was young and wanted to live. So he left his adopted father with the provisions which he had been able to smuggle from the oasis, and himself went back to Mecca. Here he persuaded a convert called Mutem ibn Adi, who had a large house, to give Mohammed sanctuary. Then he went back to the desert. He found Mohammed in a kind of coma due, partly, to the heat and, partly, to two djinns who had been keeping him company! Or so Mohammed affirmed! Zaid wasted no time. He hoisted Mohammed onto his camel and brought him back to Mecca and slipped him into the home of Mutem ibn Adi without any of the Koreishites knowing.

It was here that occurred what has become almost as much a subject for discussion as Mohammed's epilepsy and illiteracy and, while interesting, has had as little influence on the history of Islam. It is the episode known to believers as the Night Journey.

In various forms and in varying lengths, this story appears in most of the books on Mohammed. Some of the versions are inspired, some are scornful, some are colorless and prosaic. I will give it as it was told to me by my friend the Caid Madani* outside our tent one night on the Sahara Desert.

Madani was one of the few really good men whom I have ever known. Had he been an English country gentleman or an American farmer, instead of an Arab chief, his goodness would have stood out. You had only to look into his twinkling blue eyes or watch him smile to know that here was someone who was genuine. He was also an excellent storyteller. Much of his material came from the Old Testament, from the Koran, and from the Moslem "traditions," but he had an enviable way of giving the oldest yarn a new twist. The account of the Night Journey was one of Madani's pieces which was fresh to me from beginning to end. . . .

Madani settled his robes, pushed his turban to the back of his head, and looked at me thoughtfully. Then he said:

"The desert was quiet that night. No jackals yapped, no dogs barked, even the rustling of the wind had dropped. In the streets

---

*See *Wind in the Sahara*, by the same author.

of Mecca no cats prowled, and there was silence in the houses of the prostitutes. Even the bubbling of the water in the irrigation channels had ceased. It was as if everything had died with the setting of the sun.

"Mohammed had gone to rest at dusk. His body and spirit were weary from the trials through which he had been. He slept deeply on the carpet of his cousin, Mutem ibn Adi. Suddenly the heavy silence was broken. A voice as clear as a trumpet called:

"'Awake, thou sleeper, awake!'

"Mohammed roused himself and sat up. Standing before him, dazzling in the darkness, he saw the angel Gabriel. From his brightly colored wings, from his snow-white hair, from his robes embroidered with gold and glittering with precious stones, light poured. The angel repeated his call and signaled to Mohammed to follow him into the street.

"Before the door stood a mare as dazzling as Gabriel. She had wings too, glittering wings like those of an immense eagle. Her eyes were like jacinths and her head so beautiful that it was almost human. Gabriel presented the mare to Mohammed, giving her name, 'Borak.' Borak whinnied and allowed Mohammed to vault onto her back. Then, drinking the wind, she galloped up the street. As she came to the walls of the sleeping city, she spread her wings and soared into the starry night with Gabriel floating alongside."

Madani's picture of Mohammed and the mare was simple and Arab. The angel making the presentation, Mohammed mounting with the confidence of the born horseman, belonged to the lore of one people. One cannot imagine Moses or Jesus or Paul on spirited horses. Only an Arab would go on a celestial mission in such a manner.

"When they had been racing through the air for a while," continued Madani, "Gabriel gave an order, and Borak planed to earth. Mohammed was asked to dismount and pray. He was on the summit of Mount Sinai at the very place where Jehovah had given the tables of stone to Moses.

"The prayer over, they sailed away again until, once more,

an order was given and a landing made. This time the place was Bethlehem. Here Mohammed prayed at the exact spot where Jesus was born. Then they flew on.

"During the third stage of the journey they were not alone. Three times, gorgeous women appeared out of the clouds and begged Mohammed to stay with them. Mohammed did not know what to make of this, so he took no notice. However, after the third voice had implored him to wait, he asked Gabriel whether he was aware of what was going on. Gabriel evidently was aware, for he replied without hesitation:

"'The first voice was a Jew's, the second was a Christian's, the third was the voice of the world and its vanities. If you had shown inclinations to stay with any one of those women, you and your people would have become as they.'

"Before Mohammed could ask any further questions, Gabriel had spoken once more to Borak and they were diving toward earth again. This time they landed in Jerusalem outside the temple. Gabriel had Mohammed tether the mare to a ring in the wall and led the way inside. Here they found a number of prophets, among whom were Abraham and Moses and Jesus. After formal introductions, they prayed. When the praying was over, they discussed their respective missions until Gabriel said it was time to go.

"Outside the temple Mohammed found a ladder with its foot resting on Jacob's stone and leading up to heaven. Following the angel, he started to climb. This was less difficult than he had anticipated. He felt as if he were made of air, and in a few moments he was standing before the gates of paradise!"

Madani looked at me triumphantly. His smile suggested, "You didn't expect that one, did you?" I certainly didn't. Madani gave a pleased nod and went on:

"As soon as Gabriel had explained to the guardian of the gates whom he had with him, they were opened. Mohammed followed Gabriel across the threshold and found himself in the first heaven. It was made of pure silver and suspended from the stars by golden chains. An old man hobbled forward to greet the newcomers. Gabriel introduced him to Mohammed as his father, Adam. Adam took Mohammed in his arms and, embracing him, hailed him as the noblest of his children. Then he did him the honors of the first heaven.

"The whole place was filled with animals and birds and reptiles, in the midst of which stood an immense cock. So immense was it that Mohammed could not see its head, which reached up into the clouds. Adam explained that the birds and the animals were, in reality, angels who interceded with Allah on behalf of the non-human creatures of the earth. The cock's duty was to crow every morning and wake up the seven heavens.

"As soon as Mohammed had seen enough of the first heaven, Gabriel took him up to the second. It had a gate like the first, and the interior was made of polished steel. Noah lived there and was as delighted as Adam had been to meet his illustrious descendant. With Noah were Jesus and John the Baptist. Mohammed was not sure whether this was their home or if they were just visiting, but they were most cordial and spoke to him as to an old friend.

"The third heaven was more ornate than the first two. It was much bigger and studded with myriads of precious stones. Mohammed understood Gabriel to say that Joseph and David were somewhere in this heaven, but he did not have a chance to meet them. He was too absorbed by an angel of immeasurable size whose eyes were seventy thousand days' journey apart. He did not speak when Mohammed entered the third heaven, neither was he introduced. In awful silence he pored over a huge book in which he continually wrote and erased.

" 'That,' said Gabriel, 'is the angel of death, Azrael by name. He has command over one hundred thousand battalions of soldiers.'

" 'What's he doing with that book?' whispered Mohammed.

" 'He is writing the names of those who are to be born and rubbing out those who must die,' replied Gabriel.

"Mohammed felt relieved when Gabriel moved on to the fourth heaven. Like the first, it was made of silver. In the middle of this heaven was an angel five hundred days' journey in height who wept and wept and wept, until rivers of tears ran out of his eyes.

"'And that one,' said Gabriel, 'is the angel who weeps for the sins of the children of men and foretells the misfortunes that await them.'

"Mohammed showed no reluctance to leave that heaven either, and said only a few words to Enoch, to whom he had been introduced at the door.

"Up the ladder he went again, slipping from rung to rung as if he had been made of feathers. The fifth heaven was all gold. Here Aaron was waiting to greet the distinguished guest. Mohammed was hoping to have a rest and perhaps a theological discussion, when he saw a horrible-looking creature sitting on a red-hot throne surrounded by flames. His face was like burnished copper and was covered with warts and boils. His eyes sent out lightnings, and his fiery hand grasped a burning lance. Aaron noticed Mohammed's startled expression. Taking him aside, he informed him that this was God's avenging angel who controlled the element of fire. His chief duties were to execute God's vengeance on sinners and unbelievers.

"The sixth heaven was made of a curious transparent stone which Mohammed had never seen before. He looked anxiously for another monster and, sure enough, found one. This angel was not as unprepossessing as the others, but he was far from normal. Half his body was made of fire, the other half of snow. Neither did the fire melt the snow, nor the snow put out the fire. Surrounding this strange creature was a crowd of smaller angels who sang continuously:

"'O Allah, who has united snow and fire, unite all thy faithful servants in obedience to thy law.'

"'This,' remarked Gabriel, 'is the guardian angel of heaven and earth. He sends messengers to men to incline them towards you and call them to serve Allah. He will continue to do this until the day of resurrection.'

"Mohammed thought that this was the best thing which he had

heard since he left Mecca. However, before he could express his appreciation, Moses appeared and greeted Mohammed again. Then he began to cry. Mohammed took his hands and tried to comfort him, begging him to tell him why he wept and if his visit had anything to do with this grief. Moses nodded and, through his tears, said:

" 'I see before me a successor who will conduct more of his nation to paradise than I ever could my backsliding children of Israel.'

"Mohammed tried to say something consoling, but Gabriel was showing impatience, and in a few more minutes he had climbed into the seventh heaven.

"Abraham bowed Mohammed into this blissful abode, which was made of divine light and beyond the powers of description of any human voice. Its size alone could not be expressed. It was infinite. And here too was another angel unlike anything Mohammed had seen before. His magnitude was such that it made the angels of the four preceding heavens seem like dwarfs. He was bigger than the whole of the world. He had seventy thousand heads, and each head had seventy thousand mouths. In each mouth were seventy thousand tongues, and each tongue spoke seventy thousand different languages. These five billion mouths did nothing but chant the praises of Allah with their three hundred trillion tongues and their twenty-four quintillion languages."

Madani paused as if he expected me to challenge these figures, but I was not even trying to calculate. The sum which comes out after multiplying 70,000 by 70,000 three or four times does not convey anything which the human mind can grasp. To Madani and to Mohammed, they were evidences of God's infinite majesty. I could see no reason to contest this.

"Mohammed was still looking at this extraordinary creature, when he felt himself being borne away by a kind of gentle whirlwind. He did not use the ladder and, in a few seconds, found himself deposited in the lotus tree which grows beside the hidden thrones of Allah. This tree was even bigger than the angel with all the mouths. Its branches were longer than the distance between the earth and the sun. Its leaves were huge, and millions of birds flitted through them twittering verses from the Koran. The fruits on the trees were of endless varieties, and each one combined food and drink. The sustenance in one of the fruits would be sufficient to feed all the animals of the world. In each seed of each fruit lived a celestial virgin provided for true believers. Beneath the shade of the tree and beside four great rivers, which had their sources in the trunk of the tree, angels, more numerous than the sands of the sea, took their leisure. Two of these rivers watered paradise, the other two went to form the Euphrates and the Nile.

"The tree was comfortable and peaceful after the terrific angels, and Mohammed was once more hoping for a few moments to gather his thoughts. But Gabriel was still in a hurry. After a few moments of listening to the birds, Mohammed was whirled off to the House of Adoration, which was made of jacinths and rubies. Here an angel offered him three goblets filled respectively with wine, with milk, and with honey. Mohammed being a good Arab, chose the milk. Gabriel nodded approval.

" 'If you had chosen the wine,' he said, 'your people would have gone astray.' After a pause, he added, 'This is as far as I can go. In a moment you are going to see God. I'll be waiting for you in the seventh heaven.'

"With that, he turned away and, before Mohammed could say 'sword,' he felt himself snatched up and precipitated through space. In and out of regions of dazzling light and inky darkness he flew. He could feel no barriers, but it seemed as if curtain after curtain were being lifted as he drew closer and closer to that cloud-wrapped realm from where Allah watched over the world. At last the wild journey stopped and Mohammed found himself within two bow shots of the throne of God!"

Madani paused and stared ecstatically before him. Then he said:

"For a while there was great silence, and nothing was heard

except the whispering sound of the reed wherewith the decrees of God are inscribed on the tablets of Fate. . . .

"Mohammed did not raise his head at once. When he did, he found that the face of God was covered with twenty thousand veils. Even so, the glory which radiated from behind the veils was greater than fifty thousand sunrises."

Madani drew a deep breath and looked out into the night. He seemed to be uplifted by what he had said. And, truly, his words were sublime. It was the first time that I had heard the mysterious majesty of God made to sound real. After a moment, he continued:

"As Mohammed's eyes became accustomed to the dazzling atmosphere, he saw inscribed in luminous letters on the right of God's throne: 'THERE IS NO GOD BUT ALLAH, AND MOHAMMED IS HIS MESSENGER.'

"Mohammed felt reassured, but he found it hard to stand his ground when God stretched out His hands and placed one on his shoulder and the other on his chest. An icy chill froze his bones and his blood. Then the coldness faded and was succeeded by an ecstatic bliss which seemed to carry Mohammed out of himself into a state of mind so marvelous that it was impossible to describe. A deep voice, which was more soothing than alarming, said:

" 'O Mohammed, salute thy Creator!'

"Mohammed's fears disappeared. He felt complacent and was able to discuss calmly with God the details of the faith which he was to promote among the Arabs. God's final injunctions were that Moslems should pray fifty times a day. With these parting orders, the divine hold was relaxed, and Mohammed was whirled back to the seventh heaven, where he found Gabriel waiting.

"Gabriel asked no questions, but as they were passing through the sixth heaven Moses inquired what had happened at the interview. When Mohammed came to the part about the praying, Moses shook his head. He said that praying more than twice in every hour of the twenty-four was unthinkable. If Mohammed wanted his religion to stand up, he must get that changed. Mohammed, who respected the prophets who had preceded him, accordingly had himself whirled back to Allah. Allah agreed to reduce the number of prayers to forty. At this, Moses also scoffed. Mohammed went back to Allah. After a good deal of discussion with God and argument with Moses, the praying of Moslems was reduced to five times a day. Even so, Moses told Mohammed that he would be a cleverer man than he supposed if he managed to make his people pray that number of times every day of the week. Mohammed thanked Moses and said that that must be left to him. . . .

"Now he quickly descended the ladder from heaven to heaven until he reached the earth, where he found Borak. He could not see Gabriel, so he vaulted onto the mare's white back and, in a few moments, was on his carpet in Mecca."

Madani stopped. He seemed to have forgotten me. Counting his beads, he looked up at the desert sky.

"How long had Mohammed been away?" I asked after a pause.

"A very short time," replied Madani unhesitatingly. "Not more than a few hours."

For a while we sat in silence. Then I asked: "Have you ever read Dante?"

Madani shook his head. "No, what is it?"

I did not explain, but since that night on the desert when Madani told me the story of the Night Journey, I have heard it said that Dante may have been inspired by this ancient Arab legend. There are certain similarities in the two accounts of paradise.

The question which I did not put to Madani, because it would have wrecked the whole atmosphere of the storytelling, was whether he believed that Mohammed had made this journey in the flesh or in a dream. Or—and this I would not have offended Madani by even suggesting—did Mohammed invent the whole thing? Nevertheless, those are the questions which bother some writers about Islam.

My last query, as it happens, would have been superfluous, *as there is no record by Mohammed himself that the Night Journey ever took place at all.* I did not know this at the time and imagined that Madani was following his custom of giving me picturesque renderings of the Scriptures. But this was an exception. He was speaking from tradition which many Arabs accept as faithfully as the Koran. All that we have from Mohammed concerning this celestial expedition is a chapter from the Holy Book entitled, "The Night Journey." But, even in this chapter, there is nothing remotely resembling what Madani and other Arabs believe. The only indication that something of the kind occurred is in the first verse:

"Glory be to Him who carried his servant by night from the sacred temple of Mecca to the temple that is more remote, whose precinct we have blessed, that we might show him of our signs, for He is the Hearer and the Seer."

The whole account is probably a legend like those others concerning miracles which Mohammed never claimed to have performed. But if Mohammed had confirmed the story of the Night Journey by including it in the Koran, it should not cause non-Moslem critics immediately to throw doubt on it.

The story of Elijah ascending into heaven in a fiery chariot is not jeered at. The resurrection and ascension of Jesus is, by the majority of Christians, accepted. The revelation of St. John the Divine is not treated as a lot of nonsense set down by a crazy epileptic. Yet there are passages in Revelation strangely similar to parts of the story which Madani told, and no less fantastic.

Taking almost any chapter of that last book of the Bible, we find passages which would fit anywhere into the Night Journey:

Chapter IV:

And, behold, a throne was set in heaven and one sat on the throne. And he that sat was to look upon like jasper and a sardine stone: and there was a rainbow round about the throne, in sight like unto an emerald. . . . And out of the throne proceeded lightnings and thunderings and voices; and there were seven lamps of fire burning before the throne which are the seven Spirits of God. And before the throne there was a sea of glass like unto crystal; and in the midst of the throne, and round about the throne, were four beasts full of eyes, before and behind.

Chapter XIII:

And I stood upon the sand of the sea, and saw a beast rise up out of the sea, having seven heads and ten horns, and upon his horns ten crowns, and upon his head the name of blasphemy. And the beast which I saw was like unto a leopard and his feet were as the feet of a bear, and his mouth as the mouth of a lion; and the dragon gave him his power and his seat and great authority.

Chapter XXI:

And the building of the wall of it was of jasper; and the city was pure gold, like unto clear glass. And the foundations of the wall of the city were garnished with all manner of precious stones. . . . And the city had no need of sun, neither of the moon, to shine in it, for the glory of God did lighten it.

Chapter XXII:

And he showed me a pure river of water of life, clear as crystal, proceeding out of the throne of God and of the Lamb. In the midst of the street of it, and on either side of the river, was there the tree of life, which bare twelve manner of fruits, and yielded her fruit every month; and the leaves of the tree were for the healing of the nations.

And none of this is legend. It is all in the Holy Bible, as is also the passage from St. Matthew telling of Jesus' talk with Moses and Elias, and of Moses' interview with God on Sinai—Exodus, 19.

Another story, very similar to that of the Night Journey, is told by St. Irenius, who was bishop of Lyons in the second century after Christ. According to him, Jesus made the following declaration to St. John, who recorded it:

"Days shall come in which there will be vines which shall each have ten thousand branches, and every one of these branches shall have ten thousand lesser branches, and every one of these lesser branches shall have ten thousand twigs, and every one of these twigs shall have ten thousand clusters of grapes, and in every one of these clusters shall be ten thousand grapes, and every one of these grapes being pressed shall yield two hundred and seventy-five gallons of wine."

I was not acquainted with this piece when I lived among the Arabs, otherwise I would have given it to Madani to show him that Christians were just as good at setting celestial multiplication problems as Moslems.

However, whatever may be the foundations of these legends or traditions or scriptures, there is no reason to discard the parts which we individually do not think plausible. Whether we are believers or non-believers, proving that Jesus and Moses never existed or that Mohammed was an impostor leads us nowhere. Men like Madani, who had complete faith in the account of the Night Journey, as he told it, are much more content than skeptics. Regardless of anyone's personal views on the subject, the fact that Mohammed saw or did not see an angel with three hundred trillion tongues makes not the least difference to his story.

CHAPTER VIII

AL HIJRA—THE FLIGHT

(620–622 After Christ)

MOHAMMED'S CELESTIAL JOURNEY to heaven, his cordial reception by the prophets, his friendly arguments with Allah might give one the idea that he had now sufficient support to proceed with his mission and disregard the menace of the Koreishites. Two very good reasons stood against such a solution.

The first was that Mohammed was not sure himself whether he had made the Night Journey or dreamt it. The second, that God does not encourage such methods in His delegates when He wants to found a new faith.

Although Moses had been able to raise plagues in Egypt and predict an eclipse of the sun, although he had struck water in the wilderness, the nearest to an objective phenomenon which God had produced was the pillar of fire to guide the Israelites over the Red Sea.

Jesus had resurrected the dead, he had turned water into wine, he had fed multitudes with inadequate provisions, but God's only personal appearance had been in the shape of a dove over Jordan and the rending of rocks during the crucifixion.

In Mohammed's case, God did not even go that far. He left His Messenger alone to persuade the Arabs of his mission. That he succeeded without supernatural accessories adds much to the originality of his achievement.

Ten years had now passed since he had been ordered to preach and make known the nature of his message to the Meccans. During those ten years he had lost everything which he had gained during the preceding forty. It looked more and more as if something were wrong with him or with what he had in mind.

Then, one day, an incident took place which ranks in importance with the conversion of Saul of Tarsus or Henry VIII's break with the Pope.

For many centuries the Jews in Arabia had been waiting for the Messiah. Especially was this the case in Yathrib. Yathrib, as has already been stated, is the old name for Medina, or more exactly, Medinat en Nabi, the City of the Prophet. To avoid confusion, I shall continue to call it Medina.

This Medina was the home of three important Jewish tribes, the Beni an Nadir, the Beni Kainuka, and the Beni Koreiza. Although they held comparatively important positions locally, they were under the Arab sovereignty of two bedouin groups, the Beni Aus and the Beni Khazraj, who had become sedentary people and settled in these Medina oases.

This belief of the Jews in the coming of a redeemer was known to these Arabs, and when, one day, some of the Beni Khazraj heard Mohammed preaching at a fair near Mecca, his words struck a familiar chord. Without hesitation they exclaimed: "Surely this must be the prophet with whom the Jews are threatening us!" Then, realizing the importance of their discovery, added: "Let us make haste and join him!"

The men waited until no one was around and then spoke to Mohammed. They expressed their interest in what he had been saying and asked for more details. Mohammed, who was glad to find people with any inclination to hear him, arranged a meeting in the desert where there would be no risk of interruptions. There he talked far into the night. His sincerity and clear reasoning impressed the Medinese. They told him so, but pointed out that they could promise nothing on behalf of their fellow citizens until they had discussed with them what they had just heard.

This they did as soon as they reached their homes, spreading the news of an Arab prophet, one of their own people, not a Jew, who announced a true God who could put an end to their century-old dissensions.

What they said created quite a stir, and the following year a larger group of men proceeded to Mecca to hear Mohammed.

AL HIJRA—THE FLIGHT

Once more he was asked to explain his doctrines. Once more the listeners from Medina were impressed. They declared that they believed in Mohammed and what he represented himself to be. When Mohammed indicated the inconveniences which might result from such a declaration, the men remained unshaken. Solemnly in the semidarkness of the rocky desert, they swore allegiance. The following words concluded their oath:

"We will obey the Prophet in everything that is right, and we will be faithful to him in weal and in sorrow."

Then each man touched Mohammed's hand and returned to Medina. With them went a disciple of Mohammed, Musab ibn Omeir, who would help explain to the people the meaning of Islam.

Although Mohammed had divine inspiration, he always maintained a balance of common sense to meet emergencies. He understood the fire of fanaticism, but he did not want to join up with a dozen or so enthusiastic converts and have to fight the battle of Mecca all over again. Before anything further could be done, he had to be convinced that a majority of people in Medina was ready to accept him and his ideas.

This period of waiting was perhaps the most trying of Mohammed's ordeals. These Khazrajites of Medina came from the finest Arab stock. Their power and position in Arabia were unquestioned. If they accepted Islam, Mohammed would have backing which would take him a long way toward the realization of his mission. If they did not, it did not seem possible for him to struggle on alone. His task in Mecca had become almost hopeless. Every day his life and the lives of his disciples were getting increasingly precarious. In fact, so menacing was the atmosphere that he began to dispatch his people in groups to Medina. They might not find a Moslem welcome, but they would not be killed because of their creed. As party after party slipped away to sanctuary, Mohammed felt himself more and more of an outlaw. Soon he had with him no one but his immediate household: Ali, Aisha, and Sawda; Abu Bakr, with his wife Umm Ruman, their elder daughter Esma, and their son Abdallah. Zaid too was there, watchful and resourceful, keeping his head when panic hovered near. Everyone was as tense as a stretched bow. The Koreishites were no less tense than the Moslems.

The year passed without any overviolent incident. The month of pilgrimage began. From all over Arabia pilgrims flocked to Mecca. Among these was Musab ibn Omeir, the teacher who had been sent to Medina, and with him seventy Medinese converts. A meeting was arranged with Mohammed in the desert after dark.

To this meeting Mohammed brought, in addition to Abu Bakr, his uncle Al Abbas. Al Abbas was a strange character who was to play an important role in the history of Islam. He was much younger than Abu Lahab and Abu Taleb, and while, like them, had not accepted his nephew's teachings, he had a great affection for him.

Reaching the group of men which showed dimly white on the moonless desert, the courteous Arab greetings, which no crisis curtails, were exchanged. Then Al Abbas said:

"Ye men of the Beni Khazraj, my kinsman prefers to seek protection with you. Wherefore, I ask you to consider the matter well and count the cost."

Al Bara, the leader of the Medinese delegates, replied: "We have listened to your words. Our resolution is unshaken. Our lives are at the Prophet's service. It is now for him to speak."

Once again Mohammed had to repeat what he had said on the two previous occasions when he had met the men of Medina. Many questions were asked to which Mohammed replied. To these he added his previous warning about the heavy responsibilities which Islam demanded of Moslems. His attitude was sublime.

The whole of his cause, his life and the lives of his family and closest friends depended on a favorable reaction from these Medinese. He could excusably have shown the religion under its most optimistic light, but he remained true to himself. His sincerity had brought him nothing but misfortune, yet he was not

AL HIJRA—THE FLIGHT

going to give in because he was tired. He had lived and he would die with his principles.

However, the men of Medina had apparently formed their opinion of Mohammed. They set aside his warnings. All they wanted was the assurance that he would not desert them when things began to run smoothly. Mohammed shook his head.

"Never," he replied. "Your blood is my blood. I am yours, you are mine."

"Give us your hand," said Al Bara.

Mohammed stretched out his hand. Each of the seventy men touched it and swore allegiance to Mohammed and to his God. It was a dramatic moment, and of an importance which none of those robed figures standing out on the wind-swept desert realized. Had Medina not decided to adopt Islam and accept the holy outcasts from Mecca, the religion of the Koran might have died in its cradle.

Before Musab and his party made their way back to their homes, it was agreed that Mohammed should come to Medina as soon as he felt ready to do so. The clouds seemed to be rolling away. The end of the long journey appeared to be in sight. Not quite though. Mohammed had temporarily forgotten the Koreishites.

Somehow or other, the news of these secret desert meetings with the Medinese had leaked out. Simultaneously it was discovered that practically the whole of the Moslem colony in Mecca had disappeared. Whole streets had become deserted. The doors and windows were boarded up. The desert dust was already encroaching, covering the cobblestones and piling up on the porches. The climax came when Omar, in coat of mail, his helmet on his head, his bow in his hand, a tremendous sword at his side, appeared before the Kaaba. Without introduction he informed his late friends that he was off. He was not running away. He was merely moving to a place where he could organize the Moslems into a body which would repay the Koreishites for their persecutions. Menacingly he concluded:

"Let anyone who wishes to be lamented by his mother meet me in yonder valley."

No one moved. With a disdainful shrug of his great shoulders Omar strode away into the gathering dusk.

This bold declaration brought another fact to light, namely, that Mohammed had a great many more followers than anyone imagined. The situation was most disturbing. If it was allowed to go any further, the position of the Koreishites themselves might be in danger. An enemy established at Medina would be astride the main caravan tracks to Syria. Neither would this enemy have to be in great force to disrupt trade and, eventually, cut off supplies.

Abu Sofian was now governor of Mecca, as well as commander in chief. His hatred for Mohammed had increased with his promotion. When these disquieting happenings were brought to his notice, he called a meeting of the city council. Without preface he told the members exactly what was going on in Mecca. He said that this Mohammed controversy, which some of them had been inclined to scoff at, was getting out of hand. He added that if official action were not taken at once, anything might happen. The thing had become too big to be handled by individuals. This was a matter which affected every member of the Koreish tribe, every citizen in Mecca. In his opinion Mohammed must be disposed of, now and at once. When the moderate elements in the council suggested that Mohammed could be banished or imprisoned, Abu Sofian laughed. He declared that as long as the lunatic fanatic was alive, the danger remained. As long as the impostor's followers knew that he was not dead, they would make it their business to rescue him, especially now that there was all this Medinese faction to back them up.

Abu Jahl, whose loathing for Mohammed was on a par with Abu Sofian's, then spoke up. He said that there was only one way to settle the issue. Mohammed must be killed. He had thought this from the start. If this had been done five years ago the trouble would have died of its own accord. When he had let that sink in, he went on to say that as this was practically a national execution for the good of the state, he felt that one member of each family in Mecca should participate. If every family had the blood of Mohammed on its scimitars, the blood feud would be shared by everyone. After a further pause he took a vote. There were no dissensions. Abu Jahl then advised that the execution should take place that night. To this also there was complete agreement.

However, in this case too, someone had been listening who should not. Within a few minutes of Mohammed's conviction and condemnation, he had been notified. At once he realized that this time these men meant business. If he did not want to be killed and bring about the death of many others who had risked all for him, he must act quickly.

Summoning Abu Bakr and Ali, he told them what was afoot. They both agreed that Mohammed must make a dash for it. Abu Bakr said he would go with Mohammed. Ali said he would stay. He was in no particular bad odor with the Koreishites, and he would be able to look after the women and children. For the moment there was no time to lose. Already Abu Sofian and Abu Jahl, with their assassins, could be heard coming up the winding narrow street. Seizing Mohammed's cloak, Ali pushed him and Abu Bakr out of the door. Then he closed and locked it. Making sure that the shutters were barred, he went and lay on Mohammed's carpet, covering himself with the cloak.

The murderers reached the house but hesitated when they found that to get in they must use force. One of them managed to peep through the shutters. On the carpet he saw what he took to be Mohammed wrapped in his well-known mantle. This he reported, and it was decided to wait until morning and kill Mohammed as he came out of the house. Silently the men crouched through the short summer night, their drawn scimitars in their hands.

The morning breeze whispered over the desert. The dawn came mauvely from the east and showed the assassins braced to strike. As the first white rays of the rising sun hit the flat roofs of Mecca, the door of Mohammed's house opened. The men stood ready to spring. Then they held back as their astonished eyes rested on the burly figure of Ali standing on the threshold carrying Mohammed's cloak over his arm.

After the first surprise, there was a babel of questions. Finally Abu Jahl silenced the others and asked Ali where his uncle was. Ali replied that he had not any idea. He had gone out with Abu Bakr the evening before without telling where or when he was coming back. He glanced with apparent surprise at the governor of Mecca and members of the city council with their drawn swords. As no one offered any explanation, he strolled carelessly down the street toward the Kaaba.

Abu Sofian and Abu Jahl could think of nothing to say. They could not very well break into the house. Women were there, and, after all, they were relations and had been friends. Besides, it was evident that Ali was speaking the truth. They had been fooled by a cloak. However, if Mohammed had only gone out to one of his prayer meetings, he would come back. If he had started for Medina, he could be caught. A journey of that importance could only be undertaken with camels. Camels traveled slowly. They were no match for horses. A little happier, the would-be murderers hurried off to start a man hunt.

Mohammed had guessed exactly what would be the reactions of the Koreishites when they found he had gone. He had, therefore, not started for Medina with camels. He had gone on foot with Abu Bakr to Mount Thaur, about one hour's walk from Mecca. He had advised Ali of his plan and asked him to keep him posted as to what was going on.

The two fugitives reached Mount Thaur while it was still dark and concealed themselves in the innermost recess of a cave in the rocky hillside. Here they huddled, praying that their enemies would overlook their hiding place.

Soon after sunrise they heard the Koreishite horsemen galloping over the desert. When they had gone some way, however, and found no camel tracks, they realized that Mohammed had fooled them again. They, accordingly, began searching closer to Mecca. Some of them actually came to the cave where the runaways crouched. Abu Bakr began to tremble. He was a city

AL HIJRA—THE FLIGHT

man and past fifty. He had been through a lot during the past years, and this kind of escapade was completely outside his pattern of life. He was extremely frightened and said so. Mohammed was as calm as he always was under any circumstances. When Abu Bakr asked him, in dismay, what two unarmed men could do against a gang of blood-lusting warriors, he replied: "Do not worry, Abu Bakr, we are not alone. Allah is beside us."

This assurance slightly comforted Abu Bakr, but it did not halt the man hunt. The Koreishites were going to find Mohammed if it took them a month. Outside the cave a dozen horsemen debated in the hearing of the fugitives. It was then that what Moslems regard as a miracle occurred. At the entrance of the hiding place was an acacia. In this a dove had built its nest and laid its eggs. Simultaneously a spider had spun its web over the mouth of the cave. The horsemen, who were about to search the cave, saw this and concluded that it would be waste of time to go inside. No one, they argued, could have possibly passed the entrance lately.

This does not appear fantastically miraculous. The obliging way in which the dove laid its eggs in June might seem exaggerated. The spider spinning its web across the mouth of the cave is not at all improbable. The only thing which is hard to understand is the stupidity of the Koreishite warriors.

Anyway, these bloodthirsty dolts mounted their horses and rode off. The fugitives thanked God and did not move.

As night began to fall, Abdallah, Abu Bakr's son, and his sister Esma, came out to the cave. They reported Ali to be all right. Esma had been questioned, but the interrogation had not been pressed when she swore she knew nothing of the whereabouts of her father and brother-in-law. No one had bothered Aisha and Sawda. The brother and sister ran back to Mecca before dawn. Later on in the day one of Abu Bakr's shepherds brought his flock to pasture near the cave and left provisions for the two men in hiding.

But there was no question of their moving. Several times the Koreishite horsemen passed the cave, but the spider and the dove were on duty and no one thought of disturbing them. The next day the search relaxed. Esma and Abdallah, who were keeping in touch with what was going on, decided that it would be safe now for Mohammed and Abu Bakr to continue their flight. On the third night, therefore, they came to the cave with two camels and a nomad whom they could trust. Quickly Mohammed mounted and, followed by Abu Bakr, rode into the desert night. A crescent moon floated in the black sky.

The romantic attribute to this the origin of the present-day emblem of Islam. This picturesque thought has no foundation. The crescent and star are Turkish symbols dating from the days of Hazret i Ertoghrul, 1209, the grandfather of Othman I, the founder of the Ottoman dynasty. There are, moreover, several Moslem sects, such as the Shias, who do not recognize the crescent or the star as having any connection with Islam.

In order to avoid the main caravan tracks, the fugitives struck a diagonal course northwest toward the Red Sea. Medina is about two hundred miles from Mecca, and much of this distance had to be covered before there could be any question of being out of danger of capture. Soon the dawn tinged the sky and gradually disclosed a hideous desert of lava rock and stones and sand dunes. Nothing grew, nothing relieved the desolation of the landscape. There was no friendly twittering of birds to greet the coming of the light. Except for the padding of the camels' feet over the polished pebbles, there was silence in this land of thirst. The sun came up menacingly. Its rays shone nakedly without that dewy light of more temperate climates. Soon the Arabian sky was as burning brass above the two travelers' heads. Beneath them the trail reeked like molten steel. The horizon was a sea of mirages, while in the foreground gigantic sand columns whirled across the plain.

The three men went on as long as they could. Finally they had to halt and shelter under the shadow of a great rock. There was no question of finding a well or an oasis. By taking the unfrequented route to the sea, they were deliberately missing any places where they could replenish their supply of food and water.

Even so, they were not safe. The Koreish had offered a reward of one hundred camels to anyone who could bring Mohammed back to Mecca, dead or alive. The reward was nearly won.

On the second dawn of their journey from the cave, the two exiles and their guide were spotted by a nomad chief whose name was Soraka ibn Malik. Without letting any of his tribesmen know what was on his mind, he rode quickly after what looked like a safe reward. Besides being fully armed with bow and lance, he had between his legs a thoroughbred mare. The sensitive Abu Bakr saw Soraka first. He at once warned Mohammed. Mohammed glanced in the direction of the galloping nomad and continued to recite verses from the Koran. The horseman drew closer. He reached for his arrows and prepared to fit one into his bow. But before he could let fly, his horse seemed to take fright and reared so suddenly that it threw its rider.

For a nomad to fall off his horse is a disgrace. To do so before the pitying eyes of Mohammed was a dishonor. And there was nothing which Soraka could do. There he was standing in the desert, his bow flung in one direction, his lance in the other, while his mare made for the horizon as if the devil were after her. The whole situation was one with which no self-respecting Arab could cope. Soraka, therefore, did the only graceful thing possible under the circumstances. He begged Mohammed's forgiveness and promised that he would tell no one that he had seen him. Mohammed, who was also delicately situated, gave the necessary forgiveness and confirmed it with a token written by Abu Bakr on a piece of bone. With this, Soraka bade the wanderers go in peace and, picking up his arms, went in search of his mare. Mohammed, calm as usual, took up his reciting of the Koran where he had left off, and rode on.

For nearly a week the journey continued over the parched, barren, mournful wasteland. No living creatures, not even vultures or snakes, inhabited this wilderness. The only vegetation was the occasional clumps of acacia and tamarind.

On the seventh morning after the beginning of the flight, the oasis of Kuba, a few miles from Medina, was reached. As the sun brought the landscape to life, the travelers could not credit their eyes. The desolation had been left behind. Instead of being in the desert, they found themselves among hills covered with tall date palms. About them were gardens in which grew oranges and lemons and pomegranates. Irrigation channels sent water gushing over the rich soil into which fig trees and apricot trees sank their roots. It was unbelievable, even more so than it had been when Mohammed had glimpsed this paradise forty-five years ago with his mother. He immediately made his camel kneel and dismounted. Then he gave thanks to Allah for having brought him safely to the end of his journey. After that he stretched himself out in the shade to rest and recuperate.

The rest was not long. The Meccans who had immigrated before their leader knew that he would be soon on his way and had been watching for him. As soon as rumors of his arrival began to spread, crowds came flocking from Medina. Among these were many kinsmen, including Hamza and Omar and Az Zubeir, Khadija's nephew. They brought with them clean clothes and rice and honey and dates and skins filled with milk. Mohammed accepted the gifts and the warm greetings gratefully but, for a few days, he stayed in Kuba. He was extremely tired. He was also emotionally overcome at suddenly finding himself welcomed with friendly enthusiasm instead of having to parry insults and dodge blows.

On the fourth morning after his arrival his old energy returned. He accordingly announced that the time had come for him to make his entry into the city which had adopted him. Before starting, he assembled all those who had come to greet him and led the first Moslem prayer in public. This he followed by preaching his first uninterrupted sermon in daylight. After that he mounted his camel, an almost white dromedary called Al Kaswa, and rode toward the nodding palms of Medina.

Beside him was the faithful friend, Abu Bakr. Before him went Boraida, a sheik of a neighboring tribe. In his hand he carried a lance to which he had tied his turban to represent the Messenger's banner. Behind Al Kaswa padded other mounted camels. All around ran and rode warriors, brandishing scimitars and bows, crying out the arrival of Mohammed, proclaiming that they would defend him with their lives.

It was a splendid spectacle, almost unbelievable. Less than a month ago this man had been slinking about the alleys of Mecca, never sure if he would meet a dagger round the next corner, never certain of who was friend or foe, despised and detested because of what he had preached. Yet today he rode into one of the fairest cities of Arabia like a conquering king.

As the procession reached the entrance of Medina, the excitement and the shouting gathered in strength. Mohammed's elation correspondingly increased, but, with that rare sense of timing and propriety, he called a halt. Dismounting, he turned toward Jerusalem and offered a prayer of thanksgiving to Allah for having given him this triumph. Then he remounted and, letting the rein fall loosely on Al Kaswa's neck, allowed her to go as she pleased. The camel wandered through several streets of deliriously cheering crowds and finally knelt in an open space under some date palms. Mohammed dismounted again and announced that where his camel had halted of its own accord, he would build a mosque and make his home.

The hubbub redoubled with the mobs seething about the new leader, wanting to see him, trying to touch him. Finally some of Mohammed's own people cleared a way and got him into the house of a Medinese called Abu Ayub who had offered hospitality to the distinguished guest until his own living quarters could be built.

To Mohammed's surprise, he was almost immediately joined by Ali. He had walked all the way from Mecca but, outside footsoreness, he was well and as enthusiastic as ever. He brought the good news that the rest of the family would soon be arriving. Zaid was leading one party which included his own wife Zeinab, Mohammed's wife, Sawda, and his daughters Fatima and Umm Kulthum. Abdallah ibn Abu Bakr was bringing his sisters Aisha and Esma, as well as his mother, Umm Ruman.

Mohammed leaned back on his carpet and closed his eyes. He had been through a great deal. He had suffered physically and mentally, but he had never wavered from the belief that what had been revealed to him was the truth. Now his faith of thirteen years had been rewarded. His only regret was that Khadija was not with him to share his triumph. But, after all, she would know all about it and would undoubtedly be rejoicing herself in paradise. He sighed and let himself relax on the carpet. He felt that he might as well rest while he could. He had come a long distance during the past weeks. Nevertheless, in comparison to what he knew lay before him, it was but a little of the way.

Mohammed was an envoy of Allah, but he was also a realist. He knew that this apparent climax to his career was actually the beginning of his mission. If Islam was to have permanent foundations, if the people of Arabia were to see and feel as he did, if he was to carry out the orders of Allah, a tremendous task lay before him. Even so, he could not guess what this cheering morning was to prelude, neither in his life nor in the centuries to come.

The only world state based solely on religion was at that moment coming to life in the green oasis of Medina.

The date was July 2, 622 of the Christian era, known from that time as Al Hijra—(the year of) The Flight or, more precisely, The Emigration. Under the caliphate of Omar, soon after Mohammed's death, this was decreed to be the official beginning of the Moslem era. Henceforth Moslems all over the world would reckon their calendar from this day. "Before the Hijra" and "After the Hijra" would become to the people of Islam as familiar as "Before Christ" and "After Christ" to the people of Christendom. But no one thought of this. No one appreciated, while Mohammed sipped his milk and Abu Bakr repaired the ravages of the journey by hennaeing his beard, and Al Kaswa chewed her cud, that the thought generated in the dreary cave on desolate Mount Hira had come of age. No one dreamed how soon it would mature and spread like a gigantic flood, submerging great tracts of the world, and sweeping away governments and religions which had remained unchallenged for centuries.

CHAPTER IX

MEDINA

(622 After Christ)

ABU AYUB, in whose house Mohammed stayed when he arrived in Medina, was a distant cousin. He was a grandchild of those relatives to whom Amina had brought her six-year-old boy to visit shortly before her death in the desert. Abu Ayub was a militant Moslem. During Mohammed's lifetime he was beside him during all his battles. Subsequent to his death he continued as a distinguished soldier of Islam. Forty-eight years after Mohammed's triumphant entry into Medina, he was killed outside Constantinople fighting in the armies of Muawiyah, Abu Sofian's son and fifth caliph of the Moslems. A great mausoleum and mosque were erected over the place where he fell. It is still there. Up to the disappearance of the Ottoman Empire a few years ago, the sultans went there to be belted with their scimitars before ascending the throne. Abu Ayub's tomb is finer than any house or mosque which he ever knew in Arabia. It is finer than anything which Mohammed ever saw outside the seven heavens!

This is but one example of where Mohammed's preaching was to lead. These uneducated Arabs, these fugitives from the daggers of the Koreishites—Abu Bakr, Omar, Ali—would, in a short time, be deciding the fates of the once mighty and magnificent empires of the Orient. Syria, Chaldea, Byzantium, Egypt, the dominions of the Medes and Persians would be paying tribute to these obscure exiles. Their rulers, their generals, their ecclesiastics would be waiting on the pleasure of these uncombed, threadbare outcasts who now gratefully squatted on the mats of their Medinese hosts. The followers of Christ in the north and the west, the fire worshipers of Zoroaster in the east and the south would be rolling before this tide of Islam like pebbles on the seashore.

From the Persian Gulf to the Atlantic Ocean names of ex-shepherds, of ex-traveling salesmen, of ex-bankers would have taken the places of dynasties which had stood the test of ages.

Speaking from the governor's palace in the great Mesopotamian city of Basra a few years later, one of those who today waited in the dust outside Abu Ayub's house in Medina said:

"I remember the time when there were only seven Moslems in Mecca with the holy Prophet, and I was the seventh among them. We could not have any other thing for food except the leaves of the trees. In those days I received as a gift a sheet of cloth which I divided into two parts, one of which I used myself and gave the other to Sa'ad, the son of Malik, to wear. Today every one of us is governor of some province."

On this July afternoon, however, that journey from Mecca was the longest these future governors and generals and justices had ever undertaken. They had never seen such vegetation. The fertile plain in the midst of which lay Medina was something almost unbelievable to eyes accustomed to landscapes of sun-scorched rocks. The water which gurgled ceaselessly along the irrigation channels did not seem possible after living in a place where every drop was more precious than gold. To have as many dates to eat as they wanted, to find figs and apricots and pomegranates as common as the stones of the desert felt like the confirmation of Mohammed's stories of paradise.

But, although the first few days in Medina were given over to resting and praising Allah, Mohammed's mind was planning. Islam urged him on now as impatiently as in the days of active persecution. More so. It had proved itself. Now he must prove it to all those who had believed and to all those who had scoffed. He must prove it to others who had never heard of it.

Before he could attend to this effectively, however, he must provide himself with permanent quarters.

Since his orders to go out and preach ten years ago, Mohammed's instructing had, through force of circumstances, been sketchy. The various doctrines and injunctions had been brought by Gabriel in fragments. Now only were they beginning to take some shape. Practically no one except Abu Bakr and Ali, possibly Zaid, had heard all the revelations. A great many of the converts had little notion of what Islam was about. Mohammed was, perhaps, a little vague himself. Now, however, he was going to be given the opportunity, rarely allowed to originators of religions, to work out the details without interference. This is why he needed the peace of a home and a church, at once. Being energetic as well as enthusiastic, he knew that the surest way to get things done is to do them oneself.

The sagacious camel had chosen the site for the Beit Allah from which Islam was to radiate all over the world. The next step was to build it. Mohammed drank all the milk he could swallow, ate his fill of dates, slept off his tiredness, and set to work.

Within twenty-four hours of the Meccan refugees' reaching Medina, the ground had been broken for the first Moslem mosque, or *masjid*, which signifies "place of kneeling for prayer." So great had been the enthusiasm of the welcome that no one had noticed that the place Al Kaswa had selected to deposit her weary body was a graveyard. But no one cared. The people buried there had been heathens, so the bodies and bones were exhumed and thrown away to sort themselves on the Day of Judgment. The palms which used to shade the tombs were cut down. The ground was leveled and the foundations laid. Mohammed took part in all these preparations as well as in the actual building. He was assisted by Medinites as well as by Meccans.

In order to establish a working co-operation, Mohammed had put into effect a system whereby each exile was tied to a resident by a formal brotherhood. The Medinites, he called "Ansars," that is, helpers; the Meccans, he named "Muhajirin," that is, immigrants or refugees. The word is derived from *hajara*, which means "he migrated."

The Ansars not only housed and fed the Muhajirin, but they

shared all they had with them. The bond of brotherhood was considered as a blood kinship. Even when the Ansar died he was required to bequeath his belongings proportionately to his true relatives and to those by adoption. It was a masterly idea and developed a sentiment of clanship which was invaluable as a foundation for the new faith.

This clanship or alliance was essential. While the Beni Khazraj had invited Mohammed to Medina, there were others who had not. In addition to the Jewish groups, there was that other Arab tribe, the Beni Aus; there was also a troublesome man called Abdallah ibn Obei. For the moment neither he nor his satellites gave Mohammed much thought. Consequently they took no interest in what was going on at the other side of the oasis. As it turned out, this was unfortunate for them and, at the same time, fortunate for Mohammed.

The first mosque was of the simplest design. The walls were made of sun-dried bricks resting on a base of stones. The roof was of palm-branch thatching supported by the trunks of the graveyard palms. The interior of the mosque was plastered over with mud. There were no ornamentations, not even a pulpit. Mohammed had to preach from the same level as his congregation. At night the lighting was effected by fires of wood splinters. These were later replaced by small oil lamps, but the building was not changed until the caliphate of Omar, fifteen years later, when it was enlarged.

The present mosque has the same foundations as the original edifice, but that is all. Five mosques have succeeded one another on the old site. The last, which stands in Medina today, dates from the fifteenth century. It is an ornate affair with five minarets and a green dome surmounted by a golden orb and crescent. Under this dome lie the remains of the Messenger. Except for this, there is nothing about the place which is slightly suggestive of Mohammed. In fact, it has everything within it and without which he would have disliked.

Mohammed's way of living was as simple as that of Jesus. All the tawdry interior decoration of so many churches and some mosques today is the work of successors who could not see how much more suitable were the simple settings preferred by the founders of the two great faiths. The only thing to remind Moslems of the origin of the building in which they pray in the nineteen forties is the name, Masjid al Nabi—The Place of Kneeling for Prayer of the Prophet.

As a kind of annex to the mosque Mohammed built his own quarters and those for his family. These consisted of a row of humble cottages, separated one from another by palm branches cemented together with mud. There were no furnishings or draperies. Mohammed slept on a mat and did his household work himself. He even mended his clothes and cobbled his slippers.

This austere way of living is taken for granted as the privilege of a holy man. But if one gives the matter any thought, one realizes that Mohammed was by no means the traditional holy man. He had been brought up in surroundings of middle-class comforts. During his early married life he had been among the wealthiest in Mecca. Yet when he found himself in Medina, with everyone ready to give him the best they had—even after his conquests, when money and loot flowed into the state coffers—he maintained his ascetic habits.

Mohammed's principal meal consisted of gruel, dates, and milk. Sometimes there was a soup of meat and vegetables, perhaps some honey. As often as not, dates and milk would be all he took. Whatever it was, he ate it on a mat on the floor. His clothes were as simple as his food. Next to his skin, a rough wool or cotton tunic with sleeves. Over this, an ample cloak. On his head, a thick turban which had to be carefully wound. On his feet, leather sandals. Toward the end of his career he sometimes appeared in Damascene silks and an embroidered mantle. But this was rare. He disliked finery and disapproved of his followers dressing up. The Negus of Abyssinia once sent Mohammed some trousers and a pair of long black boots. The trousers he did not know what to do with, and never used them. The boots he wore occasionally, but they hurt his feet.

This way of living may have been due to his bedouin instincts.

His earliest recollections were of the austere life of the desert, which was followed by his nomadic experiences with trading caravans. In fact, the desert man's instinct is rather confirmed by the comparative extravagance in the matter of "stables."

Mohammed had few horses, because at that time the horse was much less used than it was going to be when the Moslems began their conquering wanderings. Mohammed's mounts were racing camels and mules. Of the former, he had three, including the famous Al Kaswa, and two special mules, one white and one gray, called Doldol and Shahba. He also had a number of pack dromedaries, milch camels, as well as flocks of sheep and goats. Only a nomad mentality would stint itself in clothes and food and personal luxuries and be prodigal over livestock.

However, whatever the cause of Mohammed's way of living, he made it evident from the start that Islam, in theory and in practice, was based on simplicity. He was always insisting on this ideal, always enjoining his converts to hold that thought foremost in their minds. Most of them did and carried on the tradition long after their leader's death.

During one of the campaigns in Syria under Omar's caliphate, Khaled, the Moslem commander in chief, had a parley with Manuel, the commander in chief of the Roman-Syrian army. The two generals met under a huge tent.

Manuel and his staff, in splendid uniforms, wearing swords glittering with jewels, sat on brocaded chairs. Khaled wore the fighting dress of a nomad warrior, coarse tunic, coat of mail, helmet. At his side was strapped his scimitar; in his hand he carried his lance. He was in no way distinguishable from his subordinate officers. Neither he nor his men seemed to notice the chairs which had been placed for them. After greeting the Christians, the Moslems sat cross-legged on the ground. When Manuel asked them why they did this, they replied:

"Of earth ye are created, from earth ye came and unto earth ye must return. God made the earth, and what God has made is more precious than your silken tapestries."

The next day, incidentally, Khaled and his ascetic bedouins gave the veteran imperial army of Manuel the biggest trouncing it had ever had. After which, they went on and captured Jerusalem.

One of the first problems which confronted Mohammed after he had built the Medina mosque was how to summon his people to prayer. Up till now this had been of no consequence. On the contrary, any gathering together of Moslems had to be conducted in secrecy. Every precaution had to be taken *not* to advertise that a prayer meeting was taking place. But now, among a people who wanted religious instruction, all this had to be changed.

The Jews called their congregations to the temple by blasts on trumpets; the Christians beat gongs. Mohammed considered these customs too inanimate for such hallowed purposes. He felt that the human voice could better communicate the inspiration and emotion which should be dedicated to the solemnity of the occasion.

To begin with, there was no set formula for this invocation. "To public prayer!" was deemed sufficient notice to the faithful. After a while, however, Mohammed decided that something more impressive was needed. There are various traditions of how he arrived at the final formula. None of these is important, and there seems to be no reason why Mohammed should not have composed the lines himself. They are simple, they have rhythm, and, chanted from the minarets of mosques throughout the world five times a day, now as then, they carry a heart-stirring message which moves men of any creed.

The words of the call are as follows:

Allahu Akbar.
Ash-hadu La ilaha illa Allah,
Ash-hadu Mohammed Rasul Allah.
    Hayya ala-ssalah,
    Hayya alal Falah.
    Allahu Akbar.
    La ilaha illa Allah.

> Allah is most great.
> I bear witness that there is no God but Allah,
> I bear witness that Mohammed is the Messenger of Allah.
> Come to prayer,
> Come to progress.
> God is most great.
> There is no God but Allah.*

For the first prayer of the day, the following exhortation preceded the call:

> *Assalatu Khairum Ninan-Nawm.*
> Prayer is better than sleep.

When this formula had been determined, someone had to be chosen to do the calling. There were, as yet, no mosque officials, and although Mohammed was the one who was summoning the people to pray, it was clearly not his duty to do so actively. The caller must be a man with a powerful voice which could be heard all over the city. He must also be prepared to make this his whole-time work. The choice finally fell on a Negro called Bilal ibn Rabah.

This great, polished figure, carved out of jet, had been one of the first to adopt Islam. At that time he was the slave of a Meccan called Ommeya ibn Khalaf. Ommeya was a fanatic idolator and persecutor of Moslems. When he discovered that Bilal was one of these, he did all he could to drag him back to idolatry. When Bilal refused to be dragged, he was tortured. When the tortures had no effect, Ommeya took the black man out into the desert. Here he staked him out naked under the burning rays of the Arabian sun. On his chest he placed a rock on which was inscribed: "Thou shalt remain here until thou diest or until thou hast abjured Islam." Still Bilal resisted. Nearly dead from heat and thirst, he continued to mutter, *"Ahadun—Ahadun—*One [God]—One." He would probably have died of exhaustion, had not Abu Bakr come upon the wretch and lifted the stone and

---

*Most of the lines of the call to prayer are repeated several times.

released him. Then, by paying Ommeya a large ransom, he was able to take Bilal into his service.

This was obviously the devoted, fanatical, unreasoning creature who would admirably spend the rest of his life repeating the same thing five times a day. He had almost been the first Moslem martyr; instead he would be the first Moslem muezzin. So onto the roof of the mosque he was hoisted and, at dawn, at noon, in the midafternoon, at sunset, and after nightfall, chanted to the east and the west and the north and the south the call to prayer which playwrights and film producers invariably put into their plays and pictures about the Orient to give atmosphere, without having any idea what it is all about.

As a matter of fact, Bilal's career did not end on the roof of that Medina mosque. After Mohammed's death he retired. When the Moslem armies started conquering Syria and Iraq and Palestine and Egypt, Bilal went with them. He held all manner of positions and was, at one time, appointed Moslem ambassador to treat with the Emperor Constantine's son in Caesarea. The only occasion on which he called to prayer again, after his retirement, was on the site of the future mosque of Omar in Jerusalem after that city's capture by Khaled. He eventually died in Damascus, where his splendid tomb can be seen today.

With the mosque routine settled, Mohammed now turned his attention to ordering the doctrines of the new faith. He was sure that everything was on his side, *if* he handled the situation skillfully.

This Arabia of the seventh century needed a leader. The majestic dominions of Egypt, Assyria, Persia, and Greece had consecutively passed into obscurity. Rome was on the point of disintegrating. There seemed to be no nation indicated to take their places. Mohammed was probably not fully conscious that it might be his lot to carry on the torch recently dropped by the Romans. He probably had only vague ideas about the preceding empires. He knew, however, that the Arabs, being divided into independent tribes, presented unparalleled advantages for the spread of a new faith. He knew that if he started off right, he stood a good chance of consolidating all these clans under one government—under his government.

His first step, therefore, was to impress on his original congregations that all Moslems were brothers. This he had already emphasized in his ordinances regarding the relationship between the Ansars and the Muhajirin. He also laid special stress on reciprocal charity and courtesy between all members of Islam.

Leaning on his staff, with his back against one of the palm-trunk columns of the mosque, he spoke with the kindly earnestness of a father talking to his children:

"He who is not affectionate to God's creatures and to his own children, God will not be affectionate to him. Every Moslem who clothes the naked of his faith will be clothed by Allah in the green robes of paradise."

He spoke of the strength of iron, of the strength of fire, of the strength of water, and added that stronger than all of these was charity. Neither was charity confined to the giving of alms. A smile for the sad was charity, a cup of water was charity, helping a fellow Moslem on his way was charity. He assured his listeners that whatever fortune or position a man made for himself in this world, it would not count in the world to come. The examining angel would not ask about flocks or gardens or money, but about what acts of charity the dead man had left behind him.

He asserted that charity of speech was just as important as charity of action. The courtesies of daily life were all part of what went to make a good Moslem. The salutations on entering and leaving a house, the returning of greetings by friends or strangers, the conventions of hospitality were all part of Islam.

Today one of the traits which strikes foreigners most in a true Arab are his politeness, his kindheartedness, his hospitality. There is no race which carries courtesies to such extremes as the Arab, courtesies which, moreover, are sincere. Thirteen hundred years have passed since Mohammed gave lessons in manners in Medina, but these lessons have not been forgotten. An Arab still defends his guest at the peril of his own life. He still shares with him his last date.

In addition to preaching spiritual rewards, Mohammed was attending to the practical side of his followers' lives. He began to establish customs which would gradually become laws. He made rules about irrigation and the preserving of water supplies. He caused it to be obligatory to plant a tree every time one was cut down. He established systems of taxation. His commercially trained mind made him have the dues payable in kind as well as in cash. This was not confined to agricultural produce. For example, one tax clause read: "On every adult, one dinar or its equivalent in clothes."

It is said that he sometimes made mistakes. An anecdote relative to one of these alleged mistakes is herewith reproduced as evidence of the irresponsible way in which biographers make statements about Mohammed. This anecdote appears in many of the occidental biographies of the Messenger. While it is not, as often, detrimental to Mohammed or to Islam, it is a piece of foolishness.

The date palms of Medina are among the most celebrated in Arabia. There are over one hundred varieties, some of which are famous all over the world for their aromatic odor, the flavor of the fruit, and the smallness of the stones. A date palm, however, cannot reproduce itself unless it is artificially fertilized. In January and February, Arabs, known as *nakhwali*, climb to the tops of the female palm and, to the accompaniment of hymns, insert inverted male flowers into the open female flower and bind them together. Mohammed, so say certain biographers, had never heard of this and, when he did, for some reason, stopped it. As a result the palms of Medina ceased almost entirely to produce dates. Many of them died.

In despair a deputation of desolate Arab date dealers waited on Mohammed and, while assuring him that they would fall in battle for Islam, added that they preferred not to have to undergo starvation first.

Mohammed, it is stated, listened to the complaint—then, unashamed, admitted his error.

"I am only mortal," he said. "If, therefore, I give you an order in the domain of religion, then receive it. But if I give an order of my own opinion, I am only mortal."

It is a harmless little sketch of Arab life, but without foundation. The part about the artificial fertilizing of date palms is as stated. The part about Mohammed is not. Anyone who gives the matter a moment's thought should appreciate that.

An Arab, whose staple food is dates, who has been born and bred among date dealers and date growers, would know of the sexual habits of date palms. The story makes as much sense as would an oriental writer telling of a Kansas farmer being ignorant of the rotation of crops or something similar.

Mohammed had to cope with problems material as well as spiritual. The climate of Mecca was rigorous by its heat but, owing to its dryness, was comparatively healthy. Medina was on a higher level; it was blessed with water and shade, but suffered from extremes of temperatures. The Meccan immigrants began to suffer. They developed fevers, which may have been head colds, unknown to desert people, or influenza—possibly even malaria. Soon grumblings began. Mohammed nipped them in the bud. Invoking once more the brotherhood of Islam, he insisted on the necessity of all those of the new faith making common cause. Of the needfulness of putting up with inconveniences. Of the importance of not giving their enemies any openings for the spreading of dissension. He stressed this eloquently, knowing that his future and the future of his people depended on it. So great was his personality, so sincere his enthusiasm that, in a short while, he put an end to the complaining.

This to anyone who does not know the Arab intimately was a feat more remarkable than it might appear. The Arab is fundamentally anarchistic. He is not disciplined. When he fights or works, he does it from personal enthusiasm. He has no team spirit. One never sees primitive Arabs playing games. The Arabs are the finest horsemen in the world, but all attempts to have them form polo teams have failed. An Arab on a polo pony, with "stick and ball," is almost unstoppable. His riding and his "eye" are beyond anything occidental. But he will not help another player to share the ball.

The way Mohammed welded his Arabs into a well-nigh invincible team is one of his great miracles. The credit, too, was entirely his. Not many years after his death, Islam was divided into factions, then into rival dynasties, with Moslems killing one another with the same enthusiasm as they did infidels.

Outside his building and preaching and attending to agriculture and head colds, Mohammed had also family preoccupations.

Two of his daughters were not with him. Rokaia was still with her husband Othman in Abyssinia. Zeinab was in Mecca. Her husband, Abu'l As, had refused to recognize her father as the Messenger of Allah and had stopped his wife's going to Medina. These separations worried Mohammed, especially in the case of Zeinab, who might be in danger. However, he was far from being alone. Living with him was the fat wife-housekeeper, Sawda, and his other daughters, Fatima and Umm Kulthum. Aisha, his child bride, was still with her father and mother. Although she was only ten, she was developing with that rapidity peculiar to Arab women which causes them to become old in their late twenties. At the suggestion, therefore, of Abu Bakr and his wife, Mohammed decided to consummate the marriage.

Like everything else in Mohammed's life, the ceremony was simple. Aisha was washed and dressed in a clean frock. Umm Ruman, her mother, then took her to Mohammed's quarters, where he was sitting with several friends. She placed Aisha on Mohammed's lap, saying:

"These are your family, may Allah bless you in them and bless them in you."

Having made this nebulous remark, she and the other visitors withdrew.

The marriage of the fifty-year-old man and the ten-year-old girl has caused some of Mohammed's biographers as much concern as the Night Journey and the epilepsy arguments. In each case the concern has been largely due to the writers in question looking at the matter from the angle of their own societies and their own communities. They have not considered that this kind of marriage was, and still is, the custom in Asia. They have not reflected that it is still the custom in eastern Europe, was normal in Spain and Portugal up to a few years ago, and is not unusual today in some of the remote mountain districts of the United States. And, outside the question of custom, they have not taken into consideration the particular circumstances of this particular case.

There is first of all Abu Bakr, the father of the bride. A well-to-do Meccan businessman, he had sacrificed all for Mohammed's cause. It was understandable that he would look for a stable political alliance with the leader whom he had supported during his darkest days. He had probably other less material motives. He believed in Mohammed, he respected him and liked him. He was sure his child would be well cared for in his friend's home.

Then Mohammed himself must be considered. Up to that moment there had been nothing amusing or young or gay about his life. The drudgery had been ceaseless. He was deserving of a little excitement outside being persecuted or sentenced to death. He had not even had his normal share of women. Up to the age of twenty-seven, he had remained as chaste as Aisha, and had only broken that chastity to marry a widow fifteen years his senior.

The third point, which is usually forgotten and must, therefore, be emphasized again, is that Aisha, child in years though she was, was no helpless infant abandoned to the mercy of a licentious old gentleman. If ever a young lady knew what she was about, it was the large-eyed, tiny-footed, curly-haired Aisha bint Abi Bakr. From the day she established herself in that mosque harem, she ran it. She treated old Sawda like a kind of maid of all work. When other wives were imported, she continued to have the biggest say in all domestic matters. When Mohammed strayed, she did not relax her hold. She knew that he would always come back to her. She did things in that harem against all the principles of Islam and to the deep disapproval of her father. After Mohammed's death, she did more to raise trouble among Moslems than any Meccan Koreishite. She had a fiery, headstrong, irresponsible, egocentric nature, and if she had not been a Moslem might have become another Zenobia or Theodora. That she did not meet a violent death was partly due to good luck and partly to the loyalty of her husband's successors, who, much as they felt that all she deserved was a javelin through one of her pretty breasts, defended her for old associations' sake. I have no compassion for Aisha being left at the age of ten on the lap of her husband over fifty. He was a good man, a kind man, an honest man whose love life up to that point had been little more than a formal ceremony. He deserved something young and fresh to make up for what he had missed. That he did get a great deal out of this marriage is probable, but it was due to Aisha wishing it so.

This first contact with virginity pleased Mohammed. He decided to become a matchmaker himself and, at the same time, establish another family alliance. His daughter Fatima was sixteen. For an Arab, this was grown up. Ali, who represented the coming generation of Moslems, was twenty-two. He was smaller than most of his countrymen, squarely built, with a big bearded head and large black eyes. Any lack of looks, however, was made up for by his courage and loyalty. Fatima herself was not a beauty, but she had the warmth of her mother and much of the intelligence and charm of her father. The marriage seemed a natural arrangement. That it was to lead to as much turmoil among Moslems after Mohammed's death as Henry VIII's repudiation of the Pope led to turmoil among Christians, no one suspected. But then no one suspected, Mohammed least of all, that Islam would ever become a world power. How could anyone suspect such a thing?

For the moment there were not even grounds for imagining that Islam would go much beyond the neighborhood of Medina. Mohammed was building and consolidating, but the building material was none too good. His small band of followers numbered many loyal fanatics ready to die for him, but it numbered also many who were discontented. There were thousands of Arabs also who were hostile to him. There were thousands more who had never heard of him. The situation during the past twelve months had changed vastly for the better, but Islam was still little more than an ideal in the minds of a group of friends. Alliances by marriage were, accordingly, of great political importance.

CHAPTER X

THE FIRST BATTLE

(623–January of 624 After Christ)

MOHAMMED'S SERMON ON CHARITY, his founding of a home, his building of the mosque gave him cause for a comfortable conscience. It gave him a foundation for the establishing of his religion. It did not give him security. It did not give him the wherewithal to live. Except over the sincere believers, it gave him no authority.

For thirteen years now he had been enduring insult and injury, the only reward for which had been more insult and more injury. Even in Medina he knew that it would only be a matter of months before his old enemies were on his heels again. After thirteen years of turning the other cheek, he suddenly decided to offer no more cheeks. He made up his mind to hit back.

That he was, to all intents and purposes, a starving outcast was due to the Koreishites. This was as clear as day. It was also as clear as day that the only way to remedy the situation was by putting the Koreishites in their places. They had turned their backs on peaceful overtures; it would be interesting to see what they would do with their backs toward unpeaceful overtures.

To try this out was a simple matter for Mohammed. The Arabs, in addition to being practical people, are logical. They will always see reason when reason is there to be seen. Mohammed's new followers and many of the old could not see *any* reason in letting the Koreishites make the life of their leader hardly worth while and still less in letting them do this without attempting any retaliation. There, furthermore, appeared to be no point in living on starvation diets and working for pittances when there was plenty of plunder to be had from these Koreishite folk merely by going after it. The acquiring of this plunder, which was to most Arabs a legitimate source of livelihood, could, moreover, be combined with revenge on the men of Mecca who were the cause of all their troubles.

So Mohammed had the right spirit with which to embark on the next phase of his policy. He had also the right material. These Arabs, the nomads as well as the oasis people, were not uncultured. They were as fond of poetry and music as of war and loot. They were not, however, fond of work and avoided it if they could earn enough to live on by any other method. It was clear to Mohammed, therefore, that these gentlemen of the sword would make admirable soldiers to convince the Koreishites that, so far from being defeated by persecution, he, Mohammed, was ready to carry the war into the enemy's camp.

There were other motives for Mohammed to assume the offensive. He had to do something about creating a national exchequer. He had no money, neither had any of the well-to do Muhajirin. Their businesses, their flocks, their homes had all been confiscated by the Meccans. In order to develop Islam, in order to keep the people contented, it was essential that they should be remunerated as well as fed and occupied. Raiding solved both problems.

In bringing about the revolt in the desert, Lawrence of Arabia had recourse to the same methods. He knew that it was no good preaching idealisms to bedouins about driving out the "unspeakable Turk." If they had to be under a foreign rule, these desert men did not care if it was that of the Turks, the French, the British, or anyone else, provided they had enough to eat, which meant someone to loot. Lawrence supplied them with the best implements for this purpose, and expert instruction in the best method to carry it out. The rest was easy. The descendants of Mohammed's warriors behaved against the Turks in 1916 exactly as had their ancestors in regard to the Koreishites in 623.

The other excuse which Mohammed had for resorting to force were the Koreishites themselves. Abu Jahl's monomania about Mohammed had remained at boiling point. He kept raiding parties continually on the move, attacking any isolated parties of Moslems which could be ambushed. He made forays into the suburbs of Medina and damaged crops and gardens. He let Mohammed see that his feelings had not changed, that his intentions were still as murderous. From the points of view of both sides, there could be only one solution. Fight it out!

In coming to this decision, Mohammed was setting up a principle which was to become an unofficial tenet of the Moslem faith. The jihad, or holy war, although not strictly a religious obligation, was going to do more than anything else to carry Islam round the world.

As in almost everything he did or decreed, Mohammed did not appreciate the immeasurable repercussions which the authorizing of this method of dealing with infidels would have. He obviously did not see the application of the law of the sword in terms of the distant future. The primary motive for what he was doing was, above all, exasperation against men of whom he had asked nothing but a friendly hearing and had received nothing but insults and blows. Added to this, the necessity to clothe and feed and arm his men as well as to find allies. As an Arab who had traveled much among desert people, he was aware that the tribesmen would understand a faith much better if they knew that it countenanced warfare for profit.

Mohammed has been criticized for this aspect of his teaching. The "impostor"-minded biographers have railed against him as if he were the first to preach religious wars. These people seem to forget that, from time immemorial, most wars have been fought with religion as their initial or secondary origins.

If Mohammed had read the Old Testament, he would have seen that Moses had launched a holy war some two thousand years before not far from where this fighting with the Koreishites was going to start. If he had read on, he would have learned that the judges and kings of Israel did little else but wage wars on behalf of their faiths. He would have heard of massacres beside which his casualty lists would have looked like items of accidents on a football field. He would have realized that those old Hebrews had defined laws about religious warfare unparalleled before or since.

Mohammed had no blood lust for the sake of blood lust. As a matter of fact, the infidel captive had two alternatives. He could either pay ransom and go home, or accept Islam. The Koran states:

"When the sacred months are passed, kill those who join gods with God wherever ye find them, but if they repent and pay the obligatory alms, then let them go their way."

And again:

"Let there be no compulsion in religion."

If the alternative of Islam was selected, the convert was immediately admitted to all the spiritual and temporal benefits of other Moslems. This way of proceeding was, of course, in Mohammed's interests. Nevertheless, except on one or two occasions, he never wantonly revenged himself on his defeated enemies.

Had he, however, made reprisals part of his teachings, he would have been in keeping with the times, in keeping with the Christian ethics of the period and of much later.

When the Crusaders invaded the Holy Land in 1099, they left death and destruction wherever they passed. Yet when Saladin drove the Christians out, he took no revengeful measures.

Neither did the Moslems devastate the countries they invaded, as did their fellow religious warriors of other denominations. Wherever they passed, something better sprang up than what had been there before. Like a cloudburst, they fertilized where they destroyed. That the Renaissance took place was due to the descendants of Mohammed's original followers keeping culture alive while Europe wallowed in the darkness of the Middle Ages. The architectural glories of Damascus, of Fez, of Seville, of Granada and Cordova are the indirect consequences of what Mohammed started in 623 A.C.

THE FIRST BATTLE

Mohammed undoubtedly found war expedient and then profitable, but he was not one of those Arab raiders to whom blood feuding was second nature. Had the Koreishites given him one half of a chance to spread his religion peacefully, the idea of war would not have come to him.

Up to that time, Mohammed had never fought anyone, not even with his hands. He had no training in strategy or in the leading of men in battle. His only experience of any such thing had been during those intertribal encounters when, at the age of sixteen, he had carried arrows for his uncle. Neither had he any equipped or experienced soldiers. Nevertheless he knew that he must be ready to fight if he wanted to keep himself and his faith alive. Should the Koreishites attack Medina and be victorious, it would mean the end of Islam. So he began sending parties out raiding, which taught men initiative as well as accustoming them to handle their weapons. Sometimes the raiders were under the command of Hamza or Abu Obeida, sometimes under Mohammed himself.

What is remarkable is that Mohammed, in spite of his ignorance of military matters, showed high talents as a general in every battle or skirmish in which he took part. He was brave too and, in spite of his age, able to undergo hardships with the youngest of his soldiers. In fact what Mohammed must have stood during those grueling marches and fights on the burning deserts of Arabia seems to be evidence in itself that the stories about the epilepsy are, at least, exaggerated.

However, in spite of raids and brushes with the enemy, no battle of revenge had been fought with the Koreishites and no really rich caravan had been held up. To raise Moslem prestige and to fill Moslem coffers, Mohammed needed a victory. It did not look, though, as if the Meccans were going to risk a decisive encounter far from their capital, and Mohammed was not strong enough yet to go far from his. Unless he could catch the Koreishites unawares, the situation might develop into a stalemate. To bring this about he had recourse to a ruse which has been slurred over by his admirers and condemned by his disparagers.

In the holy month of Rajab, when it was tacitly understood among all Arabs that no fighting or raiding should take place, Mohammed dispatched from Medina a man called Abdallah ibn Jahsh and six or eight nomads. Their official orders were to scout around Mecca and At Tayef and find out what the enemy was doing. Their unofficial instructions were contained in a sealed letter from Mohammed which Abdallah was to open two days after leaving Medina. When he had read it, he was to act as he felt expedient.

The contents of this letter gave Abdallah the surprising information that he could attack any Koreish caravans he might encounter. The fact that it was the closed season for raids was not mentioned, but it seems unlikely that the former Meccan idolator could have forgotten a tradition on which he had been brought up. Abdallah conveyed the injunctions to his companions, who decided that it would be a good opportunity to collect booty at no risk to themselves. As a result of this decision, an unsuspecting train of Arabs and their camels sauntering along, safe as they thought in the holy month, were ambushed and looted.

The outcry at the breach of this old-age tradition was terrific. Even in Medina the disapproval was such that Mohammed had to say that he had believed Abdallah would wait until the holy month was over before taking action. He had to confirm this repudiation of responsibility by refusing any share of the plunder.

What the truth of the matter may have been, no one will ever know, but two things stand out.

The first is the question, was Mohammed so completely illiterate? If he could not even scrawl a few instructions, who was there of sufficient integrity in his household or on his staff to be entrusted with the recording of this questionable order? Had Abu Bakr or Hamza or Ali known what Mohammed had in mind, they would certainly have raised objections.

The second is that Mohammed's notions on the principles of warfare were far ahead of the times.

"War, after all, is but a game of deception," he once remarked.

Machiavelli said something of the kind nine centuries later, and Napoleon two hundred years after him, and the Japanese only a few years ago. And they were all of them right. If war *is* going to be used as a means to an end, why quibble about the means?

However, Mohammed had not yet the prestige of Machiavelli or Napoleon, so, when the first clamor had quieted down, he did a thing to which he would soon have regular recourse in moments of quandary. He had a revelation. This revelation, as many which followed, gave Allah's counsel regarding the matter which was troubling his Messenger. He said:

"*They will ask thee concerning war in the sacred month. Say, The war therein is bad, but to turn aside from the cause of God, and to have no faith in him and the sacred temple, and to disown its people is worse in the sight of God.*"

However, while this exonerated Abdallah ibn Jahsh and cleared Mohammed's conscience and that of the Medinese, it meant nothing to the Koreishites. Every day they were getting more and more exasperated by the impertinences of their former fellow citizens. The blood feuds were beginning to mount up. It required little to make them launch an expedition which would bring on the fight needed by Mohammed to prove himself. That little thing which was to lead to such other far-reaching consequences happened very soon.

Toward the end of the year 623 A.C., Mohammed learned that Abu Sofian would have to pass comparatively close to Medina on his way from Syria with a caravan of over a thousand camels worth tens of thousands of dinars. He immediately mobilized between three and four hundred men, seventy camels, and a few horses and mules. The number of soldiers was reduced to three hundred when it was discovered that some of them were non-Moslems who were only coming out for the sake of the loot. It was a pathetic little force with most of the troops unprotected by armor and obliged to take turns in riding the camels. The Moslem cavalry which was to become so famous consisted of two horsemen.

However, Abu Sofian learned of Mohammed's intentions and, leading his caravan off the main trail, inclined it toward the Red Sea. By this maneuver, he was able to slip past the Medinese ambush and was out of their reach before they found out. To be on the safe side, he had also sent a messenger to Mecca with the news that Mohammed in person was out to capture the caravan.

The messenger rode fast and, as he rode, he exaggerated in his mind what Abu Sofian had told him. By the time he reached Mecca he was in a frenzy. Flinging himself from his camel, he stood dramatically before the Kaaba and cut off his nose and his ears. This was a sign of desperate calamity and brought all the notables running from their occupations. With blood pouring over his beard, the man cried:

"Help, O Koreishites! Mohammed is pursuing your caravan!"

The effect of this information was instantaneous. Within an hour of the alarm being given, an excited throng of one thousand soldiers, with seven hundred camels and a hundred horses, was clamoring to be taken to avenge the rumored deaths of all those who had been with the caravan, to say nothing of the plundering of its rich merchandise. Abu Jahl, now seventy years old, but still strong and wiry, was the first to arm himself. He had no doubt that he was at last going to be able to settle with Mohammed. That no confirmation had come of the capture of the caravan made no difference. This opportunity for revenge could not be missed. Before nightfall the order to march had been given.

News travels with mysterious rapidity in the desert. Mohammed heard simultaneously that the caravan had escaped and that Abu Jahl was on his way with a large army. In spite of the disparity of numbers, he decided to try battle and risk his future, his reputation, perhaps his life, in the issue of the contest. Some of his men, nevertheless, showed nervousness.

The Arabs of Arabia, before the days of organized Moslem

warfare, liked to pillage. The idea of killing did not particularly appeal to them. They disliked any prospect of being killed themselves. But Mohammed revived their spirits and assured them that Allah would give them victory. Still there were some who, with Arab common sense, suggested that it might be wiser to save the men until they could be used in some more profitable enterprise.

"For, if we fall in battle," they asked, "what will be our reward?"

Unhesitatingly Mohammed replied:

"Paradise! A drop of blood shed in the cause of God, a night spent in arms, is of more avail than two months of fasting and prayer. Whoever falls in battle, his sins shall be forgiven. At the Day of Judgment, his wounds shall be resplendent in vermilion and odoriferous as musk, and the loss of his limbs shall be supplied by the wings of angels and cherubim."

This maxim changed the whole complexion of the thoughts of this first organized group of Moslem soldiers. It did more to promote heroism, to instill disregard for discomfort, for fatigue, for life itself than any order of the day, any intensive training, any promises of earthly reward. It set an ideal in the minds of Mohammed's Arabs which they have held ever since. Instead of fearing death, they look forward to it as the deliverance from earthly pain and grief.

But Mohammed did not confine himself to giving holy inspiration this January morning of 624. He knew that Allah was there to help, but he knew too that the help would be more effective if there was co-operation.

The place where it had been decided to stand and fight was in the valley of Badr. Badr is a sandy plain enclosed on the north and east by steep hills, on the west by dunes, and on the south by a low, rocky escarpment. A brook runs through the valley from east to west, breaking out here and there into bubbling springs which had been dammed by travelers and made into reservoirs. Mohammed decided to station his "army" about the reservoir which was nearest to the enemy, and block the others.

This would give him command of the water supply so vitally important in peace and war in the desert.

The day passed quietly. Some captured scouts of the Meccan army disclosed that the enemy was resting a few miles away. They also confirmed the size of the force. This did not dismay Mohammed, and he spent the night praying in a palm-branch hut which his men had built for him near the water.

As the sun rose over the golden desert, the Meccan army, led by Abu Jahl, streamed into the valley and ranged itself out of arrow range of the Moslems. Arab battles of those days were different affairs from the bloody conflicts when the Moslems were conquering the world. They were small. They were intimate. They still belonged to the siege-of-Troy variety.

As the opening phase, champions from both sides stepped out of their ranks and insulted the enemy, recited the achievements of their own leaders, and, finally, defied someone to single combat. The second phase was the single combats. The third phase was the general mix-up when everybody fought everybody else.

The approved procedure was followed in the valley of Badr.

Protected by armor and shields, with scimitars in their hands, Otba, father-in-law of Abu Sofian, Shaiba, his brother, and Al Walid, his brother-in-law, stood before the lines of the Koreish and hurled maledictions at the Moslems who faced them.

Three young Medinese sprang forward proclaiming their eagerness to spill infidel blood or else make straight for the delights of paradise. But the Meccans yelled that they had not come all that way to blunt their swords on youths with whom they had no particular quarrel. They wanted the heads of their cousins, the renegades of Mecca—if their owners dared to risk them.

This battle, it must be remembered, was essentially a settlement of blood feuds, the time-honored demand for a tooth for a tooth. The political aspect of the conflict had not yet developed. Provided vengeance had been taken, the rest of the encounter could be left to look after itself or could even be broken off in the middle.

THE FIRST BATTLE

At the taunt of the Koreishites, Ali dashed out of the Moslem ranks, glittering in breastplate and helmet. He was closely followed by Obeida ibn al Harith, a paternal cousin of Mohammed, and Hamza, who wore an ostrich feather on his cuirass. The three champions were thus all closely related to Mohammed and fulfilled the Koreish lust for Hashimite blood.

The three duels were as rapid as they were murderous. Hamza killed Shaiba while Ali killed Al Walid. Obeida was mortally wounded but, before he fell, Hamza and Ali were able to come to his rescue. Hamza hurled himself at Otba and, with a sweep of his sword, cut off his head. In a few minutes three of Mecca's most important warriors had been sent to find out the truth about the hell which Mohammed promised them.

With a cry of rage, three more Meccans darted from under Abu Jahl's banner and assailed the Moslem champions. They too went down before the swords of Islam. A further three were dealt the same fate. There was a moment of hesitancy among the Koreishites. Mohammed did not miss his advantage. With a sharp order he sent his soldiers hurtling into a general attack.

The third phase of the Arab battle had begun. Although outnumbered by three to one, the Moslems had a great advantage due to Mohammed's forethought. They had water. The Meccans were fighting under the blazing sun of the Arabian desert without being able to refresh themselves unless they fell back on the baggage camels in the rear. The few who in desperation managed to reach the Badr brook were shot by the Moslem archers.

From the side of a hill Mohammed watched the battle, with Abu Bakr. Up to the moment of the general set-to, he had remained quiet and collected. Now, however, he passed into such a state of excitement that he lost consciousness. On coming to, his eyes had an expression of exaltation. Picking up a handful of dust, he flung it in the direction of the enemy.

"May confusion light upon their faces!" he cried wildly.

With that, he mounted a horse and, calling his bodyguard, charged into the battle, followed by Abu Bakr.

The miracle-minded say that at this point something supernatural took place. With whirring wings and flashing weapons a host of angels headed by Gabriel answered Mohammed's call and joined the fighting Moslems. That is as it may be. What did occur is remarkable enough without bringing in the angels.

As Mohammed flung the dust, one of those violent desert sandstorms got up suddenly. The burning wind came from directly behind Mohammed and blew like a blast furnace into the eyes of the enemy. Tired, thirsty, demoralized by the killing abilities of the Moslems, the Koreishites were already on the defensive. The sandstorm added to their discouragement. Mohammed's maledictions against infidels, his inspiring shouts to his now blood-lusting believers confused them. That their ranks did not break immediately was due to Abu Jahl.

Abu Jahl had no ideas about giving in. Shouting as loudly as Mohammed, he urged his horse into the thickest of the battle. The Moslem leaders saw him and closed in on him. In spite of his age, he was still a warrior who counted. With sweeping blows of his scimitar, he killed several of his attackers before he was thrown from his charger. Abdallah ibn Massoud knocked him down and leaped on his chest. Even this did not stop the old man from raining curses on Mohammed and his kind. The imprecations did not cease until Abdallah had seized Abu Jahl's head and hewn it from its body. Then he carried it to Mohammed. Mohammed looked at the gory trophy with ecstasy. Withdrawing from the fighting, he dismounted and prostrated himself.

"There is no God but Allah!" he cried. "Abu Jahl has been punished as shall be punished all enemies of Allah."

The news of the Koreishite commander in chief's death spread rapidly, and with it went panic. In a few minutes the Meccans were throwing away their armor and their swords and running for their lives. In fact so fast did they run, and so tired were the Moslems, that a great many escaped capture.

Among the prisoners was Ommeya ibn Khalaf. No one had any particular quarrel with him except his ex-slave, Bilal. In fact some of the Moslems, cooled off now that the battle was won, were talking the day over with their one-time neighbors when Bilal passed by. The moment the muezzin recognized the torturer who had staked him out on the desert, he stiffened. Addressing the group of tired warriors, he said that as long as this chief of infidels was alive he, Bilal, was not safe. Ommeya must die. Some of the Moslems tried to intercede for the Meccan, but Bilal, stubborn and black, said No! One of the soldiers whispered to Ommeya that he had better make a dash for it. This he tried to do. Bilal was after him like a flash. The race was short. Ommeya was middle-aged and getting fat. Bilal had not gained weight standing on the roof of the mosque calling people to prayer five times a day. As he caught up with Ommeya, the one-time torturer let out a terrifying shriek which faded into a gurgle as Bilal's sword went through him. The old score had been paid off and, to make quite sure, Islam's first muezzin chopped off the head of the old master and laid it at the feet of the new.

This was one of the many settlements of feuds that day, and it was the last. Mohammed summoned his men and had them collect and sort the dead. It was hot, and they had to be buried. Of these, only fourteen were Moslem while seventy were Meccan. There were also seventy-four Meccan prisoners. The Moslems were laid to rest as martyrs ready to join their spirits in paradise. The Meccans were treated like infidels and pushed into a common grave ready for hell-fire.

The fate of the prisoners had now to be settled. Omar wanted to execute them all. Abu Bakr felt that there had been enough fratricides for one day. Hamza and Ali were too tired to care. Mohammed decided in favor of Abu Bakr's judgment. Only two prisoners were officially put to death. One was a poet who had relentlessly lampooned Mohammed throughout the years when he was trying to prove himself in Mecca. The other was a man who had made a cowardly attack on his person one day when he was praying outside the Kaaba.

With the other captives, the problem was settled by letting the poor go back to Mecca after taking an oath never to fight against Mohammed again. Some of these who took the oath also became Moslems.

With the wealthy, the alternatives were conversion, captivity, or ransom. In deciding the size of the ransom, Mohammed and his lieutenants had the advantage of knowing precisely how much each prisoner could afford to pay. Among those who pleaded penury was Mohammed's uncle, Al Abbas.

Al Abbas was an opportunist. He also had a sense of humor. Studying his character, one is forever impressed with the fact that, during the whole of this Mohammed-Koreish controversy, he remained detached, watching the conflict objectively, suiting his actions to the ebb and flow of the tide.

He accompanied his nephew to meet the original delegates from Medina. He told them that he counted on them to look after his kinsman. This, however, did not prevent him from setting out to fight the said kinsman when the occasion presented itself. Neither did it prevent him from making violent objection to being treated as an ordinary prisoner and crying poverty when the amount of his ransom was fixed.

Mohammed liked his uncle. His inconsistencies amused him, and when he started moaning about his destitution, Mohammed came back quickly with:

"Maybe *you* are destitute, but where's the money you deposited in the name of your wife?"

Another prisoner of personal interest to Mohammed was his son-in-law, Abu'l As. Abu'l As had no grudge against his father-in-law, but he did not believe that he was the Messenger of Allah. These views he maintained after capture. However, Mohammed released him without ransom on a promise that he would have his wife sent to Medina. This Abu'l As agreed to do, and Zaid was dispatched to Mecca to fetch Zeinab while her husband remained with his father-in-law as a hostage.

The other prisoners were treated according to their incomes.

The division of the armor and weapons and camels left behind by the enemy caused a certain amount of discussion. However, Mohammed resorted to Allah, who revealed to him a system for allotting loot which continued as long as Moslem armies were raiding the world.

So ended Mohammed's first terrestrial battle. It was a complete victory and a vindication of Mohammed as a leader. It gave Islam the glamor which, up to date, it had lacked. It gave incentives to other tribes to adopt this faith which offered worldly rewards to the survivors and spiritual rewards to the slain. It gave Mohammed great personal satisfaction. He felt more than ever that what he stood for was right. He felt more than ever that his perseverance during those dark days in Mecca had been justified.

The Battle of Badr remained always in Mohammed's mind as a proud memory. The three hundred who, with him, had defied the Koreishites he placed in a category by themselves. During his lifetime, and long after his death, the veterans of Badr could bring up their part on that glorious day in mitigation of punishment or censure. And deservedly. It was they who had forged and tested the weapon which was going to carry Islam to so many countries of the world. Throughout the coming centuries the Syrians and the Persians and the Egyptians, the Berbers, the Romans, and the Spaniards, the Indians and the Chinese and the Malays, the Russians and the Turks were to hear that cry which had burst from the throats of the gallant three hundred as they charged over the brook at Badr:

Allahu Akbar! Allahu Akbar!

CHAPTER XI

THE JEWS

(624 After Christ)

NOT MANY PEOPLE have heard of the Battle of Badr. There is no reason why they should. From the angle of a soldier today, even from that of a contemporary Persian or Greek or Roman, it was little more than a skirmish. Had there been newspapers in seventh-century Asia Minor, Mohammed's victory would not have made headlines. Nevertheless its effect on the history of Islam and the world was as important as Constantine's rout of Maxentius at the Milvian Bridge or of Attila's defeat at Chalons. The numbers of the Koreish killed, the loot taken, the death of Abu Jahl were not in themselves of momentous consequence. There were no lessons in strategy or tactics. No special feats of valor were performed. What the victory did, however, was much more important than any such material gains. It allowed Mohammed to get his breath. It gave him the chance to say: "I told you so!"—not only to his associates and followers, but also to himself.

Mohammed needed encouragement. He needed it more now than at any other time, more than any other prophet.

Jesus and Paul died in the midst of persecution. They never reached that dangerous point where their causes were partially won and they had to prove themselves. They never had that period of anticlimax like Mohammed after his escape from Mecca. If Mohammed had not had his Badr victory or if he had been defeated there, it would have been exceedingly difficult for him to carry on. He realized nevertheless that, while he had turned the tables on the scoffers, he must not rest on this. He must follow up his success, he must keep moving.

However, the first moments of triumph were spoiled by finding Rokaia dead. She had never been well since her return from exile in Abyssinia. On the morning of the battle, she had been so weak that her husband, Othman, had remained with her instead of marching with the army. She had passed away about the same time as the ranks of the Koreishites were breaking before the Moslem onslaught.

The children of Khadija meant much to Mohammed. In all accounts of his relationship with them, one senses a fussy, parental attitude, not much in keeping with an instigator of religious wars. Rokaia's death was a great grief to her father, but it was tempered by the arrival from Mecca a little later of Zaid, bringing with him Zeinab. Zaid also brought the good news that Mohammed's unpleasant old uncle, Abu Lahab, had been so infuriated by his nephew's victory that he had expired a few hours after hearing about it.

Mohammed did not wait to remind everybody of the curse he had laid on Abu Lahab during the early days of the persecution. Soon he was able to boast about this again when Otba, the son of Abu Lahab, who had repudiated Rokaia, was killed and eaten by a lion when leading a caravan to Syria.

Thus, with the exception of this death of his daughter, everything seemed to be working out favorably for Mohammed. He had a contented group of followers, he had had his first satisfying taste of revenge, while among the local tribes his prestige was high. The only people who did not seem to appreciate him and were, in fact, doing their utmost to offset his success were the Jews.

Instead of acclaiming his victory, they belittled it. They did this in their homes and they did it in public. They mocked at the revelations. Availing themselves of Mohammed's initial liberality in allowing anyone who wished to enter the mosque, they attended his services and sneered. They challenged the authenticity of what he was putting into the Koran and produced the Bible to show how few of his declarations were original. They wrote satires about him and about the Moslems. Some of the younger Hebrews went as far as throwing stones at him. There were near attempts on his life.

Then, in a more direct manner, the Moslems were made to feel that they were in Medina on sufferance. In those days, as now, the Jews controlled many of the local banks and lent money to their clients. With things going better for the refugees, they came down on them as exacting creditors.

It may be wondered what the Jews were doing so many hundreds of miles from their native land or why they had developed this special dislike for Mohammed and his Moslems. The explanations are simple.

A great number of people are under the impression that the expulsion of the Jews from Palestine has had something to do with Great Britain or with Ibn Saud or with Adolf Hitler. Nothing could be more inexact. From time immemorial the Jews have been in the process of being expelled from their country—which they originally took themselves by force. To name only a few of the expellers, there was Sargon II about 722 B.C., there was Nebuchadnezzar in 586 B.C., Pompey in 63 B.C., Titus in 70 A.C., and the definite expulsion by Hadrian in 135 A.C. Even today barely 650,000 of the world's fifteen million Jews are in Palestine.

As each Jewish chastisement took place, the chastised wandered off into different countries. Many went into the interior of Arabia. After Titus's sack of Jerusalem, three powerful tribes, the Beni Kainuka and the Beni Koreiza and the Beni an Nadir, took possession of Medina, or Yathrib as it was then called, and made it into an agricultural stronghold. From then on, strife developed and continued between the Jews and those local Arabs who had become sedentary, the Beni Aus and the Beni Khazraj. During the years immediately preceding the Hijra, the fighting became acute and culminated in 618 A.C. by a bloodthirsty battle at a place called Boath. After this, the warring factions decided that it would make more sense to forget these futile variations of opinion. It was, accordingly, decided that rivalry and reprisals would be forgotten under one paramount chief. The man chosen to hold this office was this Arab, Abdallah ibn Obei, who was friendly toward the Jews. But, before the appointment was confirmed, Mohammed appeared with his tattered disciples and altered everything.

Abdallah did not at first appreciate the rivalry which threatened him. He did not believe in Mohammed and had no respect for his doctrines. On this score he had no hesitation in speaking his mind. Mohammed's point of view was much the same. He did not estimate Abdallah at his worth and, being not yet in a revengeful mood, would have liked to live in peace with these neighbors. His first disillusion came a few weeks only after his triumph over the Meccans.

Riding one day through the oasis on his donkey, he saw Abdallah sitting with a group of friends in the shade of a mud wall. Mohammed dismounted and joined the group. After the usual exchange of greetings, he began to talk about Islam. Abdallah and his companions were not uncontrolled fanatics like the Koreishites and listened courteously until Mohammed had finished. Then, politely but bluntly, Abdallah replied that what Mohammed had said was interesting but, unfortunately, untrue. He added that it might be a good idea if Mohammed remained in his part of the oasis and generally minded his own business. He assured him that if he did this, the rest of Medina would attend to its own affairs.

Mohammed was perturbed by this attitude, perhaps a little angry, but he still did not wish to break with the Jews, who had clearly incited Abdallah to speak in this way. In fact he drew up a charter with them whereby, among other things, it was established that Jews and Moslems were to aid each other in all matters concerning the city. They were to be allies against all common enemies, and this without any mutual obligations toward Islam or Judaism. The main clause of this charter ran as follows:

The Jews who attach themselves to our commonwealth shall have an equal right with our own people to our assistance and good offices. The Jews of the various branches domiciled in Yathrib shall form with the Moslems one composite nation. They shall practice their religion as freely as the Moslems. The clients and allies of the Jews shall enjoy the same security and freedom.

But, in spite of this concession, Mohammed still maintained that he was the Prophet promised to the Jews, while the Jews were equally emphatic that he was not. How could they be anything else without admitting that they had been wrong about their redeemer coming from their own people?

The government recognized by the children of Israel was a theocracy. That is, it was a government by God—in theory. In practice it meant a government by anyone who could effectively convince his subjects that he was the authorized interpreter of God's will. The Jews did not feel that any Arab could be this interpreter.

This stubborn, though logical, resistance of the Jews, together with the intransigeance of Abdallah ibn Obei and the lampooning and the general hostile impoliteness, soon led to open conflict between the new Medina and the old.

The first official rift was the changing of the direction of the *kibla*. The *kibla* is a niche or arch which points with mathematical precision toward the point which Moslems must face to pray. It is the first architectural requisite of every Moslem home or mosque. The only Moslems who have no *kibla* are the nomads of the desert. These have an amazing instinctive gift for turning in the direction to which their *kibla* should point if they had one.

On occasions when I was lost in the Sahara on cloudy nights, and knew the compass bearing of my camp but had no means of establishing it, I would find an Arab and have him turn in his praying direction. Where I lived, this was almost due east. With that indication, I would then ride on and invariably find my tents.

Until the disagreements with the Jews, Mohammed's *kibla* was north, toward Jerusalem. This was not, as is sometimes stated, to conciliate the Jews. Jerusalem was the direction for prayer during the days of persecution in Mecca. It was so because, in Mohammed's mind, Jerusalem was the center of all monotheistic faiths, the Holy City of the world. When, however, he saw the way things were turning out in the Hebrew section of the oasis, he reluctantly concluded that the Jews had no intention of ever having anything to do with him. He decided, therefore, that it was time for a change.

On a November morning of 623 A.C., in the middle of the prayer and after he had made two prostrations toward Jerusalem, he abruptly turned southward. The congregation turned with him. Mecca and the Kaaba of Abraham and Ishmael had once more become the shrine of those exiled Arabs and their hosts in Medina. From that day every *kibla* from Morocco to Mongolia, by way of Arabia, India, Malaya, and the Dutch Indies, has pointed to Mecca. Every Moslem in New York, in Zanzibar, in Sierra Leone, in London turns five times a day toward the Holy City in the Arabian desert. It is a stupendous thought.

No other religious leader ever had the idea of uniting his people in such a way. In no other faith is prayer so binding. For, without exaggerating, one can say that at every hour of the day Moslems somewhere are turning their thoughts and their eyes toward that sun-baked sanctuary of the wilderness.

There are many people, especially in the theatrical profession, who imagine that the east has some religious significance to a Moslem. The east, in itself, has no religious significance. It depends on where the Moslem happens to be in relation to Mecca. If he is a Sahara nomad, he prays with his face due east. If he is a Parisian, southeast will be the approved direction for prayer. If he inhabits the Maldive Islands in the Indian Ocean, it will be northwest. To a Punjabi, it will be due west. Even in Mecca the direction varies, the pilgrims all turning inward toward the Kaaba. On that November morning, the prostrations were made to the south.

The knowledge that Mohammed had officially forsaken all idea of religious understanding with the Jews spread quickly. The atmosphere was tense, with Mohammed and his men poised on one side and Abdallah ibn Obei poised on the other. The period of waiting for action did not last long. The Jews were the first to provoke; the Moslems the first to retaliate.

A woman called Esma bint Merwan resented Islam and Mohammed, especially, whom she regarded as a disturber of the peace. She had a gift for verse and wrote some disobliging couplets about Islam's Prophet and those who believed in him. Semitic people learn poetry easily, and in a short time the words of Esma were being repeated and embellished throughout the streets and gardens of Medina. The Moslems, who were not in a mood to be mocked, became angry. This delighted Esma and her friends. The lyrics multiplied and became more personal. Every day Mohammed's enemies waited for a new set of verses at the expense of these milk-drinking fanatics. They did not seem to consider that the milk drinkers might also be bloodletters. It did not take them long to find out.

One night, when Esma had finished her day's poetic lampooning and lay asleep on her mat, a Moslem called Omeir crept into her house. He was blind and, therefore, able to move easily in the dark. When he reached Esma he found that she had her baby in her arms. This he removed and plunged his sword into the sleeping woman so fiercely that she was pinned to the floor.

When Mohammed heard what Omeir had done, he went to the mosque. Addressing the congregation, he said, indicating Omeir:

"If ye desire to see a man that hath assisted the Lord and his Messenger, look ye here."

The policy to be followed in regard to the Jews had been clearly indicated. The Moslems waited only for their enemies to make the next move. It came quickly.

A very old man called Abu Afak had also that weakness for committing his thoughts to verse and choosing Mohammed as his subject. This failing cost him his life. Mohammed had not the Arab facility for writing poetry. Poems, even when not directed against him, irritated him. So, after the manner of Henry II of England, he exclaimed:

"Who will rid me of this pestilent fellow?"

There were no Norman knights to desecrate Canterbury Cathedral with the blood of an archbishop, but there were some equally enterprising Arabs to run their swords through the aged rhymer.

These assassinations increased the animosity of Abdallah ibn Obei and his supporters for the Moslems. To the Jews' animosity was added apprehension. But it did not alter their attitude or their opposition to Mohammed.

The Beni Kainuka, who lived in a *kasba* or stronghold outside Medina, in some way or another broke the charter with the Moslem Arabs. Mohammed called on their leaders and told them that, as retribution, they must either accept him as their prophet or take the consequences. The Jews challenged the ultimatum.

"O Mohammed!" their chief replied. "You think we are men akin to your race? Hitherto you have met only men unskilled in battle, and could, therefore, slay them. But when you meet us, by the Lord of Israel, you shall know we are men!"

Mohammed was taken aback by this defiance and did not immediately go into action. He thought that he had better wait for further provocation before striking.

Once again the Jews did not heed the warning. A Moslem girl was seated in the shop of one of the Beni Kainuka waiting to be served. A lighthearted Hebrew youth crept up behind her and pinned her skirt to her bodice. Arab women, then as now, never wear panties under their voluminous petticoats. The result was that the young lady walked unsuspectingly into the street with her posterior exposed. The lewd jeers of the practical jokers made her rush back into the shop blushing with shame. At the same time a Moslem who had witnessed the occurrence drew his sword and fell on the laughing Jews and killed one. Before he could kill a second, he was killed himself.

Mohammed hesitated no longer. Parading his men under the white banner around which they had fought at Badr, he led them to the Jewish stronghold. The Beni Kainuka retired within and locked the gates. Mohammed settled down outside to starve them out. This took two weeks. As soon as the Jews surrendered, Mohammed had them marched out, some four hundred of them, with their hands tied behind their backs. Then, with the same inspiration which caused Elija to slay the four hundred and fifty priests of Baal at the brook Kishon around 900 B.C., he ordered the prisoners to be beheaded. However, for the moment this satisfaction was to be denied him.

'Abdallah ibn Obei, hearing what was afoot, hurried to the scene and intervened on behalf of the Jews. He was still too powerful for Mohammed to defy openly, so the lives of the condemned men were spared. However, they were, then and there, expelled from their homes and wandered off into the desert, eventually migrating to Syria. All their possessions were confiscated by Mohammed and his men. In Mohammed's share of the loot he received several ancient swords, a great bow, and the silver cuirass which Saul had offered to David when he went out to challenge Goliath.

But while it must have been evident to the simplest-minded Hebrew that Mohammed was in no mood to brook any further impertinences, another poet set out to see if he could not better what his two murdered predecessors had failed to achieve. This lampooner's name was Kab ibn al Ashraf.

To his rashness Kab added further foolishness by not only going to Mecca and stirring up the already enraged Koreishites, but returning to Medina and boasting about it. Mohammed was in the mosque when he heard that the man was once more in the oasis. Without moving, he added to the ritual prayer:

"O Allah, deliver me from this son of Ashraf, in whatsoever way it seemeth good to Thee."

It was not long before a group of young Moslems had set out to do Allah's work. After a certain amount of crafty maneuvering and in spite of the warnings of his bride, they managed to lure the foolhardy poet out of his home. It was night and, after walking him away from frequented streets on the excuse that they were themselves plotters against Mohammed, they jumped on him and sliced him up. Then they carried the mutilated head to Mohammed, who received it with enthusiastic congratulations.

The following day Mohammed made it known that he would always justify a Moslem who killed a Jew. The edict was acclaimed by the people of the mosque, and the Jews no longer dared to venture out of doors after sunset. Finally a deputation waited on Mohammed to find out the reasons for these persecutions and a possible remedy.

Mohammed explained that the Jews had brought everything on themselves. Their poems, their criticisms, their sneers, their stone pelting had been unprovoked. All that his men had done was to retaliate. If, however, they were prepared to abide by the charter, he would see to it that they were left alone. Accordingly a fresh charter was signed, and peace reigned temporarily between the Moslems and the Jews.

During the period that Mohammed was settling these internal quarrels, which covered the greater part of the year 624, there were other preoccupations outside Medina.

Abu Sofian's mortification over the Badr defeat had nearly driven him insane. He had vowed not to shave his head or perfume himself or go near a woman until he had had his revenge on Mohammed. To begin with, his revenge took the form of raids on Medina, cutting down palms, burning crops, and killing any Moslems who happened to be around. But although the raiders were well armed and well mounted and moved in fairly large numbers, they seemed disinclined to meet Mohammed's men in any open fight. In fact whenever Mohammed was reported riding to counterattack, which he did the moment he heard the Koreishites were in the neighborhood, the enemy made for Mecca. Sometimes they left so hurriedly that minor loot in the shape of camels fell into Moslem hands.

After a while Abu Sofian found it safer to stay clear of the hornet's nest. This encouraged Mohammed, and he kept his patrols roaming constantly across the main caravan trails until the Meccans no longer dared to send their goods to the markets of Syria and the north. In a few months the trade balance began to diminish so alarmingly that Abu Sofian decided that he must take a chance. If he did not, Mecca would be ruined. He accordingly assembled one of the largest caravans which had ever left the Holy City and dispatched it by an abandoned and waterless route. But Mohammed's active intelligence service immediately reported this to headquarters.

This time the raiding party of one hundred well-mounted men was entrusted to Zaid ibn Haritha. Zaid moved swiftly and secretly and caught the caravan on the move. In a few moments it had scattered in confusion. The Koreishites who had not been killed fled, and Zaid led back to Medina the biggest prize which the Moslems had ever taken. In addition to silver bars and rich draperies and camels, there were 100,000 pieces of gold. For the first time since the Hijra, Mohammed was rich. He promoted Zaid to be a general and saw that everyone else concerned was suitably rewarded. Only the Koreishites were in despair. Staring glumly at their idols, they wondered how they could possibly rid themselves of this scourge of the devil who might soon give Mecca the status of an unimportant village.

While Mohammed had no such intentions as regards the city and had only a quarrel with certain of the inhabitants, he made it clear that aggressive action such as Zaid's would, in future, be the rule. Although he did not announce it, this was all he *could* do for the moment. He was not yet strong enough to make a general attack. He had also domestic problems to keep him occupied.

Omar's daughter, Hafsa, had lost her husband at Badr. Othman's wife, Rokaia, had died about the same time. Omar thought it might be a good idea if Othman consoled himself with Hafsa. But Othman somehow did not think so. He had heard of Hafsa's independent nature and of her violent temper, so he politely refused Omar's offer. Omar therefore went to Abu Bakr with the same proposition. And he, for the same reason as Othman, declined the honor.

Omar, who was as quick-tempered as his daughter, flew into a rage. Storming into Mohammed's apartments, he threatened to do his worst to these two snobs who disdained being his son-in-law.

With tactful words Mohammed calmed his friend, pointing out that Hafsa was perhaps reserved for something better.

"In fact, Omar," he concluded, "I'll marry her myself."

This he did and, simultaneously, betrothed his own daughter, Umm Kulthum, to Othman.

Thus, in one afternoon, Mohammed became the son-in-law of Omar and the father-in-law of Othman. These new alliances, with that of already being the son-in-law of Abu Bakr and the father-in-law of Ali, bound the leaders of Islam by even stronger ties that heretofore.

The only one who saw little to rejoice at in this welding of families was Aisha. From her point of view this tightening of parental or political bonds did not mean anything more than having to cope with a rival in the harem.

Hafsa was just twenty and as pretty as she was sensual. Aisha was twelve, but she had the mind of someone much older. She was sharp-witted, too, and gay. She summed up Hafsa quickly, took stock of her moods and used them to their full disadvantage by showing them up to Mohammed whenever the opportunity occurred. In a few weeks Aisha was satisfied that, outside the connubial intimacies between Mohammed and his new bride, she had her husband as closely attached to her as before this marriage. Even in the matter of sleeping with Mohammed, Aisha had no fears of being supplanted except from the point of view of novelty.

Once Aisha had established this, she made friends with Hafsa, and the two girls became devoted and intimate. In fact Mohammed had to intervene several times when the two young ladies were carrying their youthful exuberance too far at the expense of the stolid and stupid old Sawda.

Hafsa is chiefly known to history as the custodian of the first manuscript of the Koran. After her husband's death, Omar suggested that a master copy of the Holy Book be made before all that Mohammed had said and noted was forgotten. Abu Bakr had this done and entrusted the document to Hafsa. Why he did not give it to his daughter has not been established. He probably appreciated her capricious character. Hafsa thus became responsible for a work which has survived thirteen centuries.

Few people, even among Moslems, can quickly name all of Mohammed's wives. Yet, every one of them, with the exception perhaps of Sawda and Zeinab bint Khuzaima, played roles of varying importance in the molding of Islam.

CHAPTER XII

THE SECOND BATTLE

(625 After Christ)

EXACTLY ONE YEAR had passed since the Battle of Badr when the Meccans made up their minds that the only way to recover their prestige was to prove it. Their obsession that no good could come from Mohammed persisted. They had begun by despising him, then they had hated him, now they feared him. With fear in Mecca, life had lost its glamor and gaiety. The Meccans loved glamor and adored gaiety. To restore it, the source of fear must be eliminated.

Accordingly, in the month of January 625 A.C., Abu Sofian mustered an army of three thousand soldiers, of whom the majority had armor and two hundred were mounted on horses. These latter were under the command of Khaled ibn al Walid, Islam's brilliant cavalry leader of the future. All the other important Koreishite warriors had answered the call to arms. Fifteen bloodthirsty women had also insisted on joining the army on its mission of vengeance. At the head of these was the notorious Hind, the wife of Abu Sofian, whose father, Otba, had been killed by Hamza at Badr.

Hind was a beautiful, sensuous woman, intelligent and ruthless. This expedition against Mohammed was a great deal due to her efforts. She had refused to have anything to do with her husband or any of her lovers until her father's death had been avenged. She had not ceased to taunt the Koreishites about their defeat at Badr. She had even promised freedom to a black slave known as Wahshi (the savage), an expert javelin thrower, if he killed Hamza.

The other women were equally bloodthirsty, and pranced and

danced among the soldiers as they left Mecca, and sang psalms to one of the Kaaba idols which had been taken along on the back of a camel.

The Koreishites had no obligation, this time, to move cautiously. They had no caravan to protect. They had no haven to reach before nightfall. They were marching with one purpose, to find and put an end to Mohammed. With their superiority in arms and equipment, they could fight when and where they pleased. They accordingly followed the main caravan track which led direct to Medina. This took them through the village of Abwa, where Amina, Mohammed's mother, lay buried. Hind made an attempt to desecrate the tomb and scatter the bones. But Abu Sofian stopped her. Amina had died before there was any thought of Islam, he said. She had been in no way responsible for the crimes of her son.

In spite of the Koreishite disregard for secrecy, Mohammed's intelligence service seems to have failed him at this point. He did not hear of Abu Sofian's plans until he was already on the way. The information, moreover, came from Mecca. Al Abbas, who had eventually been ransomed after Badr, had had plenty of opportunity while waiting in Medina to appreciate the fanatical enthusiasm of the Moslems. His original idea that his nephew might one day be someone to be reckoned with had been strengthened. He had not been converted to Islam or remained in Medina, but neither had he taken any side in the discussion about sending this army out under Abu Sofian. When he had seen that the Koreishites were mustered and ready to go, he sent a messenger on a swift camel to warn his nephew. The messenger found Mohammed in the gardens of Kuba. The news took him by surprise. He immediately returned to Medina and summoned Abu Bakr, Omar, Othman, Hamza, and Ali. He also called in Abdallah ibn Obei. They had not made friends and continued to resent one another. However, in this case, with Medina being threatened by an outside enemy, Mohammed felt that the leader of the other Medinese faction should be in on this council of war.

The older men, including Mohammed, decided that the only

sensible thing to do against such a formidable force was to wait for it behind the walls of the city. Ali and Hamza were against the plan. When the younger members of the community heard what was afoot, they also backed the junior representatives of the council. Many of these had fought at Badr, some had been with Zaid during his profitable raid against the Koreish caravan. None of them had found fighting at either encounter a particularly risky enterprise. All of them had found it profitable.

"Besides," said they, "if we sit behind these walls throwing stones at an enemy which has come all this way to fight us, we will become the laughingstock of Arabia."

The clamor of the young men was so great that Mohammed, against his better judgment, decided to adopt what he knew to be an extremely foolhardy course. He announced his decision in the mosque after the Friday morning prayer. He urged his followers to be steadfast in their faith if they wanted victory. Then he retired to his quarters and spent the afternoon with Aisha.

In the meanwhile Abu Bakr and Omar mustered the Medinese soldiery. These amounted to barely a thousand men, of whom two hundred only had armor. As at the first battle, there were the same two horses. It was not much of a force to lead against the finely equipped army from Mecca. However, the die was cast and, disregarding one or two protests that perhaps it might be better to stand and await the enemy in Medina, Mohammed took over command.

He looked impressive as he came out of his quarters and surveyed the men who waited in the square of the mosque. Back and front, he wore a polished cuirass. From a leather belt a sword swung at his side. In his hand he carried a bow. On his head was his spiked helmet, around which was bound a black turban. His equipment was completed by a shield hanging from his shoulders. Satisfied that everyone was there, he placed the white standard in the hands of Musab ibn Omeir and mounted one of the horses. Once more he led his men out of the oasis to prove their God against the Kaaba idols.

Included among these thousand soldiers were three hundred

Jews and non-Moslem Arabs under Abdallah ibn Obei. Clear of Medina, Mohammed halted and made it known that he was not particularly interested in having in his force any who did not believe in Islam. Abdallah resented this and, before the engagement began, took his partisans back to Medina. Mohammed's army was thus reduced to seven hundred, less than a quarter of the strength of the Koreishites.

The place where Mohammed had decided to meet the Meccans was on the slopes of Mount Ohod. Mount Ohod was of historical interest as the burial place of Aaron. On the topmost pinnacle a stone shrine commemorated the man without whom the inarticulate Moses would never have been able to threaten Pharaoh.

Ohod was a grim place and in keeping with the bloodthirsty encounter which was to take place there. It was not really a mountain, rather a great, barren rock rising out of the desert without a blade of grass or even a thorny acacia. No animals made their homes there; there was not even the sounds of chirping birds. The only sign of life were a few prickly-backed lizards. Desolate and burning, Ohod stared grimly over the arid landscape across which the Koreishites would attack.

Mohammed placed his men on the rising ground, which gave him a slight advantage in defense against the superiority in numbers of the enemy, while the steep precipice of the mountains protected his rear. He had the swordsmen stand shoulder to shoulder in such a manner that they would oppose the Koreishite onslaught like a wall. On an adjoining mound and slightly behind the main position he established his archers. To these he gave the most stringent instructions never to move without orders from him. At all costs they were to remain at their posts and protect the Moslem flanks. Mohammed was insistent on this point. He knew how vulnerable he was without cavalry. He sensed the menace of Khaled with his mobile horsemen. He was sure, however, that the morale of his troops was greater than that of the Koreishites. If his orders were carried out, he relied on this to counterbalance the other odds against him.

While Mohammed had been making these dispositions, the

Koreishites had appeared on the plain below the hill. The two armies now faced each other, and the first phase of the Arab battle began.

The Meccans, generously assisted by the women who had brought their timbrels, flung insults at the Moslems. These were alternated by Hind, who led triumphant choruses as she danced round the idol which perched on the camel.

Talha, the hereditary standard bearer of the Koreishites, was the first Meccan challenger. As he stepped out of Abu Sofian's ranks, Ali stepped out of Mohammed's. The two men met in the middle of "no man's land." Without words or preliminary flourishes the duel began. Talha never stood a chance. Ali's scimitar flashed in the morning sun and the head of the standard bearer leaped from his shoulders and rolled away on the sand.

"*Allahu Akbar!*" cried Mohammed.

"*Allahu Akbar! Allahu Akbar!*" echoed from the eagerly watching Moslems.

Othman, Talha's brother, sprang out of the Meccan ranks and ran forward to attack Hamza, who stood, magnificent in his helmet and cuirass adorned with the ostrich feather which he had worn at Badr. Once again the Moslem sword flashed. Once again a headless Meccan stood teetering in the sunlight before crumpling on the ground. Loudly Hamza called:

"I am the son of him who gave the pilgrims drink. I am the son of Abd al Mottaleb!"

Again other members of the Talha family came out to avenge their relatives. Each time Ali or Hamza sent their heads rolling.

The smell of blood began to vapor from the shimmering desert. The Moslems stirred in their ranks. The way their champions had fared foreshadowed another Badr. Soon Mohammed could not hold them back. With a wild cry of "Death! Death!" they surged from their position on the rising ground. Like a gigantic battering ram, they hit the Koreishites head on. The Koreishite line staggered and began to waver. The superiority of equipment and of numbers seemed of no avail against this fanatic spirit. In vain Khaled tried to use his cavalry. Every time he made a move, Mohammed's skillfully placed archers sent death among his horses. It looked as if the battle were over and won. But it was not over and was far from won.

In a few years the Moslem armies would not only be ably commanded, but the troops would have a high sense of discipline which could be relied on under any circumstances. An order given would be obeyed. In 625 this discipline did not exist. The Arabs fought partly for ideals or revenge, but chiefly for plunder. They had done this from time immemorial, and instructions to the contrary or a few military skirmishes were not going to change them.

Mohammed had used his ground to offset his disadvantages in numbers and armor and mobility. Had he been able to continue these tactics, he would probably have had another victory. That he was deprived of this was due entirely to the irresponsible behavior of his own men.

As the Moslem onslaught drove a wedge into the Koreishite center, the flanks began to fold up. Hamza and Ali, with their murderous scimitars, seemed to be everywhere. Soon the enemy had fallen back behind its encampment. This was too great a temptation for the loot-minded Moslems. Instead of following through their advantage, they began to sack the camp. From their mound the archers could see what was going on. It looked as if the battle were finished and their comrades were going to collect all the material advantages. They could not believe that Mohammed had intended this. If he had, it could not be helped. The spectacle before them was more than any human Arab could stand. Without a glance behind them they ran helter-skelter onto the plain and breathlessly joined the plunderers.

Khaled had no military training, but he had that same instinct for generalship as Mohammed. He was, in addition, a dashing, daring cavalryman who handled sword and lance with the same dexterity as he did troops. During the battle he had kept his eyes on the archers. Every time they slackened their fire, he maneuvered closer to them. Now that they had abandoned their post, exposing the Moslem flank, he did not hesitate. Wheeling his squadrons, he raced at their head into the unformed ranks of the enemy. The surprise and consequent confusion was as sudden as it was violent. In two minutes the whole aspect of the battle changed. From an exulting gang of pillagers, the Moslems had become a mob of screaming victims being spitted by Khaled's lancers.

In vain did Ali and Omar try to rally the disorganized companies. In vain did Mohammed and Abu Bakr try to encourage them with invocations of Allah. The Moslems had horsemen prodding them on one side and foot soldiers, who had returned to the attack, slashing at them on the other. All they could think of was how to get away from this hellish situation. Soon even the voices of their leaders faded.

Wahshi, Hind's hired executioner, had bided his time, waiting for an opportunity to destroy Hamza and win his freedom. Just as Khaled came whirling into the battle, Hamza was challenging a Meccan called Siba, whose mother attended to the circumcising of Koreishite women. Hamza, with a preliminary "O Siba, son of Umm Anmar, circumciser of women!" had twirled his sword twice and laid Siba out on the desert. His head, however, had not been severed from his body, and Hamza bent down to finish this off. As he did so, Wahshi, who had kept as close as he dared to Hamza since the beginning of the fight, raised his arm, and the javelin swished through the air. It caught Hamza in the lower part of the back, below his armor, and transfixed him. He staggered and fell. He tried to rise, but his life blood was pumping out onto the desert. Soon he lay still. Making sure that the great warrior was dead, Wahshi cautiously approached the body and jerked out his javelin. Then he went to tell Hind.

He found her cheering on her men, who were rapidly turning the almost Moslem victory into a rout. The moment she saw Wahshi, she knew what he had come to say. A look of ecstasy spread over her lovely face. Seizing the black slave's hand, she let him lead her to where the noble Hamza, in his shining cuirass, his ostrich plume dappled with blood, sprawled. With a scream of delight she leaped upon the body and began tearing at it. She ripped off Hamza's ears, cut off his nose, and gouged out his eyes. Then, plunging her knife into his side, she lifted out his still warm liver and sank her teeth into it. Some of the other women saw what Hind was doing and, as the rest of the live Moslems had disappeared, they began also to mutilate the dead. With noses ears and fingers, they made themselves necklaces and bracelets.

In the meanwhile Mohammed's own predicament was beginning to look desperate. The majority of his soldiers had scattered before the relentless accuracy of Khaled's lancers. Only Omar, Ali, Abu Bakr, and a few others stood around their leader, who, now fighting for his life as well as his cause, discharged arrows until his bow broke. One of the enemy troopers actually reached the rock on the slopes of Ohod where Mohammed defended himself. Before, however, he could run him through, Mohammed seized a lance from one of his bodyguard and drove it into the neck of his assailant. Other Koreishites surged toward Mohammed. They were blood crazy, ready to die a hundred times in order to kill him. If it had not been for the flail-like swords of Omar and Ali, nothing would have stopped them. The air was filled with arrows and stones and javelins. Mohammed was hit, first on the mouth, then on the side of the head so violently that the metal chin strap of his helmet was driven into his cheek. Another missile deeply gashed his forehead.

Ibn Kami'a, a Meccan hater of Moslems who had killed their standard bearer, Musab, now slipped past Omar and Ali and bore down on Mohammed with drawn scimitar. It looked like the end of the Islamic ideal. But, quicker than light, Talha ibn Obeidallah, one of the original converts and son-in-law of Abu Bakr, flung himself before his master and warded off the blow. In so doing he knocked down Mohammed and laid him senseless. Ibn Kami'a was too excited to make sure what had happened. Running down the hill, he shouted that he had killed Mohammed. This information, strangely enough, saved the Moslem defeat from becoming an irretrievable disaster. For while, on the one hand, it caused most of the Moslems to abandon all attempts to counterattack, it also checked the enemy.

At Badr and as in all Arab battles of those days, the justification for hostilities was the settling of blood feuds. Abu Sofian had come out of Mecca primarily to have his revenge on Mohammed and to satisfy his wife's lust to see Hamza dead. With both these objectives achieved, the incentive to carry on the fight ceased. He therefore called off his men from chasing individual Moslems and reorganized them around his standard.

Mohammed was only stunned. Talha, though wounded, helped Omar and Abu Bakr carry their leader up to a cleft in the rocks, where a number of their own men had taken refuge. The moment they saw that Mohammed was alive, their broken spirits mended. A little encouragement and they would have gone back into battle. Mohammed restrained them. During the preceding hour he had been close to death, and he saw no point in going any closer. Besides, as far as he could make out, he no longer had an army. Before deciding what the next move should be, he wanted to collect his wits. The first thing to do was to remove the helmet chain which still bit into his cheek. Ali brought some water in his shield, and the painful operation was begun. It was not until another of the early converts, Abu Obeida, not to be confused with the martyr of Badr, had applied his teeth to the steel links, that the Messenger's flesh was freed from the imbedded metal.

As soon as this "surgery" was over and his wounds had been dressed, Mohammed put on another helmet and took a look at what was going on on the battlefield below. He saw Abu Sofian and his staff eagerly examining the bodies of the dead Moslem soldiers, evidently anxious to find out which of their prominent warriors had been killed. They were clearly disappointed for, with the exception of Hamza and Musab ibn Omeir, there were none of Mohammed's immediate lieutenants, and nowhere was Mohammed.

After a while Abu Sofian looked up at the shimmering flanks of Ohod and, seeing the group of men outside the cleft in the rock, shouted:

"Hi there! Mohammed! Abu Bakr! Omar!"

Mohammed signaled to his men to remain silent. Abu Sofian, receiving no reply, added:

"Then all are dead and we are rid of them."

The great Omar could not swallow such a taunt. Disregarding Mohammed's gestures, he stood up and bellowed back:

"Not at all. We are alive and ready to fight any of you!"

The Moslems on the hillside braced themselves. But, to the surprise of everyone, the Koreishite leader declined the challenge. Instead of calling his men and charging, he replied:

"This day shall be the return for Badr! Glory to Hubal! Hubal is ours, not yours!"

To which Omar retorted:

"Allah is ours, not yours!"

To which Abu Sofian in turn answered:

"We shall meet again in a year at Badr!"

And Omar accepted the invitation with:

"*In sha Allah* [If God wills it]."

With that, Abu Sofian had his men fall in and led them off in the opposite direction—toward Mecca.

As soon as the last soldier was out of sight, Mohammed, followed by his escort, came cautiously down onto the plain. This might be a ruse on the part of the Meccans, but he was too anxious to find out which of his friends had died for the cause, to wait. The sight of the beloved Hamza and the brave Musab and many others brought tears to his eyes. He gave orders, however, that none of the corpses should be touched or moved. They must lie where they had fallen, their martyrs' tombs to remain forever as evidence of their fidelity.

Today these graves can still be seen, over seventy of them, in the actual places where Mohammed's warriors were struck down by the lances and scimitars of the Koreishites, one thousand three hundred and twenty years ago. They are not elaborate tombs, nothing more than small heaps of red sandstone with bits of porphyry to denote the heads and the feet of the dead heroes. Only Hamza has an impressive mausoleum, which is also a mosque. Built of hewn stone, it has a minaret and a dome beneath which rests Hamza under a block of black basalt. Near him, for some reason, is the tomb of Abdallah ibn Jahsh, the leader of the raiders who attacked the Meccan caravan during the holy month, soon after Mohammed's arrival in Medina.

When the burials were completed, Mohammed bivouacked on the battlefield. Most of the surviving soldiers had rejoined their leader. A number of men and women, including Fatima, had also come out from Medina to find out if the rumor of Mohammed's death was true. They were relieved to discover him alive, but he warned them not to give thanks before they were sure of what the Koreishites had in mind. For all he knew, Abu Sofian might be reorganizing his forces to attack and sack Medina. If he decided to do this, there was nothing to stop him but Allah.

However, Abu Sofian did not attack. The Meccans had no quarrel with the Medinese. Their feelings of vindictiveness centered on Mohammed and his relatives who had betrayed the good name of Mecca. They had got Hamza. Next time they would get Mohammed or Omar or Abu Bakr. Besides, they did not much like the idea of venturing into an oasis where they might be surrounded and cut off from their base. Besides, they were tired. So they loaded their camels and proceeded slowly toward the Holy City.

Simultaneously Mohammed led the survivors of his little force back to Medina. He found it echoing to the wailing of women who had lost husbands or sons or fathers or brothers in the battle. Mohammed did not hush them. He went straight to his quarters where Aisha and Hafsa and Sawda waited for him anxiously. Tenderly they washed his wounds and brought him food and clean clothes. Mohammed spoke little. He was weary and in pain, but he was not discouraged. After several hours of heavy sleep, he got up filled with renewed energy and armed himself again. Sending for Bilal, he told him to summon the people to the mosque.

When everyone was assembled and a prayer had been said, he announced that he was marching immediately in pursuit of the Koreishites. Before anyone had recovered from their astonishment, he had mustered the men who had fought at Ohod and was on his way out of the oasis.

At nightfall of the second day the Moslem force caught up with the Meccans. Mohammed called a halt and bivouacked. As soon as it was quite dark he had his men light hundreds of campfires along the ridge above the place where the enemy rested. The effect was as he had hoped. Abu Sofian, believing that Mohammed had raised an army from his Medina reserves and was already coming to avenge Ohod, packed up his tents and sped south. Not until he reached Mecca and was safely behind its walls did he feel safe.

As soon as Mohammed was satisfied that his strategem had worked, he turned about and hurried back to Medina to tell his people that the Koreishites were really no braver than they had been at Badr.

This performance was perhaps one of the most remarkable in Mohammed's career. It showed an amazing insight into the understanding and handling of human beings.

Mohammed had been badly trounced at Ohod. It had not been through his fault. It had been the result of his men disobeying orders. Nevertheless he had been trounced. His prestige as an envoy of Allah had been lowered. If he admitted defeat, it would be lowered even more. So he did not admit defeat. Instead of letting his soldiers be fussed over by their womenfolk and give their versions of the fight, he fell them in. He was wounded himself, he was stiff, he was tired, he was fifty-six years old, but he put his legs across a horse and rode off as if he were pursuing a demoralized and routed enemy. It was masterly strategy, magnificent psychology, above anything any commander has ever conceived to revive the spirits of a shattered body of men.

Neither did he relax or give ground when he arrived in Medina. On the contrary he adopted a commanding, almost reproving, attitude. After leading a thanksgiving prayer, he entered the pulpit and began to preach.

He told his congregation that the battle of Ohod had gone as it had because his men had not yet learned to obey him. Had they appreciated that his orders were inspired, they would have carried them out and victory would have been theirs as sure as it had been at Badr. He then paused, and added one of the most important messages which he had ever delivered to his people. He asked them to realize that, whatever assistance God gave them, *he, Mohammed, was but a man like any of them.* Allah had chosen him as a mouthpiece, but that did not make him divine or immortal. He begged them to appreciate this, for he had noticed on the field of battle that the moment rumor of his death was spread, panic followed. But this must not be. *If he died, it made no difference to the cause.* Sooner or later, he *would* have to die, and then what? Did these men and women believe that Allah had promised Paradise to believers only as long as their leader was alive? Why, of course not! He said—and this is recorded in the third sura of the Koran:

"Mohammed is no more than an apostle; other apostles have already passed away before him: If he die, therefore, or be slain, will ye turn on your heels? But he who turneth on his heels shall not injure God at all. And God will certainly reward the faithful."

When the sermon was over, Mohammed left the pulpit and walked slowly between the silent ranks of his people. A year ago they had been rejoicing because of the plunder they had acquired. Today they were quieter, but perhaps rejoicing even more sincerely in the knowledge that, whether there was plunder or not, they were with a man who would never let them down.

CHAPTER XIII

POLITICAL AND DOMESTIC TROUBLES IN MEDINA

(625-626 After Christ)

BY HIS PURSUIT of the Koreishites and his frank comments on the battle, Mohammed had regained much of the standing which he had lost at Ohod. That is to say, he had regained it with the Moslems. He had, however, fallen inestimably in the opinions of Abdallah ibn Obei and of the Jews and of the other non-Moslem inhabitants of Medina. He had, likewise, forfeited the respect of the nomad tribes which pastured in the neighborhood. This he decided to offset quickly. He knew that the time to show strength is when one is weak.

During the fight at Ohod one of Mohammed's men, Al Harith by name, had taken advantage of the general confusion of the battle to settle a blood feud by killing one of his own side. This was noticed and reported to Mohammed. Mohammed took no immediate action, but when everything was quiet again he rode over to Kuba, where Al Harith lived. Al Harith came unsuspectingly to pay his respects to his general. Mohammed quickly accused him of murder. When Al Harith confessed, he had him as quickly beheaded.

In the midst of all the staggering things which were happening, this may seem a trivial matter. But it was important. A real leader must be just, he must be impartial, he must be strong. Mohammed had few enough followers and needed every ablebodied man desperately. Nevertheless he could not afford to let any of them think they could make their own laws merely because they happened to belong to the elect of Islam.

All generals who have been great have followed this principle.

Hannibal, Julius Caesar, Napoleon, Wellington made examples of officers and men who committed the smallest breaches of discipline in time of war. The same standards were maintained throughout the Moslems' victorious campaigns. It was a great deal due to this that they were so successful.

At this critical time Mohammed lived up to this maxim. When, by a justifiable mistake, one of his men killed two friends of Islam, full blood money was immediately paid.

By these gestures Mohammed indicated that, whatever anybody else might feel about the affair at Ohod, he still considered himself to be the Messenger of Allah. He was carrying out orders from above. A reverse, more or less, was not going to change his program. While most of the Medinese accepted this, many of the neighboring tribes thought it a good opportunity to shake this man's self-made position.

The inhabitants of Adhal and Kara, two towns not far from Medina, sent an embassy asking for missionaries. Unsuspectingly Mohammed sent them unescorted. On the way they were attacked by their potential hosts. Those who were not killed were made prisoners. When they refused to recant, they were delivered to Mecca, where the Koreishites put them to death.

In the same month a similar act of treachery took place. Another tribal chief expressed a desire to have the doctrines of Islam explained to his people. This time Mohammed sent a larger and all-armed party. However, it was ambushed by a different tribe from that to which it was bound, and massacred. Only one man escaped to bring the news to Medina.

Mohammed was mortified and angry. These people who could not see as he did tried his patience. Standing in the mosque, he relieved his exasperation by denouncing the murderers with curses.

"O Lord, in thine indignation, trample under foot the Beni Rial; the Beni Dhakwan, the Beni Lihyan!" he cried. "Make their years like unto the seven bad years of Joseph, for they have rebelled against God and against His Messenger."

This he repeated five times a day for a month. Then he went

out onto the desert with his men to show that he could hit as well as shout. The tribesmen did not relish this and rarely met him in an open fight. In fact they usually retreated so hastily that they had to leave their animals behind. These Mohammed took possession of and drove back to Medina, once more proving his theory that offensive action pays even when it is unwarranted.

However, he had other antagonists besides the Koreishites and the bedouins. The Jews had thought the reverse at Ohod an opportune moment to come into the open again and defy Mohammed's claims to control Medina. Mohammed went after them as quickly and as energetically as he had after the desert nomads.

Of the two Hebrew tribes remaining in the Medina area, the Beni an Nadir were the most outspoken. Mohammed even suspected them of plotting his death. He did not investigate, he did not parley. He sent an emissary with the following extremely unambiguous order:

"Thus saith the Messenger of the Lord. Ye shall go forth of my land within the space of ten days. Whomsoever after that remaineth behind shall be put to death."

The Jews were startled and indignant. Such an ultimatum had never been given them in the hundreds of years they had lived in those parts. They did not know what to do. Then that hypocritical troublemaker, Abdallah ibn Obei, appeared on the scene. He told the Jews to stay where they were. If Mohammed wanted to put them out, he must put them out! He implied that if Mohammed attempted to carry out his threat, he would stand by them. The Jews, encouraged, defied Mohammed. This was all he needed. Within a few hours of his ultimatum being rejected, he was outside the stronghold which the Beni an Nadir had established on the outskirts of Medina. With him came his soldiers. In their midst strode Ali carrying the now battle-scarred banner of Islam.

The Jews defended themselves well and warded off the first Moslem attacks. However, they were not supplied for a long siege and, unless Abdallah came to their rescue, they would be starved out. This is exactly what happened.

All that Abdallah wanted was trouble for Mohammed. Once he had stirred that up, he stayed at home. Neither did the Beni Koreiza, the other Jewish tribe of Medina, see fit to intervene. Consequently when Mohammed cut down all their date palms and ravaged their gardens, the Beni an Nadir capitulated.

Once more a Jewish emigration took place. It was an orderly emigration, and whereas many of the exiles went as far as Jericho, many attached themselves to another Hebrew community at Khaibar, not more than a hundred miles from Medina. This, they were soon to discover, was a mistake.

Mohammed had now a determined policy toward the Jews. If they would not keep the peace and recognize his authority, he did not want any of them anywhere near. He could not afford to have enemies at his back door. With every Jewish tribe which left Medina, he felt safer. Khaibar was not yet on his schedule, neither were the Beni Koreiza. But they would be.

And while he carried out these local house cleanings, he did not forget Abu Sofian's challenge for a return battle at Badr on the anniversary of Ohod. Mohammed kept the appointment. Abu Sofian did not.

There had been a drought that season, and the Meccans were in a bad way. Abu Sofian was not in a position to lead and feed an army far from its base. He, however, spread a rumor that he was mobilizing a formidable force. He went as far as demonstrating outside the walls of Mecca with twenty-five hundred men, but he did not venture more than a few miles into the desert. He hoped that, with the recollection of Ohod still fresh, this would keep the Moslems behind their walls.

The bluff nearly succeeded. The Moslems were not in a mood to be foolhardy again. But Mohammed sneered at such cowardice. He still believed in covering weakness by force. Without arguing over it, he ordered every able-bodied man on parade. Fifteen hundred, more or less armed Arabs, turned out.

It was the biggest force which the Moslems had ever mustered, five times as big as at the first battle, twice as big as at the second. Mohammed felt satisfied. Mounting his camel, he led his army out of Medina and marched on Badr. A fair was in progress, and the Moslems, finding no one to fight, did some profitable trading.

After remaining at Badr for a week with no sign of Abu Sofian, Mohammed and his men marched back to Medina. Their morale was almost as high as after their great victory. Neither did they forget to tell of how the Koreishites had failed to keep the appointment for the return match.

The Koreishites were mortified. They did a good deal of shouting, but they confined their activities to promising another Ohod soon. This did not worry Mohammed. Every day brought him new converts, every day made him surer of himself and of his followers. He began to establish reforms and institute laws which he had had in his mind for some time.

One of the things the reorganization of which was imperative was his cavalry. This going into battle with two horses was not only ignominious, but it put the Moslem armies at a great disadvantage. Mohammed accordingly created breeding centers and even forbade the raising of mules so that he could have more horses. From this nucleus was built those famous Saracen mounted units, those lightly armed, quickly moving squadrons which were to play havoc with the Roman and Greek phalanxes and become a menace to the heavily accoutered Knights Templar.

With other improvements in the military field attended to, Mohammed turned to civil affairs. As the cavalry defect had come out through practical experience, so did other matters connected with the bringing into being of this new state. Of these, one was the law of inheritance.

One of the Moslem warriors killed at Ohod was Saad ibn ar Rabi. He had left a widow and two daughters, but, according to the customs of the times, his brother inherited everything. The widow had no redress, and no one thought her case peculiar or unjust. She knew, however, how Mohammed felt about men who had died for Islam, so she scraped together a little money and prepared a dinner to which the Messenger was invited. When the fresh dates had been served and the guests had relaxed on their carpets, she told the guest of honor of her plight. Mohammed was immediately interested. He asked the woman to call on him again and he would give her a ruling.

Later he had a revelation by which he was authorized to instruct the brother in question to restore two thirds of what Saad had left to the daughters and one eighth to the widow. From that basis were developed detailed laws of inheritance which precluded anyone's bequeathing an entire property to one heir or leaving any member of a family destitute. All this is set out in the fourth sura of the Koran and has been observed by Moslems ever since.

Mohammed turned his attention also to the problem of slavery. He could not abolish it altogether any more than he could polygamy, but he eased the laws and encouraged the emancipation of slaves. What he did order was the freeing of all those who embraced Islam. He added to that order a clause that there should be no stigma attached to an emancipated slave. In fact in Islam, then and now, a liberated slave has the same opportunities as a man or a woman born free. For those who remained in bondage he laid down special recommendations. He counseled:

"See that ye feed them with such food as ye eat yourselves, and clothe them with the stuff ye yourselves wear, for they are the servants of the Lord and are not to be tormented."

And again:

"Shall I tell you the very worst among you? Those who eat alone, and whip slaves, and give to nobody."

Mohammed had never been a drinker. Even at the wedding party, when he had married Khadija, he had touched nothing alcoholic. There was, however, no question of "prohibition" among the Arabs, Moslem or non-Moslem. Shortly after Badr, Mohammed had had trouble with Hamza, who had taken too much palm liquor. At Ohod some of the soldiers had been drunk.

Still, in the Koran, the question was left open. The two hundredth and sixteenth verse of the second sura reads:

"They will ask thee concerning wine and casting of lots. Say, In both there is great evil and also advantages to mankind, but the evil of them is greater than the advantages of them."

However, when, later, Mohammed discovered that the Arabs were not sufficient masters of their emotions to follow a middle course, when he had repeated cases of the prayer ritual being wrongly carried out because of drunkenness, he issued definite orders. A divine revelation caused him to have written as the ninety-third verse of the fifth sura of the Koran, the following:

"O ye that believe! Verily wine and the casting of lots are an abomination from amongst the works of Satan. Shun them, therefore, that ye may prosper. Verily Satan seeketh that he may cast amongst you enmity and hatred through wine and games of chance."

Today the percentage of Moslems living in Moslem countries who drink wines or spirits is very small. Even those who take anything alcoholic when they travel abroad give it up when they return home.

It was at this time also that Mohammed instituted a mild form of veiling of women. The seclusion of married and marriageable females had been a custom in the Orient for a long time. It had also been practiced in Greece. But, while Jewish women went veiled, Arab women did not. That Mohammed instituted veiling, or copied it, was primarily for personal reasons.

He was beginning to get on in years. Most of his wives were less than half his age. They were attractive, good-looking, warm-blooded girls with the instincts peculiar to normally developed females. Male visitors were continually dropping by to visit Mohammed. Some of these came with petitions, others with legal or religious problems, a great many merely to pay their respects to the Master. There were quite a number, however, who made their calls with little other purpose than to have a look at the Messenger's young ladies. None of this escaped Mohammed, but it was difficult to keep such visitors away from his quarters without some definite instructions. He accordingly turned, as he always did in moments of emergency, to his God and received a revelation, which is recorded in the sixth verse of the fifth sura of the Koran, as follows:

"*O ye believers! Enter not the apartment of the Prophet, except ye be called to sup with him, without waiting his convenient time. When ye are bidden, then enter, and when ye have eaten then disperse. And stay not for familiar converse . . . and when ye ask anything of the Prophet's wives, ask it from behind a curtain.*"

A curtain, therefore, was the first restriction, the first barrier between men and women. Later on Mohammed decided that all women, when they went outside their houses, should expose as little of themselves as possible. So in the thirty-third sura we have:

"*O Prophet! Speak unto thy wives and thy daughters, the wives of the believers, that they throw around them part of their mantles. This will be more seemly that they may be honored as women of reputation.*"

The mantle eventually became the shroudlike covering in which Moslem women wrap themselves when they go abroad. But this was long after the primitive days of Islam, and the hermetic seclusion of the harem is comparatively recent and was never originally Arab.

The only women who never complied with these particular instructions of the Messenger were the nomad ladies. Then, as now, these never veiled themselves. Nevertheless it is very rare that one meets a nomad woman face to face. They have an extraordinary ability to slide out of the range of vision of any man not intimately related, or to "throw around them part of their mantles."

However, Mohammed's wives were not nomads. They were city girls with all the joy of living of others of their kind and age. Their numbers too were increasing.

Mohammed's marriage to Hafsa was quickly followed by another which was more of a formality than anything else. The bride was a widow of Obeida ibn al Harith, Mohammed's cousin who had fallen at Badr. Her name was Zeinab bint Khuzaima. She was a worthy, middle-aged person given to good works whom Mohammed took into his harem more from kindness than anything else. She never bothered Aisha or Hafsa and, eight months after her marriage, died.

The next marriage was a very different kind of alliance and caused the two younger girls in the harem much concern. The new wife was beautiful, she was proud, she was nobly born. Her husband, Abu Salama, had taken a prominent part at Ohod, where he had been wounded. Umm Salama, as she was called, nursed her husband devotedly after the battle, but he died. Mohammed was attached to this man and was troubled by his death. So was his wife, who loved her husband and had sworn that she would never remarry. On his deathbed, however, Abu Salama told her that she must not consider keeping such a vow.

For such a fine woman, there was no lack of suitors. At an appropriate time after the funeral, Abu Bakr and then Omar offered to make a home for Umm Salama. But she refused. Mohammed let a little more time pass and then proposed himself. Again Umm Salama refused. She had numbers of excuses for setting aside this honor. She was too old, she had children, she was jealous and did not like the harem life.

Mohammed countered the first objection by pointing out that he was himself much older than Umm Salama. As to the children, he said he would be only too glad to father them. As for the jealousy, he assured her that, with the aid of prayer and Allah, this would be quieted. "For," said he, "jealousy eats up virtue like fire burns up fuel." After a great deal of persuading and courting, Umm Salama gave in. The marriage took place in March of 626, one month after that to the homely Zeinab bint Khuzaima.

Aisha and Hafsa reacted badly to the marriage. They received the new wife with the required show of courtesy, but made it evident that they could be just as happy without her. Aisha admitted to Hafsa that she was exceedingly piqued. She had heard of Umm Salama's loveliness and found, to her dismay, that she was even more lovely than people said. Hafsa comforted her friend by saying that, while Umm Salama obviously had looks, she was also obviously old. At that age, beauty faded quickly. She advised Aisha to keep her jealousy for someone worthier.

Umm Salama was delighted to see the effect which her entry into the harem was having on the favorite, and did nothing to offset it. The situation soon resolved itself into an undeclared war between the two women. This war, moreover, which began as a domestic issue, developed into a political rift, the traces of which exist today in the Moslem world. It happened this way:

With Aisha and Hafsa being formally but definitely hostile, Umm Salama fell back for female companionship on Fatima, Mohammed's daughter and Ali's wife. Neither Aisha nor Hafsa had anything in common with Fatima, who was plain and self-effacing and above the average intelligence of Arab women. She was younger than Umm Salama, but had much greater feelings of affinity for her than for the rest of the family. Thus, with two wives on one side and a wife and a daughter on the other vying for the favors of a man, the seeds were planted for a relentless dynastic rivalry.

Although neither Aisha nor Hafsa appreciated it, they represented the appointed or elected caliphs of Islam—Aisha's father, Abu Bakr, would be the first caliph; Omar, Hafsa's father, would be the second.

Fatima represented the legitimate or hereditary caliphate. Ali became the fourth caliph, and his sons were the only male descendants of Mohammed. Umm Salama and other wives, who were primarily drawn into this anti-Aisha female faction for personal reasons, would thus be the precursors of what, one day, would be known as the Fatimides and Shias. The Fatimides being a dynasty, the Shias a religious sect which held that the spiritual heritage bequeathed by Mohammed devolved on Ali and his heirs.

Those who sided with Aisha became the predecessors of the Ommeyades and Sunnis—the Ommeyades being likewise a dynasty, the Sunnis a religious group which declared that the caliphate was not restricted to the family of Mohammed.

For the time being there was nothing more than plain jealousy on the part of Aisha and spite on the part of Umm Salama. To be able to upset the daughters of the powerful Abu Bakr and Omar, as well as having the Messenger make up to her, was most satisfactory. The only thing on which she had not counted was the wandering eye of her husband.

The next lady to catch Mohammed's fancy caused an even greater shock to the harem than had Umm Salama. In fact she was a shock to everyone and became the object of criticism and the subject of gossip for people outside the family circle. Her name was Zeinab, but was in no way connected with the other Zeinab who was now on her deathbed.

This Zeinab was a granddaughter of Abd al Mottaleb and a first cousin, on her mother's side, of Mohammed. She had immigrated to Medina a little before Mohammed but, for some reason, had never married, in spite of being nearly thirty. Soon after the Hijra, Mohammed had betrothed her and wedded her to his friend and freed slave, Zaid ibn Haritha. Zaid was plain. He was short and flat-nosed. He was uncultured. Outside his devotion to Islam and his master and his great personal courage, he had little to offer a lovely and aristocratic creature like Zeinab. Zeinab went through with the marriage because Mohammed insisted, but she never took any interest in Zaid. Zaid himself was no lady's man and never discovered how to handle his spoiled wife.

One day Mohammed went to visit Zaid. As no one answered his knocks and calls, he entered Zaid's house. Here he came upon the lovely Zeinab, who was half undressed. This exquisite spectacle caused him such emotion that he exclaimed:

"Praised be to Allah who transforms the heart!"

With that, he hurried away in confusion.

Zeinab had seen the look in Mohammed's eyes. She had heard

what he had said and noted the way he had said it. She appreciated what it might lead to. Accordingly, as soon as her husband returned, she told him what had happened. She left out no details and added a few of her own. As she had anticipated, the first thing which Zaid thought of was his beloved master. He went straight to Mohammed and offered to divorce his wife. Zaid's self-sacrificing proposal touched Mohammed, but he told Zaid to go back to Zeinab and think no more about it.

Zeinab, however, had other ideas. She knew what Mohammed felt about women. She was fairly sure what he felt about her. She was also more than tired of Zaid. She wanted to live as her birth had intended. So she began to make Zaid's life such a misery that, in order to escape this organized persecution, he *had* to divorce her.

Mohammed allowed the recognized period between divorce and remarriage to pass, and took Zeinab into his harem. Then the trouble began.

The two young ladies were its instigators. Denying that jealousy had anything to do with it, they passed it around that this was an incestuous union. Zaid was Mohammed's son, and marrying his wife was against all the conventions of the world. It was a scandal, a disgrace! Such a thing could not be tolerated!

Zaid, of course, was not Mohammed's son. He had been adopted and made Mohammed's heir at the same time as he had been emancipated from slavery, but he was no blood relation. Nevertheless he was referred to as his son, and many Moslems were unaware how he had become so. When, therefore, Aisha and Hafsa raised their voices in outraged protest, so did the mosque congregation. Mohammed was in a quandary. Then, quickly, he had a revelation. The revelation left no doubt as to the difference between an adopted son and one begotten. It further stated that the widow or divorced wife of an adopted son did not come within the forbidden degrees for marriage.

The young ladies were disgruntled. Aisha snapped at her husband:

"The Lord makes haste to do your pleasure!"

But that altered nothing. Zeinab was delighted. She told everyone that Allah had deigned to interfere on her behalf. He had probably arranged the marriage Himself. Aisha laughed, so did Hafsa, but they were seriously put out.

To Occidentals, especially to those who give Mohammed credit for nothing good, this marriage to Zeinab enables them to exclaim:

"I told you so! What else could you expect from this arch-deceiver?"

These men, however, approach the matter from the wrong angle. They will not transpose themselves into the society of that time or even into the society of Orientals. To Arabs today, to great men like Ibn Saud, to rulers like the Sultan of Morocco, the story of Zeinab is one which they could probably repeat a dozen times in their own lives of this mid-twentieth century. Had not Aisha put the dots on the i's, it is possible that no one would have said anything in Medina in 626.

In those days, as it is to a certain extent now, sex was almost an obsession among Arabs. It was not a banned topic as it is among so many Western people. It was regarded as a pleasurable and ecstatic and inspiring function. A normal one too.

That Occidentals have this strange hypocrisy about sex, puzzles Arabs. They are aware that the men and women of the European and American continents are in no way fundamentally different from themselves. They have the same sensations, yet they regard all matters connected with the mutual physical emotions of males and females as vices like secret drinking. Thus, to many biographers, Mohammed and Zeinab, Mohammed and Aisha, Mohammed and Juwairiya bint al Harith—an unransomed captive from a raid, who succeeded Zeinab as Mohammed's eighth wife—seemed abnormal. Yet they are not any more abnormal than the marriage habits of other rulers in that part of the world, of David and of Solomon. Mohammed never approached having a harem as large as Solomon's, and the story of Zeinab is infinitely more modest than that of Bathsheba or of

Ahinoam, Abigail's bridesmaid to whom David took a fancy on his wedding day.

Mohammed's married life must not be looked at from an occidental point of view or from that set by Christian conventions. These men and women were not Occidentals and they were not Christians. They were living at a period and in a country where the only known ethical standards were theirs. Even so, there is no reason why the codes of America and Europe should be considered superior to those of the Arabs. The people of the West have many things to give the people of the East. They have much to glean, too, and until they can prove that their way of living is on a higher moral standard than anybody else's, they should reserve judgment on other creeds and castes and countries.

CHAPTER XIV

THE SIEGE OF MEDINA
(627 *After Christ*)

MOHAMMED'S BACKGROUND in Medina is crowded with women. Yet they had no influence on his official or spiritual life. For although Aisha plagued him, delighted him, relaxed him, she had no say in the policies of his administration or the formulating of the new faith. Neither did this epidemic of marriages in 626 and 627 cause Mohammed to become obsessed by thoughts of women or make him soft. The moment he was needed he was there to lead, to organize, to encourage.

In 627 word came that the Meccans were ready to fight again. They had missed the tryst at Badr, but that did not mean that they had forgotten their quarrel with Mohammed. During the previous winter Abu Sofian had been gathering a great force, strong enough to insure victory. He had allied himself with the powerful Ghatafan Arabs, a warlike tribe of great importance in the Arabian desert. He had also found supporters among those of the Beni an Nadir who had settled in the Khaibar oases. These, in turn, had brought other Hebrews to help rid the country of this pestilential reformer and Jew baiter. Several nomad groups which had been raided by the Moslems had also joined the Koreishite standard. When Abu Sofian mustered his troops outside Mecca, he found that they numbered ten thousand. Almost every man had his individual camel, three hundred were on horses, there were few who did not wear armor. As he rode down the glittering lines, he felt proud and confident. It looked as if the annihilation of the Moslems were merely a question of meeting them in battle. This is precisely what Mohammed avoided doing.

THE SIEGE OF MEDINA

His army had grown to three thousand soldiers, but they were none too well armed, and his cavalry was untrained and did not exceed fifty. Fifty men on horses was a vast improvement on two, but it was not enough. There were still insufficient camels to transport all the troops. Added to these disadvantages, there was Abdallah ibn Obei ready to stab the Moslems in the back if things went badly for them, to say nothing of the doubtful question of whether the Jews who had remained in Medina would keep their side of their pact with Mohammed. There was also the morale of the men who subconsciously remembered the trouncing they had had at Ohod. From all points of view it would be silly to go out and challenge such a vastly superior and better-armed force. The alternative was to defend Medina. That was not a simple affair either.

For a considerable distance the city's outer fringe of houses was built so compactly that it formed an impregnable rampart. The northern approaches were guarded by a wall of steep cliffs. The Beni Koreiza, this last Hebrew tribe to stay in Medina, protected what would be Mohammed's rear. They occupied a fortified stronghold which would have to be reduced before an enemy could pass. Would they defend it? Mohammed did not know, but he had to presume so and let them think he counted on them. The immediate problem, therefore, was the unprotected south and southeast side of the city, the side where the streets ran into the gardens of the oasis. This part of Medina could be forced by an energetic attack and nullify the other defenses.

It was a Persian called Selman who brought the solution to this knotty point which was baffling the Arabs. Selman had been a Christian slave, originally brought to Medina by a Jew. His adoption of Islam had freed him from serfdom and made him a devoted supporter of Mohammed. Thus, when opportunity came when he could show his gratitude for what Islam had done for him, he did not hesitate to come forward with a plan. In his own country and in Mesopotamia, he had had experience of siege warfare. It was simple for him, therefore, to suggest that a deep and broad moat be dug along the exposed side of the city.

This seems a simple enough notion and one which anyone might have conceived, but it was new to the Arabs, who always fought hand to hand—in fact so unusual a method of waging war was it that the first reaction from Mohammed's lieutenants was that it was cowardly. But Mohammed was too hard pressed to consider the ethics of the defending of his city. He had to defend it in the most effective way, and, this seeming to be the only one which, under the circumstances, made sense, he adopted it.

There was, however, not much time. The Koreishites were on the march, and while the size of their army hampered their speed, the defenses of Medina must be ready in a matter of a few days. Neither were there any tools available, or engineers, or even workmen who had ever undertaken a task of this kind. The only one who knew anything about trench digging was Selman. He rose to the occasion.

Aided by Mohammed, the work began. While Selman instructed and advised and corrected, Mohammed flung himself with enthusiasm into the digging and picking and excavating. Stripped to the waist, his hair flowing over his shoulders, his beard sweeping his chest, he encouraged his men with words and songs as well as personal example. Gradually a deep moat, too broad for a horse to leap across, stretched itself before the vulnerable approach to Medina. When the first scouts of Abu Sofian's army appeared on the neighboring hills, the trench was ready.

Mohammed and his officers armed themselves and led the three thousand Moslem soldiers to their positions behind the moat. In case of emergencies the newly formed squadron of cavalry was placed in the center as a reserve. Long before the enemy debouched onto the plain of Medina, the defenders waited the attack.

The Koreishites had no more heard of this method of defending a city than had the Moslems a week before. They accordingly advanced in a body expecting to overwhelm the Medinese army, which they could see was much inferior to theirs. Their astonishment was great when they found themselves held up by this moat, from behind which Mohammed's archers fired at them point-blank. Retreating quickly, they established themselves at a safe distance from the arrows.

For a few days the two armies remained watching each other. The Koreishites did a lot of taunting and insulting the Moslems for waging war in this unsporting fashion. The Moslems replied by flights of arrows and showers of stones, but no actual blows were exchanged.

Abu Sofian, who had hoped to defeat Mohammed in one day and be back in Mecca within ten, became impatient. He had promised his allies easy loot—quickly. He knew that this kind of stalemate was being blamed on him. He could already sense discouragement and discontentment. Once this set in, that part of the army which had come with him for what it could get would go back to its pastures and forget about the quarrel with Mohammed.

As the moat was clearly impregnable, some other line of attack had to be considered. Mohammed's weakest point was the Jewish stronghold in his rear. If the Beni Koreiza could be persuaded to join the Koreishites, the moat would lose its value.

The Jews were not at first inclined to listen to Abu Sofian's proposal, but after a while they compromised and agreed to betray the Moslems when the time seemed opportune. This news did not take long to reach Mohammed. He realized at once in what a desperate position such an act of treachery would place him and his army. Summoning his staff, he told them how matters stood. As no one had any practical suggestions to make, Mohammed went on speaking.

In the Meccan army the Ghatafanites were the most important allies, he said. It might be worth while, therefore, to try and bribe them away from Abu Sofian by giving them one third of the Medina date harvest. The plan was received in silence. It was the first time that Mohammed had not offered a definitely aggressive means of dealing with a situation. Saad ibn Muad, the chief of the Ausite tribe of Medina, was the first to speak:

"Do you propose this by command of Allah, or is it an idea of your own?" he asked.

"If it had been a command of Allah, I would not have asked your advice," replied Mohammed, who knew his plan was poor. "However, we are in a dangerous plight, and this seems to be a way out."

Saad shook his head:

"O Messenger of Allah!" he exclaimed. "When we were fellow idolators with the Ghatafanites, they got none of our dates without paying for them, so shall we give them up gratuitously now that we are of the true faith and led by you? No, by Allah! If they want our dates they must win them with their swords."

No one contradicted Saad, and the plan was dropped. Saad pointed out that the treachery of the Beni Koreiza was only a report. He and his tribe had been in partnership with these Jews for many years without having had any trouble. Before doing anything else, he thought it might be a good idea to find out what the Beni Koreiza had in mind. He bowed himself out of the council of war and rode over to see his allies. Calling on their leaders informally and friendlily, he told them why he had come. Their response confirmed all that Mohammed had feared. Without giving Saad a direct reply to his question, they left no doubt as to how they felt about their pledge. They said:

"Who is Mohammed? And who is the apostle of God that we should obey him? There is no bond or compact between us and him."

Saad returned to Mohammed's headquarters wondering whether his ridiculing the proposal to bribe the Ghatafanites had been so clever. What the Jews had said was as untrue as it was treasonable, but that did not make it any better for the Moslems. However, he had little time to think about this, for he found the battle line flaring with excitement.

While waiting for the Beni Koreiza to make up their minds to deliver the city to him, Abu Sofian had ordered a general assault on the moat. Three Koreishite warriors, Ikrima, the son of Abu Jahl, Amr', an uncle of Khadija, and Naufal, who had been the leader of the famous caravan which Ibn Jahsh had attacked during the sacred month before Badr, had managed to jump their horses over a narrow part of the moat. They had been followed by a few others. It was a tense moment for Mohammed and his men and might have led to defeat. But, before panic could spread, Ali and a group of swordsmen cut off the invaders, who thus found themselves trapped. Mohammed simultaneously rushed reinforcements to the danger point. There was a slight lull on both sides, broken by Amr' and his companions demanding the right to settle things by single combat.

Ali immediately sprang forward and faced Amr'. When the old warrior saw who it was, he laughed. He had known Ali since he was a baby and still considered him a child. But Ali was not afraid and flung himself at the Meccan, who had dismounted and waited, gorgeous in his armor, his white beard sweeping his cuirass. In spite of his advanced years, he had remained a redoubtable swordsman. This it did not take Ali long to realize, for strike as he might, agile and quick as he was, he never got anywhere near Amr'. It looked as if he might be defeated. Soon he was being pressed back, parrying the blows which came with the rapidity of shafts of light. It looked like the end of the Lion of Arabia. But at the critical moment when Ali was literally doing no more than protect his skin, Amr' thought he sensed an attack from the rear. He turned his head. It was only for a second, but enough for Ali. Darting forward, he came in low and, with a sweeping slash of his scimitar, he cut off Amr's leg. The venerable Koreishite stood for a moment, tottering on one foot, denouncing Ali and his family. Then, picking up the severed limb, flung it at Ali with all his force. It was his last gesture. Ali was nearly stunned, but in a moment he had recovered and plunged his sword into Amr'.

In the meanwhile other duels had been taking place. Saad ibn Muad had been wounded, and Naufal, in trying to retreat, had fallen into the moat. Az Zubeir, another of Khadija's nephews, had jumped in after him and cut off his head. Ikrima had managed to get back to his side of the trench with a javelin wound. Some of the others had been killed, some had escaped. On the whole, therefore, this only hand-to-hand encounter of the battle for Medina had been a Moslem victory.

Nevertheless this did not discourage Abu Sofian. If the moat had been crossed by a few, it might be crossed by many. From then on, therefore, day and night, he kept up a continuous attack against the Moslem lines. Sometimes a cloud of cavalry would sweep down on the narrow section of the trench. Sometimes archers would creep up to another section under cover of darkness and discharge their arrows into the enemy, then slip away before retaliation was possible. Somewhere along the line, something was going on ceaselessly. There was not even time for the defenders to pray. This troubled Mohammed, and whenever he had the chance he collected as many men as he could and offered up prayers behind the lines. Even so the ritual had to be hurried and carried out on the alert. Soon the nervous strain began to tell. The army started to show signs of wear. It looked as if all the Meccan allies need do would be to keep up these harassing tactics until the Moslems were too tired to fight. For the leaders there was also the added worry of the menace of the Jews coming from the rear. So far the Beni Koreiza had not moved. They were waiting for a suitable moment when they could join in the battle without much risk to themselves. It was this caution which saved Mohammed.

Owing to the fact that on both sides of the moat were men who originated from the same districts, that neither side had a distinctive uniform, that everyone spoke the same language, it was not difficult for spies to move around without creating suspicion. Of this Mohammed decided to make use. Without consulting his staff, he sent men to work up distrust between the Beni Koreiza and the soldiers of Abu Sofian. The method of carrying this out was as simple as it was effective.

The Beni Koreiza were warned that they had better make sure that Abu Sofian intended to give them a fair deal. If they were not careful, they might find themselves fighting the Moslems alone while the Meccans looked on. It would be wise, said the spy, to demand hostages of Abu Sofian before doing anything irrevocable.

Abu Sofian and his generals were likewise advised that the Beni Koreiza had no intention of betraying Mohammed. If ordered to move against the Moslems, they would find some means of getting out of it and would be sure to demand hostages. Having planted the seeds of suspicion, the spies returned to the Moslem camp to watch them sprout.

Everything played into Mohammed's hands. Abu Sofian decided to make his big attack on what happened to be the Jewish sabbath. When, therefore, he sent a request to the Beni Koreiza to support him, he received the reply that on that particular day fighting was out of the question for the Jews. To the message was added a suggestion that before the Beni Koreiza turned on their former ally, they would like a few Meccan hostages.

The effect of this ultimatum on Abu Sofian was like a shower of cold water. He called off the assault. He took precautions to protect his own rear and flanks from any treacherous attack by the Jews. He made it clear to his men that it would take longer than he had anticipated to reduce Medina to surrender. The discouragement shifted from the Moslem side of the moat to the Koreishite.

To add to the Meccan troubles, the weather turned against them. The desert in winter can be extremely cold. This is especially the case of places high above sea level like Medina. During January and February the pastures die and the nomads move away to warmer parts of Arabia. The immigrants from Mecca had found it difficult to acclimatize themselves, with houses and the hospitality of their hosts. The Meccans, camped out on the plain, began to suffer from the climate. They caught colds, their animals died, there was nothing happening which gave them hope of acquiring the promised loot. Then it began to rain.

It was a heavy, cold rain. It was the kind of rain which does miracles for the pastures and creates misery for human beings and animals who have to live under it even for the short time that it lasts. The rain was accompanied by an icy wind which blew harder every day. Soon it was of gale force. It whistled through the scrub and screamed among the tall date palms, bending their stems as if they were bamboos. The Koreishites pegged down their tents and sat huddled inside. Their fires had been extinguished by the wet, their food was sodden, the bitter air chilled them through. It was a physical condition which no Arab can stand for long, and when a wild blast ripped up a tent and sent it flying, causing the animals to stampede, the army of Abu Sofian forgot its proud mission and vanished into the darkness of the desert.

The storm went with them, for when the morning came the sun poured its rays over oasis and plain from a clear blue sky. The Moslems breathed in the warm, scented air with relief, and their relief turned to amazement and then to excitement as they looked across the moat. Of the thousands who had attacked them with their camels and their horses, their asses and their mules, nothing was left except a few flattened tents and a number of dead animals. Once more it seemed as if a miracle had saved the Moslem cause.

In a moment the call to prayer rose above the excited exclamations. Turning toward Mecca, the army spoke with one voice: *"Allahu Akbar!"*

The hands of every man which had been raised in line with their ears were lowered and folded before them. Following their Commander in Chief, their Prophet, they intoned the morning prayer:

"Glory to Thee, O Allah, and thine is the praise, and blessed is thy name, and exalted is thy majesty, and there is none to be served besides thee."

Through the rhythmic motions they went, their voices rising and falling until, with the final, *"Peace be unto you and the mercy of Allah,"* the prayer ended. Then, slowly, the men stood up and, picking up their weapons, moved off in the direction of their homes.

Hardly, however, had they begun to disarm when Bilal's voice was heard resounding through the feathery palms which bowed to the lilt of the breeze. And it was not the usual call. It was a call to fall in on parade. For a moment the soldiers thought that Abu Sofian had played a trick on them. Seizing their swords and lances, they hurried to the mosque.

Here they found Mohammed and his generals still in their armor. Beside them Ali, also fully equipped, carried the battle flag of Islam. The horses were there, too, with their troopers. As soon as the officers reported their companies present, Mohammed gave the order to march. Riding at the head of the army, he led the way, not back to the moat, but to the stronghold of the Beni Koreiza.

The moment the Jews saw the Moslems, they knew why they had come. Hastily they shut themselves in behind their gates. Another siege began. As in the previous cases, these Hebrews appeared to have no reserve supplies in their forts. Before long they began to starve. After a while a deputation waited on Mohammed to hear his terms.

After pointing out that the Beni Koreiza had, to all intents and purposes, broken their pact with him and betrayed him to the enemy, that this was a case not only of treachery but of treason, Mohammed presented his terms. No reprisals, no recriminations, no penalties of any kind, provided the Jews recanted their faith and accepted Mohammed as their leader. This the Jews refused. The deputation retired behind the walls of the stronghold. The siege went on.

Finally the Jews had to give in or starve to death. They said they would accept any terms except Islam and begged that someone impartial should be appointed to arbitrate. They suggested that one of the chiefs of their old allies, the Beni Aus, would be a fair judge. Mohammed agreed and asked that someone specific should be designated. Without hesitation the Hebrews called for Saad ibn Muad.

Saad was not on parade. The wound he had received at the moat had become infected, and he was resting in his home. He was in great pain and unable to walk. However, when Mohammed's request to come and pronounce judgment was brought, he had himself lifted onto a donkey on which blankets and cushions had been laid. The jolting journey did not improve his temper or his spirits. By the time he reached the fortress of the Beni Koreiza, he was feeling as unfriendly as possible toward these people who, indirectly, were the cause of his wound.

It was evening, and the shadows of the date palms stretched out like long tufted serpents over the open space before the stronghold. A golden radiance covered the walls of the houses and glinted on the arms of the Moslem warriors who waited in disciplined ranks. A little in front of them stood Mohammed in breastplate and casque, his scimitar at his side. Slightly to the rear, Abu Bakr, Omar, Othman, and Ali. The other leaders a little behind them. Before them were piles of arms and carpets and household goods which the Jews had brought from their homes and laid before their conquerors. To the right and to the left were the Jews themselves. On one side, with their hands tied behind them, the men. On the other side, the women and children. The men did not speak. They knew that Mohammed was ruthless when offended. They had been guilty of treachery in wartime, and there was little hope of leniency. The only chance lay in Saad ibn Muad's remembering past associations. The women did not reason. They wept piteously for their husbands and brothers and sons and fathers from whom the Moslem swords separated them.

Saad ibn Muad was helped off the donkey and limped over to where Mohammed waited. He went through the formal greeting, and then looked at the Jews. The last time he had been to see them, they had rudely turned on him, demanding who was this apostle of God and why they should obey him. They had made a fool of him when he had vouched for their integrity. He waited a moment. Then he said:

"Will ye bind yourselves by the covenant of God that whatsoever I shall decide, ye will accept?"

The Jews bowed their heads and assented.

Saad paused again. Then, to the astonishment of the Moslems and the consternation of the Jews, he passed sentence:

"My judgment is that the men shall be put to death, the women and children sold into slavery, and the spoil divided among the army."

A murmur of incredulity rippled through the ranks of the Moslems, followed by a cry of terror from the Jews. They flung themselves on their knees, begging for mercy. They wailed and cried and tore their hair. But no one listened. A few sharp orders from Mohammed, and the women and children were dragged off in one direction and the men driven off in another. Saad was helped onto the donkey again and borne back to his home.

During the night the Moslem soldiers started digging again. This trench was not so deep or so long as the one before Medina, but it would witness more deaths. At sunrise the execution began. Mohammed, surrounded by his staff, sat where he could view the massacre. Ali and Az Zubeir directed the actual beheading. Six at a time, the Jews were driven out from the enclosure where they had passed the night. Kneeling before the trench, their heads were slashed off and their bodies pushed into the waiting grave. All day long the beheading continued until the air vapored with the stench of blood. As the sun dipped toward the west and the breeze came from the oasis, it continued. It did not stop when darkness fell. To the light of torches, the Moslem scimitars flashed and sent another Hebrew head rolling. Finally, when the last Jew had disappeared into the trench, Mohammed went back to his quarters. He took with him a beautiful Jewess called Reihana. All her male relatives had died that day of general execution. Mohammed suggested that she find comfort by marrying him. This she refused. She also refused to recant and embrace Islam. She eventually became the Messenger's slave and concubine. However, she did not live long. She probably never recovered from the massacre of the eight hundred. Aisha, who seems to have been present, said that what she saw that day haunted her ever after.

Retribution followed the author of this sentence. The donkey ride had been too much for Saad. His wound opened up again. Blood poisoning set in. About the time the last Jew died, Saad died himself. His last words testified his faith in Islam:

"Peace be on thee, O Apostle of God! Verily I testify that thou art the Messenger of Allah!"

This wholesale destruction of the Jews is naturally a matter of contention among those who believe in Mohammed and those who do not. All that can really be said is that when people become fanatical over religion, they become fanatical. They like to kill those who differ with them on matters of dogma. They usually kill cruelly and in mass.

Soon after Solomon's birth, around 1035 before Christ, David defeated the Ammonites and sacked the city of Rabbah. In the twelfth chapter of the second book of Samuel, we are told that:

"He (David) brought forth the people that were therein and put them under saws and under harrows of iron and under axes of iron and made them pass through brick kilns."

Saul, likewise, a few years earlier, for reasons that were more personal than religious, sent to Nob, the city of the priests and "smote with the edge of the sword, both men and women and sucklings."

As a matter of fact, if the Jews of Medina had given the matter a thought, they would have appreciated that Mohammed was doing nothing more nor less than carrying out the instructions laid down by their own people in the twentieth chapter of Deuteronomy:

When thou comest nigh unto a city to fight against it, then proclaim peace unto it. And it shall be, if it make thee answer of peace, and open unto thee, then it shall be, that all the people that is found therein shall be tributaries unto thee, and they shall serve thee. And if it will make no peace with thee, but will make war against thee, then thou shalt besiege it. And when the Lord thy God hath delivered it into thine hands, thou shalt smite every male thereof with the edge of the sword. But the women, and the little ones, and the cattle, and all that is in the city, even all the spoil thereof, shalt thou take unto thyself.

Mohammed was no more nor less ruthless than any other religious leaders in history who had to make their authority felt. And it must be remembered how imperative it was for him to let no doubts exist about this authority.

Mohammed stood alone in Arabia, a country equivalent in area to one third of the United States, populated by about five million people. His own dominion was not much larger than Central Park; his means of enforcing his wishes, three thousand badly armed soldiers. Had he been weak, had he allowed treachery to go unpunished, Islam would never have survived. This massacre of the Hebrews was drastic but not original in religious history. From a Moslem point of view, it was justified. From now on, the Arab tribes, as well as the Jewish, thought twice about defying this man who evidently intended to have his own way.

CHAPTER XV

THE AFFAIR OF AISHA'S NECKLACE
(627 *After Christ*)

CONTRARY TO GENERAL BELIEF, Arab women have a great deal to say in all matters pertaining to the home. Locked away in their harems or segregated in their tents, one might imagine that they would cease to be anything but conveniences for their men. It is possible that the men imagine this, but, as is usually the case where women are concerned, the men are wrong.

Arab women, without the feminine liberty of their occidental sisters, without opportunities to stir up jealousies, or run away, or even wear exciting clothes, control their husbands, get around them, and fool them in a way which is nothing less than sorcery. Arabs pay much more attention and are more considerate to the ladies of the veil than the majority of Occidentals, who should have more reason to watch their womenfolk.

Mohammed was no exception. He had a family instinct and showed the greatest regard for the wives who lived in the cottages round the mosque.

"Women are the twin halves of men," he used to declare. "A Moslem must not hate his wife. If he be displeased with one bad quality in her, then let him be pleased with another which is good."

Whether the wives in Medina did take advantage of Mohammed and fool him to any great extent has never been recorded, and only once suggested. That Aisha was the object of the one insinuation makes it open to doubt either way. That girl had more ideas in her head than a thousand monkeys, and an ability to get what she wanted which had the hallmark of witchcraft. She was also a minx. At the time of the incident in question, she was not appreciating Zeinab or Umm Salama, and, with that childish, spontaneous nature, she was capable of anything irresponsible. This is what happened:

When Mohammed made a journey or went on a raiding expedition, he always took one or two wives with him. They traveled in a kind of basketwork cradle, called a "haoudedj," over which an awning was stretched on a wicker frame, the whole thing being strapped to the camel's hump. The occupant of the cradle was completely hidden, and unless the awning was lifted it was impossible to tell whether there was someone inside or not.

Mohammed had completed that successful punitive campaign against the Beni Mustalik tribe, where he had acquired his eighth wife, Juwairah, and was on his way back to Medina with his soldiers and his camels and his loot. The last stage of the march home was a long one, and camp had been broken at dawn. As soon as she was roused, Aisha had gone to a fold in the ground to relieve the needs of nature. By the time she got back, her tent had been struck and her camel was waiting with its litter. As, however, she was about to step into it, she discovered that she had dropped her necklace. Without telling anyone, she ran back to look for it. In the semidarkness of early dawn, an agate necklace was difficult to see among the stones and scrub, and daylight had come before she found it. Clasping it about her throat, she returned to join the caravan. But there was no caravan. The only indications that anyone had been there were the remains of the campfires. The camel drivers in charge of Aisha's transportation had evidently taken it for granted that the young lady was in her litter and had placed it on the camel's back. Aisha was small and very light, so that no one would notice if she was inside or not. When the caravan moved, the men trekked away, leading an unloaded camel.

Aisha stood for a moment staring into the vast emptiness of the wilderness. The dawn had given way to the glow of morning, and the sun was already sending dazzling shafts of white light across the stony landscape. Nowhere could she see any signs of her people or her caravan. She shrugged her shoulders and sat down. It was no good getting into a panic. It was no good trying to catch up with the caravan. It was much better to stay in the last place where she had been seen and hope that her staff would have the sense to look for her when they found the litter was empty. As the day grew in warmth, she became drowsy. Pulling her mantle over her head, she curled up under an acacia. Soon she was asleep. When she awoke, the sun was high in the skies, and she was not alone.

Looking down at her from the back of a tall trotting dromedary was a youth of great beauty. Aisha rubbed her eyes. The young man smiled. Then he made his camel kneel and introduced himself as Safwan ibn al Moattel. According to Aisha's version of the story, she did not have to introduce herself. Safwan seemed to know her by sight, for he addressed her as Aisha bint Abi Bakr.

Safwan asked Aisha what she was doing sitting alone in the middle of the Arabian desert. Aisha explained. Safwan laughed. Then he offered his dromedary to take Aisha to Medina. Aisha was glad to accept. So Safwan helped her to mount, and they were off.

In the meanwhile the Moslem caravan had continued on its way without any idea that Aisha was not with it. Her disappearance was not discovered until the camel with the empty litter knelt before Mohammed's quarters. Then the excitement began.

The camel drivers, who were convinced that they had started from the camp with Aisha, attributed her vanishing to djinns. As there had been no halts during the march, this was accepted as the only plausible explanation. Mohammed, however, who disapproved of such superstitions, was organizing a search party when, through the narrow lanes of Medina, came a camel led by an extremely good-looking young man. On the back of the camel, lovely as the dawn, sat Aisha. The camel knelt before the entrance to her home. Aisha alighted and, with a smile for Safwan, went in as unself-consciously as if she were in the habit of traveling in the desert with strange youths.

Mohammed was so delighted at seeing his favorite safe that he welcomed her with hardly a question. As far as he was concerned, the incident was closed. And it might have been closed had not into the picture walked Abdallah ibn Obei.

None of my Arab friends ever told me what Abdallah looked like, and he is not described in any of the books which I have read, but he must have been an unpleasant character. Treacherous, mischief-making, discourteous, cowardly, he seems to have had the disposition of Mephistopheles and Iago and Uriah Heep and any other villainous characters in history or fiction. His life's pleasure seems to have been to distress Mohammed. The moment he heard of Aisha's singular arrival in Medina, he went to work to capitalize on it. Without any attempt to check the circumstances surrounding the incident, he immediately suggested that Safwan was Aisha's lover. He added that he did not blame Aisha. The only thing which surprised him was that this pretty girl of barely sixteen had been faithful so long to this old dodderer of nearly sixty. If everyone did not agree with him, then everyone was a hypocrite.

Only a few, however, endorsed Abdallah's gossip. Among these was Hemna, Zeinab bint Jahsh's sister. Zeinab, with her idea that Allah had personally supervised her union to Mohammed, felt that she should surplant Aisha's position as favorite. Up to that time she had failed to do so. This potential scandal seemed to offer her a chance. She did not want to do Aisha harm and, as it later turned out, did not believe the calumnies against her, but, with Abdallah supplying the foundation for rumors and Hemna ready to spread them, she let things slide. Thus, with chatter going on inside the harem and chatter going on outside, everyone in Medina soon had his version of the Aisha-Safwan affair, which did not lose in the telling. Moreover, as is usual in such cases, the husband was the last to know. When he did hear, he had no idea of what to do.

Mohammed loved Aisha. In conjunction with Khadija, but in a different way, he loved her more than any of the other women who were in his life. He could not bring himself to believe, therefore, that this little girl who had always been such a friend, as well as a mistress, could have deliberately deceived him. In fact, so perturbed was he by what he was being told that he could not bring himself to accuse Aisha directly. He accordingly avoided her.

Aisha, who also had great affection for Mohammed, noticed the avoidance but did not, at once, trace the cause. When she did, she was filled with indignation. In a flood of tears she swore her innocence and rushed to her parents' home. Her mother and her sister comforted her. They assured her that the penalty for loveliness was scandal-breeding by the jealous. If she waited without retaliation, everything would come out all right. Abu Bakr said nothing. Mohammed had not mentioned the affair to him, so he locked himself in his room and read the Koran. Neither did Mohammed consult Omar. He probably thought of his austere principles and was afraid he might advise divorce or other sanctions. However, he took the matter to Ali.

Ali was not a lady's man. He was a fighting Moslem who did not believe in all these women mixing themselves up in the life of his commander in chief. He also reflected the dislike of Fatima for her young stepmother. He replied, therefore, to Mohammed's petition for advice that all women were alike and the lady Aisha was no different from any others. This remark was brought back to Aisha. She never forgot it, and when, thirty years later, Ali's candidacy for the caliphate came up, she opposed it so violently that she raised bloody civil war among the Moslems of Arabia. In fact today the repercussions of this observation and the fury it aroused in Aisha are visible in certain Islamic schisms.

In the meanwhile Safwan was striding about Medina swearing that he had never taken the smallest interest in Aisha and had never seen her except on that one occasion in the desert. The chief object of his anger was Hassan ibn Thabit, the Moslem poet laureate to whom we are so much indebted for contemporary literature of this period. Hassan was a great personal friend of Mohammed, but he could not resist the temptation to write some stinging verses about the incident. It cost him a beating from Safwan, but it seemed worth it. In fact no one could resist the temptation to pull the story to pieces and weave it together again. It was taking a larger place in Medina than Islam's political controversies.

Finally Mohammed realized that he was the only one to blame. As long as he maintained his vacillating attitude, the scandal would continue. It was his duty to deliver judgment for or against Aisha. As in battle, he acted decisively.

At the next prayer meeting he added the following reproof to his sermon:

"O ye people, what concern is it of others that they should disquiet me in affairs touching my family, and unjustly blame them? Whereas, I myself know naught but that which is good concerning them. And, moreover, you have traduced Safwan, a man, likewise, regarding whom I know naught but what is good!"

Having said this, he went to Aisha. He found her with her parents. Sitting on the mat beside her, he began:

"Aisha, you have heard what men have spoken about you? Fear God, for indeed if you are guilty, then repent toward God, for the Lord accepts the repentance of His servants."

Aisha waited a moment to see if her parents would come to her defense. When they remained silent, she flared up and told Mohammed that she had nothing to confess about. He should know that better than anyone. She spoke violently and vehemently. Then she burst into tears.

Mohammed listened but did nothing to comfort his weeping wife. He stared at her searchingly. Then he began to sigh. Soon his eyes closed and he sank onto the mat. Abu Bakr covered him with his cloak. For a while he lay in a trance. Aisha stopped crying and watched the deeply breathing figure anxiously. Suddenly Mohammed flung the cloak from him and stood up. His eyes were alight with excitement.

"Aisha!" he cried. "Rejoice! Verily the Lord has declared your innocence."

With impulsive strides he walked out of the house. Standing

before the mosque, he announced a revelation. He proclaimed:

"They that slander married women, and, thereafter, do not bring forward four witnesses, scourge them with fourscore stripes, and you shall never again receive their testimony, for they are infamous."

For a few minutes he continued speaking, elaborating the code relative to suspected adultery. These codes eventually found their way in considerable detail into the fourth and fifth suras of the Koran.

When he had finished, he ordered that the punishment which he had just ordained should be inflicted on Hassan, Hemna, and a friend of Abu Bakr called Mistal who had helped to spread the gossip about Aisha. No one seemed to bear any ill will over this, and Hassan's devotion to Mohammed remained unchanged. Later he composed a poem praising Aisha's virtues.

Abdallah, who was really the cause of the whole trouble, was ignored. He was not a Moslem and, therefore, not subject to Koranic law. Besides Mohammed, in spite of his growing power, did not yet feel that he could quarrel openly with this mischievous individual. He never did get even with him. Abdallah predeceased him, dying as he had lived, a thorn in Mohammed's side.

The question which does not appear to have ever received a sensible or practical answer is whether Aisha was innocent or not. Hemna always insisted that the meeting with Safwan was prearranged. She may, however, have been smarting from the "fourscore stripes." Even so, Aisha's version has weak points.

How was it that Aisha, knowing that the caravan was on the point of moving, ran off without telling anybody and spent a long time looking for the necklace? The time element here is important.

An Arab camp takes quite a while to pack up and move, especially a large one such as a raiding force would require. Even when the main group of camels is on its way, there are stragglers. Neither does a camel train move fast. Two miles an hour is a good average. Therefore, to return to the camp and find no sign of the caravan, no sign of the stragglers, no sign of the hundreds of men and animals in a country where there is little cover on the near side of the horizon, must have meant that Aisha looked for her necklace for at least two hours. According to her, she then slept. Let us assume that her nap did not exceed one hour; where did Safwan appear from over three hours after Mohammed and his troops were on their way? How was it that he knew Aisha by sight, especially in view of his statement, later, in Medina, that he had never set eyes on her before? Aisha's story is either so simple and sincere that it sounds improbable or else Safwan and the necklace are one and the same thing.

Against this last supposition, there are certain contradictions. If Safwan and Aisha had been lovers, would they have arrived together in Medina and paraded their affair through the streets? Would not Safwan have ridden on his swift dromedary and warned the caravan that Aisha was not with it? The whole thing is not clear, and we shall never know. As my friend Madani used to say when we were discussing the pros and cons of Moslem versus Christian methods of handling women, "There are three things which God alone can see—the trace of a fish through water, the trace of a bird through the air, and the trace of a man through a woman."

Aisha used to say in later years that it was well known that Safwan was impotent. Is that the remark of an innocent party or of a guilty? Or is it lighthearted, irresponsible sense of humor? This she certainly had, for, on another occasion when she lost a necklace out in the desert, she halted the whole of Mohammed's army and made the soldiers look for it until it was found.

It is said that this prank brought about the decrees permitting the using of sand for ablutions instead of water. So much time was spent in looking for this trinket that the moment for prayer came before the troops had reached the wells where they were to camp. Mohammed was particular about washing. Every one of the five prayers had to be preceded by ablutions. For these he recommended running water rather than still. When, in consequence of the Moslem troops having wasted many hours hunting for the necklace, water was not available, Mohammed made sand a substitute. Accordingly most nomad Arabs do much of their washing with sand. Whether the necklace brought this about or not, the decree has made the Arabs into the most washed people in the world. While other races go dirty when they are away from water, the Arab continues to keep himself clean.

The revelation regarding the punishment of slanderers and adulterers caused Mohammed to formulate other laws connected with marriage and dissolution of marriage.

In pre-Islamic days, marriage for an Arab was merely a means for producing sons. Unless there were men to tend the flocks, the nomadic tribe ceased to exist. Women had no status in these communities which roamed the desert. A man could have as many wives as he could afford. The eldest son inherited his father's widows with the flocks and the tents. Incest between son and stepmother thus became not only lawful but obligatory. The licentiousness in Mecca was on a par with the debauchery of Sodom and Gomorrah. Prostitution was not held in disrespect.

Mohammed gradually altered all that. He advocated the marriage of the physically fit, regardless of social position or wealth. He proclaimed marriage as a foundation of society. He condemned adultery and fornication and anything which weakened the home.

In the Koran he wrote:

"*He* [God] *created for you wives of your own species, that ye may dwell with them and hath put love and tenderness between you.*"

And preaching to his people, he said:

"God enjoins you to treat women well, for they are your mothers, daughters, and aunts. The most perfect Moslem is he whose disposition is best; and the best of you are they who behave best to their wives."

The marriage rite, he decreed, was not to be a religious observance. Here again we have the desert influencing early Moslem institutions. Nomads would not be able to find a functionary whenever they happened to want to marry or a mosque in which to perform the ceremony, so the necessity of an intermediary or a sanctified spot for the uniting of men and women in wedlock was dispensed with. All that was required was a written contract between the parties concerned. The contract covered everything: the man's dowry, the woman's dowry, and what should be done with dowries in case of divorce. These regulations gave more consideration to womankind than in any occidental country of the period. In fact today a Moslem has fewer claims over his wife's property than husbands in many European communities. Thirteen hundred years ago Islam made a woman free and independent of her husband in the enjoyment of her rights of possession.

Once more in the Koran we read:

"Give women their dowry freely, but if, of themselves, they give up aught to you, then enjoy it as convenient and profitable."

And in the same sura:

"Men ought to have part of what their parents and kindred leave, and women a part of what their parents and kindred leave, whether it be little or much, let them have a stated portion."

While Mohammed decided against letting his men marry idolatresses, he had no objections to their wedding Jews or Christians. This he confirmed, in the Koran, with:

"And you are permitted to marry virtuous women who are believers, and virtuous women who have received the scriptures before you."

He clearly laid down that a Moslem should not simultaneously have more than four wives. That he himself went over the limit was partly due to his wish to have a son and partly to politics. Aisha was the only virgin girl who became Mohammed's wife. The others were all divorced or widows, and of these all but five were plain.

Mohammed made elaborate laws for divorce. He did not approve of this any more than he did of polygamy, but he knew that it was one of those things which cannot be avoided. He laid special stress on the woman implicated receiving fair treatment. In the second chapter of the Koran we note:

"Ye may divorce your wives twice. Keep them honorably and put them away with kindness. But it is not allowed to you to appropriate to yourselves aught of what ye have given them."

When one reads these and many other decrees of the same nature promulgated by Mohammed during his lifetime, one is all the more astonished at the unfairness of his detractors. They seem to have wantonly enjoyed dishonoring the female aspects of Islam, of holding them up to the scorn and ridicule of other women of the world. Although they plagued him enough, Mohammed could not have been harsh on women. For, in spite of the harem jealousies, in spite of Aisha's pranks and the other girls' exigencies, Mohammed enjoyed women from all points of view. He loved them physically, but they also interested him and he respected their intellects. The last thing that he wanted was for them to fall back into the condition of more or less slavery in which they had lived but a few years back. In one way only does he seem to have been strict with women. He never spoiled them. His harem life was as ascetic as that of his successors, a few centuries later, would be luxurious.

Although he took great care of his person—he tinted his eyelids with kohl, he perfumed his body, he dyed his hair when it began to turn gray and looked after his hands and feet—his eating and drinking and living were extremely simple. To that main meal of dates and bread and milk and occasional meat, there was little variety. Cucumbers and pumpkins were served in season, but beyond these there were few extras. Mohammed preferred rain water to any other drink. He was always glad to share each dish with anyone who happened to be there. The only things which he did not seem to care for were onions and garlic. He also refused to eat the large desert lizards which the nomads regard as a delicacy. This was partly because of a superstition that some of the children of Israel had been turned into lizards. The meals were all taken squatting on a mat and, as is still the Arab custom, everything was eaten with the fingers. Before beginning, grace was said as follows:

"O Lord, grant thy blessing on this, and feed me with better than this." If milk was part of the menu, he added: "And vouchsafe unto me an increase thereof." "For," said he, "there is no other thing which combineth both food and drink save milk alone." And he added for the benefit of strangers: "God is pleased with those who offer thanks unto Him after eating and drinking."

These frugal habits were not due to Mohammed's despising good fare. On the contrary, he liked it. As Aisha related: "The Messenger loved three things—women, scents, and food." The ascetic attitude toward meals was mainly due to being badly off, to the amount spent on other people, to the amount given away. Even when loot was coming in every week and the Moslems were becoming prosperous, this charity took so much that Mohammed never had anything to spare. He even cobbled his slippers and mended his clothes.

While attending to these domestic and legal affairs, Mohammed continued to raise livestock. In addition to his milch camels, he had two swift-trotting dromedaries. One of these was the famous Al Kaswa which had brought him from Mecca to Medina, and he had an even faster one called Al Adba. There were also the mules and donkeys and, as time went on, horses. Some of these he raced against his cavalrymen, riding always himself. Arab races are long and over rough ground. There is no pulling. Everyone is determined to win. Mohammed often did. He was fifty-seven years old, but he knew more about horse management than many of his soldiers.

He had several oasis properties. One of these had been confiscated from the Beni an Nadir. Another had been left him by a Jew called Mukerich. This man had never become a Moslem, but he admired Mohammed and wished to show him some token of his esteem. When he died, Mohammed had him buried just outside the Moslem cemetery.

Mohammed's living quarters remained unpretentious. The original small houses near the mosque had been enlarged to make room for the growing family. They were still divided into rooms by partitions made of palm branches smeared with mud. The curtains over the doors were of black haircloth. Inside the rooms were carpets and a few cushions stuffed with grain. The walls were bare, and there were no blankets. When it was cold, the occupants of the rooms covered themselves with another carpet or a cloak.

Mohammed's only personal "luxuries" appear to have been a crystal drinking goblet with silver trimmings, a copper washbowl, and an ivory comb.

There were a few slaves to help the wives who did most of the housekeeping. There was also a private secretary called Zaid ibn Thabit. During the early days in Medina, Mohammed had employed Hebrews to attend to his clerical work, but as the rift widened between him and the Jews, he replaced them by this well-educated Arab. It was Zaid who eventually collected the scattered fragments of the Koran and assembled them into the Holy Book as we have it today.

To any who have not lived among Arabs, this rather uncomfortable existence is hard to reconcile with the conventional picture of harems. It must be remembered, however, that these were desert people, and desert people are unlike any others in the world.

Meals to a nomad are not matters of course. In fact the true nomad has only one meal a day, at night before he goes to sleep. The size of his meal will depend on whether the year has been good—that is, on the rainfall. Plenty of grazing changes the outlook for flocks and for game. Even so, meat is a luxury and is not served every day. The wanderers of the Arab wildernesses eat to live.

The sedentary Arabs, the citizens, those who inhabit the oasis towns, have a little more ease in that they can supplement their perpetual grain fare with dates and vegetables. But they too must conform with the nomads for any extra luxuries. That is, they must conform with the rain which permits the nomads to have sheep and wool to sell for money which they can spend in the oasis.

A desert community has nothing whatsoever in common with a community anywhere else. It may be in Arabia or in Libya or in the Sahara, the way of living of the people is identical. It is identical with what it has been through the ages of time. It cannot change, unless some inventor produces artificial rain.

So these pretty girls who made up Mohammed's harem, these great men like Abu Bakr and Omar, these soldiers and date growers were not having a frugal existence forced on them by an ascetic or thrifty leader. They were living as was the custom of desert people. Allah had become their God. Allah was going to lead them to the fruitful valleys of the Tigris and Euphrates, to the Nile, to the Indus, to the Guadalquivir (which is Spanish for the Arab meaning "Great River"), but He was not changing their desert. Caliphs of the not so distant future would assimilate themselves to these districts where water flowed and food was abundant. They would become luxurious and fat, but their people, the people who were responsible for Islam's spread, would go on living in the same austere manner as the founder of their faith.

To an American or English or Javanese Moslem, Mohammed's life suggests something primitive, something in the order of an anchorite. It is as unimaginable as that of Jesus to the average Christian. To the Arab, it is the only way he knows.

CHAPTER XVI

THE KORAN

WHILE THE KORAN has been frequently alluded to in these pages, its substance and its role in Islam have not been considered or discussed.

The Koran is a remarkable book. It reflects Mohammed. In fact, it *is* Mohammed. Yet there are few people outside Moslems or students of Islam who have any idea what the Koran is. In spite of numbers of good translations into English and French and German, hardly any Occidentals have read it. I have heard it spoken of as a history of Mohammed, as a collection of sayings of the same kind as those attributed to Confucius, as a volume of Moslem laws, as a paraphrase of the Bible. Even Mohammed's biographers seem to avoid a concise analysis or explanation of this work on which all Islam is founded.

Without any idea, therefore, of adding fresh comments to what oriental scholars have already contributed, I will endeavor to define what the Koran actually represents.

Koran is derived from, or is an adaptation of *"qara'a,"* which means "to read or recite." Although the whole book is now called Al Koran, (The Koran) each individual revelation originally bore this title.

The Koran consists of 114 suras or chapters, the longest of which has 286 verses; the shortest, three. Each sura has a title which is taken from some word or sentence occurring somewhere near the beginning of the text. The title does not necessarily have anything to do with the subject matter of the sura.

For example, the seventy-fourth sura, entitled, "The Greeks," opens with: "*The Greeks have been defeated in a land hard by,*" which is a reference to their rout by the Persians in 615 A.C. However, a few verses further on, the Greeks are forgotten.

The longest and most famous sura, the second, is called "The Cow," but it has nothing to do with this creature, which is only once mentioned in connection with its sacrifice as ordered by Moses in the books of Numbers and Deuteronomy.

Each sura, with the exception of the ninth, has the same introduction:

"*Bismillaahir-Rahmaanir-Raheem.* [In the name of God, the Compassionate, the Merciful.]"

Ever so often, the exhortation "Say" is interjected at the beginning of a verse. This is to indicate that it is Allah who is making the revelation, for it must be borne in mind that every line of the Koran is supposed to be a divine message, transmitted to Mohammed from heaven. For example the 114th sura reads as follows:

"*In the name of God, the Compassionate, the Merciful.*
Say: I betake me for refuge to the Lord of men,
  The King of men, the God of men,
    Against the mischief of the stealthily withdrawing whisperer,
    Who whispereth in man's breast against djinn and men."

On the few occasions when the Koreishites were persuaded to listen to Mohammed, they said that the Koran was too good to be his work. Mohammed replied that they were right and wrong, for it was too good to have come from anyone but the Almighty.

In the twenty-sixth sura and in the 192d verse, it is written:

"*Verily from the Lord of the worlds hath this book come down;*
The faithful spirit [Gabriel] hath come down with it
Upon thy heart, that thou mightest become a warner
In the clear Arabic tongue."

These revelations, therefore, were made to Mohammed in Mecca and Medina at various times by an angel of God. As the various messages were delivered, they were committed to writing—not, however, on a scroll or a tablet, but on anything which was handy. The "first edition" of the Koran was recorded on shoulder bones of sheep, on oyster shells, on bits of wood and stone, on strips of leather. Some of the inscriptions were on flimsy palm branches and odd sheets of parchment. As if this method of recording God's word were not haphazard enough, further confusion was added by dropping these odd bits and pieces into a box without numbering or classification.

It was not until a year after Mohammed's death that Abu Bakr, on the advice of Omar, ordered Zaid ibn Thabit to collect these notes and "edit" them in some way that they could be conveniently read. This he did, adding passages which Mohammed had had friends memorize instead of writing them.

While Zaid undoubtedly collected every word which Mohammed wrote or dictated or committed to the minds of his colleagues, he edited them without any method. He just took the odds and ends out of the box as they came and copied each revelation without any regard to chronological order. Thus, late Medina suras were placed before early Meccan suras, and subjects which were clearly related, far apart. In fact Zaid's only system seems to have been to put the longest and best-known suras first and the shortest last. One might almost imagine him measuring them with a tape so as to have them graded like the pipes of an organ. He disregarded continuity of theme and conformity of style which developed as Mohammed matured. The result was an incoherent patchwork and conveys no idea of the evolution of any plan in Mohammed's mind or the circumstances by which he was surrounded and influenced. So general was the muddle that Voltaire, after reading the Koran, remarked:

"An incomprehensible book which violates our common sense on every page."

The only thing in favor of Zaid's method is that it was scrupulously honest. He did nothing to mold any passage or supply connecting sentences or fill in obvious omissions or suppress details discreditable to Islam. He worked with unimaginative devotion, so that when he had finished his "editing" of the Koran, a book existed which was genuinely the work of its author and its author only.

As a matter of fact this lack of order in a piece of literature is not exceptional among Arabs. One often hears poems or passages from the Koran being recited by Moslems without much attention being paid as to whether it is the beginning or the end.

It was this incoherent document which was handed to Hafsa and declared the standard and authorized text of the Holy Book.

However, not too strict attention was paid to this declaration, and soon variations began to creep into those editions of the Koran which were scattered about the growing Moslem world.

Under the caliphate of Othman, this got so bad that Hodzeifa, a Moslem general whose campaigns had taken him to Syria and Armenia and Iraq, reported that if something drastic were not done, Moslems would soon be differing about their scriptures like the Christians. Othman immediately sent for the now middle-aged Zaid and had him, with three Korcishite scholars, draw up an authorized version of the Koran from the master copy in Hafsa's box. This was done in the Meccan dialect, the purest of Arabia, and had the unpremeditated effect of standardizing the Arab language. Today Arabs in all parts of their vast empire and many Moslems in other parts of the world have this colloquial and living lingual basis for intercommunication which no other religion possesses.

When this authorized version was completed, all other copies were burned. They were replaced by the new edition with injunctions that no word or sentence must be added or subtracted. This order was conscientiously respected, and today there is no possible doubt that the Koran which is read wherever there are Moslems is the same version as that translated from Hafsa's master copy. In fact there are Moslems who affirm that some of the copies issued under the caliphate of Othman in the twenty-fifth year of the Hijra, fifteen years after Mohammed's death, still exist. Although there is no reason why this should not be, I never met an Arab who had seen such a copy. The earliest manuscript of the Koran officially catalogued belongs to the ninth century, two hundred years subsequent to Mohammed's demise. However, this is of no real importance except to collectors. What is important is that the Koran is the only work which has survived for over twelve hundred years with an unadulterated text. Neither in the Jewish religion nor in the Christian is there anything which faintly compares to this.

The only thing against this unadulteration of text is its lack of arrangement. To some extent, however, this has been remedied.

While there are indications from remarks handed down by Mohammed's followers that he intended his revelations to be arranged according to subject and not chronologically, a number of oriental scholars, European and Asiatic, have published Korans in different languages with their suras in the right order, or in the order which all evidence goes to show is the right one. This has entailed arduous work, as, among other handicaps, there are practically no historical or other landmarks in the whole of the Koran. Mohammed's name appears but five times, and there are but two references to his contemporaries. What gives clues to the dates of the suras is their tone.

The early suras are dominated essentially by poetic inspiration. The lines are impassioned, the beauty of nature is stressed. There is a feeling of a sincere inquirer after the truth, an asserter of beliefs expressed in a way deemed most likely to attract followers. The imagery, the words employed suggest the shepherd of the desert, the visionary, the poet, the prophet.

Then, when Mohammed begins to have authority, the suras become warnings. They are more prosaic, more doctrinal. It is a missionary speaking, a man aiming at conversion. As things progress for Islam, this develops. The preacher of Mecca becomes the legislator and the warrior, the dictator who calls for obedience. The poetic element fades a good deal into the background. Occasionally there are passages which speak of *"God's gifts* and *the Messenger's,*" of "*God's pleasure* and *the Messenger's.*" In fact, the evolution of the mind of the inspired traveling salesman into that of the ruler of Arabia could not be more clearly demonstrated than in these suras chronologically arranged. They invalidate Voltaire's remark on the subject and validate what Goethe said: "As often as we approach it [the Koran], it always proves repulsive anew; gradually, however, it attracts, it astonishes and, in the end, forces admiration."

Furthermore, to those who find the Koran tiresome reading, it must be borne in mind that it was not intended to be read. It was intended to be recited and heard. There is evidence, too, that Mohammed counted much on the manner of recital. He often said: "Eloquence is like magic." Today this is still the case. Arab school children learn the Koran by heart. Many remember it. My Sahara friend Madani could quote any part of the Koran suggested to him. I was not sufficiently versed to check this, but I have no reason to believe that he did not have the whole book in his head. I have sometimes heard worshipers in the mosque correct the imam when he made a mistake in the rendering of a passage.

One might almost compare the written text of the Koran to a shorthand rendering of the extemporaneous sermon of a great preacher. All the emotions of the speaker and the context and the occasion are lost in the penciled lines. If this were not sufficient handicap, the Koran suffers greatly from translation. In addition to its delivery and its subject, it depends a great deal on its phraseology. In the same way as the Vulgate, in its "pig Latin," loses the mellow beauty of the New Testament in Elizabethan English; in the same way as any version of the Old Testament other than the King James Version becomes a repetitious history and a code of laws, so does the Koran lose its inspiring rhythm when taken out of Arabic. To anyone who has not heard the sonorous majesty of an Arab reciting the Koran or listened to the call to prayer from the minaret of a mosque, it is impossible to convey what the book lacks in English or French or German. It is like Shakespeare in a foreign tongue or Wagner in Italian.

Whether one could call the Koran's suras poetry, is a matter of opinion. They are certainly not poetry as is the kasida, the best example of pre-Islamic verse, but it has great emotion and, as in Italian, the rhyming comes almost automatically.

The first half of the eighty-first sura, which follows, has a vibrating grandeur, in Arabic, difficult to surpass in any part of the King James Bible:

> *"When the sun shall be folded up,*
> *And when the stars shall fall,*
> *And when the mountains shall be set in motion,*
> *And when the camels shall be neglected,*
> *And when the wild beasts shall be huddled together,*
> *And when the seas shall boil,*
> *And when the souls shall be paired with their bodies,*
> *And when the leaves of the Book shall be unrolled,*
> *And when the heavens shall be stripped away like a skin,*
> *And when hell shall be made to blaze,*
> *And when paradise shall be brought near,*
> *Every soul shall know what it hath produced."*

Incidentally, this sura is called "The Folded Up," from the last two words of the first line.

These poetic qualities do not prevent the Koran from being a code of laws, ritual, moral, and civil; a book of common prayer and a narrative of biblical events, all in one. There are passages devoted to personal apologies, to rebukes of hypocrites, to curses and sublime revelations of the attributes of God. It has also a mystic essence which had an astonishing effect on the Arabs. It transformed the simple shepherds, the merchants, and nomads of Arabia into warriors and empire builders and constructors of cities like Baghdad and Cordova and Delhi, into scholars and dictators and mathematicians. It was undoubtedly this book which helped these men to conquer a world greater than that of the Persians or Romans in as many tens of years as these predecessors had taken centuries. While the Phoenicians had gone far afield and established themselves wherever there was trade, whereas the Jews had also gone abroad, but as fugitives or captives, these Arabs, with their Book, came to Africa and then to Europe as kings!

When, in 657 A.C., as a result of one of Aisha's little intrigues, Moslems were fighting Moslems, and Mu'awiya, son of Abu Sofian, leading Syria's Islamic armies, was near being defeated by Ali's Arab warriors, he had recourse to this mystic property of the Holy Book. The battle seemed over and the Syrians were wavering when the order was given them to place their Korans on the points of their lances. The moment Ali's men saw this, they lowered their weapons. The battle was settled by arbitration.

Today when the kadi (Moslem magistrate) fails to find in the laws which Mohammed laid down for Arab nomads a decision applicable to a case in Rabat or Agra, he places the Holy Book on his head and so renders homage to human reason and the law of progress.

A seventh of the people of the world have their actions controlled by this book. No one, so far, has been able to give a satisfactory explanation.

The Koran defies analysis. It cannot be characterized by any one epithet, for there is no one sura which sustains a uniform character throughout. Much of it is unoriginal, with thoughts borrowed from the Old and New Testaments.

The Creation, the fall of Adam, Noah, the call of Abraham, Ishmael and Isaac, Jacob and the patriarchs, are all there. The selection of the Jews as the Chosen People, the administration of Moses, the prophets and psalmists, especially David and Solomon, are recorded as items of history published for the first time. Mohammed does not even omit the promise of the advent of the Messiah.

As for the New Testament, the Koran concurs with the recognition of Jesus as this promised Messiah. It admits his miraculous conception by "the breath of the spirit of God." Likewise the immaculate nativity of the Virgin Mary, the mystic birth of John the Baptist and his role as the forerunner of Jesus are accepted. So is Jesus' rejection and persecution and condemnation to the cross. Finally Mohammed tells of Christ's bodily ascension to heaven before he was dead and his officiating there between God and men.*

While there is only one direct quotation from the Bible in the Koran: "*My servants, the righteous, shall inherit the earth* [Psalms]," there are many passages with wording extremely close to the older scriptures.

The following are average examples:

BIBLE: "Thou shalt give life for life, tooth for tooth, burning for burning, wound for wound."

KORAN: "*We have just commanded that they should give life for life, and eye for eye and nose for nose and ear for ear and tooth for tooth, and that wounds shall be punished by retaliation.*"

BIBLE: "Dust thou art and unto dust shalt thou return."

KORAN. "*Out of the ground we created you and to the same will we cause you to return.*"

A third parallel shows how Jesus and Mohammed had much the same early background. Whereas Jesus spoke of the lost sheep and the joy of finding it, Mohammed compared God's gratification at the repentance of a sinner to a nomad's delight at discovering his strayed animal in the desert.

As previously remarked, how Mohammed became acquainted with the Jewish and Christian Scriptures has remained obscure. There is this translation attributed to Waraka, but there is not the smallest evidence that Mohammed ever had access to it. His talks with Waraka were confined to theological generalities, for the primary reason that Waraka died before Mohammed began to formulate what Gabriel had told him, and long before he started to compile the Koran. The earliest known Arabic edition of the Old Testament was published nine hundred years after Christ, nearly three hundred years after Mohammed's death;

---

*Sura 3 and 4.

while the first official Arabic translation of the New Testament was some two centuries later. Arabs have amazingly retentive memories, and it is possible that Mohammed was able to store in his mind all that he had heard during his travels. It seems a stupendous feat, but it is the only feasible explanation, unless we accept unreservedly the divine origins of the Koran.

For the benefit of any who are curious to know something about the phraseology and subject matter of the Koran, the following extracts have been taken, here and there, from J. M. Rodwell's translation.

Sura XIX (this sura is entitled "MARY" and is one which is partly related to its title, the subject matter having to do with the Virgin's immaculate conception):

"And make mention in the Book, of Mary, when she went apart from her family, eastward, and took a veil to shroud herself from them. And We sent our spirit to her, and he took the form of a perfect man [Gabriel].

"She said: 'I fly for refuge from thee to the God of Mercy, if thou fearest Him, begone from me.'

"He said: 'I am only a messenger of thy Lord, that I may bestow on thee a son.'

"She said: 'How shall I have a son, when man hath never touched me? And I am not unchaste.'

"He said: 'So shall it be. Thy Lord hath said: Easy is this with me. And we will make him a sign to mankind and a mercy from Us. For it is a thing decreed.'

"And she conceived him, and retired with him to a far off place. And the throes came upon her by the trunk of a palm. She said:

"'Oh that I had died ere this, and been forgotten, been forgotten quite.'

"And one cried from below her: 'Grieve not thou, thy Lord hath provided a streamlet at thy feet. And shake the palm toward thee, it will drop fresh ripe dates upon thee. Eat then and drink, and be cheerful of eye and shouldst thou see a man, say:

" 'Verily I have vowed abstinence to the God of Mercy. To no one will I speak this day.'

"Then came she with the babe to her people, bearing him. They said:

" 'O Mary! Now has thou done a strange thing. O sister of Aaron! Thy father was not a man of wickedness, nor unchaste thy mother.'

"And she made a sign to them, pointing towards the babe. They said:

" 'How shall we speak with him who is in the cradle, an infant?'

"It said: 'Verily, I am the servant of God. He hath given me the Book, and He hath made me a Prophet. And He hath made me blessed wherever I may be, and hath enjoined me prayer and almsgiving as long as I live; and to be duteous to her that bare me, and He hath not made me proud, depraved. And the peace of God was on me the day I was born, and will be the day I shall die, and the day I shall be raised to life.'

"This is Jesus, the son of Mary. This is the statement of the truth concerning which they doubt."

Sura III (this is entitled "The Family of Imran" and has nothing to do with Imran whom Mohammed believed to be the father of the Virgin Mary. The verses quoted are directed to the Jews and Christians):

"O people of the Book, why dispute about Abraham, when the Law [Old Testament] and the Evangel [New Testament] were not sent down till after him? Do ye not then understand?

"Lo, ye are they who dispute about that in which ye have knowledge, but why dispute ye about that which ye have no knowledge? God hath knowledge, but ye know nothing.

"Abraham was neither Jew nor Christian, but he was sound in faith, a Moslem, and not one of those who add gods to God. They among men who are nearest of kin to Abraham are surely those who follow him and his messenger Mohammed and they who believe on him. And God is the protector of the faithful."

Sura II (this is from the famous long sura entitled "The Cow." The passage quoted concerns the unimportance of outward rites in religion. Its immediate context has to do with the changing of the *kibla* from Jerusalem to Mecca):

"There is no piety in turning your faces to east or west. But he is pious who believeth in God, and the last day, and the angels, and the scriptures, and the prophets; who, for the love of God disburseth his wealth to his kindred and to the orphans and the needy and the wayfarer and those who ask, and for ransoming; who observeth prayer and payeth legal alms and who is of those who are faithful to their engagements when they have engaged in them, and patient under ills and hardships and in time of trouble. These are they who are just and these are they who fear the Lord."

Sura VII (entitled "Al Araf." The beginning of the sura deals with the expulsion of Satan from heaven and the fall of Adam and Eve):

"*Then Satan whispered them [Adam and Eve] to show them their nakedness which had been hidden from them both. And he said:*

"'*This tree hath your Lord forbidden you, only lest ye should become angels, or lest ye should become immortals.*' *And he sware to them both:* '*Verily I am one unto you who counseleth right.*'

"*So he beguiled them by deceits, and when they had tasted of the tree, their nakedness appeared to them, and they began to sew together upon themselves the leaves of the garden. And their Lord called to them:*

"'*Did I not forbid you this tree, and did I not say to you, verily Satan is your declared enemy?*'

"*And they said:* '*O our Lord! With ourselves we have dealt unjustly. If thou forgive us not and have pity on us, we shall surely be of those who perish.*'

"*He said:* '*Get ye down, the one of you an enemy to the*

other, and on earth shall be your dwelling and your provision for a season.' He said: 'On it shall ye live, and on it shall ye die, and from it shall ye be taken forth.'"

Sura XXIV (entitled "Light." The three verses here quoted are an attempt to convey the magnificent rhythm of the Arabic):

"*But as to infidels, their works are like the vapor [mirage] in a plain which the thirsty dreameth to be water, until he cometh unto it, he findeth not aught, but findeth that God is with him; and He payeth him his account, for swift to take account is God.*

"*Or as the darkness over a deep sea, billows riding upon billows below, and clouds above; darkness upon darkness. When a man reacheth forth his hand, he cannot nearly see it. He to whom God shall not give light, no light at all hath he.*

"*Hast thou not seen that God driveth clouds lightly forward, then gathereth them together, then pileth them in masses? And then thou seest the rain forthcoming from their midst. And He causeth clouds like mountains charged with hail to descend from the heaven, and He maketh it to fall on whom He will, and from whom He will He turneth it aside. The brightness of His lightning all but taketh away sight!*"

These few selections should help to give some notion of the immense variety of subjects covered by the Koran. It should give some idea of the kind of mind which Mohammed must have had. It makes one wonder how he knew all this, when he thought it all out, where he learned to compose the sonorous verse-prose.

Mohammed's upbringing, his background, his early pursuits have been discussed in these pages. None of these, however, presages the author of a code of laws, of religion, of morality; of a collection of old legends and stories; of a book of prayer, and the whole thing in this lilting, resonant Arabic. Perhaps it *was* all divine inspiration.

Mohammed used to say that there were greater miracles in

nature than any which could be wrought outside of it and that the Koran was a miracle in itself. Perhaps he was right. A great many people helped to write the Bible. It took them many centuries. Mohammed wrote the Koran alone. It took him barely twenty years.

"Tell us," men used to ask Aisha after Mohammed's death, "tell us something about the Messenger's disposition."

"You have the Koran," would reply Aisha. "Be you not Arabs and read Arabic?"

"Yea, indeed."

"Then why take the trouble to inquire of me? For the Messenger's disposition is no other than the Koran itself."

To analyze Mohammed's character, to appreciate the scope of his achievement, to measure his sensitivity, a study of the Koran is essential.

CHAPTER XVII

THE TREATY

(628 After Christ)

SIX YEARS had now passed since Mohammed's flight out of Mecca. From being the homeless outcast, wondering whether he would survive the day, he now held a position of comparative importance in Arabia. Medina was his, and many of the tribes which pastured in the neighborhood were showing signs of considering him their ruler. Some still maintained the Arab attitude of distrust toward a centralized government. A few were hostile. With these, Mohammed used only one policy—force! He now had a small mobile army mounted on camels and horses. The unfriendly groups knew this and confined their hostilities to hit-and-run raids.

Two of these raids in the autumn of 627 A.C. lost Mohammed a good deal of prestige. In the first, the chief of the Oyeina bedouins ventured to the Medina oasis and surrounded a herd of Mohammed's own milch camels. The herdsmen were killed and the women carried off. Although Mohammed sent three hundred mounted men in pursuit, they succeeded in recovering only half the loot and were unable to effect reprisals on the raiders. The only survivor who returned to tell the tale was one of the herders' wives who managed to escape on a camel. When she reached her home, she announced her intention to sacrifice her mount. Mohammed intervened. Why, asked he, was she going to kill the animal which had saved her? The woman did not know. The camel's life was preserved.

Mohammed liked animals. Although he offered sacrifices at the appointed times, he did not approve of killing for the sake of killing and despised anyone who hurt living creatures. The sacrifice was a tradition of olden times which it had been impossible to eradicate from the new faith. Even so, Mohammed refused to be hypocritical about it. For the customary invocation, "In the name of God, the compassionate, the merciful," before striking the fatal blow, he substituted, "In the name of God. God is most great. God give thee patience to endure the affliction which He hath allotted thee."

He made it a matter of principle that no animals of his or of those in his employ should be roughly treated. With difficulty he put an end to the custom of tethering a camel to its master's grave so that it died there. He abolished the using of living birds as targets at shooting contests. He stopped the clipping of manes and tails of horses in this fly-infested country. Whenever he saw men overloading donkeys or mules, he arrested them. The only creatures he did not like were dogs. This was very likely because desert curs are mangy, savage animals which no one wants as pets. But they were not denied a place with other beasts in paradise.

He once told the story of an adulteress who passed a well beside which a dog lay dying of thirst. The woman took off her shoe and, tying it to the end of her girdle, drew water for the dog. For this gesture, she was forgiven her sins.

"Verily," said Mohammed, "there are rewards for our doing good to quadrupeds and giving them water to drink. There are rewards for benefiting every animal which lives."

According to the Koran, animal life stands on the same footing as human life in the sight of God. *"There is no beast on earth,"* it says, *"nor bird which flieth with its wings, but the same is a people like unto mankind. Unto the Lord shall they return."*

Whenever one sees a Moslem working a sick animal, it is nine times out of ten someone in a community overrun by Occidentals—that is to say, where Islam has been submerged. The true Arab cares for his horse and his camel as he does for his family. This has some practical elements, but it is chiefly an attitude of mind toward dumb creatures inherited from the founder of Islam.

"Fear God in these dumb animals and ride them when they are fit to be ridden and get off them when they are tired," was one of Mohammed's favorite injunctions to his people.

The second raid which threatened to shake Mohammed's growing authority was carried out by the Ghatafanites who had taken part in the siege of Medina. This time a large group of Moslems was caught unawares, defeated and massacred. The reprisals were again limited to the capture of flocks and tents and household goods. The enemy sustained no casualties.

This intertribal raiding among Arabs is a custom which began long before Mohammed and went on long after. It continues today. Nothing but an attack from an infidel or an alien enemy stops it. However, once the tribes have united to meet the invader and have driven him out, they start their raiding all over again. It is an unreasonable industry rather like stealing each other's washing. But it is a means of livelihood and goes on.

In September, Mecca and Medina once more clashed. Thinking that Mohammed was occupied by his local disputes, the Koreishites sent out a rich caravan along the seashore to Syria. Mohammed was informed. Like a hunting falcon, one of his flying columns swooped down on the Meccans and brought much silver and many camels into Medina. Among the prisoners was Abu'l As, Mohammed's son-in-law.

It will be remembered that Abu'l As was taken prisoner at Badr. As his ransom, he had been made to send his wife, Zeinab, to Medina. Zeinab was fetched by Zaid, but, before leaving Mecca, she was maltreated by some of the Koreishites with whom the defeat still rankled. This maltreatment led to a miscarriage, and Zeinab was never really well again. Consequently, she had remained under her father's protection. Now, three and a half years later, Abu'l As was once more a prisoner in Moslem hands.

Although this man had never become converted, his family ties should have made him a Moslem. In addition to being Mohammed's son-in-law, he was also his nephew in that Khadija had been his aunt. Later, he became further allied through his daughter becoming Ali's second wife. That he differed in this question of religion was just one of those things which happen in families and did not alter his esteem for his combined uncle and father-in-law.

The night the raiders brought in the looted caravan, Abu'l As managed to escape and made his way to Zeinab. No one could have been happier than she was to see her husband. She welcomed him home and, the following morning, proclaimed from the flat roof of her house that she was giving the prisoner sanctuary. Mohammed knew nothing of this until he heard the proclamation. Without hesitation he laid the matter before the mosque congregation. Everyone agreed to give Abu'l As his freedom. The generous gesture so touched the young man that he returned to Mecca to settle his affairs and then came back to Medina, where he became a Moslem. Zeinab did not survive long, which was a great sorrow to her father and to her husband. Nevertheless, Mohammed found much comfort in having with him this kinsman of Khadija, whose conversion added another link to the chain which he was gradually placing about the Koreishites.

It was in the latter part of that year that we first hear of Mohammed showing a political interest in countries outside Arabia. An envoy was dispatched to present the Prophet's greetings to the Roman, or Byzantine, emperor, Heraclius. He did not get farther than Syria, where the Roman governor received him with the courtesies due to an ambassador and sent him back with gifts. The governor had no idea whom this envoy represented or imagined for a moment that the day was not far off when it would be his sovereign's turn to send deputations to this unknown Arab. But the gesture gratified Mohammed and emphasized how far he had come during the past six years.

It was probably the realization of where his fate was leading him that made him apply his mind seriously to what he had been considering for some time: the conquest of Mecca.

The sixth anniversary of the Hijra was approaching, and there seemed as little prospect as.ever of winning over the home town by persuasion. Fighting and raiding had only widened the breach between the Moslems and the Koreishites. Abu Sofian was as firmly opposed to Mohammed and his doctrines as he had been in the days of the persecutions in Mecca. In this he was supported by Hind, by Khaled, by Ikrima, by Amr', and all the Koreishite chiefs. There was, of course, the alternative to risk everything with the army and take Mecca by storm. But even if this were successful it would go against the grain to sack the Holy City and would probably accomplish nothing permanent. The only other solution was to make peace. But how to do so gracefully? How? Then Mohammed had a brilliant idea. Why not lead his soldiers unarmed to take part in the annual pilgrimage to the Kaaba? If this were carried out during the sacred months, there could be no question of being attacked, and Mecca might be regained without any surrender on either side.

As soon as Mohammed had made up his mind about this, he spoke of it to his general staff. Their reaction was unanimously favorable. He then suggested that some of the local tribes join in. A few responded, but the majority were cautious and stayed away. They associated Mohammed with loot, and this clearly was not a looting party.

By February of 628 all arrangements had been made. Fifteen hundred pilgrims, draped in the two pieces of seamless white cloth decreed for pilgrimages, paraded outside Medina with their camels. Except for their sheathed swords and their bows and arrows, they were not armed for battle. The only precautionary measures which Mohammed took was to send a troop of twenty horsemen as a scouting force to warn him of any hostile interference. Aisha was not of the expedition, neither was Hafsa. The only wife to accompany the pilgrims was Umm Salama.

It must have been a noble spectacle to see that host of men arrayed before the fluttering palms of Medina—these Meccan exiles who had left all for the cause, these Medinese who had risked so much for the sake of an ideal. In their snowy ritual robes they sat erect, line upon line, on their tall dromedaries.

No armor or helmet glittered in the sun; even the scimitars were concealed beneath each man's left thigh. To the flank of the parade were seventy unmounted camels. These were for sacrifice and wore the ceremonial garlands about their necks. Among them, as a kind of ironic gesture, was Abu Jahl's dromedary which had been captured at Badr.

Mohammed, on the back of Al Kaswa, which had brought him from Mecca in the days of persecution, in the days when his escort was one loyal old friend, rode down the lines. There were many new faces among this throng, but there were many which belonged to the first months of Islam: Abu Bakr, the faithful; the huge Omar; the crafty Othman; Ali, the Lion of Arabia; Zaid and Bilal and the veterans of Badr and Ohod and the Battle of the Ditch. To these men, especially, Mohammed looked with pride and affection. It was because of them that he now saw before him this evidence that he had not preached in vain.

The first stages of the journey passed without incident. At Dhul Huleifa a long halt was made while the pilgrims consecrated themselves. Then, with cries of *"Labbaike Allah! Labbaike!* [Here I am, O Lord! Here I am!]" they crossed into the holy territory which surrounds Mecca.

At this point the serene atmosphere became clouded. News came that whatever might be the peaceful proclamations of Mohammed, the Koreishites did not believe them. Furthermore, that if Mohammed did happen to be sincere in his motives for paying this visit, Abu Sofian was not going to have him or his men inside Mecca under any circumstances. To emphasize this, Khaled ibn al Walid and Ikrima ibn Abu Jahl had been sent out with Mecca's crack cavalry regiment armed for war.

Mohammed made up his mind quickly. He had no intention of fighting the Koreishites, but neither had he any of turning back. Waiting for darkness, he led his men over a rugged mountain track and appeared again, behind Khaled, at a place called Hodeibiya, about three miles from the Kaaba. Here he pitched his camp. There was not much water, but his men were accustomed to campaigning and soon had cleared some of the choked-up wells. With that done, they settled down to see what the Koreishites would do next.

Everyone was on the alert, ready to retaliate the moment Khaled and his cavalry reappeared. However, Khaled had been withdrawn when it was discovered how close Mohammed was to the city. For a while there was a lull.

Mohammed had had his men impress shepherds and local people, who had ventured out to Hodeibiya to see what was afoot, that he had come to Mecca only as a pilgrim. As the Koreishites sensed the honesty of this affirmation, they began sending envoys to find out if Mohammed had any other ideas on his mind. Mohammed said no, and repeated to each one his peaceful intentions.

Orwa, the son-in-law of Abu Sofian, tried to browbeat Mohammed. He tried to provoke the Moslems. He mocked them in their pilgrim outfit and assured them that his father-in-law had no intention of allowing this rabble to enter the precincts of Mecca. In fact he became so excited that he seized Mohammed by the beard. There was a cry of consternation, and a hundred hands reached for the swords which lay concealed beneath the white robes. Orwa released the beard and said a hasty good-by. Then he mounted his horse and rode back to Mecca.

Here he confirmed what the other envoys had said about Mohammed, about a Mohammed who, in these few years, had grown beyond recognition. This despised preacher was treated like an emperor, he held court. There was nothing in this clear-headed statesman which faintly resembled the friendless visionary who had been driven out of Mecca such a short while before.

"Why," said he, "these men fight each other to get a cup of the water in which their leader has washed. They drink it, they use it to dress wounds! In their eyes, anything is sanctified which has touched Mohammed's body."

Whether this was exactly as Orwa stated or not, it is certain that the practice has survived among certain descendants of Mohammed. The Agha Khan's bath water is religiously preserved and bottled and sent to the faithful all over the world.

He may be doing his washing in the Ritz in London or the St. Regis in New York or in Monte Carlo or Rio de Janiero, the soapy water is set aside as Mohammed's was said to have been in 628 A.C.

However, such veneration for a human being was new to the Koreishites and impressed them deeply. Still they would not yield. They were slightly afraid of what Mohammed might do, but more especially they did not want to lose face. Mohammed had kept them out of Medina, he had made fools of them when they had gone up against him with ten thousand warriors, and it would be unthinkable to allow him to enter Mecca with a following which, though outwardly unarmed, was an army.

A message was accordingly sent to the Moslem camp to say that, if Mohammed would go away now, he could come back the following year and make his pilgrimage. Mohammed replied that he was prepared to discuss this and wanted more detail. No reply to this was forthcoming, and a kind of stalemate set in. Round the Kaaba the Koreishites argued and counterargued. Every time any more bellicose member of the council suggested going out and driving Mohammed away, a glance at the hillside where the Moslem campfires twinkled sobered them. Finally it was Mohammed who made the next move.

He instructed Omar to lead a delegation to the Koreishites. Omar demurred. Mecca was seething with his enemies, every one of whom had some blood-feud excuse to kill him. Mohammed saw the point of this argument and called Othman.

Othman made no objection. In the first place, he had not been in Mecca for years. His emigration to Abyssinia had taken place before the real trouble had begun, and he had no religious or individual quarrels with the Koreishites. In the second place, he belonged to the Ommeyade family and was thus related to Abu Sofian. So he made his way unostentatiously to Mecca, where a cousin met and sponsored him. He found, however, that the Koreishites were as firm as ever in their resolve to oppose Mohammed's entry into the Holy City that year. Othman was equally obstinate, and the negotiations prolonged themselves into days and nights.

Up in the camp the Moslems began to worry. Soon a rumor started that Othman had been assassinated. Mohammed summoned the pilgrims. Standing under the shade of an acacia, he called on them to make a vow to avenge Othman if anything untoward happened to him. One by one the fifteen hundred stood before their leader and, placing their hands in his, took the oath. However, before anything rash was put into effect, Othman reappeared. He had failed to change the minds of the Koreishites, but he had brought with him a man who had the authority of the council to discuss the terms for a treaty. The man's name was Soheil ibn Amr'.

Soheil was an acquaintance of the early Mecca days who had followed the anti-Moslem group when the persecuting began. He had been taken prisoner at Badr and had escaped, only to be caught again. He owed his life to Mohammed, who had chained him up in his home until the ransom came. Neither of the men liked each other. Nevertheless Soheil was an official plenipotentiary, and anything to which he agreed would be ratified.

After further lengthy discussions, the conditions of the treaty were established as follows:

Mohammed and his men were to return to Medina immediately. The following year they could come back and would have three days in which to perform their devotions round the Kaaba. During that period the Koreishites would evacuate the city and camp outside its walls. The pilgrims would have to come unarmed, except for the sheathed swords allowed to travelers for self-protection. As from this date (March 628), there would be a ten-year truce between the Moslems and the Koreishites. During that period caravans from Mecca and Medina could move through each other's territory in safety. During that period any Meccans who escaped to Medina to take up Islam without the consent of their families would have to be sent back.

Those were the main clauses in the treaty. As soon as the minor details had been fixed, Ali was called to commit the agreement to writing. Mohammed started to dictate. Using the habitual Moslem formula, he began:

"In the name of God, the compassionate, the merciful!"

Soheil stopped him. He had never heard this way of referring to God. He did not like it. He made Mohammed change the introduction to the treaty, to:

"In thy name, O God!"

Mohammed began dictating again:

"In thy name, O God, these are the conditions of peace between Mohammed, the Messenger of Allah, and——"

This time Soheil jumped up. He was partly angry, partly amused, partly impressed. That a man who had had a price on his head less than six years ago should have the self-assured impertinence to officially give himself this title was unbelievable. In spite of the Moslems who stood about him in serried ranks, all of them with swords beneath their pilgrim robes, he said:

"If I had imagined you to be God's messenger, I would not have fought you always. This is not the moment to bring up this controversy, so write as it is customary in Arabia—your name and your father's name."

There was a kind of rumble from the listening pilgrims. But Mohammed took no notice and quickly dictated:

"Between Mohammed ibn Abdallah and Soheil ibn Amr'."

When Ali had finished and a duplicate had been made of the document, the two delegates signed their names. Below came the signatures of the witnesses: Abu Bakr, Omar, Othman, for the Moslems; Huweitib ibn abd al Ozza and Mikraz ibn Hafs for the Koreishites. A note was added that Ali had transcribed the treaty. The clay seals were then attached. The original was retained by Mohammed, while the duplicate was handed to Soheil for safekeeping in the archives of Mecca.

With that, the Meccan embassy saluted the Moslems in the ancient Arab fashion and retired to their city to the accompaniment of the traditional peaceful wishes of their enemies of yesterday. But while the Moslems had spoken these conventional words of blessing, there was little genuine feeling behind them.

Most of the pilgrims, and Omar especially, were deeply mortified that Mohammed had given in to the Koreishites on practically every point. It seemed incredible to them that, after being brought all this way by their leader who had not been afraid to pursue an enemy which had defeated him, they should be halted outside their objective. It seemed even more incredible that he should humiliate himself before the Meccan envoy to the extent of neither calling his God by His rightful name nor using his own title, merely because the infidel had so demanded. Omar went as far as to ask:

"Are you really God's messenger?"

Without showing resentment, Mohammed replied that he was. When Omar insisted that his surrender that day had hardly made this seem likely, Mohammed answered that time would prove that he had acted wisely.

Omar was not satisfied. He went and consulted Abu Bakr. Abu Bakr, who knew Mohammed better than anyone, confirmed that time would show. Omar's hot temper began to rise. He left Abu Bakr and went to see what the other Moslems felt. He found them much in the same frame of mind as he. For the first time since Islam had come into being, there were signs of revolt.

Mohammed had given orders to the pilgrims to shave their heads, slaughter their animals, and carry out the traditional rites where they were. The pilgrims had refused. Three times the order had been repeated without it having any effect. The situation was one of the ugliest with which Mohammed had ever had to deal. To think things out, he retired to his tent. Here Umm Salama brought her woman's intuition to the rescue. She said:

"You can't force fifteen hundred men to do something they don't want. But you can make them look silly. Go and perform your rites and carry out your sacrifices alone, and where everyone can see you."

Mohammed realized the sense of this advice and acted on it. Putting on clean pilgrimage clothes, he stepped out of his tent into the white desert sunlight. With his face turned toward Mecca, which shimmered below him, he shaved his head and cut his nails. Thence he went over to where the sacrificial animals waited with their gay garlands. Selecting the camel of Abu Jahl, he hobbled it and drove his sword into the back of its head. In the same deliberate way he continued the sacrifice, the prayers, and the prostrations.

From under the acacias the soldiers had watched their leader with sullen interest. They expected, perhaps, some kind of exhortation, but when Mohammed went through the whole ritual with as little notice of them as if they had not been there, their indifference collapsed. As Mohammed completed the set prayer and raised his voice to thank his God for the mercies which He had shown him that day, the reclining men stirred. A moment of thundered silence was followed by a deep-throated cry. In a moment all were shaving their heads, shaving one another's head, in such haste that many gashed their scalps. In another few minutes the camp was echoing to the bellowing of camels as their sacrificers fell frantically upon them and hacked them to pieces.

Mohammed watched without any indication that anything had ever been amiss. When everything had been done which should be done, he ordered the camp struck and, mounting Al Kaswa, led the march back to Medina. He did not speak to Omar. He did not have anything to say to him. He knew he was right. He knew that his treaty would prove this.

In point of fact, that treaty was Mohammed's masterpiece of diplomacy. It was a triumph. No one, except perhaps Soheil, had thought back as had Mohammed when the Koreishite stood before him. No one, except those two, recollected the beatings, the stonings, the escape by night, the hiding in the cave. No one thought of the hazardous exile with the seventy followers. The contrast between now and then was unbelievable, miraculous. That the Koreishites were willing to treat with Mohammed at all, to recognize him as someone worthy of their attention, to admit him as the ruler of an Arab community, was beyond the bounds of all expectations. But, apart from his personal triumph over men who had vowed to capture him, alive or dead, Mohammed saw what no other Moslem did, the far-reaching effects of the treaty.

He was not a man to quibble over small details. He was like Henri IV when he became a Roman Catholic to save his throne, remarking to the disapproving Huguenots: "Paris is well worth a mass!" If Soheil's limited mentality could not reconcile itself to calling someone who had been a traveling salesman by a grandiloquent title, it did not really matter. If a Moslem phrase in referring to God was upsetting to a Koreish ear, it was not important enough to break off negotiations.

What *was* important was to have free access to Mecca. Mohammed knew that the day he and his men could set foot in the Holy City, it would not be long before they would be there permanently. From that moment he would be the decisive factor in settling who could worship at the Kaaba and who could not worship at the Kaaba, how he and God should be addressed or not addressed.

What, however, Mohammed chiefly saw in having this peace treaty with Mecca was the effect it would produce on the local tribes. He was right in this too. Within a few days of signing the document which had caused so much stir among his own people, chiefs from all around were coming to swear allegiance.

Omar was confounded. During the space of one week there had been more converts to Islam than in the six preceding years.

However, in order to make sure that there would be no doubt in the minds of his army that it had been wise to accept Soheil's terms, Mohammed had a revelation which confirmed his claims to having followed the right course. This revelation is recorded in the forty-eighth sura, and is entitled "Victory." The translation runs as follows:

"*Verily, we have won for thee an undoubted victory. In token that God forgiveth thy earlier and thy later faults, and fulfilled His goodness to thee and guided thee on the right path. . . .*

"*Well pleased hath God been with the believers when they plighted fealty under the tree, and He knew what was in their hearts. Therefore did He send down upon them a spirit of secure repose, and rewarded them with speedy victory. . . ."*

But even if these holy alliances were not sufficient triumph, the clause of the treaty relative to the returning of would-be Koreishite converts to Mecca was put to the test and invalidated by the Koreishites themselves.

A young Meccan called Abu Basir escaped from his family and came to Medina to become a Moslem. He was shortly followed by emissaries from his parents to bring him back. Although it went against the grain, Mohammed could do nothing but abide by his signature and hand the man over. However, on the road, Abu Basir overcame the guards. One he killed, the other he drove back to Medina. With his bloodstained sword still drawn, he appeared before Mohammed. Here he pointed out that, since Mohammed had fulfilled his obligation in sending him home, he was no longer responsible. Mohammed sat thoughtful for a while. Then he smiled and said earnestly to no one in particular:

"What a kindler of war! If he had but with him a body of adherents."

With that, he dismissed the young man. It did not take Abu Basir many minutes to appreciate the sense in which Mohammed's remark could be taken. Five Meccan friends of his were in Medina. These he called together and, after a short conference, led them out into the desert. In a few days they were established on the Syrian caravan track which follows the sea.

As Moslems and Koreishites were now at peace, the caravan business had started again. Long trains of camels and mules were streaming out of Mecca laden with rich merchandise. The days of Hashim and Abd al Mottaleb seemed to have come again. But not for long. Abu Basir was there to see to that.

Soon other young men who could not escape to Medina because of the treaty heard what was going on along that Red Sea trail and joined Abu Basir. In no length of time it became more dangerous for Meccan caravans to take the road than in the days of open war with the Medinese. Neither could the Medinese or their leaders be blamed. That it was reported that Mohammed never heard of another exploit of Abu Basir without smiling could not be held against him as a violation of the treaty.

Finally things got so bad that a deputation of Koreishites called on Mohammed and begged him to come to their assistance. Mohammed demurred. He said that this was not his business. The Koreishites begged all the more. When Mohammed finally gave in, it was on condition that the clause in the treaty relative to refusing sanctuary to converts should be ruled out. The Koreishites accepted. Mohammed had proved that he was as able a statesman as he was diplomat and general.

The highwaymen were immediately recalled to Medina. All answered the call but Abu Basir. The ingenious young man had been wounded during one of the raids and never recovered. Before he died, however, he heard Mohammed's commendations for the services which he had rendered to the Moslem cause and the assurance that a martyr's portion awaited him in paradise.

While regretting the loss of a potential leader, Mohammed felt satisfied with the general situation. In fact everything was working out more serenely than he had expected. Next year he would be in Mecca. From there anything might happen. In the meanwhile he had a great many things to do to consolidate the recent gains. He had also two or three small accounts to settle with those who had not yet had the intelligence to recognize him as the Messenger of God.

CHAPTER XVIII

THE EMBASSIES

(628 After Christ)

MOHAMMED NEVER LIVED to see the might of the Moslem Empire. He never had any real grounds during his lifetime to make him feel that there might be such an empire. Yet he believed in it. He believed in it in the same way as he had believed in his inspiration when he had only four followers. Now that he saw the rapid conversions of individuals and whole tribes, which followed his return from Hodeibiya, he became convinced that the time was not far off when the world would be ripe for Islam. It was true that there were still a few local groups which denied his sovereignty, but these he would deal with appropriately. Those on whom his thoughts now rested were the nations outside his present realm. He felt that these needed only a word of encouragement to become Moslems.

With this in view, envoys were chosen to go and give that encouragement. Some traditions say that in the same way as the apostles of Jesus found themselves on the Day of Pentecost able to speak in many tongues, so did Mohammed's ambassadors receive a miraculous gift of languages. That is as it may be. What Mohammed did do was to choose his representatives from the ranks of former commercial travelers. These men had been abroad, they knew the customs of foreigners and would not become bewildered as might Abu Bakr or Omar if they found themselves outside the familiar setting of the desert. They could also make themselves understood among Greeks and Romans and Persians.

In order to give the ambassadors some insignia of authority, Mohammed had a large silver seal or medal struck on which was engraved: "Mohammed the Messenger of God." It was an innocent and artless idea and caused a good deal of amusement to Abdallah ibn Obei and his friends. This did not prevent it, however, from soon meaning more than a Roman eagle.

The first mission went again to Heraclius. This one was halted at Bosra, where the governor took charge of the message and forwarded it to the Emperor. The silver seal interested Heraclius, and he had the epistle translated. What was his surprise to hear a summons from an Arab he had never heard of to give up the worship of Jesus and Mary and embrace the true faith, the faith of one God! Heraclius had the letter and the seal preserved as a curiosity, but took no further action.

The next embassy went to the Persian court. Chosroes had but lately been assassinated by his son Siroes, who received Mohammed's strange document. Siroes was not so much taken aback by the text of the message as that Mohammed addressed it: "Mohammed son of Abdallah, Messenger of Allah, to Chosroes [he believed him to be still alive] King of Persia."

The impertinence of this desert Arab placing his name before the King's incensed Siroes. Tearing the letter into pieces, he wrote to his viceroy in Yemen as follows:

"There is in Medina a madman of the tribe of Koreish who pretends to be a prophet. Restore him to his senses or send me his head."

Mohammed shrugged his shoulders when he heard of this, but all he said was:

"Even as he tore the letter, so shall Allah rend his empire."

The prophecy was realized rapidly. In less than twenty years Persia was a vassal state of the Moslems. Her ruler one of the men whom the "madman of the Koreish" had trained.

The chief of the Beni Hanifa, a Christian tribe of central Arabia, received the envoys with entertainment and gave them gifts. He, however, stipulated that he would join Islam only if he might have a share in the rule. Mohammed replied that if he had asked the share of an unripe date he would not have given it him. To this, he added a comprehensive curse which seems to have been effective. Next year the ambitious chief was dead.

In Abyssinia the envoys had an easy time. From the earliest days of the Call, the Negus had always befriended the Moslems and given them sanctuary. There were still sixty of them living at his court, among whom was Jafar, the son of Abu Taleb and half brother of Ali. This did not prevent Mohammed from having the same messages delivered to the Negus as to the Romans and Persians. It is said that the Negus accepted Mohammed's pious suggestions and acted on them. Of this there is no confirmation in works of history. While the Abyssinians had the deepest respect for Mohammed and what he stood for, they were already Nestorian Christians whose fundamental beliefs differed little from those of the Moslems. Today, moreover, the Abyssinians are still Christians. Whatever did transpire between the Arabs and the Abyssinians, it was all gay and cordial.

The embassy had another mission of a less religious nature to carry out on Mohammed's behalf in Abyssinia. There were several female Moslems living in Addis Ababa, of whom one was Umm Habiba, the daughter of Abu Sofian. She was the widow of Obeidallah ibn Jahsh, one of the first converts and one of the original fugitives from Mecca. Obeidallah's mother had been a daughter of Abd al Mottaleb, so he was a cousin of Mohammed. He was also the brother of Zeinab, whose divorce from Zaid and marriage to Mohammed had caused such a scandal. If this were not an already complicated enough relationship, Mohammed wished to add further ties by marrying this kinsman's widow. He had also in mind to mortify Abu Sofian and, simultaneously, strengthen his position in Mecca. Abu Sofian might denounce this alliance, but he would have to admit that the despised preacher was his son-in-law. As a matter of fact, all that Abu Sofian said when he heard about the marriage was:

"That camel is so rampant that no muzzle can retain him."

Umm Habiba, however, was pleased to marry Mohammed, and the Negus conducted the marriage by proxy. When this was done, Jafar and the other refugees made ready to accompany the bride back to Medina.

Another embassy was dispatched to Egypt. Mukaukis, the Roman governor, treated Mohammed's letter seriously and received the envoys courteously. He would not, though, commit himself on the matter of Islam. Before the messengers started on their return journey, he gave them valuable presents for their master. These included jewelry, Egyptian linen, honey and butter, a she ass, a white mule, and a thoroughbred stallion. To these conventional gifts he added two Copt sisters of great beauty called Miriam (Mary) and Shiren.

Whether Mukaukis had any idea of Mohammed's susceptibility to women or was merely rounding off the already great variety of gifts, has not been said. Whatever his motives, he could not have selected a present which pleased Mohammed more or caused a greater commotion in his home.

The moment Mohammed set eyes on this fair, curly-headed beauty he lost his heart to her. So did Hassan the poet. Mohammed quickly warded off the dangerous rivalry by giving his friend Mary's sister, Shiren.

For some reason, however, Mohammed did not marry Mary and brought her into the harem as a concubine. The uproar which greeted this was unanimous. Everyone from Aisha to Zeinab declared themselves outraged. Making a solid front, all the wives turned against Mary. In fact life was made so unpleasant for her that Mohammed moved her to an apartment in upper Medina. Neither was this looked upon with approval. The harem had decided that it hated Mary and carried the hatred to a point which nearly ended in wholesale divorce.

Mary was probably not the true cause for this crisis, but she appeared at a time when jealousies between wives had reached boiling point. To try and keep the peace, Mohammed had allotted one night to each wife in rotation. When he traveled outside Medina, he had the women draw lots for the privilege of accompanying him. This did not prevent him from always preferring Aisha, who knew it and used it to her advantage.

The two political parties still existed in the harem, Aisha and Hafsa and Sawda standing together against the others. Sawda had joined the two senior wives, partly because they had been her immediate successors and partly from self-protection. She was getting old and had always been unattractive. With Aisha sponsoring her, she felt safer from divorce. In fact, to make certain of this protection, she gave up her night with Mohammed to the young favorite.

Thus Aisha's position had remained unchanged, and there were few subjects which Mohammed was not ready to discuss with her. One of these was Khadija. Mohammed always placed Khadija in a different category from these girls who excited him and amused him but also plagued him. He continued to interest himself in her relatives and irritated Aisha by speaking of her as the best among women. One day Hala, Khadija's sister, came on a visit to Medina. She had much the same tone of voice as Khadija. When Mohammed heard her speak in the courtyard of the harem, he nearly fainted. As soon as she had left, Aisha said irritably:

"Why are you always dragging in those dreary Koreishites? Why do you always think about that toothless old woman whom Allah replaced by a better?"

Mohammed's face clouded.

Sternly he rebuked Aisha.

"No, indeed, Allah has not replaced her by a better. She believed in me when I was rejected. When they called me liar, she proclaimed me truthful. When I was poor, she shared with me her wealth. There can never be another like Khadija."

Outside the question of Khadija, however, Aisha did much as she liked in the harem. On one occasion she broke up one of Mohammed's marriages before it was consummated.

The lady in question was Esma, the sister of a princely desert chief. Her home was in Najd, and Mohammed sent a special escort of his camel corps to fetch her. To Aisha's and Hafsa's surprise and annoyance, they discovered that this essentially political bride was also very good-looking. Aisha decided to get rid of her, and took Hafsa into her conspiracy.

Dismissing the slaves, they said that the sister of so great a chief and the descendant of kings could only be prepared for her wedding by the Messenger's favorites. While they hennaed the unsuspecting girl's hands and combed her hair and perfumed her ready for the bridal carpet, they talked to her in a friendly, sisterly fashion. Among other things, they told her that if she met Mohammed's embraces with: "I take refuge from thee in Allah!" he would think much more of her than if she submitted immediately like all the other women with whom Mohammed had slept. The poor creature who had never seen such a madhouse as this harem or met such a crowd of crazy young women did as they suggested. She did not realize that this formula had been invented by Aisha and indicated that the woman using it did not wish to have physical relations with her husband.

Mohammed was taken aback when his bride made this protest. He thought he had heard wrong and approached her again. Esma met him with the same words. With parrotlike insistence, she repeated what Aisha had taught her. Finally Mohammed gave up. The next day Esma was sent back to Najd. She never understood why and, in later years, spoke of the lack of gallantry of the Messenger of Islam.

When, therefore, Aisha had to accept as a rival a Copt slave whose chief crime was to be prettier than any Arab, she could not contain her rage. The other wives, with the same objection to Mary, were not as outspoken as Aisha, but were not submissive. The atmosphere of the harem became charged, and the day that Hafsa caught Mary with Mohammed in her own apartment there was an explosion. Within fifteen minutes of the scandalous news being reported, the place was in pandemonium. In vain Mohammed tried to calm the infuriated women with promises and exhortations. Nothing seemed to calm their passion. They were like a band of maniacs. Finally he lost his temper too.

"Hell is inhabited by women!" he cried and added: "You women are more contemptuous of Allah than of me. I shall not visit you for a month!"

With that, he retired to a turret near the mosque and locked himself in. Such violence from this usually mild-mannered man had the effect of a bucket of cold water on the harem. After a few unassured assurances to one another that he would come back as soon as he had thought it over, the wives went back to their rooms. Here they waited apprehensively. But Mohammed did not return. He did not return that night, or the next day, or the next night. The rumor began to circulate that he had repudiated the whole harem. The city bubbled with excitement. There had not been so much running to and fro with reports and counterreports since the affair of Aisha and the necklace.

Abu Bakr and Omar alternately upbraided their daughters and sat gloomily in their houses. Apart from having their leader upset, the repudiation of Aisha and Hafsa might change the whole of their futures.

At last, when Mohammed had remained incommunicado for over three weeks, Omar could not stand the suspense any longer. He penetrated to the turret and asked Mohammed if he had divorced his wives. To begin with, Mohammed would not reply. After a while, when Omar began to show angry impatience, he shook his head. Partially relieved, Omar went out and told the people who hung around the mosque, seeking the latest gossip, that the Prophet's desertion of the harem was only temporary. He also reassured Abu Bakr.

Toward the end of the fourth week of absence, Mohammed reappeared in the harem. He went straight to Aisha's quarters and sat on her mat. He did not smile and looked at her reproachfully. But instead of being impressed, Aisha laughed and said:

"I thought you told us you were going away for a month?"

Mohammed had to laugh too. Taking Aisha in his arms, he said:

"This month has only twenty-eight days."

This reconciliation did not, however, keep Mohammed from Mary the Copt. He had installed her in this apartment in the town and continued to visit her regularly. A year after her arrival, she bore him a son whom they called Ibrahim. Mohammed was so happy and could not understand the gloom which the news spread over the harem. However, the child died before it could walk, and Mohammed grieved. Nevertheless he went on keeping Mary, who survived him by five years.

It must not be supposed that because Mohammed had much of his leisure plagued by his women, he was a henpecked husband. Considering the circumstances, he handled his wives with skill. He really knew a great deal about women. One of his counsels on this tortuous subject, which has baffled men throughout the ages, is the height of wisdom and shows profound understanding. In fact it is so wise that its application in any community, in any country, at any time might avoid the ceaseless misunderstandings between males and females. He said:

"Be charitable to the women sprung from your ribs. If you try to straighten a rib you will break it. Accept women as they are with all their curvatures."

He was not like his old friend Abu Bakr, who, in spite of having married four times, used to say:

"Women are an evil, but the greatest evil of all is that they are necessary."

The fact is that Mohammed was versatile. He could turn his mind and his energies to anything. On the one hand he was sending embassies to the rulers of the civilized world, while on the other he was devoting himself to a curly-haired concubine and getting himself into trouble with a crowd of jealous wives. And concurrently he was forming an army which could move quickly and strike hard. Subordinate officers were being trained, the men were becoming disciplined, the weapons were being improved. The strategy and tactics employed by bedouin raiders were being laid aside. In August of 628 Mohammed put his new fighting machine to the test by leading it against the Jewish settlement at Khaibar, which flanked the road to Syria.

These Jews who were going to be attacked were not unwarlike people. Like all their brethren of that era, they were warriors to be counted with. Descendants of the fighting Jews, of Abner and Joab, they could give battle as well as any Arab.

The reason for this expedition was threefold:

First, because Mohammed did not like Jews in his neighborhood. In spite of repeated warnings, they never seemed to learn a lesson. Whenever the opportunity offered, they started to make trouble for the Moslems. This was especially the case with the Beni an Nadir. After having been allowed by Mohammed to leave Medina unmolested, they had thought of nothing better than to ally themselves with the Koreish. Some of them had settled in these Khaibar oases.

Second, Mohammed wanted to make up for the disappointment which he had imposed on his men at Hodeibiya.

There was probably a third reason. He wished to maneuver his new army.

Khaibar was a territory comprising, as well as gardens and cultivations and dateries, several castles, in the center of which was a main stronghold which had defied many sieges. It was the kind of campaign which would show Mohammed if his army was trained up to his expectations.

The Moslem force consisted of sixteen hundred well-armed warriors, of whom nearly two hundred were finely mounted cavalrymen. Everyone else had a fast-trotting dromedary. Mohammed's regular staff was as usual with him: Abu Bakr, Omar, Othman, and Ali, also Zaid. Umm Salama had drawn the lucky lot and was once more with the army. There were other women too.

For the first time perhaps in the history of warfare, Mohammed was taking with him wives of Moslem soldiers to attend to the wounded. Women had accompanied armies on campaigns as concubines, as inciters to valor, like Hind and her companions at Ohod, but never before had anyone thought of females in their rightful roles on the battlefield.

The army also carried for the first time the great, somber standard known as Okab, the Black Eagle. It had been made out of a mantle belonging to Aisha. In later years it became one of the most glorious emblems of Islam as the ensign of Khaled and his Saracen light cavalry.

Several of the tribes which had refused to join the expedition to Mecca offered their services. Mohammed refused them. He said that if they could not disturb themselves for unprofitable ventures, he saw no reason why they should do so for the profitable.

The distance between Medina and Khaibar is a little over a hundred miles. An army moving normally would take five days to reach it. Mohammed knew that the only way to defeat this strongly fortified enemy was by surprise. He covered the distance in three forced marches, reaching the enemy territory before dawn on the fourth morning. No one had the least suspicion of this impending attack. The first thing the Jews knew about it was the Moslem helmets and breastplates reflecting the rays of the rising sun. A cry rang out and was echoed from garden to garden, from field to field, from castle:

"Mohammed! Great Jehovah! Mohammed and his soldiers!"

With that, everyone scattered and took refuge in the castles and cities.

Mohammed knew that on this occasion there would be no question of a spectacular victory or of starving garrisons into surrender. He was fighting the flower of Judaism, and it would need all his generalship and all the bravery of his men to conquer.

He began the campaign by reducing individually the minor strongholds. When this was done, he marched against Al Kamus, the main fortress of Khaibar. It was a formidable-looking place with frowning walls built out of the living rock. All accesses were strongly fortified, and within the ramparts was a well-equipped and well-provisioned garrison. Before delivering the attack, Mohammed gathered his army before him and offered up the following prayer:

"O Allah! Lord of the Seven Heavens and of all things which they cover! Lord of the Seven Earths and all which they sustain! Lord of the evil spirits and of all whom they lead astray! Lord of the winds and of all whom they scatter and disperse! We supplicate Thee to deliver into our hands this city and the riches of all its lands. To Thee we look for aid against this people and against all the perils by which we are environed."

"*Amin! Amin!*" resounded from the companies and squadrons.

After a moment of meditation everyone set to work on the grimmer task of battle. Mohammed found then that what he had set himself to accomplish was even more formidable than he had anticipated, and was aggravated by the difficulty of feeding his troops.

Arabs never carry much food with them. They rely on the hospitality of their friends and the plundering of their enemies. In this case the Jews had had time, while the outer castles were being reduced, to set fire to their cultivations and drive their livestock inside the city. Siege warfare was also unfamiliar to these nomads accustomed to desert raiding, and their defense of the moat at Medina had taught them nothing about assaulting fortresses. However, Mohammed seemed to have an inspirational knowledge of conditions of which he was as inexperienced as his men. He had a number of improvised siege engines put together on the spot. The most effective of these were palm-trunk battering rams which, eventually, made a small breach in the walls.

Into this Abu Bakr led a heroic attack, but he was driven back. Then Omar tried, but while he reached the mouth of the breach, he had to retire, losing most of his men. Finally Ali went up against the wall, bearing the black standard. As he charged, he chanted:

"I am Ali the lion, and like a lion howling in the wilderness, I weigh my foes in the giant's balance."

Ali was no giant, but he made up for his lack of height by his great breadth and prodigious strength. Today he was formidable in a scarlet tunic over which he wore his shining breastplate and backplate. On his head gleamed a spiked helmet encrusted with silver. In his right hand he brandished Mohammed's own scimitar, Dhul Fikar, which had been entrusted to him with the black banner.

Again and again Jewish veterans rushed at Ali. Again and again they staggered away with limbs or heads severed. Finally the champion of all the Hebrews, a man called Marhab, who towered above the other warriors, planted himself before Ali. He wore a double cuirass, and round his helmet was a thick turban held in place by an enormous diamond. He was girt with a golden belt from which swung two swords. He did not use these, however, and killed right and left with a long three-pronged spear. For a moment the battle paused and the combatants rested on their arms to watch the duel.

Marhab, like Goliath of Gath, had never been defeated. His size alone frightened opponents before they came close to him. His barbed fork disheartened the most skilled swordsmen.

Marhab attacked first, driving at Ali with his trident. For a moment Ali, unaccustomed to this form of weapon, gave ground. Then he steadied himself and fenced with the Hebrew. A feint and a parry sent the spear flying. Before Marhab could draw one of his swords, Ali's scimitar had cloven his head through his helmet and turban so that it fell on either side of his shoulders.

The Jews, seeing their champion dead, retreated into the city. Mohammed gave the signal for a general assault. The Moslems surged forward. Ali led the onslaught. He had lost his shield during the duel and, to replace it, had torn a door from its hinges, which he carried before him. But he had little need for it now. With the Moslems pouring through the breach like a torrent in flood, the inhabitants took refuge in their homes. Those who did not surrender were massacred.

The city was then sacked. Not finding the treasure which they believed to be there, the Moslems tortured the Khaibar chief and put him to death. The other Jews were banished, all of them except the chieftain's bride, Safiya.

Safiya was the daughter of the ruler of the Beni Koreiza who had died in the general execution of Jews after the Battle of the Ditch. She was an exceedingly good-looking girl and a scheming opportunist. The moment she was brought before Mohammed, she made it clear that she wanted to be friendly. Mohammed, who needed little encouragement with a pretty woman, threw his cloak over her, which indicated that he took her under his protection. When, shortly after this, he screened her from his soldiers, they knew that another wife was being added to the harem. The wedding celebrations were combined with the banquet in honor of the taking of Khaibar. The Jews had stored many good things in the city against the siege, and these were freely fed to the Moslem soldiers, who had been on half rations for some time.

When the feasting was over, Mohammed brought his camel and made it kneel before Safiya. Then, offering her his own bended knee, he helped her mount. Thus he took her to the bridal tent.

Safiya's introduction to the harem nearly stirred up another storm. But Safiya was as clever as she was beautiful and handled the situation with tact and firmness. She quickly appraised the politics of the Mohammed household and decided to be on Aisha's and Hafsa's side. It was not easy, though, and she had to accept a lot of taunts about her origins—in spite of the fact that she had become a Moslem. However, when she had replied to one of Aisha's more biting reproaches, "How can I be inferior to you when Aaron is my brother, Moses is my uncle, and Mohammed is my husband?" Aisha felt reproved. From that day Safiya became the fourth of the anti-Ali clique. Later she played quite a part in the Medina and Moslem politics. She did not die until forty years after Mohammed.

For the moment it was honeymoon time outside Khaibar, a honeymoon which nearly ended in calamity and the extinction of Islam.

The man with the trident whom Ali had slain had a sister called Zeinab. Zeinab had none of the fickleness of Safiya. She disliked the Moslems and detested Mohammed. She accordingly prepared and cooked a kid for the Medina general staff. This she thoroughly poisoned before serving. Mohammed loved broiled kid and eagerly dipped into the dish. However, as he began to chew the first mouthful, he gave a yell and spat it out.

"This is poisoned!" he cried.

Only one of the other officers had started to eat. He had swallowed several pieces of meat. In a few moments he was writhing on the floor. In an hour he was dead. Mohammed suffered much pain and was inconvenienced by the poison for quite a while, but he was not incapacitated.

When Zeinab was brought before him, he asked why she had done this. Her reply, if not sincere, showed presence of mind. She said:

"You have inflicted grievous injuries on my people. You have slain my father and my uncle, my brother and my husband. Therefore, I said to myself, if this man is a prophet he will know that the meat is poisoned and will reject it. If he is an impostor, he will die and it will be better for the whole world."

Some contemporaries say that Zeinab was executed. Others state that Mohammed was flattered by her explanation and let her go.

With Khaibar no longer in Jewish hands, with enormous spoils—animals and armor and carpets and weapons—there was nothing further to do but go back to Medina. The fertile lands of the Jews had been divided. One half was to be considered as a kind of crown domain to be administered by Mohammed. The other was allotted to individual soldiers who had taken part in the siege. The state coffers were brimming with gold pieces, so was the privy purse. As Mohammed slowly led his army home, he counted up his gains. From all points of view the balance was much in his favor. If this Jewish poison did not cut his life short, he was on the threshold of realizing most of his ambitions.

As he came within sight of the Medina palms bowing to the lilt of the wind, he had another pleasant surprise. During his absence his cousin Jafar and the refugees from Abyssinia had arrived. As soon as the army was sighted, they rushed out to meet it. It was a joyful reunion.

The last time Mohammed had seen these people, it had been in the dim alleys of Mecca, as, in groups, they crept away to exile. No one dared to lift his voice in farewell, no one had any idea if they would see each other again. How different it was now. The greetings were boisterous and filled with laughter.

In the harem waited Umm Habiba. She was not so young and

not attractive like Mary or Safiya. Consequently she was not an immediate cause for trouble. Everyone knew that Mohammed's interest in her was more political than physical. She, however, deliberately placed herself in the camp of Umm Salama and Zeinab and Fatima. During the political upheavals which followed the Messenger's death, she became the bitter and often dangerous enemy of Aisha. For the moment the serenity in the army and the church spread into the harem. With Safiya and Umm Habiba accepted, Mohammed felt comfortable in spite of the poisoning. All he waited for now was the great day when he would lead his men back to their home town.

CHAPTER XIX

THE FULFILLMENT OF THE TREATY
(629 After Christ)

SUCCESS did not turn Mohammed's head, but it made him overconfident. He had thought continuously about this first return to Mecca. He had seen himself as the conquering hero coming in his glory to prove that the Meccans had been wrong while he had been right. This dream would one day be fulfilled, but it was not for this seventh year after the Hijra and the six hundred and twenty-ninth after Christ.

The winter of 628 was occupied by various minor campaigns under the respective commands of Abu Bakr and Omar. At the turn of the new year Mohammed proclaimed that he was going to exercise his rights according to the treaty of Hodeibiya and make the pilgrimage to Mecca.

In February of 629, therefore, the Moslems once more paraded in their white pilgrim clothes before the oasis of Medina. All those of the original group who had survived Khaibar were there. Many others had come to fill the gaps made by the casualties, and increase the numbers. When Ali took the count of the muster, there were over two thousand Arabs whose only thought was to pray in the Holy City. Every one of these men was mounted on a dromedary, while on the flank of the parade were the sacrificial camels garlanded for execution.

In observance of the treaty, the pilgrims were unarmed except for their sheathed swords. However, to make quite sure that Abu Sofian had not arranged all this in order to lead Mohammed into a trap, other precautions were taken. A force of a hundred cavalry under Mohammed ibn Maslama, who had fought in all the battles of Islam, scouted ahead of the main body of pilgrims.

THE FULFILLMENT OF THE TREATY

In the rear, likewise, traveled a reserve of armor and bows and arrows.

On this occasion Abu Sofian seems to have wished to keep his side of the bargain. The moment it was announced that the Moslems were in sight, he evacuated Mecca. With carpets and bundles of provisions, the Meccans scrambled up the steep sides of the hills which overlooked the Holy City and camped. The die-hard anti-Mohammeds retired to a distance so that they would not have to see the desecrating of their shrines. The majority of the other citizens squatted on the rocks to watch the performance.

Slowly the Moslem column emerged from the gully which ran into Mecca from the north. At its head, Al Kaswa padded slowly along. Mohammed, who had often ridden down this road with the Syrian caravans, looked neither to left nor to right. Around him rode the chief companions: Abu Bakr and Omar, Othman and Ali, Zaid and, a little behind, Bilal. Seething through the defile came the rest of the pilgrims on their camels. As they caught sight of the Kaaba, a shout went up:

"*Labbaike Allah! Umma Labbaike!* [We are here, O Allah! We are here!]"

Outside the enclosure of the Beit Allah, the cavalcade halted. When everyone had caught up, a procession was formed and slowly entered the sanctuary. Mohammed rode first to the corner of the Kaaba and touched the Black Stone with his staff. He then began the seven circuits of the shrine. This was an ancient ritual belonging not only to Mecca but to faiths from time immemorial. Circling the maypole or the sacred fire or the walls of Jericho had similar origins. It had nothing to do with Islam. As they went, the pilgrims chanted:

"There is no God but Allah. It is He that hath upheld His servant and exalted His people. Alone hath He put to flight the host of the confederates."

This done, Mohammed led the way up the hills to Safwa and Marwa, where he rode from one to the other seven times. This part of the pilgrimage commemorates Hagar's frantic rushing to and fro between these two points when she was looking for water for Ishmael.

The sacrificial victims were then lined up and slaughtered. After that, all the pilgrims shaved their heads.

The main body of the pilgrims had now performed the initial rites of the lesser pilgrimage, but there remained those who had been mounting guard in case of treachery. Mohammed had these relieved, and they went through the same devotions as the others.

That night the pilgrims camped in Mecca. They did not say much, and they kept close together. The long-waited-for homecoming had not, somehow, been up to their expectations.

Oriental cities depend a great deal on their inhabitants for their personalities. The bazaar, the gossip on the flat roofs, the coffeehouses, the music, the general going and coming of men and women and donkeys and camels and mules and horses are of much greater significance to a town than the daily round of an American or English community of the same nature. To find Main Street or High Street deserted, to have the bars or teashops without patrons, to see no one looking out of the windows does not shock or depress an Occidental. But to an Oriental this absence of life means pestilence or national disaster.

Then, in addition to this ghostly atmosphere, this absence of sound, there was something more personal. Many of these Arabs were coming home after an absence of seven years. Through religious differences of opinion, they had lost touch with their friends and their relatives. They had quarreled with them. Still they had hoped that this pilgrimage would bring about some sort of reconciliation. It had not. Abu Sofian had seen to that. He had not sent soldiers to bar the way to the Moslems, but he had damaged them much more than by fighting them. The pilgrims could not even visit their homes. Every door and window had been barred and locked. A few women and old men had stayed behind, but they did not venture out. So the pilgrims huddled round the Kaaba, hoping that their leader would do something to relieve the gloomy tension.

He did nothing. He left them. He went up into the inner chamber of the Kaaba and remained there meditating. The place was still filled with idols, but he did not seem to see them. He was back in what he regarded as the emblem of his faith, the temple which Abraham had raised to God. The homesickness of his companions did not occur to him. Excepting during the early days of his marriage to Khadija, he had never known home life like other Meccans. He had been on the road or else he had been dodging persecutions. Mecca meant for him chiefly the divinely ordained center of the Moslem faith. . . .

When the hour came for the morning prayer, Mohammed left his retreat. He summoned Bilal and had him climb onto the roof of the Kaaba. Standing in the white sunlight which blazed down and reverberated from the rocky hills, the Negro, the first muezzin of Islam, made the ritual call to prayer. As the cry rang out clearly over the silent city, "*La ilaha illa Allah! Mohammed Rasul Allah!*" the dozing pilgrims stirred. The words, proclaiming the unity of the one God and the mission of His Messenger, rose and fell. To east and west, to north and south, to the Meccans perching on the rocks, the creed of the Moslems was published. It was dramatic, it was sublime, it was perfectly timed and staged. Every Meccan on that shimmering cliff knew that, below the black feet of this ex-slave, 360 idols sat staring sightlessly before them. But none of them protested. None heaved thunderbolts or caused the earth to quake. The Kaaba remained, square and solid, while the Negro, who a few years ago was carrying water like a beast of burden, desecrated it.

The pilgrims felt the inspiration. Their apprehension disappeared. An electric excitement spread through the men who had sat so sadly through the night. Pressing eagerly forward, they surrounded the Kaaba. When every one of the two thousand was in his place, Mohammed led them in prayer. Harmoniously the thousands of deep voices intoned the words which their leader had taught them in the early days of Islam. Rhythmically they lifted and dropped their hands and bowed their heads and bodies until the prayer was over. For a few moments they sat in silent contemplation. Then they dispersed slowly. Their hearts were glad. The disappointment of the previous evening had been swallowed up in the realization that nothing really mattered, homes or friends or relatives, provided they belonged to the true faith.

To a lesser degree this emotion reached up to the Meccans. Many of them expressed their feelings openly. Abu Sofian became restless. He had been afraid that this might happen. Jealously he watched the time and, on the morning of the fourth day of the pilgrimage, he sent Soheil and Huweitib, who had signed the treaty, to tell Mohammed to leave.

Mohammed, who was feeling at peace with the world, suggested that it would do no harm if he stayed a little longer. The two envoys shook their heads. Mohammed had agreed to stay three days. Those three days were over. He must go without delay.

Mohammed shrugged his shoulders and gave orders for the evacuation of Mecca, but he was annoyed. He was annoyed because he had hoped for some kind of compromise with the Koreishites. There was also a more personal reason. He was about to be married for the last time.

The eleventh and ultimate bride was Maimuna bint al Harith. She was the sister-in-law of Mohammed's peculiar uncle, Al Abbas. She was also the aunt of Khaled, the D'Artagnan of the Koreishites. Her age was twenty-six, and she was a widow. The courtship had been carried out through Al Abbas, who was still not a Moslem but kept in with Mohammed for the same opportunist and family reasons as before. The young lady was nice-looking and brought with her Meccan connections which Mohammed needed.

Mohammed would have liked to have the Koreishites sponsor this wedding, but he had misjudged their tempers. All they wanted was that he should go. So he led his men about ten miles from Mecca to a place called Sarif. Here the marriage took place.

Maimuna was attended by Salma, the widow of Hamza, who had remained in Mecca, and an unmarried daughter called Omara. Omara was young and pretty, and attracted the attention of

Mohammed's staff. Ali, especially, wanted to have her for his wife. However, Mohammed thought otherwise and gave her to the older cousin, Jafar.

Although Maimuna outlived Mohammed and the other surviving eight wives, she never held any great place in her husband's life or took any part in the development of Islam. Her only claim to fame is that she insisted on being buried at the place where she had been married. Her tomb can be seen today outside Sarif in a valley known as Wadi Fatima.

The two thousand pilgrims now continued on their way to Medina. In spite of that moment of inspiration after the prayer, they still felt that the pilgrimage had been a failure. They still felt that Mohammed was not acting toward the Koreishites with enough audacity. Mohammed was sure of the contrary. Once again he was proved to be right. . . .

It was about midsummer, and the Medinese went to work at dawn so as to escape the fierce heat of the day. From the south two men came riding with a small retinue. They were fully armed and, to the farmers' alarm, they wore the accouterments of the Koreishites. The alarm increased when one of the cultivators recognized Khaled ibn al Walid, as the first warrior, and Amr' ibn al As, as the second. Messengers were sent running to warn Mohammed of the coming of these enemies of all Moslems. Mohammed heard them without showing concern. He was in the mosque when Khaled and Amr' and their staff arrived. Saluting him, they begged to be admitted into the brotherhood of Islam.

These two were quickly followed by Othman ibn Talha.

A warm satisfaction glowed in Mohammed. The two Koreishite generals who had fought him in every battle and skirmish, whose tactics had once defeated him, were now officers in his army, while this Othman ibn Talha, as one of the custodians of the Kaaba, represented the first important defection from the religious and political groups in Mecca.

Numbers of less important Koreishites quickly succeeded these leaders. Mohammed once more felt that the time was fast approaching when he would be able to forget the treaty and be accepted by everyone except, perhaps, Abu Sofian and a few old die-hards.

Yet it was not quite time and, before he could put his project into effect, he had to suffer some unexpected reverses. It seemed almost as if Allah were testing his Messenger up to the very last moment.

A series of raids against tribes which had not yet adopted Islam ended unfortunately, or else achieved nothing. While they were incidents, annoying in themselves, they were of no great importance to Mohammed's general policy. When, however, an envoy of his was killed at Muta in Palestine by the son of the amir who governed in the name of the Emperor Heraclius, Mohammed resolved on reprisals.

Muta was about a hundred miles south of Jerusalem, on the Dead Sea. It was far outside Mohammed's domain or, for that matter, any Arab domain. The Romans were in command here, and Roman soldiers, with native levies under Roman officers, assured the peace. It was a veteran army accustomed to and equipped for modern warfare. This meant nothing to Mohammed. He believed in his troops, and having never seen anything but more or less desert warfare, could not imagine any other.

Without any more foresight than if he had been going up against the Jews at Khaibar or the Koreishites at Badr, he mobilized three thousand armed men on camels with a complement of cavalry. Zaid was appointed commander in chief, with Jafar as his second in command. In the event of both these men being killed or wounded, Abdallah ibn Rawaha, one of the old guard, was to succeed him. Khaled was appearing for the first time in the ranks of the Moslem army, but he was not suggested as a possible alternative commander.

Mohammed's self-confidence or ignorance or innocence in the handling of this affair is hard to reconcile with his usual practical-mindedness. He was sending an expedition against the most famous soldiers of the world and placing in supreme command, not Ali or Omar or even Abu Bakr, but his ex-slave who, brave as he was, had never held such a position before.

THE FULFILLMENT OF THE TREATY

The Roman government heard of the proposed invasion of imperial territory and made up its mind to indicate to this crazy man from Medina that he must confine his follies to his Arabian deserts. The local garrisons were called up. In a few days an imposing force of two hundred thousand modernly equipped soldiers stood ready under the orders of Theodorus, brother of the Emperor.

In the meanwhile Zaid and his three thousand warriors, on their desert camels, and his two hundred horsemen were hurrying gaily toward Syria expecting to surprise their enemies, thrash them, and return with the loot. Their astonishment was great, therefore, when on arrival at Maan they heard that the Romans had thought them worthy of turning out with their crack divisions. They accordingly halted and began to discuss what they had better do.

Zaid and Jafar pointed out that the object of their mission had been to teach a lesson to a local chief, not to fight Roman legions. Abdallah opposed this. He said that Mohammed had sent them out to fight infidels. If Allah was really with them, what difference would it make how outnumbered they were? Besides, how perfectly foolish they would look if they returned to Medina with nothing to show after riding all those hundreds of miles. The latter argument probably caused Abdallah's advice to win over the more cautious element on the staff.

The advance was ordered to be continued, and the little band of Arabs rode on toward a place called Belka, where the enemy was reported to be in position.

As the sun sent its first parching rays over the dreary shores of the Dead Sea, the Roman army was sighted. The Arab column stopped in its tracks. Never had any of the Moslems seen so many men all together, such fine equipment, such armor and weapons, such an orderly parade. They gazed in wonder as line upon line of plumed, breastplated soldiers maneuvered before them as if they had but one mind.

There could be no question now of changing tactics and refusing battle. The Moslems would have to fight and hope that

Allah would not desert them. The only thing which might help them would be a choice of position. A retreat was accordingly ordered to more advantageous ground near the village of Muta.

Simultaneously the Roman phalanxes began to advance. Like lumbering tanks, they bore down on the lightly equipped Arabs. Zaid could not resist this comparatively immobile force. He forgot the favorable position which he held and ordered the charge. Had there been a few more Moslems, the outcome of the battle might have been different. Moving with lightning rapidity, the infantry and the cavalry inflicted great damage on the closely formed ranks of the Romans. But they could not keep it up against the vastly superior numbers.

Zaid went down mortally wounded. Jafar leaped to his side and seized the standard. The hand by which he held it was slashed off. He placed it in the other hand. This was struck off too. He clasped the standard to him with bleeding stumps. A blow from a sword felled him. Another killed him. Abdallah took Jafar's place, and the battle ebbed and flowed around him. Then he was killed. There being no other appointed commander, a young officer seized the standard, shouting:

"Rally, Moslems, rally!"

Once again the fight raged about the standard which some providence seemed to preserve. But the day was lost and the ranks were beginning to give. Then Khaled showed his superior generalship. By voice and example, he reorganized the demoralized Moslems. He could not halt the retreat or counteract the defeat but, by skillful maneuvering, he stopped the rout and put an end to the panic. Slowly fighting every yard, making use of folds in the ground, disputing the smallest vantage point, he gradually drew his men off the field of battle. When night fell he had a badly mauled command, but one which was still a command.

In the morning, feeling rested, he had the audacity to advance against the enemy. This feint gave the Romans the idea that the Moslems had been reinforced, and they retreated to more suitable positions to meet the Arab attack. But Khaled was not going to risk what only good fortune and daring generalship had saved from a complete disaster. He hung about on the skirts of the enemy until dusk, and then made as quickly as possible for Medina. Although he was unable to find the bodies of Zaid or Abdallah, he found Jafar's, which he carried back with him.

News of the defeat had preceded the returning soldiers, and they were met outside the oasis by jeering citizens. It was another example of how little these Arabs knew of the outer world, how much they trusted in what Mohammed told them. They had no idea of who the Romans were, nor could they see any reason why their army should leave them without defeating them. This attitude was greatly responsible for their eventual spectacular victories. To them a Moslem was better than anybody else. He worshiped the only true God. He was under the leadership of this God's own envoy. He had a guaranteed safe-conduct to paradise. Such a spirit led to discounting whatever might be the reputation of the enemy and made death in battle a premium rather than a misfortune.

Mohammed, hearing the jeers, came out and quickly took the side of the soldiers. He quieted the booings and complimented Khaled. He then assured the officers and men that they would soon have other opportunities to retrieve what little prestige they might have lost at Muta.

What Mohammed could not speak evenly about were the deaths of Zaid and Jafar. Especially the loss of Zaid caused him great distress. Zaid had been his friend and companion for over thirty years. He had been one of the first converts, he had been beside him during the darkest days in Mecca and during the early difficult times in Medina. He had fought in every battle and had sacrificed himself to the extent of giving his friend and master his wife. Now he was dead. Mohammed wept unashamedly.

Jafar was given an imposing military funeral. The army paraded in full strength. Mohammed preached the farewell oration. He assured all that he knew Jafar to be in paradise. He ended his sermon by lauding Khaled and conferring on him the title of Sword of God. By this title he was thenceforth known and feared. For, although he had many spectacular victories with his crack cavalry divisions, he probably never excelled what he accomplished with a handful of inexperienced nomads against soldiers who had conquered the whole of the then known world.

Before anyone had time to comment or conjecture on Mohammed's defeat, he was on the move again. In the same way as he had followed up the Meccans after the trouncing at Ohod, he followed up Muta by taking the offensive.

Amr' ibn al As was placed in command of an expeditionary force of camel-mounted warriors and sent to the Syrian border. His objective was nomad tribes who were reported to be going to take advantage of the Muta defeat to attack the Moslems. Amr' marched fast and reached the approaches to Syria in ten days. Here he found the reports about the nomads well founded and a large body assembling to cross into Arabia. He sized up the situation quickly and ignored the fanatical counsels of some of his lieutenants. Sending a messenger to Mohammed, he said that if he was reinforced he could answer for the outcome of the encounter. If he were not, he and his men would do their best, but it might lead to another Muta.

Mohammed immediately dispatched troops under the command of Abu Obeida, seconded by Abu Bakr and Omar. Such an array of great names might have suggested that Mohammed did not trust Amr'. But before any of the relieving generals could express their views on the subject, Amr' had intimated that he had been appointed to lead this expedition and would continue doing so as long as he lived. Moreover, such was the democratic spirit of the Moslems that no one minded this lately converted Koreishite having his way.

The following morning Amr' attacked. The enemy, unaware of the arrival of reinforcements, were caught off balance and defeated. Amr' sent a messenger to Mohammed with the good news. He did not return at once and remained on the borders of Syria raiding and skirmishing and showing the enemy that if Muta had been a reverse, it had only affected a fraction of the Moslem forces. When he was sure that everyone understood this, he made his way back to Medina.

This was followed by a general submission of tribes from all over the country. Nomad chiefs who had sworn that they would die before they recognized Mohammed, appeared at Medina and swore allegiance. The reception was always cordial, and a friendly ear was given to grievances and petitions. In fact, by the end of 629, Mohammed felt that he could count on the majority of the tribal organizations from the borders of Yemen to the borders of Syria. The moment had come, he decided, to have done with the impertinences of Abu Sofian. He had stood them for sixteen years, he saw no reason why he should stand them for seventeen. All he required to do this was a valid excuse to break the treaty. The excuse came unexpectedly from the Koreishites themselves.

CHAPTER XX

THE ABDICATION OF ABU SOFIAN
(630 After Christ)

IN JANUARY OF 629 the Beni Bakr, a tribe allied to the Koreishites, attacked and pillaged another tribe which had sworn allegiance to Mohammed. Among the pillagers were a number of Koreishites in disguise. The survivors of the raid hurried to Medina and begged for redress. With a happy smile Mohammed assured them that they could count on it.

This was reported to Mecca. A few minutes after receiving the information, a meeting of the city council was called. It was an apprehensive meeting. There were no harangues inciting the Meccans to fight, there were no vain threats against Mohamhamed, there was no kind of bravado at all. The Koreishites knew that, unless someone had an extremely intelligent idea and a quick one, Mecca would soon cease to be an independent city. And no one had half an intelligent idea. No one could think of anything which could possibly halt Mohammed except perhaps appealing to his better feelings. This was the last thing anyone wanted to do. But what else was there? With Khaled and Amr' on the other side, with these hundreds of tribes now Moslems, diplomacy seemed the only way of escape.

The approach to the problem having been decided, the next question was, whom to send? Without exception, every member of the council detested Mohammed. He had been a troubler of their peace for nearly twenty years. Everything had been tried to destroy him, and everything had failed. To have to go now and admit that he had been right, to beg his pardon, to ask for tolerance was bitter to taste and hard to digest. But it had to be done, and it had to be done by someone who could convince Mohammed of the sincerity of his gesture.

The eyes of the members of the city council turned toward Abu Sofian. Abu Sofian protested. How could he, the archenemy of this bogus prophet, this ridiculous commercial traveler, humiliate himself before him? The more Abu Sofian talked, the more convinced the Koreishites became that he was the man to go to Medina. Besides, there was Umm Habiba. Abu Sofian had not seen his daughter for some time, and she must have latent affections for her father, in spite of her unbeseeming marriage to Mohammed.

Finally Abu Sofian agreed to this degrading mission and set out for Medina. When he got there, further humiliations awaited him. Mohammed, appreciating that the Koreish must be in a bad way to have to send their leader as their deputy, refused to see him.

Abu Sofian, who had already swallowed much pride, became incensed. But no one took any notice. He visited Abu Bakr and Omar and Ali, but they all treated him with the same indifference. He went to Fatima, who was not any more encouraging. His daughter's only gesture, when her father called on her, was to roll up Mohammed's mat lest an infidel body might rest on it.

Seeing that no one had any intention of discussing anything whatsoever with him, Abu Sofian went into the courtyard of the mosque and made an announcement. He said:

"Hearken unto me, ye people! Peace and protection I guarantee for all."

Hardly raising his voice, Mohammed commented:

"It is thou who sayest this, not we, O Abu Sofian."

When Abu Sofian reached Mecca again and reported on his trip to Medina, the people were dismayed. But, even then, they did not suspect what little respite they were to have before Mohammed struck.

He had now at his disposal a force which could really be called an army. It was officered by men who had served under him in battle and in raids for six years. They knew his methods, they had confidence in him and confidence in themselves. The rank and file consisted of nomad cameleers and horsemen, hard wanderers of the desert to whom fighting was a sport. No longer allowed to drink, their looting controlled, they had become disciplined. Added to these natural physical qualities, they were now well equipped and armed. To carry out this attack on Mecca, Mohammed could muster ten thousand trained men and as many animals.

But although this was the biggest Moslem command which had ever been put into the field, Mohammed was running no risks. The march to Mecca was to be carried out in secrecy. All the roads to Mecca were barred. All movements of nomads stopped. An efficient counterespionage service kept track of everyone. The only attempt to convey information to the enemy was frustrated.

Hatib, one of Mohammed's early followers, felt anxious about his family in Mecca and dispatched a female slave with a letter of warning. Mohammed heard of this through his intelligence corps, so that the woman was captured and brought back. Hatib nearly paid for his selfishness with his life. He was spared only when he pleaded that he had fought at Badr.

On January 1, 630, the army began to move. Az Zubeir, with two hundred cavalry, led the vanguard. Mohammed led the main body. In the rear traveled a few women, among whom were Zeinab and Umm Salama.

Omar was in charge of co-ordinating the advance and the march. With great skill he led the troops by unfrequented passes through the stony hills. No trumpet calls were permitted, no cheering, no shouting. About halfway between Medina and Mecca scouts reported that a party of men and women were traveling over the desert from the direction of the Holy City. Their leader turned out to be the irrepressible Al Abbas. He did not explain how he knew what was afoot, he just appeared and greeted Mohammed as if it were quite normal to find him parading across Arabia Deserta accompanied by ten thousand armed warriors. With him was his entire family. After passing the time of day, he unashamedly informed his nephew that he had decided to become a Moslem. With the same lack of self-consciousness, he and his relatives then made the profession of faith. Mohammed, who realized that while his uncle always went with the tide, he had always remained friendly, said good-naturedly:

"Uncle, you are the last of the emigrants as I am the last of the prophets."

Al Abbas shrugged his shoulders. Sending his family on to Medina, he joined the Moslem army.

Day by day it crept closer until, at Man Azzahran, it camped within sight of Mecca. Then only did Omar permit the lighting of campfires. To the consternation of the Koreishites, who had no idea what Mohammed was planning, they suddenly saw the hills to the north ablaze with thousands of splashes of red flame. They could not, however, believe that all of them represented soldiers. It was probably a ruse to make them think that the army was bigger than it was. To make sure, Abu Sofian and Hakim, one of Khadija's nephews, and Budeil, the chief of one of the few local tribes which had remained with the Koreishites, went out to reconnoiter.

Before they got anywhere near the camp, they saw a large white creature looming in the darkness. They were wondering what defensive measures to adopt when the creature stopped beside them. To their surprise, it was Al Abbas. Fearing that the Koreishites might do something rash and be massacred for their pains, he had somehow borrowed Mohammed's white mule and ridden out to warn anyone he could find of the strength of the Moslem army. Running into Abu Sofian, he advised him to come with him and surrender to Mohammed before daylight, when the assault on Mecca would begin.

Abu Sofian, who had very little pride left, agreed and climbed onto the back of the mule behind Al Abbas. The other two Meccans retraced their steps to report what was happening.

As the Messenger's familiar mount penetrated the lines of the camp, the soldiers on all sides sprang to attention. No one noticed who was on the mule, and the two men were not halted until they met Omar. He, with his customary lust for blood, gave a gleeful snort and made ready to cut off Abu Sofian's head. Al Abbas had quickly to intervene and claim privilege as the sponsor of his fellow rider. Omar turned away reluctantly, and the mule continued to Mohammed's tent.

Mohammed made no gesture when his uncle saluted and told him who was outside. He dared not express the delight which the news gave him. Not only was he returning with interest all the humiliations which Abu Sofian had inflicted on him, but he now had the means of having Mecca delivered to him without bloodshed. Although this huge army had been mobilized, Mohammed had no longing for physical revenge, no wish to hurt people who had hurt him. He wanted no more fratricidal killing. All he said to Al Abbas, however, was:

"Take him to your tent and bring him to me in the morning."

These orders Al Abbas complied with, and spent most of the night convincing Abu Sofian that the days of a Mecca independent of Mohammed were over. Immediately after the morning prayer he waited on Mohammed with his prisoner.

For a few moments Mohammed looked Abu Sofian over as he stood before him, partly cringing, partly raging, and still rather contemptuous. Then he said:

"Abu Sofian, have you not yet discovered that there is but one God?"

Abu Sofian nodded.

"Had it not been so, I would not be in my present plight," he grumbled.

"And am I not this God's Messenger?" went on Mohammed.

Abu Sofian hesitated. He looked about him anxiously. To acknowledge this was more than he could bear. Quickly Al Abbas intervened.

"This is not the time for hesitancy!" he cried. "Believe and testify, or else——"

"Or else," concluded Omar, who stood menacingly at the

entrance to the tent, "your head will be severed from your body."

Abu Sofian waited no longer. He made the profession of faith.

Mohammed remained silent for a few minutes. He could not believe that this archpersecutor of Moslems had acknowledged him. True, he had done it through fear, but to be able to inspire fear in this old rascal who had so often tried to kill him was almost past credibility. After a while he said:

"Hasten to Mecca, Abu Sofian, and tell the people to remain indoors. All those who will do so will be safe."

Abu Sofian withdrew. Outside he found the camp in a hum. Companies and squadrons, battalions and regiments were falling in. The sun flashed and glinted on the polished helmets and the steel breastplates. The banners of the tribes, hundreds of them, danced in the breeze. Tall camels gurgled and bellowed. Horses neighed and pawed the ground. Abu Sofian had never seen so many men, so many animals, such fine arms. Catching sight of a body of horsemen in dark mail and carrying long lances, who sat in their saddles like carved statues, he asked who they were:

"They are Mohammed's personal bodyguard, chosen from the foremost warriors of Mecca and Medina," replied Al Abbas.

Abu Sofian did not wait to hear more. Down the stony hillside he rushed back to Mecca. Summoning the city council, he told them what he had seen. He warned everyone that it would be useless to resist. There was little remonstrance. The majority of the Meccans did not want to resist. They had been impressed by the behavior of the Moslems at the pilgrimage the previous year. They were tired of fighting. Many of them were beginning to think that they had been wrong about Mohammed from the start. Accordingly men, women, and children retired into their houses and, closing the doors, waited for the triumphal entry of the Moslems.

In the meanwhile Mohammed had dressed and armed himself as if for battle. Wearing a scarlet tunic, over which gleamed his cuirass, he had on his head a spiked helmet around which was wound his black turban. Except for his sword, he was unarmed.

Mounting on Al Kaswa, which knelt before his tent, he rode out to review his troops. Before the march past began, he handed to Ali the great banner which he had already carried so bravely at Khaibar.

In spite of Abu Sofian's declaration of faith, Mohammed did not trust him any more than at the time of Ohod. He consequently did not expose his army to any surprise move on the part of the Meccans. In fact he caused his forces to surround the city and enter from four different points.

From the south Khaled led the cavalry of the allied bedouin tribes; from the north came another group of nomads, these on camels, under Az Zubeir; from the west the Medinese under Saad ibn Obada and from the east Abu Obeida at the head of the veteran refugees. Behind this last contingent rode Mohammed with his staff, supported by Ali in command of the black armored lancers which had so impressed Abu Sofian.

With the precision of well-disciplined troops, the regiments and battalions moved off from the camp. Slowly the columns wound down the worn tracks which led to the Holy City. Nowhere was there any opposition. It looked as if the bloodless victory which Mohammed had hoped for would be his. Then, without warning, Khaled's force was attacked.

Safwan ibn Omeiya, Soheil ibn Amr', and Ikrima ibn Abu Jahl had found it too much to sit in their homes while this breaker of treaties took over their city and their liberties. They did not care how big an army he had. They were warriors, and their instinct was to fight.

It was their misfortune that they chose to oppose Khaled's column. With any of the others they might have had a temporary success. With this firebrand they stood no chance. The shower of Meccan arrows had hardly fallen before Khaled's and a thousand other scimitars had flashed from their scabbards. Lying close to their horses' necks, the cavalry charged. Before Mohammed could send a messenger to stop what he had done so much to avoid, two Moslems and twenty-eight Meccans had been laid low.

At the time of this untoward event Mohammed was watching

the occupation of Mecca from a kind of platform a little below the cemetery where Abu Taleb and Khadija were buried. Here he had had his tent pitched and remained until the occupation of Mecca was completed.

Everything still seemed incredible to him. From where he sat he could see the home of Abd al Mottaleb, where he had played as a little boy. He could see the home of Abu Taleb, where he had been brought up, and the home of Khadija, where he had been so happy. He could see the alleys where he had walked as a young man and the spot where he had joined his first caravan. He could not remember how often he had ridden down this same road returning from some distant trading expedition or the number of times he had passed this place on the way to his silent vigils on Mount Hira. And now all this was his. The descendant of old Hashim, whose family had degenerated until no one in it counted, was reviving the greatness of the name. Today he, Mohammed ibn Abdallah, ibn Abd al Mottaleb, ibn Hashim, Messenger of the Lord, was master of Mecca! . . .

As soon as he was assured that the Moslem troops were in control of the city, Mohammed exchanged his uniform for his pilgrim dress. Then he mounted Al Kaswa and rode to the Kaaba. Here he repeated the rites of the year before—the touching of the Black Stone and the making of the seven circuits of the shrine. After a pause he called those surviving few who had believed in him before the Hijra, those men who had stood with him at this very spot and risked their lives for the cause. He was about to put into execution what had been in his mind from the earliest days of his mission. He was going to break up the Kaaba idols.

One after another the 360 stone images, including the great god Hubal and the statues of Abraham and Ishmael, were brought out of the shrine and dashed to pieces. As each effigy was shattered, Mohammed recited from the seventeenth sura:

"Truth is come and falsehood is vanished. Verily, falsehood is a thing which vanisheth."

Some of the Meccans who had come out of their houses to see what was going on held onto themselves as this sacrilege was carried out. When, however, the last emblem of age-old idolatry had been trampled under foot without anything calamitous happening, they looked at one another with relief. Hurrying to their neighbors who had stayed indoors, they spread the astonishing news. By the time they had brought the incredulous to the Kaaba square to see for themselves what was taking place, Mohammed had added to his desecrations by obliterating the paintings on the walls of the shrine.

When this was done, a crier was sent through the city to tell all those who wanted to acquire the benefits of Islam to destroy any private idols they had in their homes. After the pitiable defeat of the stone deities outside the Kaaba, the Meccans had no hesitation in throwing their images out of the windows.

With that settled, Mohammed summoned Othman ibn Talha and returned him the keys of the Kaaba, thus reinstating him as the hereditary keeper. Simultaneously he restored his crafty uncle to the guardianship of the bitter well of Zemzem.

Al Abbas accepted it without comment and continued to behave as if he and Islam had been one and the same thing since its beginning. This double-minded opportunist never did anything outstanding during his lifetime, unless one counts his achievement in keeping in with both parties for so long, but his name has lived for ever in the annals of Islamic history. He was the direct ancestor of the dynasty of the Abbaside caliphs under whose rule Arab civilization and culture rose to its greatest height. These Abbasides, who were in power from about one hundred years after Mohammed's death until the middle of the thirteenth century after Christ, gave Baghdad its fabulous golden age. Harun al Rashid (Aaron the Just) was one of the many illustrious descendants of Al Abbas, a rascal, but the only man of that period of Meccan turmoil who never lost his sense of humor.

With these two investitures confirmed, Bilal mounted to the top of the Kaaba for the second time and raised voice in the summons to prayer. Once again, to north, south, east, and west, he called, the words ringing clearly over the flat roofs of Mecca. As the last invocation died away, Mohammed turned toward the now purified shrine and began the prayer. The soldiers in the immediate neighborhood turned also. So did the soldiers in the streets and on the hillsides, ten thousand of them, turn and confirm their faith in one God and His Messenger, Mohammed.

A short pause followed while Mohammed rode to a small hill not far from the Kaaba, where he accepted conversions from the men and women of Mecca.

The first to take the oath was Abu Kuahafa, Abu Bakr's father, who approached Mohammed leaning on his son's arm. Mohammed told his old friend that he should not have inconvenienced the aged man and rather taken him to see him. In fact during the whole of the ceremony Mohammed did not cease to emphasize that he was no more than a human being like any of those who now stood before him—the son of Koreishite parents.

Very few people were punished for past wrongs to Mohammed, and only four who had murdered were executed. Among the proscribed was Wahshi, who had killed Hamza at Ohod. He ran away, however, and the next time that Mohammed saw him he had become a Moslem, which saved him his head.

The most surprising conversion was that of Hind. She had been unable to flee from Mecca and boldly presented herself before Mohammed. When Mohammed saw her looking up at him with her lovely eyes, he could not repress a gesture of disgust. Hind's proud stance left her. She fell at Mohammed's feet begging forgiveness. This public humiliation of the woman who had done more than anyone to blacken him satisfied Mohammed. He forgave Hamza's murderess and accepted her as a Moslem. But Hind never believed and, until she died, she detested and despised Mohammed.

Ikrima, the son of Abu Jahl, managed to get away. When, however, he heard that Mohammed was being lenient to converts, he returned. He found a considerate welcome from his blood enemy.

There were reasons for this. The acknowledgment of Mohammed as the Messenger of Allah by the son of Abu Jahl was a triumph which justified moderation. There was also need for first-class officers in the growing Moslem army. Ikrima was one of the best in Arabia. Soon after his conversion he was given a command. He quickly vindicated Mohammed's decision and became a valiant leader, eventually dying for Islam on the field of battle.

In fact all these converts became much more fanatic than their brethren who had turned Moslem in the days of persecution, when there were no battles to fight outside personal ones of self-defense.

Immediately after the surrender of Mecca and the conversion of the people, Khaled and Amr' were dispatched to destroy images and groves in the neighboring villages and oases. This they did, but whenever they, and especially Khaled, encountered any who showed hesitation about professing the faith, they immediately killed them. This was contrary to all Mohammed's ideas. He had behaved with forbearance and magnanimity in Mecca. He had forgiven and, apparently, forgotten the innumerable slights and wrongs which he had suffered during his persecution. He had behaved rather like Joseph in Egypt. When he heard of the way that Khaled was propagating Islam, he raised his eyes to heaven and cried:

"O Lord! I am innocent in thy sight of what Khaled hath done!"

He confirmed his contrition more practically by censuring Khaled and sending money to compensate the relatives of those who had been slaughtered.

When all the ceremonies were over, Mohammed looked over the city, bathed in the golden light of evening. Around him stood the faithful few who had been with him from the start. They looked different too. They were relaxed and chatted without that alertness of men who must always be sure that their swords are not stuck in their scabbards. Stretching out his arms toward the sun-kissed roofs of the city, Mohammed said:

"Thou art the choicest place on earth to me and the most

delectable. If thy people had not cast me forth, I never had forsaken thee."

The Meccans greeted this with words of gratitude, with tears. The Medinese, however, turned to one another in dismay.

"Alas," said they, "Mohammed is now conqueror and master of his native city, he will doubtless establish himself here and forsake Medina."

These remarks were carried to Mohammed. Quickly he reassured those who had shown him kindness when he had no friends.

"No!" he said. "When you plighted to me your allegiance, I swore to live and die with you. I should not act as the servant of God or His Messenger were I to leave you. Where you live, there will I live, and there too shall I die."

This pledge he carried out. In fact he only twice returned to Mecca before his death.

Now he was tired. He needed rest. In a few days he had become one of the most powerful rulers in Arabia. He was pope, he was caesar. Before the year was over, he would be the only ruler who counted, the founder of a nation, of an empire, of a faith. But this did not elate him as much as the thought that the Kaaba, the center of the world, was now cleaned of its infamous idols. If he died that night, he would consider the most important part of his mission accomplished.

Mohammed did not die that night. He had still a little while to live, but the climax of his career was that golden evening when everything he had striven for was his.

It is rare to find men fulfilling all their ambitions during their lives. It is even rarer to find those few who do, not losing their sense of values. On this January evening of 630 A.C. and in the eighth year of the Hijra, Mohammed slept on his mat in the same way as he had slept when he traveled commercially for the house of Khadija bint Khuwailid.

CHAPTER XXI

THE FORGING OF AN ARMY
(630–631 After Christ)

IT MIGHT BE SUPPOSED that anything following the taking of Mecca would be anticlimax. It was not. On the contrary, climax upon climax continued to pile themselves in adventurous succession into Mohammed's already overtumultuous life.

Although the majority of the Meccans had embraced Islam, some of the older families had not. They had accepted Mohammed as their leader, but did not see the necessity of believing as he did. This did not suit Mohammed's designs for the Holy City or for any Arabian community. He had no pretensions to temporal power, but until all of his "subjects" were Moslems he did not feel that he had justified himself before God. He was considering going out to preach again when unexpected news halted him.

The impression on the minds of the Moslem general staff was that the fall of Mecca would be the signal for the rest of Arabia to surrender unconditionally. The contrary occurred.

The great tribe of Hawazin, which pastured around At Tayef, where Mohammed had tried to take refuge from persecution two years before the Hijra, had always dismissed him as an impostor. These tribesmen were proud people and, in their hilly retreat, had always managed to maintain their independence. Mohammed's triumph decided them to hit him hard before he had that complete control of Arabia which would mean an end to their liberties. They accordingly called to arms their many affiliated clans which lived in the same mountains. Among these were the Sa'adites with whom Mohammed had spent his early childhood.

As soon as Mohammed heard about this revolt, he decided also to hit hard before it made any headway. He had every means for so doing. Since the taking of Mecca, his army had been increased by a contingent under Abu Sofian and now numbered twelve thousand. At the head of these he set out to meet the confederation of tribal levies from At Tayef.

These had mobilized quickly and had mustered in great numbers. To counteract the cavalry and greater military experience of the Moslems, they had furthermore taken advantage of their rugged country.

In order to reach the fertile valleys behind the Autas mountains where these rebellious tribes grazed their camels and their sheep, a narrow defile had to be traversed. The name of the defile was Hunayn. It was a dark and dismal place with precipitous sides and little room for an army to advance except in small groups. There was no scope for cavalry to maneuver, once engaged in the gully. Camels too would be at a disadvantage. The Moslem advance guard was, however, led by Khaled and his still untried bedouin troopers. Behind these surged the main body of horsemen and cameleers and foot soldiers. Mohammed, riding his white mule, brought up the rear with his veterans.

Mohammed did not ride in the rear of the column for the sake of safety. He did not consider such a contingency. He was as confident today as he had been cautious a few weeks before. He had no doubt in his mind that his army could defeat any enemy. He regarded the whole expedition rather in the light of a big raid which would give his recruits experience and furnish his soldiers with loot. This view was shared by his officers and men. When, therefore, the Hawazin tribesmen sent avalanches of rocks onto the Moslems and followed them by showers of arrows and then by yelling swordsmen, everything in that dark gorge became turmoil.

It is singular how often these tactics have routed first-class troops. It is even more singular how often first-class troops have allowed themselves to be caught in such a situation. Roland was routed this way at Roncesvalles, so was Varus in the Teutoburger forest. Lawrence of Arabia used this stratagem successfully against the Germano-Turkish forces not far from this place where Mohammed now saw his glittering advance guard rushing helter-skelter toward him like stampeded cattle. In a few minutes this proud army which had been promenading so splendidly up the defile had become a mob of disorganized men being hacked at by yelling tribesmen who seemed to multiply out of the dark cliffs. In vain did Mohammed command and entreat his soldiers to rally. Panic, which has destroyed some of the finest battalions in the world, had taken charge. Trying to halt the rout was like trying to stem a tidal wave.

Mohammed was so mortified that he called on his veterans, who had stood fast, to follow him to death. He drew his sword and, spurring his mule, rode toward the seething ranks of the enemy which were themselves immobilized by the narrowness of the pass. Al Abbas sprang after his nephew. He seized the mule's bridle and, raising his voice, yelled at the Moslems to remember who they were and what they represented. Al Abbas had a voice as loud as a hundred trumpets. In the enclosed rockiness of the valley, it reverberated and echoed. The Moslems paused. Al Abbas redoubled his shouts. The Moslems turned to face up the gorge. Those who had fought at Khaibar and Muta suddenly felt shame. With the same ferocity with which they had made for safety, they now made for the enemy.

"*Ya Labbaike Allah!* [Here we are, O Lord!] *Ya Labbaike!*" they yelled as they flowed up the hill.

Charging Moslems, Moslems rushing to die for their cause, have always been irresistible. They were no less so on this February morning of 630. What had begun as a disorderly panic turned into a desperate battle. The hill tribesmen did their best, but, against these fanatics, well armed and now well disciplined, they gave ground. Soon they were running as quickly as had the Moslems.

Their rout was complete. Pressing on them with the weight of his army, Mohammed drove them out of the defile and into the open valley. Here they attempted a stand, but they were now at the mercy of the cavalry. The rout degenerated into a massacre.

Soon the few survivors were fleeing for their lives. Soon they had fallen so far back that their camp was in Moslem hands. In addition to the casualties inflicted, Mohammed's soldiers had to their credit 6,000 old men and women and children, 4,000 pieces of silver, 40,000 sheep and goats, 24,000 camels. It was the most spectacular victory which Mohammed had ever won.

He, however, withheld his congratulations. He felt much as he had after Ohod. He knew that if it had not been for his uncle's voice of thunder he and his veterans might have ended their days in the defile. He recognized the unpardonable weakness of self-confidence. In the nineteenth sura, he wrote:

"Now hath God helped you in many battles. But on the day of Hunayn, when ye prided yourselves on your numbers, it availed you nothing. The earth with all its breadth became too straight for you, then you turned your backs in flight."

Among the prisoners taken after the battle was a withered old woman who demanded to be brought before Mohammed. When she saw him she addressed him familiarly by name. Mohammed was puzzled until the old lady introduced herself as Sheima, his foster sister of the days when he was brought up by the Beni Sa'ad nomads. Mohammed did not hesitate to have Sheima come and sit on the mat beside him as she had when they were both babies in the shepherds' camp. A little later Halima also made her way to the commander in chief's tent. She was wizened and bent with age, but spoke to her illustrious foster child as she had fifty years back. Mohammed treated her with the same deference as Sheima, and the three sat on the same mat and laughed over childhood anecdotes which Halima remembered.

However, meeting these links with the past did not deter Mohammed from dealing severely with the tribes which had dared to question his authority. Especially did he want to teach a lesson to the people of At Tayef who had treated him so roughly ten years before. He felt also that if he could destroy the notorious idol Allat, it would finally convince the other Arabs of the futility of worshiping images.

But the men of At Tayef were stout warriors. They shut themselves up in their city, well armed and with plenty of provisions. Mohammed, likewise well armed, tried all manner of attacks. He used new siege weapons and massed assaults, but everything failed. His casualties began to mount alarmingly. Some of his best officers fell. Abu Sofian lost an eye. Finally, after laying waste the dateries and the vineyards, he decided that it would be wiser to raise the siege. He accordingly marched his army to Al Jirana, where he divided the loot of the campaign. In doing this he allotted as large proportions to the newly recruited converts as to the old. To Abu Sofian and Ikrima he was especially generous. He even sent a message to Malik, the commander in chief of the At Tayef tribes, offering to return him his personal property if he surrendered and became a Moslem. Malik, who realized that it would only be a matter of time before he would *have* to surrender, agreed to the proposal. He could not convince his followers of the wisdom of this move, but his coming alone gave Mohammed sufficient satisfaction for the moment.

None of this, however, pleased the old guard.

"See," they said, "how he scatters gifts to all these newcomers and gives us but our bare share!"

Mohammed heard about this and, as usual, taking the initiative, attacked the trouble at its base. Calling a parade of the Ansars and the Muhajirin, he addressed them as follows:

"I came among you marked as a liar, yet you believed me; persecuted, yet you protected me; helpless, yet you aided me. Think you I do not feel all this? Think you I can be ungrateful? You complain that I bestow gifts upon these people, and give none to you. It is true, I give them worldly gear, but it is to win their worldly hearts. To you, who have been true, I give—myself! They return home with sheep and camels; you return with the Messenger of the Lord among you. For, by Him in whose hands is the soul of Mohammed, though the whole world should go one way and you another, I would remain with you. Which of you, then, have I most rewarded?"

The sincerity of the earnest words sank deeply into the hearts of the veterans. Without hesitation they replied:

"O Messenger of Allah, we are content."

Mohammed was, of course, right. These newly converted tribes had little idea of what Islam meant. All that impressed them was force and its resultant loot. By convincing them that he represented both these elements, Mohammed won them to him. The cultivating of the faith could come later.

When all these matters had been settled, Mohammed returned to Mecca to complete the rites of the pilgrimage which the campaign had interrupted. With this done, he led his men back to Medina.

The route he chose took him past Abwa, where his mother lay buried. He halted the army and sat for a while beside Amina's tomb. It was fifty-four years since he had stood holding black Baraka's hand while the villagers shoveled sand and stones over his mother's shrouded body. But he remembered the scene. He remembered the tears of the slave nurse. At the time he was not so sure what the weeping was all about. Death was as strange to him then as it was familiar now. Today he wished that his mother had lived to find salvation in the new faith.

The return to the home town was in triumph. Not only had Mecca fallen to the Moslem army, but the battle of Hunayn had been fought and won. Aisha and Hafsa were relieved to see their husband safely home. They were unquestionably jealous of Zeinab and Umm Salama, who had been on the expedition, but their curiosity made them listen to the tall stories which the two camp-following wives had to tell. Mohammed, also, was glad to see Aisha. Within a few hours of his arrival, he had resumed his usual routine and wife visiting. Nothing which had occurred during the past months was allowed to alter his way of living. There was a great deal of money available and a great deal of glory to celebrate, but this made no difference. The money was given to the poor, and the glory was celebrated with the same humble food in the same unfurnished apartments of the mosque.

The democratic relationship between the crownless king and his warrior subjects was the same as it had been in the early days of hardship and discouragement.

The remainder of the spring and early summer of 630 was given over to establishing and promulgating laws and receiving deputations from the tribes coming to swear allegiance. Then, in the midsummer of that year, on the eve of his sixtieth birthday, Mohammed undertook what was, perhaps, the hardest physical ordeal of his life. He mobilized and marched a great army of men and horses and camels across the burning deserts of Arabia to impress on the Roman emperor that the days were over when *Romanus sedendo vincit* (The Roman conquers by sitting still).

It came about this way.

Mohammed's fast piling up victories and his now established sovereignty in Arabia made the Emperor Heraclius realize that he should have followed up Muta with an invasion. Perhaps it was still not too late. He accordingly called on the Syrian tribes to assemble round the Roman eagles and help destroy the Arabian dictator.

To meet this threat, Mohammed had two courses open to him. The first, to let the Romans venture into his own desert country and meet them where it suited him. The second, to attack himself. The first course was the easier, but might lead to losing some of the newly allied tribes. He chose the second. The choice encountered almost universal disapproval.

Although reared in these waterless countries, Arabs are not immune to heat. Any Arab who can drive his flocks into hill country in midsummer will do so. Those who cannot get away keep under any shelter they can find during the middle of the day and pasture their animals, as far as possible, before sunrise and after sunset. The prospect, therefore, of setting out over these waterless, sun-scorched wildernesses, in armor, and marching all the way to Syria to meet a formidable enemy had little inducement. To the average member of the Moslem rank and file, it made no sense. A majority refused to take any part in the mad venture. Abdallah ibn Obei, who had been eating his heart out at Mohammed's succession of triumphs, appeared prominently again. Darting about among the discontents, he made mischief. He painted the picture of the desert in midsummer worse than it was. He added to this the certain defeat which the Arabs would find at the end of their body- and heart-breaking march. He suggested that megalomania had caused Mohammed to lose his reason. No born Arab who was not crazy would consider such a scheme.

Mohammed did not insist. From the earliest campaigning days, he had never encouraged any to follow who were not filled with fanatic zeal. To those who came to him with excuses, he commented caustically. Thus when some begged off because it was harvest time, he replied:

"Your harvest lasts for a day! What will become of your harvest throughout eternity?"

To the general complaint against the heat of the Arabian sun in summer, he retorted:

"Hell is hotter!"

The old guard, however, behaved with the same loyalty and trust as they had always. Omar laid his savings before Mohammed. Othman brought one thousand gold pieces. Abu Bakr subscribed four thousand drachmas. Mohammed knew that it was about all his friend had, but he insisted on handing it over. Even Al Abbas came forward with a generous contribution.

Finally everything was ready. As the shadows of the palms began to lengthen, Mohammed paraded his men. In spite of the many tribes absent from the muster, a great host had turned out, larger than any before. Interminably, the ranks stretched out before the oasis. Thirty thousand cameleers, ten thousand cavalry and a great transport train, over forty thousand in all. It seemed hard to believe.

At Badr, there had been three hundred ill-armed fanatics; at Ohod, seven hundred; at Khaibar, only two years before, sixteen hundred had marched under the Moslem banner.

With his usual perverseness, Abdallah ibn Obei appeared on parade. As usual, he and his contingent started with the army. As usual, they deserted as soon as the troops were clear of the Medina area. This time Abdallah added mischief to desertion.

Mohammed had appointed Ali to command the Medina garrison during his absence. On returning to the oasis, Abdallah spread the rumor that Ali had been left behind because Mohammed was jealous of him. When Ali heard this, he mounted his fast dromedary and rode after the army. Mohammed had to use great tact to pacify his deputy and convince him that he had been given this inactive post because he wanted a tried leader in charge if there was a tribal revolt while he was away. Ali returned to Medina and pulled Abdallah out of his house. He told him that, while Mohammed was unaccountably lenient with his mischief-makings, *he* was not. If Abdallah did not behave while he, Ali, was in command, he would know what to expect.

The crossing of the desert by the Moslem army was a grim ordeal. No marching was carried out until after sunset, but this was not much compensation. The dusk brought relief from the direct rays of the sun on helmets and breastplates, but the night was not long enough for the country to cool off. In the daytime the only shadow was afforded by rocks which were so hot that they could not be touched. The ground was as blistering to the feet as burning coals. The scarcity of water added to the misery. The hot wind made life intolerable. None of the men, not even the oldest nomad, had undergone such a trial of heat and privation.

Mohammed rose above himself. His behavior was exemplary. He was not a nomad, he was not young or even middle-aged. In addition to the actual physical test, he had to cope with a thousand responsibilities. Yet he never faltered. In just over a week he brought an entire force with all its baggage train to Tebuk, on the frontier of the Roman Empire. Had he been a shepherd or a cameleer driving his herds across the desert, the achievement would have been remarkable. To lead forty thousand men and animals was on a level with the march of Cyrus' ten thousand Greek mercenaries from Babylon to the Black Sea in 401 B.C.

Tebuk was a fertile oasis. Gardens and palms and abundant

water made the Moslems think of paradise. Neither were there any Romans to spoil the picture. The inhabitants were friendly, and the army gave itself up to an orgy of bathing and nursing wounded feet.

As there was no one to fight, Mohammed sent out flying columns into the neighboring districts to demand submission of the local chiefs. Jews and Christians and idolaters flowed into the Moslem camp without demur. The only column which came back with bloodstained lances was, as might be expected, Khaled's.

His command consisted of the new regiments of Moslem cavalry, numbering in all about five thousand. Khaled moved so fast that he caught an important Christian chief named Okeidir outside his city walls on a hunting expedition. Khaled, remaining true to his principles, killed every one he could except Okeidir. He spared his life only on condition that he surrender unconditionally. This he did and was taken back to Mohammed with two thousand camels, eight hundred sheep and goats, and a great store of arms. Mohammed received Okeidir so cordially and so differently from what Khaled's behavior had led him to expect that he voluntarily abjured Christianity and became a Moslem.

For some months Mohammed remained in Tebuk receiving homage from tribes from all over the country. Then, as no Romans appeared, he suggested to his staff that it might be a good idea to go and look for them. Omar, however, opposed this. He pointed out that the main object of the expedition, to prevent an invasion of Arabia, had been accomplished. That, in addition to this, tribes ranging from the Red Sea to the Euphrates valley had made submission. That it would be much better to let well enough alone. Mohammed was persuaded. The return march to Medina was undertaken during the comparatively cool month of December.

The reception of the army by the Medinese was clamorous. As soon as the dust of the long column was sighted, the citizens poured out of the oasis, cheering and singing and applauding. Even so, Mohammed did not take the attitude of a conquering hero. As the people thronged about his mule, he addressed them by name. He let the children climb up his stirrups and ride behind him and before him. He behaved like the father of a huge family returning from a hunting trip.

The only people who kept away from the rejoicings were those who had thought it too hot to march. Not only did they feel ashamed, but they were disappointed. The army had suffered few casualties and had brought back much loot.

Mohammed, also, took a stern attitude toward all these who, for no reasons but their own comfort, had stayed at home. He placed an interdict on them and forbade the old guard to have anything to do with them. It was a kind of general excommunication which ostracized them from mosque and social intercourse. Not only were they branded as cowards, but they were denied any spiritual comforts. Revelation after revelation came to the Messenger about these shirkers which were duly transcribed in the Koran. He dictated:

"If there had been plunder near at hand and an easy journey, they had surely followed thee. But the way seemed long unto them. They will swear by God unto thee. . . . If we had been able we had surely gone forth with you. . . . They destroy their own souls, for God knoweth they are liars."

And many more verses like it.

For a month Mohammed continued this persecution. Then he relaxed the interdict and pardoned the delinquents. He knew that, from now on, he would not have to worry about absenteeism from battle. He had also further cause for gratification.

As if Allah had decided that Abdallah ibn Obei had plagued Mohammed long enough, this tiresome man sickened and died soon after the return of the Tebuk expedition. Mohammed went to see him several times, and, before he was buried, said prayers for him. When the ever bloodthirsty Omar protested, Mohammed shrugged his shoulders.

"It doesn't matter," he said, "if you pray for a hypocrite or not. If you pray all day and all night, and the man *is* a hypocrite, God knows it and will not forgive him."

Mohammed could afford to be magnanimous over Abdallah's death. With him out of the way, he had no one to contend with. In fact within a few days of Abdallah's burial the dissident Medinese acknowledged Mohammed as their only leader.

* Soon he had further cause for satisfaction. Although the siege of At Tayef had been raised; although its chief, Malik, had gone over to the Moslems; although armed bands continued to raid the neighborhood—the city had not yet surrendered. In spite of having their gardens and dateries ravaged and their flocks seized every time they ventured far from the walls, the inhabitants had managed to hold out. At last a deputation made its way to Medina and offered to surrender the town if it were permitted to retain its idol, Allat. Mohammed shook his head. The ambassadors then asked if Allat could be spared for three years, for two years —maybe for one year?

"Not even for one week!" declared Mohammed uncompromisingly.

Nothing else which the men of At Tayef could say would shake this decision. Soon they became too tired to argue. Before they left Medina, they had agreed to unconditional surrender. Mohammed, however, did not trust them as it concerned the destruction of Allat. So he sent Abu Sofian and Al Moghira ibn Shuba, one of Islam's early converts, to see that this part of the treaty was observed.

Delegating this Koreishite leader as one of the iconoclasts was an astute gesture. Without any proclamation, it made it clear that however anti-Moslem a man had been, he could always become the instrument of Allah's will. However, when Abu Sofian took up a pickax and aimed a blow at the great stone figure, he lost his nerve. Either fear of what the idol might do to him or of the reactions of the citizens of At Tayef made him miss his mark. To triumphant shouts from the onlooking idolaters, he fell flat on his face. It was a critical moment which might have led to the Hawazinites changing their minds. But Moghira was a veteran Moslem. Seizing the pickax, he hacked Allat to pieces. With that, he called his companions and, mounting his camel, left the women of At Tayef to weep over the remains of their protector.

With the turn of the year, the time came again for the pilgrimage to Mecca. This time Mohammed did not go. In his place he sent Abu Bakr and Ali. He did this with a purpose. Although most of Mecca and the tribes of Arabia had adopted Islam, there were still a number of idolaters who, from force of habit, made the Meccan pilgrimage. There were no idols to worship, but this did not prevent these men from observing their pagan rites. For it must be noted that while the religion of the Arabs had been changed, most of the age-old ceremonial had been retained or adapted to the new way of thinking. Mohammed never denounced the cult of the Kaaba which he considered dedicated to Allah ever since the days of Abraham. Nevertheless, he did not wish this misinterpreted, so he decided that the heathens and heretics must adopt his teaching or be kept away from Mecca. He did not, however, wish to involve himself in what, in reality, was a comparatively minor matter for him in his present position. So he stayed at home and let his lieutenants attend to these details.

When the pilgrimage was in its final stages, Ali called everyone together and made known Mohammed's latest decree, which amounted to a general denunciation of all infidels.

Idolaters who refused to accept Islam were to be put to death. Jews and Christians did not have to forfeit their lives. They were to be warred against, but, on making submission to the Moslems and paying tribute, they were to be allowed to continue in their faiths. The edict concluded as follows:

"I am ordered to declare unto you that no unbeliever shall enter paradise. No unbeliever shall, after this year, perform the pilgrimage. Whosoever has a treaty with the Messenger, it shall be respected until its time expire. Four months are given to the tribes that they may return to their homes in security. After that, the obligations of the Messenger cease."

THE FORGING OF AN ARMY 313

When Ali had finished speaking, the pilgrims dispersed. In groups and companies and alone, they made their ways to their homes. As they went, they spread the news that, from now on, Islam was the faith for every part of Arabia. From the end of this ninth year after the Hijra and the six hundred and thirty-first after Christ, no one who did not believe in the inspired teaching of Mohammed would be permitted to set foot within the sacred area of Mecca.

This order is still enforced in 1946, thirteen hundred and fifteen years after it was promulgated.

CHAPTER XXII

THE LAST PILGRIMAGE

(632 After Christ)

MOHAMMED'S ORDER relative to the Moslem attitude toward Christianity has, with few exceptions, been maintained. This is contrary to what Occidentals generally suppose.

To the average American or European who professes a religion, any faith which is not Christian is wrong. Even within the Christian fold, the various denominations consider each other as respectively misguided. There is little tolerance between church and chapel, and none between cathedral and mosque. This is not so with Islam.

While the Moslem faith unconditionally condemns idolatry, it unreservedly recognizes Christianity.

In the second sura of the Koran and again in the fifth, Mohammed wrote:

"Verily, they who believe, and the Jews and the Sabeans and the Christians—whoever of them believeth in God and the last day, and doth what is right, on them shall come no fear, neither shall they be put to grief.... And thou shalt certainly find that those to be nearest in affection to them [who believe in Islam] are those who say, We are Christians."

Discussing the conditions under which Jews and Christians could remain on Moslem soil and be considered part of the community, Mohammed added:

"He who wrongs a Jew or a Christian will have me as his accuser."

Again and again he recommended this tolerance toward the faith which so resembled his own. In all his treaties with Christians, he invariably guaranteed their liberty of worship.

When Omar became caliph and captured Jerusalem, he gave rigid injunctions that neither Christians nor their churches should be harmed. When the Moslems invaded Spain in the eighth century, everything Christian was respected. It continued to be so until the disintegration of the Arab rule in Europe during the fifteenth century. It did not continue when the Christians regained the upper hand. Forced conversions by the Holy Inquisition took the place of Moslem benevolence.

This active intolerance has ceased, but its germ remains. Yet there is no reason why it should. After all, the quarrel between Islam and Christianity is really a quarrel between near relations; and, like most quarrels of that kind, is based chiefly on misunderstanding. Nothing will be achieved by trying to discredit Mohammed. Nothing will be gained by dismissing the Koran as a lot of incoherent nonsense. Much will be attained by studying Islam impartially. As that clear-thinking member of King George's Privy Council, Ameer Ali, wrote a few years ago:

"The true Moslem is a true Christian, in that he accepts the ministry of Jesus and tries to work out the moral preached by him. Why should not the true Christian do honor to the Preacher who put the finishing stroke to the work of the earlier masters?"

Why not? Why should Occidentals assert that their beliefs are more authentic than those of other sects? It is true that there are 585 million Christians in the world against 300 million Moslems. But of these 585 millions, not more than 70 per cent attend to their religious obligations with any regularity, whereas 95 per cent would be nearer the ratio of Moslems who practice Islam as laid down by Mohammed thirteen hundred and thirteen years ago, when he was about to make his valedictory pilgrimage to Mecca.

Before actually setting out, however, he had to receive deputations from rulers who, if they did not all embrace Islam, recognized Mohammed's temporal rule. Among these were one of

Heraclius' Syrian governors and the King of Oman. These men, like many others, saw the handwriting on the wall and interpreted it correctly. To be safe in Arabia depended on the good will of Mohammed.

To Yemen, at the southern tip of Arabia, Ali was ordered to go and convince the inhabitants that a time had come when they should cease to regard Mohammed and his people merely as traders. Ali had never been entrusted with such a mission. He did not like the idea. He would fight anyone from a Koreishite to a Roman, but preaching frightened him. Mohammed assured his nephew that inspiration would come. Placing one hand on his mouth and the other on his heart, he prayed:

"O Allah! Loosen his tongue and guide his spirit."

To give Ali further confidence, he furnished him with three hundred well-armed horsemen.

This was lucky. Ali proved to be as poor a preacher as he was a good soldier. The people of Yemen laughed at everything he said. Some threw stones. When they started shooting arrows at him, he decided that sermons might be mightier than swords, but they did not suit his notions of making converts. In a few minutes the Book had been exchanged for the lance. Before the day was over, the Yemenites were sorry they had not let Ali go on talking. When he reached Medina, he drove before him prisoners and camels and sheep and goats. He also assured Mohammed that Yemen was part of Islam.

From another southern state, Hadramaut, came princely envoys to join the Islamic cause. This pleased Mohammed even more than the Oman alliance. The people of Hadramaut belonged to a rich, civilized race which lived in splendid cities overlooking the Gulf of Aden. Their homes must have been the fathers and grandfathers of the world's modern skyscrapers. Today, as then, as centuries before, the architecture of these towns was more like that of New York of the future than Arabia.

The Hadramautites were great travelers and traders. As Mohammed anticipated, their attachment to Islam caused the faith to spread outside Arabia. It was these dwellers in tall houses who carried it to Malaya and Java and the Philippines. It was probably through them, unwittingly, that the Moros of Mindanao got their designation. To the Spaniards who first put the Philippines on the map, any Moslem was a Moro—this from the Latin *Maurus*, a citizen of the North African kingdom of Mauretania. Finding people who had the same religious practices as the Moslems of the Mediterranean, the Spaniards decided they came from similar stock and called them Moros.

And so it went on. From north, south, east, and west the tribes and the states and the principalities sent their delegates to confirm their adherence to this obscure man of the desert. No one seemed to find it peculiar that this individual, following no higher trade than traveling salesman, possessing no peculiar mental culture, and not distinguished at the outset by any claim to power, should be in this exalted position. It was taken as a matter of course—then as today. It will no doubt continue to be so, with increasing fervor, until the end of the world.

No Jew or Buddhist or Christian ever saw his faith grow before him with such miraculous rapidity. No other religious leader was ever so rewarded in his lifetime. It seems almost as if God had wished to emphasize that Mohammed was the last of His prophets and Islam the last of His religions. With the exception of Brigham Young, no other man of note has since that time attempted to set up a new creed. A few impostors appeared in Arabia, but their followers were not numerous and their sovereignty short-lived.

One of these, Moseilma, had a gift for oratory. His sermons, which he claimed to be inspired, brought him followers. Others were added whom he duped by conjuring tricks. He wrote a Koran of his own which did not amount to anything, but had the originality of placing man's soul in his abdomen! Feeling overconfident one day, he sent an embassy to Mohammed with a letter which began as follows:

"From Moseilma the prophet of Allah, to Mohammed the prophet of Allah! Come now, let us make partition of the world. Let half be thine and half mine."

Mohammed's reply was short and pointed:

"From Mohammed the Prophet of Allah, to Moseilma the liar. The earth belongs to God. He bestows it on such of His servants as He pleaseth."

With that, he dismissed the matter. Moseilma was, however, not discouraged and continued to preach and gain supporters. He eventually became a sufficient nuisance for Abu Bakr, as first caliph, to send Khaled with an army against him. After a stiff fight, Moseilma's men were defeated. He was himself killed by Wahshi, now an ardent Moslem, with the same javelin with which he had transfixed Hamza at Ohod.

But that hardly worth mentioning incident was the most which Mohammed and his people had to contend with in the way of rivalry. During the next seven centuries the Moslems would be the aggressors, carrying Islam to countries which its founder had never heard of.

Today Mohammed was beginning to feel the strain. He probably had no definite premonition of his approaching death, but he did not want to be caught unawares. He accordingly made preparations for a full-dress pilgrimage to Mecca. This was to be the greater or unabridged pilgrimage which had not been performed since the Hijra.

Early in March of 632, draped in the seamless white pilgrim robes, he mustered his men. Forty thousand answered the call. The nine surviving wives were also on parade in their camel-borne litters. With the exception of Ali who was on a mission to Yemen, every member of the old guard was present. Ali, however, reached Mecca in time to take part in the pilgrimage.

The great procession moved by easy stages across the desert. There was no longer any necessity to send out advance guards or even to carry weapons. The country for hundreds of miles around was solidly Moslem. At what had been nomad camping places, mosques had been built. The few shepherds passed on the line of march could belong to none but the true faith. It was the triumphal climax to hard work and great courage. Mohammed no longer felt his age, and Al Kaswa, which had carried him in flight nine years before, padded along as if she understood the part she had played in this drama of the desert.

THE LAST PILGRIMAGE 319

Sarif, a few miles outside Mecca, was reached on the tenth day. Here the pilgrims bathed and rested. On the following morning the cavalcade wound its way down the rocky slopes of the barren hills which guarded the Holy City. As the sun rested its first rays on the Kaaba, Mohammed passed through the gate of Beni Sheiba by which he had entered as conqueror on the last visit. Coming within full view of the shrine, he raised his hands and cried:

"O Lord! Add unto this house in dignity and glory, the honor and the reverence which Thou hast already bestowed on it. And they that for the greater pilgrimage, and the lesser, frequent the same, increase them much in honor and dignity, in piety, goodness and renown."

Not feeling strong enough to make the seven circuits of the Kaaba on foot, he did so on the back of Al Kaswa.

During the succeeding days he performed the rites of the greater pilgrimage which have been observed with the same detail ever since. In fact, when, for certain uncontrollable reasons, and nothing to do with the cult, Mohammed had to hurry certain ceremonies, these hurryings were noted and continue today! There is nothing written regarding the carrying out of the pilgrimage. Those present that day committed everything to memory and passed it on. When, in 1853, Sir Richard Burton succeeded in outwitting the interdict against non-Moslems going to Mecca, he went through precisely the same ritual which Mohammed observed in 632, including the unintended hurryings.

The first of the series of ceremonies took the pilgrims outside Mecca to Mina. Here the usual prayers were said and the night was spent in camp. The following morning the procession, now greatly increased by the Meccan contingent, marched to Mount Arafat, some ten miles from Mecca.

Arafat is the place where Adam and Eve are supposed to have been reunited after the long separation subsequent to their expulsion from Eden. It is not really a mountain. It is rather a huge block of granite two hundred feet high rising out of a kind of pebbly basin in the middle of other hills. Neither can it have been very steep, as Al Kaswa carried Mohammed to the summit.

From this commanding station he informed the waiting throngs that Arafat and its valley were holy stations for pilgrimages. After that he made formal prayers, concluding with:

"This day I have perfected your religion unto you, fulfilled my mercy upon you, and appointed Islam to be your faith."

This stage of the pilgrimage had taken longer than had been anticipated, and the next stopping place was not reached until late. In consequence Mohammed had to rush the afternoon and sunset prayers into one. It did not occur to him to mention that this was due to circumstances and could have been avoided by better timing. So the pilgrims took this rush to have some mystic significance. Consequently it became one of the illogical observances which Sir Richard Burton commented on, twelve centuries later.

At dawn the following day the tens of thousands of pilgrims followed Mohammed in the morning prayer. Thence the procession returned to Mina. As he went, Mohammed cried loudly:

"I am here, O Lord! I am here! There is none other God but Thee! I am here! Praise, blessing, and dominion be to Thee. I am here! No one therein may share with Thee. I am here, O Lord! I am here!"

Arrived near Mina, Mohammed and his pilgrims hurled small pebbles at a projecting rock known as the Devil's Corner. According to tradition, Abraham had encountered Satan at this spot and driven him away with stones.

With the stone throwing over, the camels brought for sacrifice were slain until the valley ran with blood. The ceremonies ended with the shaving of the head and part of the face and the cutting of nails. The hair and the nails were ordered to be burned. It is, however, probable that Mohammed's were conserved. Today there are mosques in all parts of the Moslem world in which, in contradiction to all of Mohammed's injunctions on the subject, one or two of his hairs are kept and reverenced. These hairs are supposed to have come from the shaving rites of this pilgrimage.

With these holy observances completed, the pilgrims were

permitted to put on their normal clothes. Ali then announced that the time had come for eating and rest. The flesh of the sacrificial animals was distributed, and for two days everyone forgot about everything but making up for restrictions of the preceding weeks. On the third day Mohammed mounted his camel and, taking position in the middle of the Mina valley, preached the valedictory sermon:

"O people, listen to my words, for I know not whether another year will be vouchsafed to me after this to find myself amongst you at this place.

"Your lives and property are sacred and inviolable amongst one another until you appear before the Lord, as this day and this month is sacred for all. And remember you shall have to appear before your Lord who shall demand from you an account of all your actions. . . .

"O people, you have rights over your wives, and your wives have rights over you. Treat your wives with kindness and love. Verily you have taken them on the security of God, and have made their persons lawful unto you by the words of God. . . .

"Keep always faithful to the trust reposed in you, and avoid sins.

"Usury is forbidden. The debtor shall return the principal, and the beginnings will be made with the loans of my uncle Abbas son of Abd al Mottaleb. . . .

"Henceforth, the vengeance of blood practiced in the days of paganism is prohibited and all blood feud abolished. . . .

"And your slaves! See that you feed them with such food as you eat yourselves, and clothe them with the stuff you wear; and if they commit a fault which you are not inclined to forgive, then part from them, for they are the servants of the Lord, and are not to be harshly treated. . . .

"O people! Listen to my words and understand the same. Know that all Moslems are brothers one unto another. You are one brotherhood. Nothing which belongs to another is lawful unto his brother, unless freely given out of good will. Guard yourselves from committing injustice."

Then, raising his voice, he cried:

"Know you what month this is? What territory this is? What day?"

To which the people replied:

"The sacred month. The sacred territory. The great day of pilgrimage."

At each reply, Mohammed added:

"Even thus sacred and inviolable has God made His life and the property of each of you unto the other, until you meet your Lord.

"Let him that is present tell it unto him that is absent. Haply he that shall be told may remember better than he who has heard it."

He now paused while the people stood silent and attentive. Then he gave instructions abolishing the system of triennial intercalation of the year as contrary to God's arrangements of the months. In other words, the Moslem year is lunar. This, of course, causes Moslem feasts to vary in season every so many years. With that established, he concluded the sermon:

"And now on this very day has time performed its cycle, and returned to the disposition thereof existing at the moment when God created the heavens and earth. You people, truly Satan despairs of being worshiped in your land for ever. But, if in some different matter, which you might be disposed to slight, he could secure obedience, verily he would be pleased. Wherefore beware of him.

"Verily I have fulfilled my mission. I have left that amongst you, a plain command, the Book of God, and manifest Ordinances which, if you hold fast, you shall never go astray."

He paused once more and then, impulsively and with great emotion, he cried:

"O Lord! I have delivered my message and accomplished my work!"

The tens of thousands of pilgrims answered as one man:

"Yea, verily thou hast."

And Mohammed cried again:

"O Lord, I beseech Thee, bear Thou witness unto it."

The army of pilgrims was then dismissed and silently trooped over the stony country toward Mecca, five miles away. Mohammed stayed a little longer to rest and meditate. Then, accompanied by his staff and his wives, he made for Mecca also.

He went straight to the Zemzem well and drank a cup of bitter water. Thence he climbed inside the Kaaba, where he prayed for a while. It was very hot in the unventilated shrine, and Mohammed left it thirsty. He stopped, therefore, at the first open door he came to and asked for a drink. All that the householder happened to have was water in which raisins and dates had been steeped before being delivered to the pilgrims. Al Abbas' son, Al Fadl, begged his cousin to come as far as his home, where there was plenty of fresh water and milk. But Mohammed would not wait and drank the water, cloudy with date dust. Some of the pilgrims took note of this, and today there are many who regard swallowing a cup of this fouled liquid as part of the pilgrimage rites.

Three days were allowed for the Medina contingent to recuperate before returning home. The atmosphere was cordial and different from what it had been at the time of the last visit. Relatives met relatives, and friends recognized friends without that watchful glance for the concealed sword. Parties were given, and the brotherhood of which Mohammed had preached was put into practice. It was perhaps less gay than in the days of Abu Jahl and Abu Lahab, but it was more sincere.

Mohammed was happy. His mind was at peace. He had completed the pilgrimage and established a ritual which he knew would continue. But, although all the official ceremonies had been attended to, he had a private rite to perform before he could return to Medina completely satisfied.

After the last evening prayer had been said, he slipped away from the crowd, which drifted out of the Kaaba square. Mounting his mule, he rode out of Mecca by the northern road. In a few moments he had left behind him the narrow streets of the Holy City with their sounds of laughter and feasting. He passed up the rugged path down which he had so often ridden as a young merchant returning from trading expeditions. Soon he was out in the open country. He could no longer hear anything but the wind hissing through the desert scrub. After a while he turned his mule westward. A few yards brought him to two rough stones marking the head and foot of a grave. For a few moments he paused and looked down at the tomb. Then he rode on. Old Abu Taleb had died an unrelenting disbeliever in Islam. There was nothing his nephew could do but remember him with grateful thoughts and hope that his kindness had not been overlooked in the hereafter.

The ground was growing rougher now. There was practically no track, and the mule stumbled in the darkness. For a quarter of a mile Mohammed guided it through stones and scrub until he came to another tomb. It was no more ornate than Abu Taleb's. Three uncut stones marked it: one at the head, one at the feet, one in the middle. Mohammed dismounted and sat beside it. Beneath the hard, arid ground lay his beloved wife Khadija, his first convert, the only woman for whom he had really cared.

Silently he prayed. Then he wrapped himself in his cloak and remained motionless, lost in meditation. He seemed to see his life racing before him.

His childhood with the nomads of the desert, his youth with Abd al Mottaleb and then with Abu Taleb. His first wonderful journeys into foreign countries, his first realization that there were other landscapes than the desert, other people than the Koreishites. Then the unforgettable day when Khadija had summoned him and put him in charge of her caravans, of her business. This was the end, so to speak, of Mohammed's carefree career. From then on—with the marriage, with the new leisure—the thoughts accumulated during the voyages had had time to sort themselves. Gradually everything had changed.

He saw again the cave on Mount Hira and heard the awful words of Gabriel. He felt Khadija comforting him and listened to Waraka and Ali and Abu Bakr and Zaid pledging their trust in him. He heard the gibes and insults of the Meccans, followed by the threats of death until he was obliged to flee for his life. The Medina scenes surged toward him, merging themselves one into the other. The first mosque, the first home, Badr, Ohod, the Ditch, Khaibar, his following growing until, once more, he saw Mecca. . . .

Mohammed closed his eyes as the incredible triumph which had been his loomed up in the night. He felt overwhelmed by what God had done for him, by what God had done for his people. It was staggering! Then his senses seemed to travel on into the future, and everywhere the triumph continued. He saw many of the old faces as the Moslems sped relentlessly to north, south, east, and west like great rays of light: Abu Bakr, the faithful, and fierce Omar and the silent Othman, ruling one after the other in his place. And Ali the valiant and Khaled and Amr'. Wherever they went, followed his teaching, until Persia and Egypt and Mesopotamia knew his name. Then the old faces faded and new ones took their places, but they all looked forward with the same purpose. On and on went the banners of Islam, across North Africa to the Atlantic; northward, after that, through Spain and into France. East they went too. Across the Persian Gulf to India and China. In Malaya and in the Indies, in East and West Africa, what he had taught his people here in Mecca spread relentlessly.

Mohammed opened his eyes, breathless. He almost expected to see the warriors of his vision in helmets and mail massed beside him. But he was alone. Dimly, a few yards away, the white mule dozed. The sky was black and picked out with myriads of bright stars. The desert breeze stirred among the stones of the graveyard. Mohammed's tenseness relaxed. Gently he touched the ground which covered Khadija. It was due to her that all this had happened, due to her that all this would be. For a long while Mohammed did not move. He did not move until he was certain that this woman he loved knew that, in spite of any appearances to the contrary, she was the only one who had ever meant anything serious to him.

CHAPTER XXIII

THE DEATH OF MOHAMMED
(*June 632 After Christ*)

DEATH seems to come more easily in hot climates than in cold. In northern latitudes, the painless agonies of the Arabian deserts are rare.

The Arabs die gracefully and without giving trouble. They fade out like a nursery fire. They do not prelude leaving the world with phases of senility and decrepitude. There is none of that obligation to care for a doddering, complaining old man so common in occidental communities. He may be a nomad chief, he may be a merchant, he passes on with due consideration for his family and his friends.

An Arab gives little indication of his age. He may be sixty, he may be eighty, his way of living has little changed since he was a young man. Then, one evening, he will not feel so strong. The next day he will stay in the house or in the tent. A week later he will be dead. Within a few hours he will be buried in the oasis cemetery or under a heap of stones in the desert. Everyone will remember him gratefully and wish him well in the next world. No one will breathe that so frequent occidental sigh of relief at seeing the last of the old nuisance.

This sensible attitude and lack of fuss are primarily due to the Moslem's feeling no apprehension about death. On the contrary he regards it as a blessed relief from all the tiresome complications of life on earth. He reflects those words of Mohammed:

"The world is as a prison and as a famine to Moslems, and when they leave it, you may say they leave famine and prison."

Mohammed died according to tradition. To within a few hours of ceasing to live, he was ministering to his people. . . .

Soon after the return from the Mecca pilgrimage, Mohammed set about organizing an expedition against Syria. He had never reconciled himself to the Moslem defeat at Muta. He had never forgiven the Romans for killing his friend Zaid. He decided that now was the time to retaliate.

To make the revenge even more spectacular, he appointed Zaid's son, Osama, as commander in chief of the army. Osama was the son of Baraka, Mohammed's black nurse, who had been Zaid's first wife. He was a clever boy and subsequently confirmed Mohammed's trust in him, but he was only twenty. The veterans did not like the idea of attacking the still redoubtable Romans with a lad, who had little military experience, as their leader. Mohammed was, however, unmoved by the protests. He was establishing the precedent, observed ever since among Moslems, that age and social standing do not necessarily make the best generals. He was ingraining in them the message of democracy which they were to carry to the world. Without discussing the nomination, he summoned Osama to the mosque and handed him the banner of Islam with recommendations to bring it honor. Osama accepted the banner and, without further argument, took over command.

The army marched on the afternoon of May 27 and camped that night at Al Jurf, which is close to Medina. This was as far as it got for some time. Before "Fall in" had sounded the following morning, news came that Mohammed had been taken seriously ill.

No one has stated definitely what was the cause of Mohammed's fatal sickness. His followers attributed it to the poisoned meat which he had been given at Khaibar. This does not seem likely.

In the first place, the attempted poisoning had taken place four years before. In the second, Mohammed had never swallowed any of the poisoned kid. He had spat it out the moment he had tasted it. Thirdly, Mohammed's health had been excellent ever since. He had led that heart- and body-breaking expedition to Tebuk. He had conducted the campaign against the Hawazins and besieged At Tayef. He had conquered Mecca. A man with a pernicious poison slowly eating him away would surely have been unable to undergo such ordeals.

Some suggest that Mohammed died of malignant malaria. Or was it typhoid? The symptoms according to reports were as follows:

During the course of his sickness, he ran a violent fever. He had acute intestinal and back pains. He sickened and died with great rapidity. He went through the phases which millions used to go through in the Orient until the introduction of antienteric inoculations. There was, furthermore, every opportunity for him to contract such a disease.

Owing to water being so scarce in the desert, Arabs have a way of drinking anything available. It does not seem to harm them nine times out of ten. We have seen how Mohammed quenched his thirst in Mecca from a bucket in which dirty dates had been washed. We know that in Medina he used an uncovered cistern near the mosque to drink from. We must also appreciate that this man of sixty-two had put into those years four times as much as any normal being. A constitution which had absorbed persecution and privation, and had never been allowed to rest, finally began to give.

However, whatever the ailment, Mohammed woke on the morning after delivering the standard to Osama with a violent headache and burning pains inside. Dizziness followed. But he did not allow anyone to know how bad he felt and continued to go about his duties and visit his wives in turn. Nevertheless he sensed that this might be the beginning of the end. To Fatima he went as far as confiding that he had not much more time to live. When she burst into tears, he reprimanded her.

"Why weep, my daughter?" he remonstrated. "Be comforted, for you are the first of my people who will rejoin me."

As it happened, Fatima did die six months after her father.

On the second night of his illness, Mohammed left the room of Maimuna, whose turn it was to entertain, and slipped out of the mosque dwelling with a slave. Once more he made for the graveyard.

For a while he sat meditating among the rough headstones of the men and the women who had died in the faith. Then he prayed, speaking to those who had gone before:

"Verily both you and I have received fulfillment of that which our Lord did promise us. Rejoice, you dwellers in the grave, for your lot is better than the lot of those that are left behind. God has delivered you from the storms with which they are threatened, and follow one another, each darker than that preceding it. . . . O Lord, have mercy on them that lie buried here."

Then, turning to the slave, he added:

"The choice has verily been offered me of continuance in this life, with paradise thereafter, or to meet my Lord at once; and I have chosen to meet my Lord."

Once more addressing the graves, he added:

"Peace to you, O people of the graves! May God forgive us and you. You have passed on before us, and we are following you."

He then returned to Maimuna's room. The next day he felt worse. The fever had increased, and the pain gnawed at his inside. Mohammed decided that he needed nursing. He made up his mind that Maimuna was not the nurse he wanted. He wanted Aisha. Al Abbas happened to be there when Mohammed expressed this wish, and he tried to put him off. It was obvious that Mohammed was dying, and it occurred to his uncle that if the Prophet of Islam gave up this world in the arms of his sister-in-law, it might have interesting repercussions. And so it might. No one had yet been appointed to succeed as leader of the faithful, and any hint, such as spending his last moments with a relative of Al Abbas, who would capitalize on it to its fullest extent, could be construed as Mohammed's intentions. However, Mohammed was not yet sufficiently ill to have his inclinations questioned. Supported by his uncle and by Ali, he insisted on moving to Aisha's apartment.

Aisha was barely twenty. She had never nursed a sick person before or been close to death. But she rose to the occasion and devoted herself to the last days of her dying husband. Mohammed reacted vigorously to the affection which this girl showed him. His strength began to return and his thoughts to clear. When he heard that Osama had not yet left for Syria and was being held back on account of adverse criticism on the appointment from the veterans, his old spirit showed itself. He called for water and, having bathed, dressed and went into the mosque. The congregation had just assembled for the general prayer. Mohammed led it as usual, after which he said:

"Ye people! What is this I hear, that some of you oppose my appointment of Osama to command the Syrian expedition? Now, if you blame my appointment of Osama, you should have blamed my appointment of his father, Zaid. And I swear by the Lord that he was fitted to command, and his son is well fitted also. Truly Osama is one of the men most dearly beloved by me, even as his father was. Wherefore do you treat him well, for he is one of the best among you."

He let his eyes travel over the congregation. They still had that alertness, that commanding expression which allowed no questioning of their authority. The logical, lucid reasoning was as convincing as ever. Satisfied that he had made his point, he went on:

"Verily, the Lord has offered unto one of His servants the choice between this life and that which is nigh unto Himself, and the servant has chosen that which is nigh unto the Lord."

Abu Bakr seems to have been the only one in the mosque who recognized what Mohammed meant. Tears filled his eyes as he tried to hold back his sobs. Mohammed turned to his old friend.

"Verily, the chiefest among you all, for love and devotion to me, is Abu Bakr!" he said feelingly. "If I were to choose a bosom friend, it would be he, but Islam has made a closer brotherhood among us all." Addressing the Meccans among his listeners, he continued: "Hold in honor the 'ansars' of Medina. The number of believers may increase, but that of the helpers never can. They were my family, and with them I found a home. Do good to those who do good to them, and break friendship with those who are hostile to them."

After a few more wise counsels and requests, he left his place by the pulpit and returned to Aisha.

The journey to the mosque and back had tired him, and he spent a restless night. In the morning he did not feel able to lead the prayers. He accordingly gave Abu Bakr orders that he should lead them in his place. This was the nearest he ever did to appointing a successor. It is, nevertheless, clear that this was what he intended. When he had been available, no one but himself had led the prayer. When he had not been available, any of the original converts who happened to be there had done so. Today he could have ordered Omar or Othman or Ali to deputize. By singling out the trusty colleague, by choosing Aisha as his nurse and her quarters as his sickroom, Mohammed manifestly indicated that he meant the caliphate to pass to the man who had shared the good with the bad since the start of Islam.

During the next few days the fever took such a hold on the Messenger that he could not leave his mat. As his temperature became unbearable, he dipped his hands in a bowl of water beside him.

"O Lord, assist me in my hard condition," he prayed. "O Lord, assist me."

At times he was delirious, but on the whole his mind registered all that went on about him. He complained little. He recognized his old companions as they came to see him. He even gave instructions that any savings which he possessed should immediately be given to the needy. Then, like the last flame of a dying fire, he was feeling better. That indomitable will power, that strength which, up till now, had never deserted him, welled up again.

Water and clean clothes were brought and, after a thorough bathing, he had Ali and Al Abbas help him into the mosque. He reached it when Abu Bakr was in the middle of the prayer. The murmurs of joy and surprise which rippled round the congregation made Abu Bakr turn. He immediately stopped the prayer, but Mohammed signed to him to go on. When he had finished, Mohammed sat on the step of the pulpit and, once more, spoke to the people.

"I have heard that the rumor of my death filled you with alarm, but has any prophet before me lived for ever? Everything happens according to the will of God, and has its appointed time, which is not to be hastened or avoided. I return to Him who sent me, and my last command to you is that you remain united, that you love, honor, and uphold one another, that you exhort one another to faith and constancy in belief, and to the performance of pious deeds. By these alone, men prosper. All else leads to destruction."

With an effort he forced himself to his feet and, raising his voice to almost its old pitch, said:

"I do but go before you. You will soon follow me. Death awaits us all, let no one then seek to turn it aside from me. My life has been for your good, so will be my death."

He stood for a moment looking eagerly at the robed figures which crowded in the mosque. Then, slowly, supported by Ali, he walked through the silent ranks and back to the sickroom. He had made his last public appearance. He had spoken his last speech.

Once more with Aisha, he laid himself wearily on the carpet and let his young wife undress him. For a while he rested, clasping Aisha's hand. The fever was intense, but he did not moan or complain. As Aisha wetted his burning face with a damp cloth, he smiled. Slowly words and sentences broke from his throat.

"O Lord, I beseech thee assist me in the agonies of death. . . . O Gabriel, come close to me, come close to me."

This he repeated several times. Then, after a period of silence, strength ebbed back. His eyes wide open, he said clearly:

"O Lord, grant me pardon and join me to the companionship on high. O Allah, be it so among all the glorious associates in paradise."

THE DEATH OF MOHAMMED

His limbs relaxed. His head fell back on Aisha's lap. The hand she held lost its burning fever. For a minute there was rigid silence. Then, gently, Aisha laid her husband's head on the pillow. She straightened his clothing and closed his eyes. She looked down anxiously, almost hopefully, at the dear face. Its calm banished any idea that Mohammed was in a trance. The faint suggestion of a smile which relaxed her husband's lips did not belong to this world. Holding back her tears, she quickly kissed the forehead of the first man she had ever known, of the only man for whom she had cared. Then she went into the courtyard where the other wives waited apprehensively.

The cries of despair from the harem quickly spread to the neighborhood of the mosque. Consternation and fear blazed through the ranks of the people who had so lately seen their leader alive. No one, not even Omar, would admit that he might be dead. In fact Omar stood before the throng which milled around the doorway of the Messenger's living quarters and announced that Mohammed had merely swooned. He repeated his statement loudly and with increasing conviction.

It was an extraordinary scene, an extraordinary situation. While Mohammed had never in manner or by word suggested that he was of any different substance from his followers, while he had emphasized his mortality, the people had subconsciously come to regard him as someone allied to the superhuman. What he had said a few hours before in the mosque, they had accepted as a kind of formula. They did not associate their master with anything which could decompose.

This was natural. From the degradations of poverty and persecution, these men of Mecca and Medina had found themselves raised to a position where they counted above any other community in Arabia. Seemingly unsurmountable obstacles had stood in their way, but over all of these they had been successfully guided. In fact they had a justifiable feeling that whenever troubles, great or small, threatened them, all they had to do was to go to Mohammed, who would solve them. It seemed preposterous to imagine that this man would no longer be within their reach to support them against the storms of the world.

Omar himself was a convert. In the space of one hour he had changed from being one of the most violent opponents of Islam to being one of the most violent proponents. He too placed Mohammed on a level far above anyone else in the universe. For that reason he denounced the women who wailed in the harem as hysterical creatures who had no idea who or what their husband was. The situation was becoming tense when Abu Bakr appeared.

Abu Bakr had been so reassured by Mohammed's appearance in the mosque that he had gone to visit one of his wives who was spending the summer in a Medina suburb. The moment the news of Mohammed's death reached him, he jumped onto his mule and hurried back to the city. Disregarding the crowds which pressed about him, asking a thousand questions, he walked into the harem and straight to the death chamber. He found his daughter sitting beside the body. Abu Bakr did not say anything to Aisha, but motioned her to lift the sheet which covered the corpse. For a moment he looked sadly at the finely drawn features of his friend. Then he knelt beside him and kissed the broad forehead.

"Sweet you were in life and sweet you are in death," he said gently.

He touched the long black hair which curled back from the massive head.

"Yes, you are dead," he went on. "Alas, my friend, my chosen one, dearer than father or mother to me, you have tasted the bitter pains of death."

Once again he kissed Mohammed's forehead and, replacing the sheet, went slowly out into the courtyard where the wives continued to weep.

He then became aware of the tumult outside the walls. He hurried toward it and heard Omar's booming voice reiterating that Mohammed was in a trance. Abu Bakr tried to silence Omar, but he was too excited to take any notice. For a moment he looked troubled. This was a crisis which he had never foreseen. Finally he raised his hands and began to speak himself. The people, hearing the familiar voice, quietened. Sternly he spoke, sternly and clearly:

"Has not the Almighty revealed this verse unto His Messenger, saying, 'Verily thou shalt die and they shall die.' And again, after the Battle of Ohod, 'Mohammed is no more than an apostle. Verily other apostles have deceased before him.' What then? If he were to die or be killed, would you turn your heel upon him and abandon his doctrine because he is dead?"

He allowed the words to sink in. Then he concluded with emphasis:

"Let him then know, whosoever worshipeth Mohammed, that Mohammed indeed is dead, but whoso worshipeth God, let him know that the Lord lives and does not die."

A dreadful silence followed these words. Abu Bakr had spoken with authority. He had quoted passages from the Koran which everyone had heard Mohammed quote. There was no question of the sincerity of their leader's great friend. Some eyes turned toward Omar as if he might voice some contradiction. But he stood apart with bent head. Quietly the men and women who had so noisily protested a few moments before dispersed. With heavy hearts they made their ways back to their homes. Soon the square outside the mosque was empty save for Omar and Abu Bakr. They too went their way, grieving and unable to find words to exchange at this tragic hour.

However, in spite of his personal sorrow, Abu Bakr kept his head. He knew that at this moment Islam stood in grave danger. The shock of Mohammed's death had been great, but the reaction might be greater. Unless a leader were appointed immediately, rival factions would appear. In this surmise he was justified.

The Medinese had assembled after Abu Bakr's speech and decided that if Mohammed was really dead, there was no reason why they should remain under the governorship of one of the Meccan immigrants. Now was the time and the chance to make themselves independent. Abu Bakr sensed this trend of thought, so, rousing Omar from his house, where he had gone to mourn, he made him accompany him to where he had heard that the Medinese had gathered. The two men arrived in time to witness Saad ibn Obada designated as the new chief. Abu Bakr acted with the same forcefulness as would have Mohammed.

He said that, while he had the greatest respect for the people of Medina, the other tribes of Arabia would never recognize their sovereignty. Only members of Mohammed's tribe, the Koreishites, would stand the least chance of holding the country together. If the people wanted Islam to continue, they must bear that in mind. He allowed this to be absorbed and then added that, in making this recommendation, he was not advocating himself for election. He did not mind who succeeded Mohammed, provided the successor was a Koreishite.

Abu Bakr had spoken fluently and without playing up Mohammed's death. He had placed the matter unsentimentally in the hands of the Medinese for them to decide. They did so unanimously, electing him caliph, or successor, of Islam. Omar seconded his friend and confirmed the appointment publicly the next day in the mosque. After explaining how he had been in error about Mohammed's death and telling the people to place their faith always in the Koran, he concluded:

"And now, verily, has the Lord entrusted your affairs in the hands of him that is the best among us all, the companion of His Messenger, the sole companion, the second of the two when they were in the cave alone. Arise, swear fealty to him!"

With one accord the people surged toward Abu Bakr. Then, one by one, they placed their hands in that of Islam's first caliph and swore allegiance.

When that was over, Abu Bakr took his place in the pulpit whence no one but Mohammed had spoken before. It was the most telling moment in the history of Islam, one of the most telling in the history of the world. If Abu Bakr failed now to hold his congregation, this religion built on an ideal would return to what it had been—an ideal.

Abu Bakr had none of the glamor of his friend. He was an

old man not far from death himself. His only claim to greatness was his unshakable belief in the cause and his unquestionable sincerity. It was these two qualities which gave him victory on that memorable morning. Without attempting to reproduce Mohammed's eloquence, he stated soberly what he had in mind.

"Ye people!" he said earnestly. "Ye people, verily have I become the chief over you, although I am not the best among you. If I do well, support me; if I err, then set me right. In truth and sincerity is faithfulness; in falsehood is perfidy. Know also that wickedness never abounds in any nation, but the Lord visits that nation with calamity. Wherefore, obey me, even as I shall obey the Lord and His Messenger. Whensoever I disobey him, obedience is no longer binding to you. Arise to prayer! And the Lord have mercy on you!"

While all this had been going on, the body of Mohammed had been washed and perfumed with musk and aloes. It had then been wrapped in three coverings and laid in state in Aisha's room. The people were allowed in by companies. Each group paused to look at the face of the dear leader. Then each one moved on. The visiting of the body went on for the whole day, the women following the men, the children and the slaves following the women.

When the time came for the burial rites, it was discovered that no one had a clear idea where Mohammed's tomb should be. Some wanted the grave dug beneath the pulpit in the mosque. Others said that the most appropriate place was under the spot where Mohammed took up his position to lead the prayers. A few suggested that he would have liked to lie with his people in the Moslem graveyard. Abu Bakr solved the problem by announcing that Mohammed had once said that a prophet should invariably be buried where he had died. As no one could contradict this, this site for the grave was agreed to.

A deep hole was, accordingly, dug under Aisha's room. Upon its floor was placed Mohammed's green mantle. Onto this the shrouded corpse was gently lowered by Ali and Osama and

Al Fadl. A vault of unbaked bricks was built over it, and the rest of the grave was filled in with gravel and sand.

Thus, on Tuesday June 9, 632 A.C., in the eleventh year after the Hijra, Mohammed was left to rest in peace for the first time during the sixty-two arduous years of his tumultuous life. Today he still rests in the same tomb. It is no longer visible to the public. An ornate mosque surrounds the one-time humble living quarters of the harem. Over the actual burial chamber a superb dome has been built. Here, from all over the world, men and women come to pray within sight of the place where the founder of their faith lived and died. In so doing, they are disregarding Mohammed's repeated injunctions that his tomb should never be regarded as an object of worship. They are helping to establish the legend that he belongs to the company of saints and angels. They are doing him a disservice.

Mohammed's unique position in religious history is due to the fact that he inspired all he did without being a saint or an angel, without having any attributes which were not strictly human. Outside his tremendous personality, he had nothing in life to distinguish him from other Moslems—neither titles, nor riches, nor a different mode of living. The mosque in Medina, like the mosques in Damascus and Fez and Delhi, are as well-favored works of art as any ecclesiastical architecture of the world, but they have nothing in common with Mohammed the son of Abdallah and his wife Amina.

CHAPTER XXIV

MOHAMMED AT HOME

The successes which crowned the end of Mohammed's earthly career are inclined to make one forget the domestic or familiar aspect of his story. The movement which he started, the stupendous effect of his teaching, the universal significance of Islam today blurs the more intimate portrait of this man *during his lifetime*.

I seldom think of Mohammed as God's Messenger whose followers make up one seventh of the world's population. I seldom think of him as the inspirer of the soldiers whose conquests were exceeded only by those of Britain's imperial armies. I seldom think of him as the author of that amazing book of laws and theology and verse, the Koran. I think of him rather as the boy who made good among his own people. I think of him as the scoffed at, persecuted young man with an ideal who forced his family to acknowledge him to have been right. For what Mohammed did with the sword and from the pulpit was far less of an achievement than confounding the saying about prophets being without honor in their own countries and changing the minds of his relatives. And that must be borne in mind, if one is to appreciate this "success story" of the desert. For that is what it is. Not quite, perhaps, the log-cabin-to-White-House formula, but something akin. At any rate, a situation where the personal and family elements predominate.

In the first place, the setting was intimate. With the exception of the two expeditions to Syria, the whole of the drama was played in an area no larger than the state of Connecticut. The people involved were not numerous and were, for the most part, related. The issue, to begin with, was essentially one of jealousy and misunderstanding. It was, moreover, a justifiable misunderstanding. That it led to such violent and bitter feelings was unfortunate, but quite intelligible.

Up to this point we have looked at everything which happened during those eventful years at the beginning of the seventh century from the angle of Mohammed. But there are always two sides to a controversy, and the angle of the Koreishites and the people of Mecca has merits deserving of examination.

Here was a city which, for centuries, had been building itself up as one of the great religious and trade centers of Arabia. By combining business with "church," the Meccans had found prosperity. They ate and drank their fill, they made love, they made money, they enjoyed life to its extreme limits. Everything they undertook flourished. It was natural, therefore, for them to attribute some of this good fortune to the idols who lived in the Kaaba. It was natural for them to see no reason for a change.

The members of the Koreishite tribe were, perhaps, the most prosperous and the most looked up to in the community. They held important posts in the administrative, the religious, and the social enterprises of the city. They also controlled most of the big banking and trading concerns.

In spite of its geographical isolation and evil climate, Mecca was one of the most civilized places in that part of the world. From the imported silks and linens to the jewelry and perfumes, it had every luxury. The Meccans felt themselves to be thrice blessed. They could see no cause or excuse for disturbing their prosperity.

Then, from nowhere, there appeared a middle-aged man with all kinds of peculiar ideas. He was of good family, a full-blooded Koreishite, but with no standing among the merchant princes of the city. In fact he was a failure. Despite all his family connections, he had never done anything of note. He had remained an honest, but a quite unenterprising, commercial traveler.

His first enormity had been to marry the biggest heiress in Mecca. His second, to advocate reforms which would change the easy and luxurious existence of this desert community. The effect was to arouse a protest, mild at first, but growing in intensity as the defiance of Mohammed became accentuated. The uncles and cousins and nephews and parents-in-law were scandalized. Scandalized to begin with, soon alarmed. Mohammed barred their way like a kind of impassioned prohibitionist, denouncing, loudly, not only everything which gave pleasure and prosperity, but the actual gods which helped bring about this happy state. *There was, however, nothing national in the revolt. It was essentially personal, essentially local.* As the story unfolds itself this is emphasized. The abolitionists and the anti-abolitionists. The Red Rose of Lancaster and the White Rose of York.

At the Battle of Badr, at Ohod, at the siege of Medina, everybody knew everybody else. When Hamza slew Siba, just before being killed himself because *he* had killed the opposing commander in chief's father-in-law, he could mention by name his victim's mother, who circumcised the women of Mecca. After the rout at Ohod, Abu Sofian challenged Mohammed to a return fight next year. He did so as might the captain of a rival football team. Mohammed kept the appointment, but Abu Sofian did not. Hence ridicule, which annoyed them more than the lost battle. During the siege of Medina the near relationship of the combatants was made use of by Mohammed to create mischief in the enemy ranks.

When, eventually, Mohammed returned to Mecca for the first time, the personal element was again foremost. The Meccans wanted to save face. They were beginning to recognize that this busybody relation of theirs was a bigger man than they thought, but they wished to give in gracefully. Mohammed understood this perfectly and did everything to make their surrender easy.

When peace was made, no one was more happy than the onetime antagonists. There was no ill feeling like that between two warring nations. The eager fraternization and party giving was an immense sigh of relief that the family squabble was over.

The conversions of the outlying tribes, of the Yemenites and the Omanites, seem almost intrusions in this intimate difference of opinion among close relations.

In Medina, also, it was a big home. A big home in a small

village. Mohammed helping to build the mosque. Mohammed making local laws, arranging marriages, marrying himself. That harem, with all the female jealousies and intrigues and small-town gossip, was as familiar as Main Street. Neither were these men, whose descendants would one day rule so much of the world, grandiose figures. I can see them all, I can identify them with the Arabs with whom I used to share my life on the Sahara Desert:

Abu Bakr, the friend who believed in his friend because he was his friend. He is rather timid and quite unused to this hand-to-mouth existence. Wondering, perhaps, at times, what it would have been like to grow old a millionaire in Mecca.

Omar, choleric, huge, a warrior by trade and instinct. His only notion of dealing with infidels, to convert or kill.

Othman, rather a nebulous character. Less sincere than Abu Bakr, less warlike than Omar, definitely more of a diplomat than both of them.

And Ali! The honest, ugly, swashbuckling soldier. Mohammed is his hero, fighting his hobby. He belongs essentially to the camp and is quite unsuited to the council chamber or the court. Yet he, like the other three, will one day become caliph and rule over countries which, until a few years before, he had never heard of.

Neither does Mohammed appear to me as the saint of his admirers or the impostor of his disparagers. Aisha, who had no illusions about her husband, said of him:

"He was gentle and noble—just a man who laughed often and smiled much."

This analysis in part explains Mohammed's success. No man who could not laugh often would have come through all those trials. No man who had not the common touch could have inspired such sincere friendship or the love of Khadija and Aisha and probably of his other ladies. He could not have drawn children to him. Often, in the mosque, he had a child in his arms while he spoke. He was often seen walking in the oasis holding a child by each hand.

"A man cannot live without constant effort," he declared. "The effort is from me, its fulfillment comes from God."

He never let God slip into the background, he never allowed his own position to turn his head. Whether one reads pro-Mohammed writers or anti-Mohammed writers, they are all agreed that a patriarchal simplicity always pervaded their subject's life.

That is, of course, one of the fundamental strengths of Islam—its thorough simplicity. It is one of the causes of its remarkable spread.

If St. Peter returned to Rome, he might be puzzled by the gorgeous ritual, by the gaudy vestments and the strange music in the temple associated with his name. The incense, the images, the incantations would not bring back to mind anything which his Master had taught. But if Mohammed dropped into any mosque between London and Zanzibar, he would find the same simple rites as in his brick and palm-beamed house of worship in Medina.

Mohammed was essentially human. He appreciated the weaknesses of other men. He understood their passions and realized that the inartificial has far more permanent appeal than what is complicated and gilded.

Moslem missionaries have a quite different approach toward proselytizing than missionaries of other sects. In the first place, they do not go out furnished for that deliberate purpose. There are no holy orders in Islam, and the preacher is likewise the merchant and the administrator. Then there is forbearance and sympathy and respect for native customs and prejudices, even for some of the more harmless of the beliefs.

Neither is there any color bar for a Moslem. Be the believer black or white or yellow, it does not matter. He is treated with rigorous equality.

Mohammed denounced and abolished caste, class, color, and race distinctions.

The greatest evidence of the democratic policies of Islam is in the pilgrimage to Mecca. Here Europeans and Asiatics and

Africans, coolies, princes, merchants, and warriors, meet in the same humble garb which Mohammed and his followers wore for the last pilgrimage in 632. They all eat the same food, share the same tents, and are treated with no distinction whether they come from the docks of Sierra Leone or the Nizam's palace in Hyderabad. They are Moslems. That is sufficient distinction. They follow the example of the founder of their faith who ruled Arabia but had no compunction about dining with a slave or sharing his dates with a beggar.

Could a man who was not inspired have brought such an international brotherhood into being? Does not the scoffing of the anti-Moslems rather reflect on themselves? Why should an impostor have left a creed which has grown ever since he died? Today the numbers of followers of the Moslem faith increase by a quarter of a million every year! And this without any persuasive disciples to preach the message of Islam.

Mohammed had no Paul. The original disseminators of his faith were his soldiers. That they left Islam so firmly rooted wherever they went makes one wonder what would have happened had there been a great Arab missionary to preach the Koran like those early Christians. There were never any great Moslem propagandists in the direct sense. The religion was found likable to the people with whom it came into contact and was accepted. On the other hand, Islam has never taken hold upon a country fundamentally different from its birthplace. Spain was admirably governed under the Moslems for five hundred years, but when the Christian kings returned with their Holy Inquisition, the Moslem faith faded and died. It is, moreover, unlikely that Europe would have been Islamized if Charles Martel had been defeated at Tours. This religion belongs to uncomplicated people whose souls are close to nature.

The Arabs really are uncomplicated. Mohammed was uncomplicated. The objection that he complicated his life with many wives is not justified. He was merely following a custom. A country and an era cannot be judged by another country or another era. That harem, like the rest of Mohammed's story, belongs to the family background which dominates all throughout his life.

The misfortune of many of Mohammed's biographers is that they judge unhesitatingly without assessing the contributing circumstances. The majority know nothing of the Arabs. An oasis dweller or a nomad or a stevedore at Beyrouth is just another Arab—usually a dirty Arab.

It would be interesting to see a biography of St. Paul written by a Moslem. It is more than likely that it would be more tolerant than the majority of those published by Christians on the subject of Mohammed.

"O Lord, forgive us our sins and our mistakes in this our work, and set our feet firm, and help us against the unbelieving people!" prayed Mohammed.

His only refuge from sin was God, and he never tolerated hypocrisy. When men came to him and said, wishing to impress: "I am unmarried," or "I eat no meat," or "I pray continuously," he replied: "Praise be to Allah, I fast and I eat, I keep vigil and I sleep and I am married. Whosoever is not worthy to follow my custom does not belong to me."

And to one who inquired what he enjoyed the best, he disarmingly answered: "The things of the world which appeal to me most are little children and women and perfumes, but I have only found complete felicity in prayer."

And so let this honest man, who kept a sense of humor in spite of his trials, rest until that day when everyone's worth will be known, until—

"Men shall come forward in throngs to behold their works,
  And whosoever shall have wrought an atom's weight of good
    shall behold it,
  And whosoever shall have wrought an atom's weight of evil
    shall behold it. . . .
  For, unto God belongeth the sovereignty of the heavens and of
    the earth and of all that they contain, and He hath the power
    over all things." (Koran, Suras 99 and 5.)

EPILOGUE

WHILE the story of Mohammed ended on that June morning six hundred and thirty-two years after the death of Christ, the story of Islam did not. The young and the old, the women as well as the men who had played leading parts under their leader's administration, carried on his traditions according to their lights. I say "according to their lights" because, during the years immediately succeeding Mohammed's death, conflict and intrigue took the place of the harmony which had marked the brotherhood of Islam during his lifetime. It is, in fact, miraculous that what Mohammed had brought into being did not die with him. It is further evidence of the man's personality and the fundamental strength of the faith which he had founded.

As already shown, Abu Bakr became the first caliph. His reign did not exceed two years, but they were years of consolidation and the first steps in expansion. The people were still bewildered at no longer having Mohammed to lean on, and they accepted all that Abu Bakr decreed. In the military field Khaled ibn al Walid and Amr' ibn al As confirmed the promise they had shown for generalship. During Abu Bakr's caliphate they carried the Moslem banner into Iraq and Syria. Bosra, Damascus, and other Roman strongholds fell before their brilliantly led armies.

In 634 Abu Bakr sickened. As in the case of Mohammed, various causes were attributed to his fatal illness. As in the case of Mohammed it was due more than anything else to overfatigue. Aisha nursed her father as she had nursed her husband, devoting herself with the same affectionate concern to his last moments.

Appreciating the precarious position in which Islam had found itself after the death of Mohammed, Abu Bakr took the precaution to appoint a successor. Omar rather reluctantly accepted to be the second caliph. With this assurance, Abu Bakr died. He was buried underneath Aisha's apartment in a grave beside his friend with whom he had shared every peril and privation and triumph since the earliest days of the Call.

Omar was fifty-three when he assumed office, but he did not look his age. His austere way of living had retained him his noble appearance and his virility. No one questioned his authority. Aisha herself, whose father's short reign had given her no time to make herself any official position in Medina, decided that it was safer to co-operate with the new caliph.

Although Omar had shown disinclination to succeed Abu Bakr, once he had the reins of government in his hands, he did not relax the hold. Assuming the title of Amir al Momirin' (Commander of the Faithful), he ordered the continuance of the conservative, domestic policies begun by Abu Bakr. He likewise encouraged the spread of Islam by conquest. It was during Omar's sovereignty that the first serious Moslem empire building began.

Chiefly under the leadership of Khaled and Amr', the Moslem armies swept on like great tidal waves, overwhelming all that stood in their way. Between 634 and 644 A.C. the conquest of Syria was completed, with the Roman Byzantines being decisively defeated near Lake Tiberius. Jerusalem and Aleppo, Antioch and Caesarea were besieged and captured. The seacoast of Asia Minor rapidly came under the rule of Medina. Before long this rule extended north to the Amanus mountains and east to the farthest limits of Mesopotamia. Persia was then invaded, subjugated, and occupied. Toward the west, Amr' drove into Egypt and took Memphis and Alexandria. Within a few months of the appearance of the Moslems, another proud nation had sworn allegiance to these desert Arabs and accepted their religion. At the same time, also, the Babylonians on the other side of the Middle East had become Islamized.

Yet, in spite of these victorious contacts with the richest empires of the world, the Caliph maintained his asceticisms and insisted that his followers should be as he. In fact he at one time deposed Khaled, believing that he was becoming luxurious and deflecting loot to his personal use. This was not the case and, on his death in 640 A.C., it was found that the Moslem cavalry leader's entire property consisted of his charger and his arms. It was not until much later that these Arabs forgot their desert origins and adopted the easy ways of townspeople.

In 644 Omar was assassinated by a Persian named Firuz who had been brought captive to Medina. Omar was praying in the mosque when the man fell on him from behind and stabbed him three times before he could defend himself. The wounds were not immediately fatal. Nevertheless Omar would not make any definite pronouncement as to who should succeed him. Instead he appointed a council of six to designate the next caliph. Then he asked Aisha if she would permit him to be buried beside his two friends. Aisha approved. As soon as he was dead, therefore, the First Commander of the Faithful was laid to rest beneath Aisha's room. This was the last time that the tomb of the Messenger was opened.

The six counselors appointed by Omar met as soon as the funeral was over. The caliphate was first offered to Ali with the conditions that he govern according to the Koran, the traditions of Mohammed, and the regulations established by Abu Bakr and Omar. Ali accepted the first two conditions, but refused the third. The offer was, accordingly, withdrawn and Othman was approached with the same terms. Being less honest than Ali, he accepted them without demur. Thus, in 644 A.C. Othman ibn Affan, Mohammed's son-in-law and a member of the Ommeyade family of Mecca which would one day rule the Moslem empire, from Cordova and Damascus successively, became the third caliph of Islam.

Although the march of empire continued under Othman's sovereignty, although the first Arab fleet was brought into being at this time, although Cyprus was captured and the Byzantine navy annihilated, it had none of the high-principled stamp of the preceding reigns. Othman had never been an outstanding figure when Mohammed was alive. Today he showed that he lacked the qualities of his predecessors. He was easily swayed and had no scruples in replacing military leaders and governors by his favorites, regardless of their competence. He also made the mistake of offending Aisha.

The slight in itself was small, but it was of a kind to arouse all of Aisha's most vindictive instincts: Othman reduced her pension to the level of that of the other widows!

Aisha had always deemed herself Mohammed's favorite. During her father's and Omar's reigns, she had been held in the same regard as when her husband was alive. The last caliph had begged her permission to be buried beneath her room. But with her two protagonists dead, she knew that it might require all her wit to maintain her position. When, therefore, Othman made his indirect attack, Aisha resolved that he was no worthy successor to her husband. Once she had settled that, all that remained was to find the best way to get rid of the enemy. The excuse or the methods employed had no bearing on the situation. When Aisha wanted something done, it was carried out regardless of ethics. In this case Othman gave Aisha every assistance.

The favoritism was becoming more and more blatant. Old friends of Mohammed, tried warriors, statesmen of integrity were being sacrificed daily to satisfy some whim of the Caliph. Aisha missed none of his vacillating policy. She brought it to the notice of the old guard. She never missed an opportunity to stir up the growing dissatisfaction.

The story of Othman's waverings and treacheries and of Aisha's intrigues is too long to go into here. However, a situation finally developed where the Moslems were so incensed by Othman's behavior that they demanded his abdication. This, Othman refused. The temper of the people turned ugly. In a short time the Caliph found himself besieged in his house. The atmosphere had changed from one of requests to one of threats.

Othman became alarmed. He sent a message to Aisha, begging her to intervene. Aisha sent a message back to say that she was sorry but she was busy, she was about to make the pilgrimage to Mecca. Before Othman could appeal to her again she put this into effect. Before she had gone very far, however, word reached her that the Medinese had taken the law into their own hands and executed their caliph. Moreover, so great was their disgust at his behavior that his body had been unceremoniously buried in the public cemetery.

Aisha's reactions were unexpected. She denounced the murderers of Othman and called on the Ommeyades to proclaim a blood feud. Within a few days of the death of a man which she had indirectly contrived, she used that death to sow the seeds of civil war!

To add to the confusion, there were now four candidates for the caliphate. These were Ali, Mohammed's adopted son, cousin, and son-in-law; then, Zubair and Talha, relatives of Aisha who had her full support; and finally Mu'awiya. Mu'awiya was the son of Abu Sofian and Hind. He was also head of the Ommeyades and was, this moment, governor of Syria.

Ali acted quickly. Before anyone could make up his mind about the succession, he proposed himself. There was little opposition. Mu'awiya was in Damascus and unaware of what was afoot. Zubair and Talha had been temporarily deserted by Aisha, who was keeping an eye on what was taking place from the vantage point of Mecca. The other notables were too preoccupied by the murder of Othman to think. Consequently Ali was able to force his candidature. On July 18, 656, in the thirty-fifth year of the Hijra, he was elected fourth caliph of Islam.

The news was extremely displeasing to Aisha. She had never forgotten or forgiven Ali's attitude in connection with the affair of Safwan and the necklace. She had always been jealous of Mohammed's regard for him, both as a man and as a son-in-law. She had always resented him as the father of Mohammed's only surviving male heirs. To have him as the head of Islam was something which she could not accept. She therefore made up her mind to resort to any methods to put him out of her way. In this, Ali, like Othman, played into Aisha's hands.

While Ali was a brave soldier and a brilliant strategist, he was no statesman or diplomat. While on the field of battle he made up his mind in a moment, in the council chamber he was undecided. Within a few weeks of taking office it was evident that he would be as easily swayed by favorites as Othman, and that only the supporters of the Fatima succession need hope for important positions in the military and civil administration of the Moslem domains. He also showed no inclination to punish the murderers of Othman. Aisha immediately capitalized on these weaknesses to denounce the new caliph. She even suggested that Ali had had something to do with Othman's killing. In this she was supported by Mu'awiya, partly because, as head of the Ommeyades, he represented the blood feud and partly because he coveted the caliphate.

What followed is as fantastic a tale as ever came out of Arabia.

Aisha, assisted by Talha and Zubair, raised an army in Mecca and marched to Basra, at the junction of the Tigris and Euphrates. Basra was an important stronghold and was divided in its allegiance to Ali. The support of its citizens would add greatly to Aisha's cause. A period of feminine intrigue followed Aisha's arrival which culminated in Aisha's getting possession of the city.

Ali, in the meanwhile, though loath to use violence against his father-in-law's favorite, could not permit open rebellion. He accordingly marched on Basra and tried to settle the matter diplomatically. There were, however, too many hotheads in both camps, too many men with personal ambitions at stake and few with that Moslem unity which Mohammed had bred. Consequently an inadvertent skirmish on December 4, 656, led the two armies to joining battle.

Aisha led her troops in person. To do this she occupied a scarlet pavilion protected by chain armor which was strapped to the back of her camel. The encounter was long and fierce. Again and again the superior leadership of Ali made Aisha's soldiers waver. Again and again they were rallied by the voice and example of their commander. The battle surged back and forth around Aisha's camel until the red pavilion was bristling with darts and arrows and javelins. Warrior after warrior died at the feet of the camel. Aisha herself was slightly wounded. Finally one of the enemy managed to hamstring the camel. This was the signal for a general charge by Ali's army. With no one to encourage them, Aisha's men broke and fled. A few only remained beside their leader. These, with the aid of her brother, cut her loose from the pavilion and carried her into the city. Here she was followed by Ali and his troops. Ali, who was as good a soldier as he was a poor statesman, had his men in hand, and there was no massacre, nor even looting. He called on Aisha as if he had been visiting her in the old days of the mosque harem. Aisha did not reciprocate the friendly attitude. She received Ali contemptuously and in silence. All she said was:

"You have conquered. Show forbearance."

This Ali did. Furnishing Aisha with camels and an escort, he sent her to Mecca and thence to Medina.

Ali's troubles were, however, not done with. Although his victory over Aisha had given him the sovereignty of Arabia and Persia and Egypt, Mu'awiya was still in command in Syria. He was still using the excuse of the blood feud to fight Ali and had greatly added to his cause by gaining the support of Amr' ibn al As and his army. This defection from the caliphate was also a personal matter, in that Ali had deposed Amr' from the governorship of Egypt, which he had so brilliantly conquered.

Even so, Ali was as loath to unsheathe the sword against these fellow Moslems as he had been to attack Aisha. He did his best to come to some peaceful arrangement, and it was only when he was convinced that the Ommeyade faction was bent on fighting it out that he marched into Syria at the head of ninety thousand men.

It was a curious situation. Ali, the cousin and son-in-law of Mohammed, on one side, at the head of an army in the ranks of which marched veterans of Badr and Ohod, and Khaibar. On the other side, Mu'awiya, the son of Mohammed's archenemy, seconded by Amr', who had also led the Koreishites against Mohammed. The official cause of the conflict, Ali's supposed connivance in the murder of Othman, one of his ex-colleagues of the early days of Islam and, at that time, the bitter enemy of the two men who were now ready to fight to avenge his death! On *both* sides, fanatical Moslems. In fact it was during this campaign that the incident, already reported in this book, took place, when the soldiers of Mu'awiya placed their Korans on the points of their lances and thus stopped Ali's men charging to victory.

Although militarily this civil war ended favorably for Ali, the diplomacy of Mu'awiya won the peace. By a complicated sequence of intrigues, the son of Abu Sofian was declared the rightful successor to Othman. At the same time Amr' invaded Egypt and deposed Ali's viceroy. It looked as if Islam would be divided indefinitely by rival claimants to the caliphate. However, before hostilities could recommence in earnest, Ali was assassinated.

A group of fanatics belonging to the Karigite sect decided that these dissensions among Moslems were contrary to all of Mohammed's ideals and would lead to the ruin of Islam. They further made up their minds that Ali and Amr' and Mu'awiya were responsible. They accordingly made a vow to rid Arabia of them. Two of the plots miscarried. Mu'awiya was wounded, but not severely. A case of mistaken identity caused an imam who was leading the prayer in Egypt to be struck down in the place of Amr'. Only Ali fell beneath the regicides' swords. His murder took place in the Mesopotamian city of Kufa on the Euphrates in 660 A.C., the thirty-ninth year of the Hijra. He was sixty-three years old. He was buried where he fell. A magnificent tomb covered by a splendid mosque was erected in his honor. Around it grew up a fine city known as Meshed Ali, the Tomb of Ali. Today it is one of the principal shrines of the Shias.

The news of Ali's murder was received in Medina early in 661. The people were shocked. To them Ali was the last link with the great days when Mohammed lived. Aisha's reactions were, as usual, unexpected. Whatever may have been her personal feelings about the death of her enemy, she immediately gave orders for public mourning. She had the Medinese assemble in the old harem. Here, standing above Mohammed's grave, she pronounced a eulogy of the dead caliph, enumerating the valorous things which he had done for Islam. It looked almost as if another inter-Moslem conflict were imminent. But the working of Aisha's mind always led to surprises. Within a few days of the funeral oration she recognized Mu'awiya as the fifth caliph, thus removing from his path the only possible obstacle to his dominating the whole of Islam. This was, of course, in Aisha's interest. She had disposed of the two men who had offended her. She had caused Mohammed's surviving wives to fade into insignificance. She had shown the Moslems that she was someone who had to be reckoned with. She now wished to end her days as a kind of legendary figure, as "the Mother of all Believers," as a kind of unofficial successor to the Messenger. The best way to achieve this would be with a strong government and an ever spreading Islamic domination.

This is exactly what occurred. From the day Mu'awiya became the undisputed caliph, the might of Islam rolled on. Before the Hijra was a hundred years old, the Moslem Empire extended from the south of France, through Spain, North Africa, Egypt, Arabia, Syria, Mesopotamia, Persia, and as far as the borders of India, with footholds in Italy and Greece and the countries south of the Danube. Further conquests were being prepared. Before long the Koran would be the holy book of northern India, of parts of China and of what are now the Malay States and the Dutch Indies. In East and West Africa, too, the muezzins would be calling the people to prayer with the words first used by Bilal from the roof of the original mosque in Medina.

Aisha's mind could not grasp such geography, but she was content. She knew that what her husband had taught was being given its due, was being accepted by many. She herself lived much as she always had. That is, she did not become luxurious and seemed anxious to have everyone forget the days when she had tried her hand at politics. She interested herself in her people, helping them with charity and advice. Her counsels, moreover, were not always of a spiritual nature. They ranged from commercial and financial recommendations for businessmen to styles in dress and choices of cosmetics for women.

When, finally, she died, Aisha was sixty-four, two years senior to Mohammed at his death and about the same age as Khadija when she died. Although several suggestions had been made that she should be laid beside her husband and her father, she had expressly forbidden it. She had felt that it would be in bad taste. She was, therefore, buried in the first of all Moslem cemeteries in Medina, where most of the original converts already had their graves. Every citizen, from the highest to the lowest, attended the funeral. The governor of Medina pronounced the farewell oration. A period of mourning was observed in the neighborhood. It was the last important political event in Medina. From now, the center of Islamic government would shift to Damascus and Baghdad and Cairo and Cordova. Mecca and Medina would become shrines, holy cities to which pilgrims from all over the world would come to sanctify themselves in the settings where the founder of their faith had lived his earthly life.

Aisha was almost the last link with the Mohammedan era. She was the very last who could trace back her connections with Mohammed to the pre-Hijra days. With her interment, the personal element in the administration of Islam ceased. Her name is little known outside the Moslem world, but there is no doubt that, with Khadija, she had as much influence as anyone in bringing into being this religion which today unites one seventh of the world's population.

PRINCIPAL ACTORS IN MOHAMMED'S DRAMA OF THE DESERT

ABDALLAH IBN OBEI, the Medina rival of Mohammed.
ABU BAKR, Mohammed's close friend, and first caliph of Islam.
ABU JAHL, Koreishite chief who hated Mohammed.
ABU SOFIAN, Koreishite chief. Mohammed's violent antagonist.
ABU TALEB, Mohammed's uncle who brought him up.
AISHA BINT ABI BAKR, Mohammed's favorite wife.
AL ABBAS, Mohammed's uncle who helped Mohammed but did not become a Moslem till late.
ALI IBN ABU TALEB, Mohammed's cousin and adopted son.
BILAL, Islam's first muezzin.
FATIMA, Mohammed and Khadija's daughter. She married Ali.
HAFSA BINT OMAR, Mohammed's fourth wife, to whom was entrusted the MS. of the Koran.
HAMZA, Mohammed's uncle and foster brother. One of the early supporters of Islam.
HIND, wife of Abu Sofian.
KHADIJA, Mohammed's first wife.
KHALED IBN AL WALID, the Meccan cavalry leader who became one of Islam's famous generals.
OMAR IBN AL KHATTAB, Meccan warrior who became one of Mohammed's early supporters. He was second caliph of Islam.
OTHMAN IBN AFFAN, another of Mohammed's early supporters. He became third caliph of Islam.
ROKAIA, Mohammed's and Khadija's daughter, who married Othman.
UMM KULTHUM, another of Mohammed's and Khadija's daughters who also married Othman.
ZAID IBN HARITHA, Mohammed's freedman and adopted son.
ZEINAB, Mohammed's and Khadija's daughter, who married Abu'l As.

MOHAMMED'S WIVES AND CONCUBINES
[*in the order of their marriages to Mohammed*]

KHADIJA BINT KHUWEILID, predeceased Mohammed.

SAWDA BINT ZAMA, widow of Sakran, an early convert who had died in Abyssinia.

AISHA BINT ABI BAKR.

HAFSA BINT OMAR.

ZEINAB BINT KHUZAIMA, widow of Mohammed's cousin Obeida. She predeceased Mohammed.

UMM SALAMA BINT ABI UMAYYAH, widow of Abu Salama, who died of wounds after Ohod.

ZEINAB BINT JAHSH, divorced wife of Mohammed's freedman Zaid.

JUWAIRAH BINT AL HARITH, captured after the raid against the Beni Mustalik.

REIHANA, Jewish concubine taken after massacre of Beni Koreiza. She predeceased Mohammed.

UMM HABIBA BINT ABI SOFIAN, widow of Obeidallah, an early convert who migrated to Abyssinia.

MARY THE COPT, concubine presented to Mohammed by the governor of Egypt.

SAFIYA, Jewess of the Beni Koreiza, taken after the fall of Khaibar.

MAIMUNA BINT AL HARITH, sister-in-law of Mohammed's uncle Al Abbas.

GLOSSARY

ABD. Servant or slave. Thus, "Abdallah" means "servitor of God."

ABU. Father. Thus "Abu Bakr" is "father of the young camel."

AL or EL. The. Thus, "Al (or "El") Koran" means "The Koran."

ALLAHU AKBAR. God is great.

AMIR. Commander. Thus, "Amir al bahr" means "commander of the sea." From this has come the title "admiral."

ASSALAMU ALAIK, ASSALAMU ALAIKUM. "Peace be unto you" (in the singular or plural).

BEDOUIN. Roaming tribes of the desert; used adjectively, synonymous with "nomad." Bedawi means desert dwellers.

BEIT ALLAH. The house of God. The expression was used before as well as during Mohammed's time to indicate the temple or mosque or any sanctified place in which to pray.

BEN or IBN.* Son of. Thus "Ibn Saud" means the son of Saud.

BENI or BANU.* Children of. This expression is used chiefly to denote tribes. Thus "Beni Saad" means "children (or "members") of the Saadite tribe."

BENT or BINT.* Daughter of. Thus "Fatima bent (bint) Mohammed" means "Fatima, daughter of Mohammed."

CALIPH. Successor. The title used by the rulers of the Moslem Empire after Mohammed's death.

DJINNS. Supernatural beings usually inhabiting the desert. They can be good or evil.

HADJ. Pilgrimage to Mecca.

HADJI. Meccan pilgrim.

HIJRA. Emigration. It refers especially to Mohammed's flight

---

*N.B. Arabs have no surnames. Arab men and women and families distinguish themselves by affixing to their first names those of their fathers or mothers or by calling themselves the children of some clan.

from Mecca to Medina in 622 A.C. and is used as the basis for calculating the Moslem era. Before and after the "Hijra."

IBN or BEN. Son of.

IMAM. A mosque official who leads the prayer.

IN SHA ALLAH. If God wills it.

ISLAM. The religion of Moslems which Mohammed founded. The word means "submission to the will of God."

JIHAD. Moslem holy war, proclaimed in times of national emergency against non-Moslems.

KAABA. The Meccan shrine, originally idolatrous, today the focal point of Islam.

KADI. The Arab judge, attorney, official receiver.

KASBA. Fortress.

KESOUA. Embroidered black cloth cover for the Kaaba in Mecca.

KIBLA. The niche in every mosque and Moslem home which indicates the direction of Mecca toward which the face must be turned when praying.

KORAN. The Bible, prayer book, book of laws of the Moslems.

MASJID. Place of kneeling for prayer, or mosque.

MOSLEM. A follower of the Islamic faith. It means "one who has surrendered himself to the will of God."

MUEZZIN. The mosque official who calls Moslems to prayer from the minaret of the mosque five times a day.

NABI. Prophet. But not foreteller in the sense of the Greek word προφητης. "Nabi" really signifies "preacher."

RAMADAN. The month of fasting. Owing to the Moslem year being lunar, it varies in seasons.

SIMOOM. Fiery desert wind.

SURA. Chapter of the Koran.

BIBLIOGRAPHY

The Spirit of Islam, *Ameer Ali*.
The Life of Mohammed, *Sir William Muir*.
Islam and the Arabian Prophet, *Dr. G. I. Kheirallah*.
Mahomet and His Successors, *Washington Irving*.
History of the Arabs, *Dr. Philip K. Hitti*.
Essays on the Life of Mohammed, *Ahmad Khan Bahadur*.
Mohammed, *Tor Andrae*.
Mohammed and Mohammedanism, *R. Bosworth Smith*.
Mahomet, *G. M. Draycott*.
Mohammed, *R. F. Dibble*.
Aisha, Beloved of Mohammed, *Nabia Abbott*.
The Pilgrimage to Mecca and Medina, *Sir Richard Burton*.
The Crescent and the Rose, *S. C. Chew*.
The Arab Heritage, *P. K. Hitti, N. A. Faris, G. L. D. Vida, J. Oberman, J. L. la Monte*.
The Origins of the Islamic State, *Dr. Philip K. Hitti*.
The Mystical Elements of Mohammed, *J. C. Archer*.
The Apostle of God, *Edward Gibbon*.
Life of Mohammed, *George Bush*.
Heroes and Hero Worship, *Thomas Carlyle*.
Men of Might, *A. C. Benson* and *H. F. W. Tatham*.
Sayings of Mohammed, *Abdallah Al Mamun Al Suhrawardy*.
Meet the Arab, *John van Ess*.
The World of the Arabs, *Edward J. Byng*.
Life of Muhammad, *Sufi M. R. Bengali*.
Vie de Mahomet, *Emile Dermenghem*.
La République Marchande de la Mecque, *Henri Lammens*.
La Mecque, Ville Interdite, *Jean Barois*.
Mahomet, *Etienne Dinet*.
The Koran, *translated by J. M. Rodwell*.
The Koran, *translated by Marmaduke Pickthall*.
The Koran, *translated by George Sale*.

INDEX

Aaron, 111, 180, 242, 273
Abbasides, 296
Abdallah, Abu Bakr's son, 122, 127, 131
Abdallah ibn Obei, Mohammed's rival in Medina, 136, 167, 168, 170, 171, 172, 178, 179, 190, 191, 205, 221, 224, 262, 306, 310
Abdallah ibn Jahsh, Moslem leader, 154, 155, 187
Abdallah ibn Massoud, Moslem warrior, 160
Abdallah ibn abd al Mottaleb, Mohammed's father, 22, 25, 26, 27, 30, 338
Abdallah ibn Rawaha, Moslem general, 282, 283, 284
Abd al Mottaleb, Mohammed's grandfather, 22, 24, 25, 26, 47, 57, 65, 69, 74, 181, 200, 259, 295, 321
Abd ar Rahman, early Moslem convert, 65
Abd Shems, Koreishite clan, 65
Abraham, 11, 12, 13, 50, 54, 83, 100, 109, 112, 169, 239, 242, 279, 295, 312, 319
Abu Affak, Medinese Jew, 170
Abu Ayub, Mohammed's Medinese cousin, 131, 133, 134
Abu Bakr, Mohammed's closest friend and first caliph of Islam, 2, 52, 65, 79, 82, 105, 121, 122, 125, 126, 129, 132, 133, 134, 140, 145, 146, 154, 159, 174, 178, 184, 185, 199, 214, 222, 223, 231, 234, 251, 253, 256, 261, 266, 269, 271, 276, 277, 286, 289, 307, 312, 325, 330, 331, 334, 335, 336, 342, 346
Abu Basir, Meccan convert to Islam, 259, 260
Abu Jahl, Koreishite warrior, 74, 75, 76, 78, 79, 105, 124, 125, 126, 150, 156, 158, 160, 164, 251, 257, 298, 323

Abu Kuahfa, Abu Bakr's father, 297
Abu'l As, cousin of Khadija and Mohammed's son-in-law, 145, 162, 248, 249
Abu Lahab, Mohammed's uncle, 22, 27, 66, 68, 69, 165, 323
Abu Maslama, Moslem warrior, 276
Abu Obeida, Moslem warrior, 153, 286, 294
Abu Selama, early Moslem convert, 65, 198
Abu Sofian, leader of the Koreishites, 65, 66, 69, 73, 80, 81, 105, 124, 155, 156, 158, 161, 173, 177, 178, 185, 188, 193, 204, 207, 211, 212, 239, 250, 263, 276, 278, 282, 287, 289, 291, 292, 293, 301, 303, 311, 341, 350
Abu Taleb, Mohammed's uncle, 22, 30, 31, 32, 33, 34, 42, 46, 52, 57, 70, 74, 80, 81, 82, 122, 295, 324
Abwa, burial place of Mohammed's mother, Amina, 29, 178, 305
Abyssinia, 6, 23, 25, 74, 80, 145, 165, 263, 274
Adam, 11, 16, 51, 54, 100, 110, 239, 243, 319
Aden, 316
Adhal, village near Medina, 191
Africa, 5, 20, 239, 317, 325, 354
Agha Khan, 252
Aisha bint abi Bakr, Mohammed's favorite, 105, 121, 127, 131, 145, 146, 147, 175, 187, 198, 199, 200, 201, 202, 215, 218–25, 229, 239, 245, 264, 265, 266, 273, 305, 329, 330, 331, 332, 333, 337, 342, 346, 349, 350, 351, 352, 353, 354, 355
Al Abbas, Mohammed's uncle, 22, 30, 122, 162, 178, 280, 290, 291, 292, 293, 296, 302, 307, 321, 329

361

Al Bara, Medinese chief, 122, 123
Al Fadl, son of Al Abbas, 323, 339
Al Harith, Moslem warrior executed after Ohod, 190
Al Jirana, city near At Tayef, 303
Al Jurf, city near Medina, 327
Al Kamus, capital of Khaibar, 270
Al Kaswa, Mohammed's favorite camel, 130, 131, 132, 135, 138, 229, 251, 257, 277, 294, 295, 318, 319
Allat, pagan idol, 50, 51, 82, 106, 311, 312
Allah, 10, 51, 56, 57, 78, 82, 83, 85, 92, 100, 101, 112, 113, 114, 115, 127, 130, 139, 140, 157, 162, 186, 189, 198, 208, 212, 231, 233, 256, 279, 283, 311, 329
Allah Ta'ala, Kaaba idol, 50, 51
Al Moghira ibn Shuba, destroyed the idol at At Tayef, 311
Al Mottaleb, Mohammed's great-uncle, 24
Al Rabba, Kaaba idol, 82
Al Uzza, Kaaba idol, 82
Al Walid, Koreish warrior, 158, 159
Aleppo, 43, 347
Alexandria, 73, 347
Ali, Mohammed's nephew and fourth caliph of Islam, 52, 53, 57, 65, 70, 82, 121, 125, 131, 133, 134, 137, 154, 159, 161, 175, 178, 181, 182, 183, 184, 191, 199, 209, 212, 214, 215, 222, 239, 251, 254, 269, 271, 276, 277, 280, 289, 294, 308, 312, 316, 320, 325, 329, 331, 342, 348, 350, 351, 352, 353
Alilat, Kaaba idol, 18, 51
Almsgiving and charity, 94, 102, 142, 152, 229, 331
Amanus Mountains, 347
Amalekites, 13
America, 20, 203, 231
Ameer Ali, Privy Counselor, 315
Amina bint Wahb, Mohammed's mother, 22, 26, 27, 28, 29, 48, 105, 133, 178, 305, 338
Amina, Omar ibn al Khattab's sister, 78
Amr' ibn al As, Koreishite and, later, Moslem general, 73, 250, 281, 286, 288, 298, 346, 352
Amr', uncle of Khadija, 209
Antioch, 43

Animals, 97, 110, 246, 247, 248
Ansars, original Medinese converts, 135, 136, 142, 303, 330
Arabia, 4, 10, 19, 24, 31, 36, 42, 44, 99, 156, 166, 169, 217, 231, 262, 290, 300, 305, 340, 354
Arians, seventh-century Christian sect, 89
Arafat, Mount, 16, 319
Asia, 5, 18, 20, 146
Assyria, 16, 141
At Tayef, 32, 106, 154, 300, 301, 303, 304, 311, 312, 328
Attilla, 164
Atlantic Ocean, 134, 325
Autas Mountains, 301
Azrael, angel, 100, 110
Azrafel, angel, 100
Az Zubeir, Mohammed's eldest uncle, 36
Az Zubeir, Khadija's nephew, 65, 130, 209, 215, 290, 294

Baal, 172
Baalbeck, 43
Babylon, 3, 308, 347
Badr, battle of, 157, 158, 159, 163, 164, 171, 174, 177, 178, 181, 185, 188, 193, 195, 248, 254, 290, 307, 352
Baghdad, 238, 296, 355
Bahira, Nestorian monk, 33, 86
Baraka, Mohammed's nurse, 26, 29, 33, 47, 53, 305, 327
Basra, 134, 351
Beit Allah, 11, 40, 135, 277
Bible, 86, 117, 165, 232, 238, 240, 245
Bilal ibn Rabah, Islam's first muezzin, 140, 141, 160, 161, 187, 212, 251, 277, 279, 296, 354
Belisarius, 20
Belka, village near the Dead Sea, 283
Beni Aus, sedentary Arab tribe in Medina, 120, 136, 166, 208, 213
Beni Bakr, tribe allied to the Koreish, 288
Beni Dhakwan, nomad tribe, 191
Beni Hanifa, Christian tribe of central Arabia, 262
Beni Kainuka, Jewish tribe in Medina, 120, 166, 171

INDEX 363

Beni Kahzraj, sedentary Arab tribe in Medina, 120, 121, 122, 136, 161
Beni Koreiza, Jewish tribe in Medina, 120, 166, 193, 205, 207, 210, 212, 214, 215, 216
Beni Lihyan, nomad tribe, 191
Beni Mustalik, nomad tribe, 219
Beni an Nadir, Jewish tribe in Medina, 120, 166, 192, 193, 204, 230, 269
Beni Rial, nomad tribe, 191
Beni Saad, nomad tribe which helped to bring up Mohammed, 27, 28, 48, 300
Beni Soleim, nomad tribe, 32
Bethlehem, 108
Beyrouth, 43
Black Stone, 11, 12, 40, 53, 277, 295
Boraida, Medinese chief, 130
Borak, Mohammed's celestial charger, 108, 109, 115
Bosra, 32, 50, 262, 346
Budeil, friend of Abu Sofian, 291
Buddha, 1, 19, 317
Burton, Sir Richard, 319
Byzantium, 18, 20, 23, 73, 132, 249, 348

Caesarea, 141, 347
Caesar, Julius, 191
Cairo, 73, 355
Caliphs, 52, 54, 65, 69, 79, 133, 199, 222, 231, 331, 336, 342, 346, 347, 348, 349, 351, 352, 354
Chaldea, 133
China, 19, 163, 325, 354
Chosroes, king of Persia, 18, 19, 262
Christ, Jesus, 1, 12, 33, 54, 63, 70, 71, 89, 91, 96
Christianity, 6, 7, 20, 26, 64, 84, 91, 314, 315
Christians, 18, 33, 54, 83, 87, 89, 98, 109, 139, 152, 227, 236, 242, 312, 315, 317
Circumcision, 92
Collyridians, seventh-century Christian sect, 89
Communism, 94
Confucius, 1, 232
Constantine, Emperor, 141, 164
Constantinople, 18, 97, 133
Cordova, 152, 238, 348, 355
Corinthians, 6
Crescent and Star, 127

Crusaders, 152
Cyprus, 348
Cyrus, 308

Damascus, 38, 43, 141, 152, 338, 346, 348, 355
Dante, 115
David, king, 16, 37, 100, 110, 172, 202, 216, 239
Dead Sea, 282, 283, 284
Delhi, 238, 338
Dhul Huleifa, village near Mecca, 251
Deuteronomy, Book of, 216, 233
Divorce, 227, 228
Drinking, 93, 96, 113, 195, 196

Eden, Garden of, 16, 29, 319
Edomites, 13
Egypt, 18, 42, 50, 73, 119, 133, 141, 163, 325, 347, 354
Eisenhower, General, 3
Elijah, 116, 172
England, 19, 231
Ephraim, Saint, 98
Epilepsy, attributed to Mohammed, 55, 57, 63, 145, 153
Esau, 13
Esma, Abu Bakr's daughter, 122, 127, 131
Esma bint Merwan, Jewess who attacked Mohammed in Medina, 170
Esma, daughter of Prince of Najd, 265, 266
Euphrates, 113, 231, 309, 351, 353
Europe, 18, 19, 20, 146, 203, 239
Eutychians, seventh-century Christian sect, 89
Eve, 16, 243, 319
Exodus, book of, 117

Fasting, 101, 102
Fatalism, 95, 96, 101
Fatima, Mohammed's daughter, 53, 131, 145, 147, 187, 199, 223, 274, 289, 328, 351
Fatimides, sect which followed descendants of Ali and Fatima, 54, 199, 351
Fez, 152, 338
Firuz, murderer of Omar, 348
France, 19, 325, 354

INDEX

Gabriel, angel, 11, 56, 57, 59, 60, 61, 67, 100, 108, 109, 112, 114, 134, 160, 232, 240, 241, 324, 332
Galilee, 63
Gambling, 196
Genesis, Book of, 13, 16
George VI, of England, 20
Ghatafanites, nomad Arab tribe, 204, 207, 248
Goethe, Johann, 237
Goliath of Gath, 172, 272
Gospel, 100
Guadalquivir, 231
Granada, 152
Greece, 3, 18, 141, 164, 194, 196, 261, 308, 354
Gregory, Pope, 18

Hadramaut, 316
Hadrian, 166
Hafsa, Mohammed's fourth wife, 2, 174, 175, 187, 198, 199, 201, 235, 265, 266, 273, 305
Hakim, Khadija's nephew, 291
Hagar, concubine of Abraham, 12, 13, 25, 278
Hala, Khadija's sister, 265
Halima, Mohammed's nomad foster mother, 27, 28, 47, 303
Hamza, Mohammed's warrior uncle, 22, 46, 75, 76, 82, 130, 153, 154, 159, 161, 177, 178, 181, 182, 184, 185, 186, 195, 341
Hannibal, 191
Harem, 53
Harun al Rashid, 296
Hashim, Mohammed's great-grandfather, 22, 23, 24, 26, 31, 57, 65, 259, 295
Hassan ibn Thabit, Moslem poet, 222, 224, 264
Hatib, Moslem warrior, 290
Havilah, 17
Hawazinites, mountain tribe near Mecca, 36, 106, 300, 301, 311, 327
Hedjaz, 16
Hell, 99
Hemna, Zeinab bint Jahsh's sister, 221, 224
Henry II of England, 170

Henry IV of France, 258
Henry VIII of England, 120, 147
Heraclius, Roman emperor, 19, 20, 249, 262, 282, 306, 315
Herodotus, 18
Hind, Abu Sofian's wife, 65, 177, 178, 181, 183, 250, 269, 297, 350
Hira, Mount, 54, 56, 60, 63, 64, 67, 83, 132, 295, 324
Hitler, Adolf, 166
Hodeibiya, camp near Mecca, 251, 252, 253, 254, 261, 269, 276
Hodzeifa, Moslem general, 235
Homer, 5
Houris, 96, 113
Hubal, Kaaba idol, 25, 186, 295
Hunayn, 301, 303, 305
Huweitib ibn abd al Ozza, Koreishite noble, 255, 280

Ibn Saud, 202
Ibn Kamia, Koreishite warrior, 184
Ibrahim, Mohammed's and Mary the Copt's son, 267
Ikrima, son of Abu Jahl, 209, 210, 250, 251, 294, 297, 298, 303
Illiteracy of Mohammed, 57, 63, 154
Immaculate conception, 90, 241, 242
India, 19, 163, 169, 325, 354
Indus, 231
Inheritance, laws on, 194, 195, 227
Inquisition, Holy, 315, 344
Iraq, 141, 235, 346
Irenius, Saint, 117
Ireland, 20
Isa, Jesus, 90
Isaac, 83, 239
Islam, 8, 9, 10, 11, 26, 49, 52, 53, 57, 61, 63, 65, 74, 83, 84, 91, 92, 96, 103, 121, 133, 134, 138, 142, 152, 167, 190, 195, 213, 217, 222, 231, 232, 254, 258, 261, 281, 296, 298, 313, 319, 330, 335, 343, 352, 354
Ishmael, son of Hagar, 11, 12, 13, 16, 25, 50, 83, 169, 239, 278, 295
Israelites, 64
Italy, 19, 354

Jacob, 13, 84, 109, 239
Jafar, son of Abu Taleb, 263, 274, 280, 282, 283, 284, 285, 286

Japan, 19, 155
Java, 231, 317
Jehovah, 64, 108, 270
Jeremiah, 16
Jericho, 193
Jerusalem, 18, 19, 24, 43, 79, 87, 109, 131, 139, 141, 166, 168, 243, 282, 315, 347
Jesus Christ, 4, 12, 50, 54, 63, 64, 72, 83, 87, 88, 99, 100, 103, 104, 108, 109, 118, 119, 136, 164, 231, 240, 242, 261, 262
Jews, 18, 19, 50, 54, 83, 87, 89, 109, 120, 136, 139, 151, 165, 166–73, 180, 190, 191, 205, 207, 211, 227, 230, 236, 239, 242, 268, 270, 271, 272, 312, 314, 317
Jihad, holy war, 151
Joan of Arc, 63
John the Baptist, 54, 63, 104, 110, 240
John the Divine, 116, 117, 118
Joseph, son of Jacob, 110, 191, 298
Judaism, 17, 26, 64, 84, 91
Judas Iscariot, 88
Jurhumite kings, 25
Justinian, Emperor, 18
Juwairah bint Harith, Mohammed's eighth wife, 202, 219

Kaaba, 11, 13, 16, 18, 24, 25, 30, 34, 35, 36, 40, 50, 51, 53, 54, 55, 65, 67, 71, 74, 76, 79, 80, 81, 88, 90, 102, 123, 156, 161, 169, 250, 253, 258, 277, 279, 295, 297, 299, 312, 319, 323, 340
Kab ibn Ashraf, a Medinese Jew, 172
Kara, village near Medina, 191
Karigites, fanatic Moslem sect, 353
Kasim, Mohammed's son, 53
Kedar, tribe of nomads, 16
Kesoua, covering of the Kaaba, 11
Khadija bint Khuweilid, Mohammed's first wife, 41, 42, 43, 44, 45, 46, 47, 49, 53, 54, 55, 57, 58, 59, 61, 64, 65, 69, 81, 82, 105, 165, 221, 248, 265, 295, 299, 324, 325, 342, 355
Khaibar, Jewish group of strongholds near Medina, 193, 204, 268, 269, 270, 271, 272, 273, 276, 327, 352
Khaled ibn Walid, Meccan and, later, Moslem cavalry leader, 138, 141, 177, 180, 182, 250, 251, 269, 280, 281, 282, 284, 286, 288, 294, 298, 301, 309, 318, 346, 348

Khuzaima, Khadija's nephew, 42, 46
Kibla, niche in Moslem mosque or home indicating direction of Mecca, 100, 168
Kishon, brook, 172
Koran, 2, 11, 55, 56, 60, 61, 68, 69, 72, 78, 85, 87, 97, 99, 100, 107, 113, 116, 123, 129, 152, 165, 175, 189, 195, 196, 197, 226, 227, 230, 232–45, 303, 310, 314, 335, 352
Koreish, Mohammed's tribe, 22, 23, 24, 26, 40, 41, 46, 67, 69, 70, 74, 80, 82, 119, 122, 124, 149, 153, 164, 173, 178, 182, 187, 191, 206, 211, 233, 248, 269, 280, 281, 287, 289, 324, 336, 340, 352
Kuba, oasis near Medina, 130, 178, 190
Kufa, city on Euphrates, 352
Kuss ibn Saida, Christian bishop of Nejran, 34, 86
Kwala bint Hakim, Amina's sister and Mohammed's aunt, 105

Lawrence, T. E., of Arabia, 150, 301
Lourdes, 63

Maan, city of Syria, 283
Machiavelli, 155
Madani, Arab chief of the Sahara, 107, 108, 112, 114, 115, 116, 118, 225, 237
Maimuna bint al Harith, Mohammed's last wife, 280, 281, 328
Maisara, Khadija's slave, 42, 44, 45, 47
Makalah, daughter of Ishmael, 13
Malaya, 163, 169, 317, 325, 354
Manat, Kaaba idol, 82
Man Azzahran, camp near Mecca, 291
Manuel, Roman general, 138
Malik, governor of At Tayef, 303, 311
Marhab, champion of Khaibar Jews, 272
Maronites, seventh-century Christian sect, 89
Mary, Mohammed's Copt concubine, 264, 265, 266, 267, 274
Mary, mother of Jesus, 12, 50, 63, 100, 240, 241, 262
Mariamites, seventh-century Christian sect, 89
Marriage, 226, 227, 228
Martel, Charles, 344

Marwa, hill outside Mecca, 277
Matthew, Saint, 91, 98, 117
Mayas, 20
Meshed Ali, city on the Euphrates, 353
Mediterranean, 20, 87, 317
Mecca, 3, 7, 10, 12, 13, 14, 15, 16, 22, 23, 24, 25, 26, 27, 29, 31, 35, 41, 49, 51, 54, 58, 65, 67, 74, 80, 83, 94, 100, 102, 106, 108, 112, 120, 123, 128, 137, 154, 156, 164, 169, 172, 177, 191, 193, 204, 211, 226, 234, 246, 253, 254, 273, 276, 278, 288, 298, 300, 305, 318–25, 340
Medina, 3, 7, 15, 25, 26, 29, 120, 121, 122, 123, 124, 128, 130, 131, 133, 137, 142, 149, 153, 162, 172, 180, 187, 188, 191, 194, 200, 204, 207, 209, 220, 234, 246, 254, 276, 281, 288, 299, 305, 308, 342, 347, 355
Mesopotamia, 205, 325, 347, 354
Messiah, 239
Michael, angel, 63, 100
Mikraz ibn Hafs, Koreish statesman, 255
Mina, hill outside Mecca, 319, 320, 321
Miracles, 8, 63, 72, 73, 90, 104, 116, 119, 145, 166
Mistal, Medinese citizen who slandered Aisha, 224
Modernists, 83
Mohammed and the mountain, 7
Mohammedanism, 8
Mongolia, 169
Morocco, 169, 202
Moros, 317
Moses, 1, 37, 54, 63, 64, 72, 83, 87, 91, 99, 100, 104, 108, 109, 112, 114, 119, 151, 180, 233, 239, 273
Moseilma, rival prophet of Mohammed, 317, 318
Moslem, 8, 9, 19, 84, 87, 92, 101, 102, 105, 107, 122, 134, 142, 152, 158, 159, 165, 169, 207, 259, 261, 288, 290, 302, 312, 321, 326, 344
Mosque, 92, 94, 135, 136, 139, 141, 237, 281, 320, 338
Mu'awiyah, abu Sofian's son, 133, 239, 350, 351, 352, 353
Muezzin, 140, 141, 161
Muhajirin, Mecca immigrants, 135, 136, 142, 159, 303
Mukaukis, governor of Egypt, 264

Mummery, 6
Musab ibn Omeir, early Moslem convert, 121, 122, 123, 179, 184, 185
Muta, village near Dead Sea, 282, 284, 285, 286, 306, 327
Mutem ibn Adi, early Moslem convert, 107

Napoleon, 155, 191
Naufal, Koreishite warrior, 209
Nebuchadnezzar, 166
Negus of Abyssinia, 6, 137, 263
Nejran, 34, 50, 86
Nestorians, 33, 50, 74, 89, 90, 263
New Testament, 50, 63, 86, 237, 242
New York, 169
Nile, 113, 231
Noah, 16, 54, 83, 100, 110, 239
Nocturnal journey, 107–18, 145
Nurses, army, 269

Obeida ibn Harith, Mohammed's cousin, 65, 159, 198
Obeidallah ibn Jahsh, early Moslem convert, 263
Ohod, battle of, 180, 185, 188, 190, 193, 195, 198, 205, 307, 352
Okaz, fair of, 34
Okeidir, Christian Arab chief, 309
Old Testament, 17, 50, 63, 86, 91, 107, 151, 237, 240, 242
Oman, king of, 316
Omar ibn Assad, Khadija's uncle, 43, 45, 46, 47, 178
Omar ibn al Khattab, Mohammed's warrior friend and Islam's second caliph, 76, 78, 79, 80, 123, 130, 132, 133, 136, 138, 161, 174, 183, 184, 185, 199, 214, 222, 231, 234, 251, 253, 255, 256, 261, 266, 269, 271, 276, 277, 286, 289, 292, 307, 310, 314, 323, 331, 333, 334, 335, 336, 342, 347
Omara, Maimuna's daughter, 280
Omeir, a blind Medinese, 170
Omm Jemil, Abu Lahab's wife, 66, 68
Ommeya ibn Khalaf, Bilal's master, 140, 160, 161
Ommeyades, 69, 200, 253, 349, 350, 351
Orwa, son-in-law of Abu Sofian, 252
Osama, son of Zaid and Baraka, 53, 327, 328, 330, 337

INDEX

Otba, father of Hind, 158, 159, 177
Otba, Abu Lahab's son, 66, 69, 165
Otabayah, Abu Lahab's son, 69
Othman Ali, Nizam of Hyderabad, 52
Othman ibn Affan, Mohammed's friend and son-in-law and Islam's third caliph, 2, 65, 69, 74, 145, 165, 174, 178, 214, 235, 251, 253, 255, 269, 277, 307, 325, 331, 342, 348, 349, 350
Othman ibn Talha, guardian of the Kaaba, 281, 296
Othman ibn abi Talha, Meccan warrior, 181
Othman I, sultan of Turkey, 127

Palestine, 36, 93, 141, 166
Palmyra, 43
Paradise, 81, 96, 97, 109, 115, 157, 189
Paran, district near Mecca, 17
Paul, Saint, 91, 104, 108, 164, 344
Pentateuch, 100
Persia, 18, 19, 23, 36, 133, 141, 162, 164, 169, 205, 233, 238, 262, 325, 347, 354
Peter, Saint, 343
Pharaoh, 180
Philippines, 317
Pilgrimage, 102, 250, 251, 276-280, 318-323, 343, 344
Pius XII, Pope, 20
Polygamy, 91, 92, 96, 98, 227
Pompey, 166
Pork, eating of, 93
Portugal, 146
Praying, 101, 114, 115, 210
Psalms of David, 100, 240
Pyrenees, 63

Ramadan, 56, 101, 102
Red Sea, 3, 87, 119, 128, 156, 260, 309
Reihana, Jewish concubine, 215
Revelation, Book of, 116
Rokaia, Mohammed's daughter, 66, 68, 74, 145, 164, 174
Roland at Roncesvalles, 301
Rome, 18, 19, 23, 141, 163, 165, 194, 238, 249, 261, 282, 283, 284, 306, 308, 327, 343, 346

Saad, nephew of Amina, 65
Saad, ibn ar Rabi, Moslem warrior, 194
Saad ibn Muad, chief of the Ausites, 208, 209, 213, 214, 215
Saad ibn Obada, early Medinese convert, 294, 336
Sabellians, seventh-century Christian sect, 89
Safwa and Marwa, hills near Mecca where Hagar nearly died, 277
Safwan ibn al Moattel, Aisha's desert friend, 220, 221, 223, 225, 350
Safwan ibn Omeiya, Meccan leader, 294
Safiya, Mohammed's tenth wife, 272, 273, 274
Sahara Desert, 4, 107, 169, 231, 237
Said, Omar's brother-in-law, 78
Saladin, 152
Sale, George, 6, 7, 99
Salma, Hamza's wife, 281
Sarah, Abraham's wife, 12
Sargon II, 166
Sarif, village near Mecca, 280
Saul of Tarsus, 120
Sawda bint Zamah, Mohammed's second wife, 105, 121, 127, 131, 145, 147, 175, 187, 265
Selman, Persian Moslem convert, 205, 206
Seville, 152
Sex, 203
Shah Jahan, 97
Shaiba ibn Rabia, Koreishite warrior, 158, 159
Shakespeare, 6, 238
Sheima, Mohammed's foster sister, 303
Shem, son of Noah, 16
Shia Moslems, 53, 128, 199, 353
Shur, 17
Siba ibn umm Amnar, Koreishite warrior, 183, 341
Sierra Leone, 169, 344
Sinai, Mount, 63, 108, 117
Siroes, king of Persia, 262
Shiren, sister of Mary the Copt, 264
Slavery, 195, 321
Soheil ibn Amr', Koreish statesman, 254, 255, 256, 257, 258, 280, 294
Suleiman the Magnificent, 97
Solomon, 202, 216, 239
Sorak ibn Malek, nomad chief, 129

Soubirous, Bernadette, 63
South Sea Islands, 20
Spain, 4, 19, 146, 163, 315, 317, 325, 344, 354
Suez Canal, 73
Sulimaneieh Mosque, 97
Sunnis, 200
Syria, 18, 23, 36, 42, 50, 52, 73, 93, 98, 124, 133, 138, 141, 163, 172, 173, 235, 248, 249, 268, 283, 286, 306, 327, 346, 352, 354

Taj Mahal, 97
Talha, cousin of Abu Bakr, 65, 350, 351
Talha, Meccan standard bearer, 181
Talha ibn Obeidallah, early Moslem convert, 184, 185
Talmud, 50
Tebuk, city on Syrian border, 308, 309, 327
Thaur, Mount, 126
Theodorus, brother of emperor Heraclius, 283
Theodora, Empress, 18, 147
Thuweiba, Mohammed's first foster mother, 27
Tiberius, Lake, 347
Tigris, river, 231, 351
Titus, Emperor, 166
Torah, 50
Trinity, Holy, 88
Turkey, 150, 162
Tyrius, Maximus, 12

Umm Kulthum, Mohammed's daughter, 69, 131, 145, 175
Umm Ruman, Abu Bakr's wife, 121, 131, 145
Umm Salama, Mohammed's sixth wife, 198, 199, 200, 219, 250, 256, 269, 274
United States, 4, 94, 146

Vandals, 20
Veiling of women, 196, 197
Venice, 23
Voltaire, Arouet de, 234, 237

Wahshi, Hind's slave, 177, 183, 297, 318
Wales, 20
Waraka, cousin of Khadija, 46, 49, 50, 58, 59, 60, 64, 86, 240
Washington, George, 3
Washing, 101, 225
Wellington, Duke of, 191
Women, 23, 24, 96, 97, 196, 197, 203, 218, 224, 226, 227, 228, 265, 268, 269, 321

Yahu, 64
Yathrib, 29, 30, 120
Yemen, 16, 23, 36, 262, 287, 316
Young, Brigham, 317

Zaid ibn Haritha, Mohammed's adopted son, 52, 57, 64, 82, 106, 107, 121, 131, 134, 162, 165, 173, 179, 200, 201, 248, 251, 269, 277, 282, 283, 284, 285, 326, 330
Zaid ibn Thabit, Mohammed's secretary, 230, 234, 235
Zanzibar, 169
Zeinab, Mohammed's daughter, 145, 162, 165, 248
Zeinab bint Jahsh, Mohammed's seventh wife, 131, 200, 201, 202, 219, 221, 264, 274, 290, 300
Zeinab, Jewess who tried to poison Mohammed, 273, 274
Zeinab bint Khuzeima, Mohammed's fifth wife, 176, 198
Zemzem well, 12, 13, 25, 30, 296, 323
Ziporah, wife of Moses, 64
Zoroaster, 133
Zubair, Aisha's cousin, 350, 351